FAITH AND FEMINISM

FAITH AND FEMINISM

Ecumenical Essays

EDITED BY

B. Diane Lipsett
and
Phyllis Trible

WJK WESTMINSTER
JOHN KNOX PRESS
LOUISVILLE • KENTUCKY

First edition
Published by Westminster John Knox Press
Louisville, Kentucky

14 15 16 17 18 19 20 21 22 23—10 9 8 7 6 5 4 3 2 1

Book design by Sharon Adams
Cover design by Lisa Buckley
Cover art by Ansgar Holmberg, CSJ, used with permission. A woman wearing a hat and clouds behind her © ImageZoo/Alamy.

Library of Congress Cataloging-in-Publication Data

Faith and feminism : ecumenical essays / edited by B. Diane Lipsett and Phyllis Trible.—First edition.
    pages cm
  Includes bibliographical references and indexes.
  ISBN 978-0-664-23969-5 (alk. paper)
  1. Women and religion. 2. Feminism—Religious aspects. 3. Bible and feminism. I. Lipsett, B. Diane (Barbara Diane) editor.
  BL458.F35 2014
  202.082—dc23
                                                                              2014009141

Most Westminster John Knox Press books are available at special quantity discounts when purchased in bulk by corporations, organizations, and special-interest groups. For more information, please e-mail SpecialSales@wjkbooks.com.

In Memoriam
Sylva Billue
1941–2007

Contents

Chapter 7   Learning in the Presence of the Other:
             Feminisms and the Interreligious Encounter   103
             Mary C. Boys

Chapter 8   Speaking from behind the Veil:
             Does Islamic Feminism Exist?   115
             Hibba Abugideiri

Chapter 9   The Emergence of Muslim American Feminisms   135
             Yvonne Yazbeck Haddad

Chapter 10   Sarah and Hagar: A Feminist European Perspective
             on Actual Controversies   161
             Ulrike Bechmann

Chapter 11   The Woman of Jericho: Dramatization
             as Feminist Hermeneutics   183
             Ulrike Bechmann

PART 3   THEOLOGY AND ETHICS

Chapter 12   Ecological Theology in Women's Voices   189
             Elizabeth A. Johnson

Chapter 13   Daily Life Challenges as the Criterion
             for Biblical and Feminist Theological Hermeneutics 203
             Ivone Gebara

Chapter 14   Do You Understand What You Are Reading? African
             Women's Reading of the Bible and the Ethos
             of Contemporary Christianity in Africa   217
             Mercy Amba Oduyoye

Chapter 15   With Running Mouth and Hands on Hips:
             Sapphire and the Moral Imagination   233
             Emilie M. Townes

Chapter 16   Why Do Men Need the Goddess? Male Creation
             of Female Religious Symbols   245
             Rosemary Radford Ruether

             Selected Bibliography   251

             Index of Bible References   255

             Index of Authors and Editors   257

             Index of Subjects   261

Preface

In 2006 Westminster John Knox Press published *Hagar, Sarah, and Their Children: Jewish, Christian, and Muslim Perspectives,* edited by Phyllis Trible and Letty M. Russell. That collection of essays grew out of the annual Phyllis Trible Lecture Series housed then at the Divinity School of Wake Forest University in Winston-Salem, North Carolina. The present book, *Faith and Feminism: Ecumenical Essays,* offers a second collection that also grew out of the lecture series.

Unlike the first, this book focuses not on a single subject but rather explores a variety of religious topics from a variety of feminist perspectives. The fifteen contributors come from five continents: Africa, Asia, Europe, North America, and South America. In backgrounds, they speak multiple and different languages. In ages, they span five decades. In religions, they represent Judaism, Christianity, and Islam. In methods and content, they cover a spectrum of disciplines. In turning oral presentations into written compositions, which range from the scholarly to the conversational, they have produced a collection of plenty.

Assembling this collection involved considerable work by Diane Lipsett, currently on the faculty at Salem College in Winston-Salem. For six years, she chaired the lecture series with efficiency and style. In coediting the book, she has attended to academic matters, to correspondence with the contributors, and to the complexities and challenges of the computer. Together we have benefited from the feminist value of collaboration.

Special thanks belong to donors and friends who supported the series across the years and encouraged the making of this book: in particular, to the Rev. Dr. Darla D. Turlington, a former student of mine at Union Theological Seminary, New York, later a pastor in New Jersey and now a resident of Florida; and to Mr. Randall Greene, my favorite businessman, biblical enthusiast, and sometime student, who flew parishioners from his church in Connecticut to the lectures.

When Diane Lipsett and I considered the dedication for the book, our choice came easily. Sylva Billue, the founder of the lecture series, was a true friend, generous donor, and dedicated feminist. To this day we miss her as we mourn her untimely death in 2007 in a road accident in Winston-Salem, North Carolina. *Requiescat in pace.*

—Phyllis Trible

Contributors

*with countries of origin
and current professional locations*

Hibba Abugideiri (Sudan)
Villanova University
Villanova, Pennsylvania

Wilma Ann Bailey (United States of America)
Christian Theological Seminary
Indianapolis, Indiana

Ulrike Bechmann (Federal Republic of Germany)
Karl-Franzens-University of Graz
Graz, Austria

Mary C. Boys (United States of America)
Union Theological Seminary
New York, New York

Ivone Gebara (Brazil)
Theologian, Philosopher, Writer
São Paulo, Brazil

Yvonne Yazbeck Haddad (Syria)
Georgetown University
Washington, DC

Elizabeth A. Johnson (United States of America)
Fordham University
Bronx, New York

Hisako Kinukawa (Japan)
Japan Lutheran Theological School
Tokyo, Japan

B. Diane Lipsett (Canada)
Salem College
Winston-Salem, North Carolina

Susan Niditch (United States of America)
Amherst College
Amherst, Massachusetts

Gail R. O'Day (United States of America)
Wake Forest University School of Divinity
Winston-Salem, North Carolina

Mercy Amba Oduyoye (Ghana)
Women in Religion and Culture Institute, Trinity Theological Seminary
Legon, Ghana

Rosemary Radford Ruether (United States of America)
Claremont School of Theology and Graduate University
Claremont, California

Emilie M. Townes (United States of America)
Vanderbilt University Divinity School
Nashville, Tennessee

Phyllis Trible (United States of America)
Emerita, Union Theological Seminary
New York, New York

Abbreviations of Modern Versions of the Bible

ESV	English Standard Version
JPS	Jewish Publication Society
KJV	King James Version
NAB	New American Bible
NIV	New International Version
NRSV	New Revised Standard Version
REB	Revised English Bible

Chapter 1

Testimonies in Tongues

B. DIANE LIPSETT AND PHYLLIS TRIBLE

Faith and Feminism unlocks storehouses of words old and new. The subtitle *Ecumenical Essays* indicates that these words, these tongues, belong to women of faith around the world—women who speak in diverse settings and situations. Though all the contributors claim the noun "feminism," their developments of it range widely.[1] To present their testimonies and engage the results marks the purpose of this book. Where dissonance and harmony intersect among writers, there readers confront choices, which, in turn, become their own testimonies.

Two biblical stories, often associated with each other, provide orientation for reading: the Tower of Babel in Genesis 11:1–9 and the Day of Pentecost in Acts 2:1–13. In choosing to begin with these stories, we editors write from within our own scholarly disciplines and our own faith commitments.[2] For us, these stories offer entry into storehouses of words old and new. Even as the stories may confuse, they also clarify and challenge faith and feminism.

THE TOWER OF BABEL

The Tower of Babel, as traditionally labeled, concludes a series of five stories (with intervening content) that probe the mythical beginnings of humankind: creation and expulsion from the garden of Eden (Gen. 2:4b–3:24); fratricide as Cain kills Abel (4:1–16); mixed marriages of heaven and earth (6:1–4); Noah and the flood (6:5–9:28); and, at last, the Tower (11:1–9). A classic interpretation traces the motifs of sin, judgment, and grace throughout these stories, until the last.[3] The God who let Eve and Adam live, who put a protective mark on Cain, who countered the breach of boundaries in mixed marriages to find favor in Noah and save him and his family—that God offered no grace in the story of the Tower. Instead, announcing judgment upon sin—the pride of one people striving to make a name for themselves and take over heaven—God punished them. So runs the classic view. Recent interpretations, however, have sought to uproot it.[4] With variations, they offer a positive reading of the story, one in which God corrected the stated desires and actions of the people by decreeing cultural differences, not as judgment and punishment but as virtue and value.

Internal features of the Tower Story—its design, content, and gaps—may well produce conflicting interpretations. A balanced structure yields two episodes (11:1–4 and 6–9) linked by a transitional verse (11:5). In *episode one* the narrator and all the people of the earth speak. No God is present. The narrator identifies the generic people as linguistic creatures, with "one language (*sepah*) and the same words." They migrate to the land of Shinar (Babylon), settle there, and speak to one another about building projects. Two human speeches ensue (vv. 3, 4), each introduced by the invitational particle and phrase, "Come (*habah*), let us . . ." The people first make bricks, and then they propose to make a city and a tower "with its top in the heavens." Their reason is to "make a name for ourselves; otherwise, we shall be scattered abroad upon the face of the whole earth" (v. 4). One people seek identity through unity of language and location. Are pride and fear intertwined in their words?

At this juncture comes the *transition* (v. 5). YHWH enters the story through the narrator. Whether intentional or not, irony takes over. The deity "came down to see the city and the tower"—surely, then, not with "its top in the heavens." The report becomes the link to *episode two* (vv. 6–9). It features direct speech of the deity. Taking no account of the city or the tower, YHWH observes human and linguistic unity, to follow it with a judgment about human power: "See (*hen*), one people and one language (*sepah*) to all of them, and this is only the beginning of what they will do. Nothing that they will propose to do will now be impossible for them" (v. 6). Do these words suggest that YHWH is threatened by the power of the people?

The Hebrew word translated "language" (*sepah*) is literally "lip" (cf. v. 1). It connotes common speech. Prefacing both it and the noun "people" with the adjective "one" reinforces the connection. Unity of people in language (and location) appears undesirable in YHWH's purview, indeed a threat. But a threat to whom? Or to what? As one people in all the earth, speaking one "lip," surely the people cannot be threats to themselves. Is YHWH threatened by human unity and language? Is heaven threatened by "all the earth"?

Whatever the answer, YHWH announces a decision in the heavenly court. Its introductory word, "come" (*habah*), parallels the introductory word in the earlier speeches of the people (cf. vv. 3, 4). The emphasis on language continues as the Hebrew word *sepah* (lip) appears twice more in the divine speech, "Come let us go down and confuse their *language* there so that they will not understand one another's *language*" (v. 7). What is the intent of this divine decision—to punish? correct? promote diversity? Whatever the motive, the divine words render judgment as they provide an etiology for linguistic diversity. The language of YHWH decrees the confusion of human "lips" to achieve lack of understanding.

The divine words cease. The narrator takes over, reporting a second divine act accompanying the worldwide scattering of all the people. Repetition underscores the action. An inclusio begins and ends with the words, "So YHWH scattered them abroad over the face of all the earth …" (vv. 8, 9b). In the center of the inclusio the narrator reports the termination of the people's urban goal: "and they left off building the city" (v. 8b). Then the narrator incorporates an etymological note, with words used earlier by YHWH: "Therefore it was called Babel, because there YHWH *confused the language* of all the earth" (v. 9a).

Five times, in five strategic places, the word "language" ("lip") has appeared: once in the opening narrated sentence (v. 1); three times in divine speech (vv. 6, 7); and once in the closing narrated speech (v. 9). From beginning to end, language has moved, along with the motif of scattering, from singularity to multiplicity, from unity to confusion.

Certainty and uncertainty allow diverse interpretations of the Tower Story. For certain, language is paramount. For certain, the plans of the people for unity in location and for a "name" do not please YHWH. For certain, YHWH decrees that their language be confused so that they will not understand one another. For certain, YHWH scattered them and confused their language. Yet throughout, the divine motivation and intention remain murky. Does YHWH bring judgment, correction, or sanction for cultural differences? Whatever the answer, for certain, diversity pervades all the earth, with linguistic and interpretive confusion the identifying characteristics.

Whether prescriptive or descriptive, punitive or corrective, judgmental or confirmatory, this story describes well the world—to this day. And alongside the Tower stands its New Testament companion, the Pentecost Story.

THE PENTECOST STORY

From mythical Babel to historical Babylon and on, confusion of languages and cultures spread across the ancient Near East. As millennia passed, the linguistic scattering included Sumerian, Akkadian, Hebrew, Persian, Greek, Syriac,

Aramaic, and Latin. One conquering people after another promoted their speech as they encountered the speech of others. Languages became tongues of power and promoted the power of tongues.

In time, aspects of the historical narrative focused on Jesus of Nazareth, who lived during the Roman occupation of the land of Judea. According to the Gospel of John (19:19–22), when Jesus was crucified, Pontius Pilate, the Roman prefect, had the inscription over the cross written in the three languages of Hebrew (Aramaic), Greek, and Latin. Pressured to revise the inscription from "King of the Jews" to "he says, he was king of the Jews," Pilate refused. "What I have written, I have written," he declared. Words mattered. One utterance (Pilate's) overruled the tongues of those around him.

As the subsequent narrative about Jesus moved from crucifixion and resurrection to ascension and the aftermath, it focused upon a memorable occasion of language and location (Acts 2:1–47).[5] The location was Jerusalem, where followers of the risen Jesus gathered after his ascension (1:12–26). Though men dominated (1:13, 15, 21–23), the gatherings included Mary the mother of Jesus as well as certain other women (1:14). Similar to the beginning of the Tower Story, on the day of Pentecost, the Jewish Feast of Weeks, the followers of Jesus are "all together in one place" (Acts 2:1). But the crowd that witnesses the strange, subsequent event is not one people. Nor do they actually dwell in one place. Unlike mythic and generic humankind, who wished to "*reach heaven,*" this wider group of characters is historically and specifically identified as "devout Jews from every nation *under heaven* in the city" (v. 5).

The story unfolds in three episodes (2:1–4, 5–11, 12–13). In narrated discourse, *episode one* (vv. 1–4) reports the occasion—its location and the events that transpire. A sound "from heaven" like violent wind fills the one room, and "divided *tongues*, as of fire" appear to rest on those gathered. Filled thereby with the divine spirit, the gathered begin "to speak in other *tongues*, as the spirit gives them ability to speak." Repetition of the Greek noun "tongue" (*glōssa*) and the verb "to speak" (*laleō*) presage the genre of testimony. The adjectives "divided" and "other" indicate the diversity of languages (*glōssais*, v. 4) that emerge under the power of the spirit from heaven. With echoes of the Tower Story, heaven reaches down to earth. Language multiplies.

Introduced by the narrator, *episode two* (vv. 5–11) shifts focus from speaking to hearing, from testimonies to reception, from tongues to ears. Three times the verb "hear" (*akouō*) appears: near the beginning, in the middle, and at the end (vv. 6, 8, 11). Accordingly, hearing encloses speech to shape the outcome of the occasion.

In the beginning (vv. 5, 6), "devout Jews from every nation under heaven" gather at the sound, and they are "bewildered" (*sunechuthē*). Again similar to the Tower Story, a cosmic vantage point (heaven) intensifies the motif of sound. Further, the initial response, "bewildered," echoes the confused tongues ("lips") of Babel. But why the bewilderment? Hearing and speaking give the answer. "Because each one heard them speaking in the native language of each." The confusion that reigns is truly "worthy of Babylon."[6] Yet again, however, circumstances and conditions differ. Whereas in the Tower Story God deliberately confused language so that humankind would not understand one another, in the Pentecost Story the bewilderment resulting from the heavenly sound (no explicit reference yet to God) yields a different outcome. The hearers understand the speakers. Whatever the speakers were speaking (glossolalia? xenologia? ordinary words?), the text does not say. Instead, it reports what the hearers hear. Testimony yields to reception.

In the middle of episode two (vv. 7, 8) the hearers take over from the narrator. "Amazed and astonished," they ask, "'Are not all these who are speaking Galileans?'" Next they pose a rhetorical question: "And how is it that we hear, each of us in our own language?" What they hear is "the native speech of each" (*ta idia dialektō*), discrete languages and dialects, perhaps even familiar accents, not confused tongues. Babel it is not. Is to hear in this way the embrace or the rejection of diversity? Is it assimilation or a unity that preserves difference? Has the language of the other been honored or domesticated?

Expanding the middle of episode two, the hearers elaborate on their amazement. Speaking as a collective character, a chorus, they follow their rhetorical question ("How is it that we hear?") with a listing of the disparate nations and regions they represent—some fifteen (vv. 9–11a). Cultural, geographic, and linguistic diversity is paradoxically recited in unison. The crowd then expresses the testimony of the others: ". . . in our own languages," they say, "we hear them speaking about God's deeds of power" (v. 11b).

At the close of this second episode, the word "tongue" (*glōssa*), which occurs twice in the first episode, reappears; the verb "hear" makes its third internal appearance; and the verb "speak," which occurs twice at the end of the first episode, also reappears. Tongues speak and repeat. Testimonies matter as the story moves to its conclusion.

Episode three alternates between narration and direct speech (vv. 12, 13). It reports two verbal responses to the Pentecostal event. They posit tension within the crowd, now divided into "all" and "others." The first response comes from the group described as the "all" who "were amazed" (cf. v. 7) and "perplexed." Speaking to one another, they wonder what to make of the happening. "What is going on?" or "what does this mean?" they ask. Is it as though Babel has come to Jerusalem—and yet, paradoxically, "in our own native language"? But the group described as the "others" sneers at the whole event. They deem the "all" speaking other languages not inspired but "filled with new wine." No puzzlement do they express but rather negative judgment.

A sermon follows (2:17–36), with three thousand converts (2:41). Beyond the confines of this story, Acts narrates the spread of testimony and reception beyond the Jews to the Gentiles (Acts 15). The movement that prompted such speaking extends from region to region, from country to country, and embraces not just multilingual Jews and proselytes (2:10), but diverse languages, peoples, and cultures.

The Pentecost story, however, remains open-ended. Uncertainty about what has happened, wavering between affirmation and negation, persists within it. Tension, even division, characterizes its participants. Not unlike humankind in Babel, some witnesses experience confusion of tongues. But unlike Babel, many witnesses show receptivity to these tongues, a receptivity that extends to the speaking and the hearing of all. As with the story of Babel, so Pentecost testifies to the power and diversity of testimony. Both texts offer fitting backgrounds for the various stories in this book.

FEMINIST STORIES

From this biblical background we enter the contemporary world of scattered peoples and confused tongues. In it faith meets faiths. Women speak their stories and hear the stories of others. But the speaking and hearing do not always coincide—nor need they. The results may yield blessing, perplexity, or even dismissal. (So Scripture reports the human condition under heaven.) Nonetheless, whatever the outcomes, here the beginnings share a base in defining feminism.

As a generic word, feminism signifies, first, a particular perspective on the subject of gender. Negatively stated, this perspective opposes in all forms the paradigm of male dominance and female subordination. Positively stated, feminism advocates the full humanity of female and male. From this base the perspective reaches out to speak in multiple ways on a host of subjects world-wide—e.g., on race, ethnicity, age, generations, geography, and points of view. In judgment and for blessing, feminism embraces the whole earth of Babel even as in this collection it tells specific stories that embrace three religions. Though not comprehensive, the fifteen essays testify to an ecumenical purview.

Contrary to surface appearance, the book contains multiple languages in tongues ancient and contemporary. Beneath the English surface (and sometimes level with it) reverberate ancient Hebrew, Aramaic, Greek, and Latin; contemporary Arabic, Portuguese, Japanese, German, and Ghanaian languages. Along with these recognized forms of speech come dialects and clichés reflective of individual cultures. Though readers cannot embrace all these tongues, they need not become "confused" (as humankind at Babel) or "bewildered" (as the crowd in Jerusalem). Translation and interpretation offer ways for deepening communication.

Congruent with this multiplicity of tongues, the book witnesses to a scattering/multiplicity of continents, countries, and cultures. Africa, Asia, Europe, North America, and South America appear. Within the five continents, nine countries come to the foreground: Ghana, Japan, Germany, Austria, Canada, Sudan, Syria, the United States, and Brazil. Within these countries, numerous cultures interact: for example, religious versus secular; rural versus urban; guilt versus shame; educated versus uneducated; tribal versus democratic; rich versus poor; homogeneous versus varied; and so forth. Sometimes openly and other times discretely, such differences emerge within the essays. To generalize, then, about a continent, country, or culture on the basis of a single contribution falsifies reality. Correspondingly, to generalize about feminism or feminists on the basis of these fifteen essays falsifies reality. Nonetheless, the testimony of each contributes to a larger whole. Like the hairs of the head or the sparrow who falls to the earth, individual tongues and testimonies merit attention.

The three parts of the volume, each with five essays, follow disciplinary divisions: biblical studies, interreligious ventures, and theology and ethics.[7] Sections shape expectations and allow harmonies and dissonances to emerge. Yet the divisions are not rigid. Conversations, debates, and disclosures pull beyond the boundaries of the sections, cutting across the fixed organization.

Biblical Studies

Close textual interpretation opens the volume, as *part one* offers studies of Genesis and Gospels (Mark and John) with an array of methods and critical approaches. Three essays treat Genesis, sacred to both Jews and Christians. In the first, Phyllis Trible juxtaposes two ancient creation stories—the Akkadian *Enuma Elish* and the biblical version of Genesis 1:1–2:4a—with literary and rhetorical analysis attentive to ecological consequences (chap. 2). In the *Enuma Elish*, Trible finds stark contemporary relevance in the myth's persisting threat of environmental chaos. In Genesis 1, questions of hierarchy find distinctive answers. Trible shows that male and female created in the *imago Dei* (Gen. 1:26–27) manifest no gender hierarchy but "gender identity without prejudice."[8] Further, the humans are created without specification of race, ethnicity, class, or any such category that could invite domination. What, then, of the divine directive that humankind is to have-dominion (*radah*) over the animals and subdue (*kabas*) the earth (Gen. 1:28)? These troubling verbs, Trible shows, are both circumscribed and defined by the beautiful liturgy in which they occur. According to Genesis 1, humans are creatures *within* nature, with no license to exploit or savage the earth but with responsibility to preserve and promote the goodness of God's creation. In several ways, Trible prepares for the volume's other biblical studies and for its further critiques of hierarchy and domination.

Testimonies of female characters and gendered bodies in Genesis follow. Wilma Bailey works to recover an oft-neglected story and woman, the character Leah, co-wife with her sister Rachel of the patriarch Jacob (Gen. 29–30; chap. 3). Bailey joins patient analysis of scenes wherein Leah names her children to a range of cultural explorations—forced marriage, barrenness, the opening of wombs, strategies of sexuality, enslaved women's bodies, and more—to present Leah as a dynamic literary character, gaining agency and self-assurance. In Leah, Bailey finds assurance that God notices the pain of those marginalized in society and works with them toward remedy.

Susan Niditch turns to two female "tricksters" of Genesis—Rebecca (Gen. 27) and Tamar (Gen. 38)—with an approach that intertwines folklore, feminist, and cultural studies (chap. 4). While Niditch values feminist critique of male power imposed on female characters, she explores how Genesis creates subversive openings that both criticize men and delight in women's self-assertion and creative survival. Rebecca and Tamar find distinctively feminine means of achieving their goals—for Rebecca, clothing and cooking; for Tamar, seduction. In an extended look at the tale of Jacob, Esau, Rebecca, and Isaac (Gen. 27), Niditch traces how the motif of hair and hairlessness further subverts gendered expectations: the manly, hairy son (Esau) loses his position to the smooth, hairless underdog in gender (Jacob). Without claiming female authorship for these stories, Niditch asks whether female voices, perspectives, or sympathies may be detected in such trickster tales and gender subversions.

Two contributors explore Christian Gospels. Asian feminist New Testament scholar Hisako Kinukawa weaves together reflective autobiography; sketches of feminist theology in Asia, particularly Japan; and critical exegesis of the Syrophoenician woman in the Gospel of Mark (7:24–30; chap. 5). Kinukawa joins other feminist interpreters interrogating why Jesus insults and refuses a Gentile woman seeking healing for her daughter. Distinctively, Kinukawa asks why Jesus' refusal uses imagery of food or table fellowship: "Let the children be fed first, for it is not fair to take the children's food and throw it to the dogs" (7:27 NRSV). Drawing on postcolonial criticism, Kinukawa shows that political relations between Tyre and Galilee (rival colonies of the Roman Empire), including inequities in food distribution, help account for Jesus' language and the woman's insistence that she, like Galilean peasants, be identified with those whose needs Jesus must meet.

The language of literary-theological analysis enters with Gail R. O'Day's reading of embodiment and friendship in the Gospel of John (chap. 6). Reflecting longstanding feminist critiques of spirit/body dualisms, O'Day urges *incarnation* as the defining category for understanding John's story of Jesus: "The Word became flesh and dwelt among us" (John 1:14). In that embodiment, flesh—that is, ordinary human life, including mortality—is redeemed. For O'Day, friendship in John is a theological motif related to embodiment, one that she says renders a spirit/flesh dualism impossible, "because human beings live and love as friends in our bodies, just as Jesus did."[9] When Jesus at the farewell meal in John washes his disciples' feet (an act anticipated by Mary of Bethany washing Jesus' feet), he lays down his role as host to become servant and friend, just as he will later lay down his life for his friends.

In addition to these five essays in biblical studies, varied testimonies of feminist biblical interpretation are heard elsewhere in the collection: in further ecological references to Genesis (Johnson); in exegeses of Abraham, Sarah, Hagar, and a conquest story from Judges (Bechmann); and in allusions to Hebrew prophets, Song of Songs, and Woman Wisdom (Ruether). Moreover, contributors trace the myriad ways that culture shapes biblical hermeneutics in Europe (Bechmann), Africa (Oduyoye), Latin America (Gebara), and Asia (Kinukawa). The move from biblical texts to testimonies embraces a collaborative effort to understand.

Interreligious Ventures

The essays in *part two* promote interreligious understandings. A scholar of religious education and longtime participant in interreligious dialogue, Mary C. Boys opens the section (chap. 7). Boys describes sustained interaction between persons of different faith traditions as a pilgrimage to "thin places" that entails a "thick religiosity." Knowing about the religious Other, she holds, deepens knowledge of one's own tradition and convictions, along with encouraging humility and a sense of the mystery of God. In our time, such knowledge "is especially important among the so-called 'Abrahamic religions,' that is, Judaism, Christianity and Islam, which share profound commonalities and deep differences, as well as many tragic historical encounters."[10]

Some of these encounters are traced in the two extended introductions to Muslim feminisms by Hibba Abugideiri and Yvonne Yazbeck Haddad. Both scholars invoke the damaging historical legacy of colonialism for Muslim women: colonial powers in the Middle East depicted Muslim women as needing the West's liberation from the oppressions of their religion, culture, and men—a devastating rhetoric persisting in the United States today, voiced even by some Western feminists. Against such prejudice, Abugideiri introduces Islamic feminism, with its own distinctive history, objectives, and strategies (chap. 8). Her particular focus falls on contemporary American Islamic scholar-activists who share a "critical faith-centered approach," locating struggle in readings of the Qur'an oriented toward Islamic gender justice. Such Muslim feminists give priority to the Qur'an as the source of liberation, critique Islamic patriarchy, and emphasize the right of scriptural interpretation to redress gender injustice.

Similarly, Haddad highlights the work of Muslim American scholars and activists in "negotiating gender through the Qur'an" (chap. 9). Her essay further surveys five decades of social, religious, and political contributions from Muslim American women, with particular emphasis on the years since 9/11 and the subsequent "war on terror." As Islamophobia has intensified, Muslim feminist expressions have varied widely: some progressive, some pietistic; some traditionalist, others denouncing Islam. Toward the close of Haddad's essay, a series of vivid cultural snapshots captures younger women reflecting on their Muslim American identity and making myriad social contributions—from public policy to literature, from activism to entertainment.

Struggles and responses in the European context are evoked by Ulrike Bechmann as she blends exegesis, critical hermeneutics, and sociopolitical analysis with nuanced evaluations of European interreligious dialogues (chap. 10). Starting with the Genesis narratives of Abraham, Sarah, and Hagar, Bechmann traces the symbolic meaning of Sarah and Hagar in the European religious context, illuminating European anti-Semitism, Islamophobia, and stances toward the Israeli-Palestinian conflict. Bechmann identifies two approaches to European interreligious dialogue: (1) an institutional male-dominated approach with Abraham offered as a unifying figure, often at the expense of recognizing difference, and marked by a biblical hermeneutic of acceptance; (2) feminist examples of interreligious dialogue related to Sarah and Hagar, which acknowledge difference and histories of conflict, and are marked by a biblical hermeneutic of protest.

In a creative conclusion to *part two* (chap. 11), Bechmann turns to another problematic biblical text sometimes dangerously presumed relevant to contemporary Israeli-Palestinian conflict: the conquest of Jericho (Josh. 6). Through a dramatic reading, Bechmann gives voice to a hospitable woman of Jericho welcoming an Israelite visitor the day before the city's destruction. Thereby, the feminist hermeneutic of protest in interpreting Scripture, one that emerges in more than one religious tradition, gains imaginative force.

Within *part two,* testimonies converge and diverge. Abugideiri, Haddad, and Bechmann concur, for instance, that the *hijab* (the veil) and other forms of traditional Muslim dress have become key symbols of religious identity. More Muslim women are choosing to veil, finding therein a complex repertoire of meanings,[11] including expressions of cultural and religious identity, empowerment, and activism. Yet some observers, including some Western secular and Christian feminists, continue to see women who veil as subjugated, degraded, or male-dominated. As Boys sensitively shows, the encounter with the religious Other can disclose how one's own religion is complicit in misrepresentations, exposing "the tribalism, racism, and xenophobia enmeshed in home traditions."[12] Overall, contributors to *part two* highlight ways that religion, spirituality, and scriptural interpretation are powerful sites of resistance rather than sources of oppression.

Theology and Ethics

In *part three*, each of the influential ethicists and theologians who contribute looks to the past, reflecting with candor and critique on a history of feminist or womanist contributions. Then, in varied tones—some hortatory, some sober, none sanguine—each urges a changed future.

Elizabeth A. Johnson contributes to ecofeminist theology in an essay rich in vibrant imagery drawn from nature (chap. 12). Her compressed yet extensive review shows how women theologians and ethicists have already made decisive contributions to "this life or death project" of reclaiming the natural world as essential to both theory and practice—in Christian anthropology, theology of God, and ethics. Feminist ethics, in particular, underscores the connection between ecological devastation and social injustice; poor people suffer disproportionately from environmental damage. To Christology, then, Johnson offers a fresh contribution, exploring how Jesus' proclamation of the reign of God revealed divine solidarity, not just with humans, but with the suffering of "all creatures' living and dying."[13]

A call for solidarity with suffering pervades Ivone Gebara's essay (chap. 13). Focused on Latin America but with broad resonance, Gebara points to an existential and theoretical gap between what common believers experience as faith and an analytical way of reflecting about religious subjects, including biblical studies and feminist religious studies—a contrast between living religion and thinking religion. With notes of sorrow and urgency, Gebara urges feminist theology to find, beyond the critique of patriarchal images and interpretations, new language to address deep human aspirations and needs and to find new forms of solidarity with and among poor women. She calls for a new understanding of transcendence—no longer metaphysical, but rooted in compassion and solidarity. The lived experience of women and all those who face poverty, suffering, or marginalization is, for Gebara, not just a *resource* for biblical and theological hermeneutics, but a *test*, a means for judging authenticity or adequacy—a *criterion*.

A biblical hermeneutics rooted in life experience remains pressing in Mercy Amba Oduyoye's study of how African women have appropriated the Bible (chap. 14). Discussing a range of interpreters, Oduyoye highlights writings from the Circle of Concerned African Women Theologians. African women interpreters critique injustice in both the Bible and African cultures, expose the legacies of colonialism, and seek to enhance women's development and participation in religion and society. Relevance matters: for example, interpreters seek resources of spiritual care for those with HIV/AIDS (including critiques of theologies of punishment); they find biblical precedents to celebrate women's empowerment, resilience, and survival (e.g., Jairus' daughter, the hemorrhaging woman, and Ruth); they value texts that voice divine opposition to poverty and colonization (e.g., the Magnificat). Reading the Bible becomes one strategy for "building a world that accommodates diversity and justice."[14] Seeking a cultural analysis adequate to diversity, Emilie Townes confronts the difficulty religious traditions have in addressing race and racism and, more particularly, challenges the ways "coloredness remains inadequately interrogated in the household of God" (chap. 15). Emphasizing history, memory, and imagination, Townes draws from literary and womanist writers (especially Toni Morrison) and from theorists of race to insist race is that not an essence, something fixed or objective, but a complex set of social meanings enmeshed in political struggle. Moreover, race cannot, Townes insists, be collapsed into "uninterrogated coloredness." "Uninterrogated whiteness" holds particular danger, because if "whiteness" seems "colorless" then "[t]he values, belief systems, privileges, histories, experiences of White folks are marked as normal or neutral or natural."[15] For more faithful encounters with race and color, Townes urges not blame, but a relentless and inclusive recovery of history, a willingness to understand ourselves as both victims and perpetrators, and a womanist social ethic that embraces all segments of society.

In the final essay (chap. 16), Rosemary Radford Ruether puts to brisk test the assumptions of some feminists that female symbols for the divine are "remnants" of a pre-patriarchal women-centered religion or that female religious symbols are intrinsically empowering to women. Drawing from Judaism and Christianity, Ruether evaluates a series of female images for the divine. From

Hebrew prophets imagining Israel as an unfaithful wife, to the Song of Songs as an allegory for the love relationship between God and the soul or church, to Woman Wisdom appearing in texts that depict no female sages or students, Ruether finds no suggestion of women's empowerment. In Christianity, Marian worship and Christian love mysticism also disappoint. Only a few female mystics—Hildegard of Bingen and Julian of Norwich, for instance—suggest how women interpreted such gendered symbols for themselves. Rather than grasping for such female images, Ruether urges a deeper, more thorough symbolic and social restructuring: "creating a truly nonsexist symbol system that no longer values one gender against another . . ."[16] At the close of the collection, her testimony leaves hearers and readers with a bold and sober challenge.

DEVELOPMENTS OF FAITH AND FEMINISM

Clearly, feminism is (or perhaps feminisms are) constituted by a multiplicity of testimonies, projects, and debates. Much as Babel suggests that the encounter with voiced difference may displace a hearer, so some essays in the collection may cause disorientation and surprise. Much as Pentecost suggests that common identity is not required for a collaborative struggle to understand, so some essays may prompt new coalitions and solidarity among readers.

Throughout, certain themes recur. A reader pursuing treatments of *embodiment* may move with interest from hairy and smooth men to barren and bearing women (Niditch and Bailey). She or he may compare two readings of flesh, *sarx*, in the Gospel of John: one stresses *sarx* as ordinary human life (in contrast to sin) and human flesh as the embodiment of God in the world (O'Day); another reads *sarx* as all flesh (in contrast to exclusively human flesh) and therein discovers God's identification with all life forms (Johnson).[17] A reader pursuing feminist critiques of other dualisms and hierarchies may compare two views of the relation of humanity to the natural world: one arguing that a "pyramid of privilege" must be replaced by a "circle of the community of life" (Johnson); the other elucidating a "hierarchy of harmony," resisting exploitation but not treating all hierarchies as irredeemable (Trible).[18] Throughout the collection runs strong attention to complex *intersections* between analyses of sex and gender and other forms of social identity and power, including race, class, nationality, religion, colonial histories, and more. Postcolonial criticism proves particularly cogent for some interpreters (see, e.g., Kinukawa, Abugideiri, Haddad, Oduyoye). Understanding the *religious Other* emerges as a desideratum (see particularly Boys and Bechmann).

The feminist concern to critique the status quo, tradition, or canon also includes the commitment to critique feminism. Ruether challenges feminists who treat female symbols of the divine as intrinsically empowering to women. Townes challenges communities of faith who falter in their willingness to interrogate race and color. Gebara speaks of "fatigue melded with indignation"[19] as she laments how slight an effect feminist theology appears to have had in chang-ing traditional religious devotion among poor women and other people facing suffering. Abugideiri, Haddad, and Bechmann voice urgent critiques of how Western feminists perpetuate colonial and prejudicial attitudes toward Muslim women. Analyzing feminism as a complex term, Abugideiri states emphatically, "The West is no longer viewed as the locus from which all feminisms derive and against which they must be measured."[20]In this collection, some contributors speak out of personal struggles as women in a man's world; some speak at more academic levels; and some mix the two approaches. Again, some speak grounded solidly in faith; some speak skeptically, cautious of faith. Overall, the essays move from Judaism to Christianity to Islam; from the private to the public; from the personal to the political; from the experiential to the academic; from the scholarly to the colloquial; from research to exposition; from teaching to preaching; from confusion to comfort; from clanging to harmonious cymbals; and always from text to testimony. As these tongues now find diverse hearers, testimony yields to reception.

Notes

1. Corollaries of the noun "feminism" and/or the adjective "feminist" include, for example, "womanist" in African American cultures, "mujeristic" in His-panic cultures, and "Musawah" in Muslim cultures. Of these designations, "Musawah" ("equality" in Arabic) is perhaps the least familiar. For an introduc-tion, see Elizabeth Segran, "The Rise of the Islamic Feminists," *The Nation* 297 (December 23/30, 2013): 12–18.
2. In studying these texts, we benefitted from the doctoral dissertation of Sarah J. Ryan, "Identity Development in a Multicultural Setting," New York Theologi-cal Seminary, 1996, 36–47.
3. For the classic interpretation (as old as Augustine), see, e.g., Gerhard von Rad, *Genesis: A Commentary* (Philadelphia: The Westminster Press, 1972), 147–55.
4. For the recent interpretation (as new as the twenty-first century), see, e.g., Theodore Hiebert, "The Tower of Babel and the Origin of the World's Cul-tures," *Journal of Biblical Literature* 126 (2007): 29–58. Cf., John T. Strong, "Shadowing the Image of God: A Response to Theodore Hiebert's Interpre-tation of the Story of the Tower of Babel," *Journal of Biblical Literature* 127 (2008): 625–34. For a mediating position, see Bernhard W. Anderson, "The Tower of Babel: Unity and Diversity in God's Creation," in *From Creation to New Creation* (Minneapolis: Fortress Press, 1994), 165–78. On the ambivalent view of unity in diversity within the story itself, see Terence E. Fretheim, "The Book of Genesis," *The New Interpreter's Bible*, vol. 1 (Nashville: Abingdon Press, 1994), 410–14. On contrasting ways of reading the story, see Joel S. Badden, "The Tower of Babel: A Case Study in the Competing Methods of Historical and Modern Literary Criticism," *Journal of Biblical Literature* 128 (2009): 209–24.
5. The complete narrative about Pentecost extends from Acts 2:1–47. We confine our study to the first major section, 2:1–13. For interpretation of this section, we rely primarily upon the commentaries of Richard I. Pervo, *Acts: A Commentary,* Hermeneia (Minneapolis: Fortress Press, 2009), 58–75, and Joseph Fitzmyer, *The Acts of the Apostles,* Anchor Yale Bible Commentary (New Haven: Yale Uni-versity Press, 1998), 231–46.

6. Pervo, *Acts: A Commentary*, 59.
7. Each essay began as a public lecture delivered at the Phyllis Trible Lecture Series. The series was conducted annually at the Wake Forest University School of Divinity from 2003–2013, with a distinct theme each year. Across two days in early March, four speakers delivered lectures, interacted with their audiences in formal question periods and at informal receptions, and then participated in a closing panel discussion.
8. Phyllis Trible, "The Dilemma of Dominion," 26.
9. Gail R. O'Day, "Sacraments of Friendship: Embodied Love in the Gospel of John," 89.
10. Mary C. Boys, "Learning in the Presence of the Other: Feminisms and the Interreligious Encounter," 110.
11. Hibba Abugideiri, "Speaking from behind the Veil: Does Islamic Feminism Exist?" 116; Yvonne Yazbeck Haddad, "The Emergence of Muslim American Feminisms," 142, 149–52; Ulrike Bechmann, "Sarah and Hagar: A Feminist European Perspective on Actual Controversies," 166–67.
12. Boys, "Learning in the Presence of the Other," 104.
13. Elizabeth A. Johnson, "Ecological Theology in Women's Voices," 198.
14. Mercy Amba Oduyoye, "Do You Understand What You Are Reading? African Women's Reading of the Bible and the Ethos of Contemporary Christianity in Africa," 227.
15. Emilie M. Townes, "With Running Mouth and Hands on Hips: Sapphire and the Moral Imagination," 239.
16. Rosemary Radford Ruether, "Why Do Men Need the Goddess? Male Creation of Female Religions Symbols," 248.
17. Cf. O'Day, "Sacraments of Friendship," 86–87, and Johnson, "Ecological Theology," 199–201.
18. Cf. Johnson, "Ecological Theology," 193, and Trible, "Dilemma of Dominion," 29.
19. Ivone Gebara, "Daily Life Challenges as the Criterion for Biblical and Feminist Theological Hermeneutics," 214.
20. Abugideiri, "Speaking from behind the Veil," 118.

PART 1
BIBLICAL STUDIES

Chapter 2

The Dilemma of Dominion

PHYLLIS TRIBLE

From galaxies to genes, from the skies above to the ocean below, from the waters of the womb to the dust of death, the environment surrounds, shapes, and subsumes us. No matter how casually we may think of it, the environment holds us within mystery and majesty and within misery and madness.

Ancient peoples did think of it, seriously. Their mode of expression was the narrative.[1] In the beginning was the story or, rather, the stories—powerful, contrasting witnesses to the creation of the universe and all therein. This article juxtaposes two of these stories: the unfamiliar Akkadian version called the *Enuma Elish* and the familiar biblical version of Genesis 1:1–2:4a. Focusing on the entwined topics of gender, power, and responsibility, we relate the ancient stories to contemporary reflections on ecology.

THE *ENUMA ELISH*

Thanks to archaeological discoveries of the nineteenth century, a story of primeval origins surfaced among the ruins of the great library at Nineveh in ancient Assyria. Though the library flourished during the reign of King Ashurbanipal in the seventh century BCE, the story itself dated much earlier, sometime between 1700–1200 BCE. It came from the land between the Tigris and Euphrates Rivers, from Mesopotamia known now as Iraq. Written in Akkadian, it recounted the ascendancy of the city Babylon, the capital of the Mesopotamian world. No small event, the recounting encompassed the universe.[2]

The story develops through an omniscient narrator and speaking deities. Taking its title from the opening words, *enuma elish*, meaning "when on high," it begins before the heaven and the earth appear and even before the emergence of the gods. It begins in chaos. That concept means, first, lack of order, form, activity, and structure. Second, chaos comes to mean evil, that which threatens even if the violence be passive. Described as a watery abyss, chaos appears in two kinds: the male Apsu, who is sweet water, and the female Tiamat, who is salt water. Sexuality marks chaos. Of the two figures, Tiamat is the stronger. At first, she is "not an evil force."[3] Later she becomes vengeful and violent, giving birth to monsters and becoming herself the chaos dragon monster. In the beginning, the female dominates.

Primeval Parents and Their Children

From preexistent chaos, from primeval parents, spring the gods. Generation after generation they come. In time, their youth, energy, dancing and singing—their noise—disturb the parents, particularly Apsu. The first deity to speak, he appeals to Tiamat to destroy the children and their offspring—smash them to bits, so that rest, sleep, and inactivity can return to the watery abyss. Tiamat replies with the maternal instinct of protection: "What?" she asks. "Should we destroy that which we have built forth? Their ways [the ways of the children] indeed are most troublesome, but let us attend kindly!"

All is not well in chaos. When the children and the grandchildren learn what the male parent is proposing, they act quickly and in kind. One of them, Ea, god of running water, marshes, and wisdom, kills Apsu while he sleeps. Ironically, the rest Apsu sought for his life becomes his death. After the triumph, Ea retires to chambers that he has built on the remains of Apsu. There, with his consort Damkina, Ea begets the most wonderful of all children, perfect in all ways—the most wonderful Marduk.

> Greatly exalted was he [Marduk] above them, exceeding throughout.
> Perfect were his members beyond comprehension,
> . . . .
> He was the loftiest of the gods, surpassing was his stature.

Only superlatives identify Marduk. Truly, the savior figure has been born.

Salvation is needed because mother Tiamat, who earlier showed sympathy for the younger generations, now reverses allegiance, seeking revenge for the murder of her husband, Apsu. Angry and ready to fight, she calls a council meeting of her supporters. She sets up animals of terror, such as vipers, dragons, lion-demons, mad dogs, scorpions, and centaurs. They are to serve the gods in battle. Then, from among the gods of the council, Tiamat elevates one, Kingu, as commander-in-chief of her army. "To avenge Apsu, Tiamat wrought this evil." Violence grows in the primeval environment.

When the younger generations learn that the fierce mother plots their demise, they react in fear, unwilling or unable to take her on. Even Ea, killer of Apsu, recoils from confronting Tiamat and her forces. Fear of the female—of the chaos dragon monster, the epitome of violence—overwhelms the gods. (No feminist perspective here.)

The Victory of Marduk and Its Aftermath

The threatened gods implore Marduk the perfect to save them from Tiamat. Replying to their request, he downplays the threat by ranking male over female. "What male is it," he asks, "who has pressed his fight against thee? [*It is but*] Tiamat, a woman, who opposes thee with weapons!" Marduk, this son of Ea, this child of the fourth (or fifth) generation, this "wisest of all the gods," agrees to take on primeval mother Tiamat—but for the price that after victory he be declared the undisputed authority among the gods; that all the gods recognize his supremacy; that they declare him king. For the threatened gods, the price is none too high. Gladly they assent. Their song rings out across chaos:

> O Marduk, thou art indeed our avenger,
> We have granted thee kingship over the universe entire.

The environment and all therein will belong soon to Marduk.

A gory battle unfolds. With savage defiance, Tiamat confronts Marduk. She plans to swallow him. When she opens her mouth, however, he quickly sends in the east wind. It expands her body. Into her swollen belly he shoots an arrow, thereby ripping apart her insides. He splits her heart, crushes her skull, severs her arteries, and stands upon her carcass. Next he destroys her troops, including the leader Kingu. Upon viewing his destructive work, Marduk assumes a different posture. The violent warrior becomes the creative artist. From the halves of Tiamat's mangled body, he makes the heaven (the sky) and the earth. Thereby Marduk contains and controls, but does not eliminate, the chaotic watery abyss. He holds it in place by making the firmament. Then he sets the luminaries and regulates the years, months, and days. A seven day cycle he sets up. All in all, Marduk fashions the cosmos—an environment composed of defeated chaos.

Only near its end does the *Enuma Elish* turn attention, and then but briefly, to earth and its inhabitants. Marduk, described again as an "artful" creator, orders his father, Ea, to make "savage man" on earth and to make him from the blood of the defeated Kingu. The language "savage man," with the surrounding discourse, does not even recognize the female in the human realm—in contrast to her prominence in the divine. "Mankind," the male creature composed of controlled chaos, is assigned one task: to work on earth for the gods in heaven. He lives within the destroyed body of Tiamat, the mother without activity or power.[4] In ancient Babylonia, human beings (but only males counted) serve by blood, decree, and definition as slaves of the gods.

After slaying Tiamat the chaos dragon monster, reigning in her rebellious retinue, and arranging for the making of "savage man," Marduk claims his rewards. The gods build him a city (Babylon) and a shrine (Esagila) in which to rest. They throw a party, a great banquet in heaven. They exalt Marduk by bestowing on him fifty names that begin with "Marduk" and conclude with "Lord of the lands." These names proclaim Marduk as "supreme" in heaven and earth. Among other accomplishments, he creates grain and herbs, regulates grazing and watering places for the land, causes rich rains over the wide earth to provide vegetation, and opens wells to apportion water. On the other hand, Marduk exercises violence and destruction, multiplies spears, uproots all the evil ones, purges his enemies and their progeny, and destroys the gods of Tiamat. Yet Marduk's work is never done. In and around him evil persists.

The epilogue of the story contains another ecological reference. It instructs humans (all made from the blood of Kingu, all savages, and all males) to rejoice in Marduk so that "their land may be fertile." On this reference to "fertile land" hangs the greening of the earth, surrounded and ruled by violence, blood, and savagery.

Reflection

Reflecting on the *Enuma Elish* as it shaped Mesopotamian life, we observe that the setting and action occurred in the watery abyss among the gods, even though the story itself functioned for the earth and its inhabitants. The real and the true belonged to the divine realm. Earth took its meaning from heaven where controlled chaos reigned. Furthermore, the story did not happen just "once upon a time, long, long ago." Ever present, it happened repeatedly. Year after year, at the Babylonian New Year festival, the story was reenacted, with the king and his slave people assuming the roles of Marduk and his armies and with enemy countries viewed as Tiamat and her retinue. Establishing and maintaining the supremacy of Babylon and its god Marduk sealed the political purpose of the story.[5]

To live by the *Enuma Elish* is to experience an environment threatened forever by chaos. To live by this story is to fear "the persistence of evil,"[6] over which no final victory obtains. If at first the narrative seems alien, remote, and inappropriate, second thoughts bring revised understanding with contemporary relevance. Narratively, how do human beings account for all the evils and miseries of the world? for natural disasters? for conflict and confrontation? for violence, suffering, and despair? for disease, poverty, ignorance, and arrogance? for the clutter and pollution of the earth? Why do such things keep happening? For sure, "sin" does not cover the answer. Perhaps the chaos-dragon monster Tiamat and her forces still lurk in the universe. Perhaps we need a savior figure to deliver us, even if that deliverance is not permanent. In surprising, chilling, and disturbing ways, this ancient story resonates with contemporary struggles, including our environmental predicament. After all, humankind could profit from a savior figure. But King Marduk exacts his price—and Mother Tiamat always regroups.

GENESIS 1:1–2:4a

No doubt some readers chafe at the story told in the *Enuma Elish* because they know that the Bible, in its very first chapter, narrates a different beginning for the heavens and the earth. Many scholars have observed that Genesis 1:1–2:4a both reflects and counters the Babylonian creation story.[7] A prevailing, if questioned, view holds that in its final form Genesis 1 (shorthand for 1:1–2:4a) is the work of Judean priests living in the Babylonian exile of the sixth century BCE.[8] Their poetic composition—a liturgy in style and content[9]—gives voice and vision to an environmental theology over against the culture in which they were enslaved; over against the theology espoused in the *Enuma Elish*. Furthermore, this liturgy does more than reflect and counter evil chaos. It testifies to God the transcendent creator who "saw" (*yr*) as "very good" (*tob me'od*) the environment that God made. Together verb, adjective, and adverb bespeak an aesthetic dimension to the divine perspective.

Overview

The judgment "very good" comes, however, not as divine speech but as narrated discourse. From beginning to end, the omniscient narrator shapes the story and so controls the content. To explore the shape, content, and environmental meanings of Genesis 1 in conversation with the *Enuma Elish*, we attend to the beautifully ordered structure of introduction, body, and conclusion.[10]

Introduction

The introduction (1:1–2) uses the unique verb "create" (*bara'*) of which, throughout the Bible, only God is the subject. Unlike the situation in the *Enuma Elish*, this God (*'elohim*) appears without competitors and beyond sexuality.[11] Unlike Marduk, Elohim does not fight to become the sovereign Elohim already is.

As traditionally translated, the seven word Hebrew clause that opens Genesis makes the absolute statement, "In the beginning God created the heavens and the earth." But the absolute is relative. An alternative translation uses a temporal clause: "When God began to create . . . ," or "At the beginning of God's creating of . . . ."[12] Similar in form to the opening clause of the *Enuma Elish*, "when on high," this temporal clause yields not the absolute beginning but rather the beginning of creation. "When God began to create the heavens and the earth . . . ."

Immediately Genesis, in contrast to the *Enuma Elish,* drops the heavens to focus on the earth. Three references suggest that Elohim did not create out of nothing (*ex nihilo*) but rather out of preexistent chaos that lacked order. First the earth was *tohu wabohu,* often translated "chaos and desolation" (1:2).[13] Second, *hoshek,* that is, primeval darkness, covered the face of the deep (*tehom*).[14] Third, the primeval waters (*ha-mayim*) existed, over which the wind (*ruach*) of God swept.[15] In form, syntax, and vocabulary, the opening lines of Genesis witness to the presence of chaos at the beginning of creation. To be sure, strikingly unlike the *Enuma Elish,* Genesis reports no struggle or battle with these manifestations; yet neither does it proclaim or secure the absolute aloneness of God. Furthermore, as these references signal lack of order, they lead invariably to a troubling question: Are they morally neutral or do they represent evil? Do they hint at evil, at a threat with which God the creator must contend? The opening words of the Bible are neither grammatically nor theologically tight.[16]

Body

The temporal introduction, "When God began to create . . . ," plus its expansion leads to the body of the liturgy (1:3–31), whose overall structure is also temporal. Corresponding roughly to the order of events in the *Enuma Elish* (beginning with the luminaries and moving to the appearance of the human), six days of God's creative acts come as matching pairs: days one and four, two and five, three and six.

Each of the days begins with the words, "And God said." Throughout the liturgy God is the only character to speak. On days one, two, and three God "said" into being: (1) *light* separated from darkness (1:3–5); (2) the *firmament* (or dome) separating upper waters from lower waters (1:6–8); and (3) the *earth,* surrounded by the seas, putting forth vegetation (1:9–13). On days four, five, and six, God filled these structures. God filled (4) light with the *lights,* greater and lesser, plus the stars, to separate and rule day and night (1:14–19);[17] God filled (5) the firmament that holds back the waters with *aquatic and aerial animals,* fish and birds (1:20–23). Among the aquatic animals, God "created" (*bara'*) "the great sea monsters" (*hatanninim hagedolim*)—perhaps a tantalizing polemic, certainly irony, directed against the chaos dragon monsters of the *Enuma Elish.*[18] Moreover, God "blessed" all the aquatic animals (as well as the aerial)—so different a picture from the treatment, status, and behavior of sea monsters in the *Enuma Elish.* Next, God performed (6) two tasks to fill the earth: bringing forth *animals* of every kind, wild and domestic, and, climatically, creating *humankind* to inhabit the earth and eat its produce (1:24–31). Whereas in the *Enuma Elish* animals of all sorts, living in the watery abyss, are portrayed as monsters belonging to Tiamat and then to Marduk, in Genesis land animals, both wild and domestic, belong to that which is "good." Whereas in the *Enuma Elish* humankind (male) is the slave of the gods, in Genesis male and female are in the image of God. They receive dominion and blessing. (More on this later.)

As these six days of creation progress, each becomes narratively longer than the preceding. A hierarchic structure unfolds. "Day the six," on which God creates animals and humans, becomes the most expansive of all. Amazingly, the vast cosmos—"the spacious firmament on high, with all the blue ethereal sky"[19]—receives less (daily) emphasis than do the earth and its creatures. (To this remarkable feature we shall return.)

Beginning with the temporal clause that introduces God's creative work, Genesis 1 has expanded to six days in which God establishes order, sets boundaries, assigns roles, and perfects the cosmos. "All things bright and beautiful; all creatures great and small; all things wise and wonderful: in love God made them all."[20] Unlike the labors of Marduk, this divine work has happened without violence or competition. Accordingly, Genesis 1 moves to its conclusion.

Conclusion

Day seven, plus a coda, concludes the liturgy (2:1–3 and 4a).[21] Reminiscent of the seven day cycle that Marduk instituted, this numeral, itself a symbol of perfection, plays out repeatedly in the account.[22] Seven resides in the number of its words (35), the length of sentences (seven words each), and the phrase "the seventh day," repeated three times. (Cf. the seven-word Hebrew clause at the beginning, 1:1). On this day of perfection God "rested."[23] As in the conclusion of the *Enuma Elish,* Marduk rested, so in the conclusion of the Genesis liturgy, Elohim rested. Yet again comparison becomes contrast.

If the two stories correspond in using the motifs of seven and rest, they also diverge significantly. In the *Enuma Elish,* rest opposes work; in Genesis 1 rest completes work. Rest does not come after work; rather, it fulfills work. It is not inactivity but a special kind of activity. The occurrence of the verb *bless* (*brk*) underscores the difference.[24] As on day five God worked to *bless* aquatic and aerial creatures (1:22) and on day six God worked to *bless* humankind (1:28), so on day seven God worked to *bless* the day itself (2:3). Setting it apart, God made it holy. No such action describes Marduk at rest. In Genesis 1 rest does not signal divine inactivity but rather divine blessing.

Contrasts with the *Enuma Elish* continue on the seventh day. Whereas Marduk speaks volumes while inactive, God says nothing while active. Whereas Marduk rests in a place (a shrine or palace), God rests in time (day seven). Fitting the pattern of the entire Genesis liturgy, the temporal supersedes the spatial. Further, when God's work ends, creation is completed, finished once and for all. Unlike creation in the *Enuma Elish,* it is not repeated year after year. Remembered and recited, yes; repeated, no. The exiled Jews, unlike their Babylonian captors, need not fear an unstable, insecure, and dangerous universe. How different is Elohim the artist from the "artful" creator Marduk.

The last sentence of the Genesis liturgy, the coda, echoes its opening phrase, thereby forming an inclusio. "When God began to create the heavens and the earth" (1:1) reappears in modified form to become the summary, "These are the generations of the heavens and the earth when they were created" (2:4a

NRSV).[25] Replacing the active verb of creating with the passive, the omniscient narrator signals that God's work is completed. The circle of creation closes.

The Good Beginning

Throughout this majestic liturgy runs the divine judgment "good" (*tob*). Seven times (again, the number of perfection) appears the evaluation, "And God saw that it was good, indeed "very good" the seventh time (Gen. 1:4,10,12,18, 21, 25, 30). Throughout, this adjective renders pragmatic or functional judgment. The creative works of God perform as God intended. They do what they are supposed to do. Light, for example, becomes light and not something else. The repeated refrain, "and it was so," seals the point (1:9, 11, 15, 24, 30). Creation fulfills its purpose and so is "good."[26] The adjective "good," accompanied by the verb "see," also renders aesthetic judgment.[27] The cosmos, and all therein, is beautiful. God brought forth a universe that delights the eye, truly pleasing the beholder.[28] From "the spacious firmament on High" to "all creatures great and small," the Supreme Artist has been at work. And for certain, the adjective "good" renders moral judgment.[29] Everything God created is "good," not evil. Indeed, the word "evil," along with its corollaries of discord and violence, never appears. In describing creation, the evaluation "good" testifies to the character of the Creator. How different from the warring and competitive deities of the *Enuma Elish* is Elohim.

Pragmatic, aesthetic, and moral: the environment Elohim created works as intended, manifests beauty, and exudes integrity. Emphatically these meanings climax when, on "day the six," God saw everything that God had made and, lo, it was "very good."[30] Nonetheless, may not the absence of the word "evil," along with the preexistent presence of chaos and desolation (*tohu wabohu*), darkness (*hoshek*), and the deep (*tehom*) in the introduction (none of which God created) draw attention to evil? What is not said may well threaten through omission. That possibility leads to further reflection with exegesis.

Reflection

How beautifully Genesis 1 depicts the cosmos and all therein. It yields a green earth. Who, then, would not choose this liturgy, rather than the *Enuma Elish*, for an environmental narrative? How can anyone find problems with it? Traditionally, the religions of Judaism and Christianity have not found problems. Indeed, Genesis has inspired a theology of triumph and thanksgiving that embraces the environment:

> For the beauty of the earth
> > For the glory of the skies
> For the love that from our birth
> > Over and around us lies:

God of all, to you we raise
   this, our hymn of grateful praise.[31]

Alas, however, as we look around, all too often we see not "the beauty of the earth" but a garbage heap, not the "glory of the skies" but a polluted canopy. If honest, we must temper our hymns of ecological triumph and turn to confession.

For the clutter of the earth
   For the smog-filled skies above
For the mess that scars our birth,
   Spoiling now the work of love,
God of all, to you we frame
   this, our dirge of guilt and shame.[32]

Whence comes the ecological mess? However complex the answers, pivotal problems may reside in Genesis 1. They appear on the day that the liturgy highlights, designating it "day *the* six" rather than simply "day six" (which would have paralleled "day one," "day two" and so forth). First on this longest day or this day of most words, God by fiat assigns earth the task of producing (or bringing forth, *ysa*) the animals, domestic and wild, in all their variety (1:24). "Let the earth bring forth living creatures of every kind."[33] Earth becomes God's agent. Nature carries responsibilities on behalf of God. Animals are not, as in the *Enuma Elish*, creatures of terror and violence made in heaven by a chaotic deity. Second, on this longest day God by fiat makes humankind. For that special task God enlists the divine council, those hosts who do God's bidding in heaven. Though with difference, a parallel to Marduk's calling upon the assembly of the gods comes to mind. "Let us," intones God. "Let us make *'adam* (humankind) in our image (*selem*), after our likeness (*demut*)" (1:26). In all creation the words "image" and "likeness" pertain only to humankind. Accordingly, humankind stands apart, exalted as the representative (the image) of God on earth.[34] Again, what a contrast to Marduk's ordering the making of "savage man," from the blood of the defeated Kingu, to be slave of the gods.

The contrast continues. God moves the human vocabulary from the singular noun *'adam* to the plural pronoun *'otam*. "Let them [not "him" or "the one"] have-dominion (*weyiredu*) over the fish of the sea and over the birds of the air and over the domestic animals and over the wild animals and over all the earth and over every creeping thing that creeps upon the earth" (1:26).[35] Dominion over the earth, its surroundings, and its inhabitants: with this vocabulary God gives humankind great power, so unlike the "slave man" of the *Enuma Elish*. Yet "dominion" emerges as the first of two verbs that may signal trouble for the ecological bliss of Genesis 1. (More later.)

Following God's hortatory proposal, using the ordinary verb "make" ("Let us make, *'asah* . . ."), comes the narrator's declarative poem, using the unique verb "create," *bara'*. Arranged as a chiasm (A, B, B', A'), the first two lines of the little poem lock in the phrase "image of God" by surrounding it with the unique activity of God.

```
           A                      B
So God created humankind ('adam) in God's image;

        B'              A'
In the image of God created God it.³⁶
Male and female created God them. (1:27)
```

Whereas the chiastic arrangement of the two lines emphasizes God's image as central, it fails to explicate the phrase "image of God." The third line discloses the meaning. It gives a gender identification that parallels the phrase "image of God." "Male and female created God them."³⁷

Male and female are the *imago Dei*.³⁸ How different from the "savage male" of the *Enuma Elish*; how different from hierarchies of sexuality that would subordinate female to male; how different from role distinctions between the sexes. And how different from established priestly theology.³⁹ No ranking, no division of duty, no rule over another, no separate spheres of operation: "male and female" as "the image of God" (not as God but as God's image) recognizes gender identity without prejudice.⁴⁰ But the identity 'adam does not specify race, ethnicity, class, or any comparable category. To the contrary, 'adam embraces humankind. Further, no natural context or substance (e.g., no blood of a rebellious god as in the *Enuma Elish*) accompanies this divine act. Even though the word 'adam may connect to the word 'adamah (ground) as it occurs in 1:25 (cf. 2:7), thereby relating animal ("everything that creeps upon the ground") and human to yield an ecological connection, in this liturgy the method and material for God's creating 'adam remain mysteries.

Humankind in the image of God male and female: God "blessed" (*brk*) them and spoke directly to both of them in assigning responsibilities:

> Be fruitful and multiply and fill the earth and subdue it;
> and have dominion over the fish of the sea and over the birds of the air
> and over every living thing that moves upon the earth.
>
> (1:28 NRSV)

With the vocabulary "bless," "be fruitful," "multiply," and "fill," the storyteller and God repeat motifs that apply to the aquatic and aerial animals of day five. Major links within creation continue even as striking differences emerge. The troubling verb "have-dominion" (*radah*), unique to humankind, reappears, along with its parallel "subdue" (*kabas*)—the second verb that may disturb the ecological bliss of the liturgy.

Two Troubling Verbs: Interpretive Background

More than forty years ago (1967), Professor Lynn White argued, in an article for *Science* magazine, that by separating "man" from nature the biblical accounts of creation (both Genesis 1 and 2), as traditionally interpreted, granted "man" power to "exploit nature for his proper ends."⁴¹ White contended that nature has been "de-divinized" and the human has become its lord, to the detriment of both nature and humankind. Across decades, White's thesis continues to attract attention.[42]

Writing in 2000, the biblical theologian Norman Habel argued that Genesis 1 contains two conflicting stories: an "earth-oriented" story (1:1–25) and a "human story" (1:26–30).[43] By claiming verses 24 and 25 for the "earth-oriented" story and dropping verse 31, he disregarded the literary integrity of day six, which extends from verses 24 to 31. The "human story," he averred, "violates the spirit of the Earth-oriented story that precedes it." Giving humans power to have-dominion over animals and to subdue the earth devalues the earth. For Habel, the harsh verb *kabas* (subdue) is beyond redemption. Overall, he maintained that Genesis 1 itself does not resolve the conflict between the two stories. For certain, the "human story" has contributed adversely to the ecological crisis.[44]

The structure, vocabulary, and content of Genesis 1:1–2:4a, however, resist Habel's reading. Although earth-conscious, Genesis 1:1–23 (the introduction through day five) is not totally "earth-oriented," as he claims. Within these twenty-three verses, the word *'eres* (earth) occurs but ten times: two times in the introduction; never on days one and two; and eight times across days three (the creation of earth), four, and five. By comparison, within the over eleven verses of Genesis 1:24–2:4a, which Habel (omitting 1:24–25 and 1:31–2:4a) designates "the human story," the word *'eres* occurs twelve times: ten times within day six alone and one time each in day seven and the coda.

In reporting the creation of animals and humankind, "day the six" stresses the word *'eres*, repeatedly in divine speech.

> "Let the *earth* bring forth . . . wild animals of the *earth*," said God (v. 24).

> "God made wild animals of the *earth*," reported the narrator (v. 25).

> "Let humankind have-dominion over wild animals of the *earth* and every creeping thing that creeps upon the *earth*," said God (v. 26)

> ". . . fill the *earth* and subdue it," said God (v. 28).

> ". . . have-dominion over . . . every living thing that moves upon the *earth*," said God (v. 28).

> "I have given you every plant . . . upon the face of the *earth*," said God (v. 29).

> "To every beast of the *earth* . . . and to everything that creeps on the *earth* . . . I have given every good plant for food," said God (v. 30).

After these ten occurrences of *'eres*, the word appears twice more: (a) within the narrated phrase "the heavens and the earth," which introduces day seven (2:1), and (b) within the coda (2:4a). Rather than the conflict that Habel posits between "two stories," emphasis upon the earth pervades the Genesis liturgy (with the exceptions of days one and two) from start to finish.[45]

The Focus in "Day the Six"

Although throughout "day the six" the narrator and God portray earth prominently and positively, the focus of this day belongs to God's creating humankind male and female and assigning them the verb "have-dominion," with animals and the earth as the objects, and the verb "subdue," with earth as the object.

Accusations against these two verbs mount when readers consider their appearances elsewhere in the Bible.[46] Occurring some twenty-seven times, the Hebrew word translated "have-dominion" (*radah*) carries negative meanings: to have power, especially over enemies.[47] Most often associated with royal power, the verb signifies use of force accompanied by violence and destruction (e.g., Deut. 20:20; 1 Kgs. 5:30; 9:23; Neh. 9:28). Perhaps, however, one text hints through negation at royal rule of a positive sort (Ezek. 34:4).[48] This verb also describes treading or trampling the winepress (Joel 3:13), an action of coercion, even if with good results. Never does God appear as subject or object of the verb, though God does use it to authorize human (royal) activity. When in Genesis 1 God assigns humankind dominion, the negative uses of the verb elsewhere would hardly commend it here.

Similarly, the parallel verb "subdue" (*kabas*), appearing some fourteen times in the Hebrew Bible, denotes force.[49] The settings range from military conquests of land and people (e.g., Num. 32:22, 29; Josh. 18:1; 2 Sam. 8:11) to individual predicaments of enslavement (Jer. 34:11; Zech. 9:15) and, once or twice, to sexual assault (Esth. 7:8; cf. Neh. 5:5). In one instance, however, this force does form a positive parallel to the verb "have-compassion" (*rhm*), with God as subject, "subduing [or "treading under foot"] our iniquities" (Mic. 7:19). But not unlike the verb "to have-dominion," the verb "subdue" bears negative meanings of violence and exploitation—hardly commendation for its use in Genesis 1.

Immediate Context

Given these disturbing meanings, what do biblical interpreters say about the two verbs as God uses them in Genesis 1? Do they give humankind license to exploit, rape, and savage the earth? Do they authorize destruction of the environment? Drawing upon the parallels elsewhere in Scripture, one might reach that conclusion. Drawing upon the context in Genesis, however, one might not. Two interlocking rubrics guide the latter view: (1) Context encloses texts to circumscribe meanings. (2) Discounting context distorts texts.

The contextual approach to the verbs *radah* and *kabas* focuses on the adjective "good." "Everything God created, lo, it was very good" (Gen. 1:31). This context is altogether different from other contexts of war, violence, enslavement, and assault in which these verbs appear. Here in Genesis the pragmatic, aesthetic, and ethical components of the "good" enclose the verbs "have-dominion" and "subdue." Do these verbs, then, with predominately negative associations elsewhere in the Bible, subvert the context of the "good"[50] or does the context subvert the negative meanings of these verbs? Do these verbs give humankind permission to rape the earth or do they exhort humankind to preserve the goodness of the earth? Do they authorize license or delegate royal and priestly responsibility?[51] These questions signal the dilemma of dominion.

Context plays another role in considering a related judgment against the ecological integrity of Genesis 1. This judgment maintains (as White and others have noted) that to have-dominion over the animals and to subdue the earth separates humankind from nature and so places humankind over against nature. But again, context suggests otherwise. A motif of separation runs throughout creation; it is not limited to humankind versus nature.[52] At all levels nature itself is divided. The firmament separates the waters from the waters; the dry land separates the waters under the heavens; the lights separate day from night. Moreover, plants and fruit trees, fish and birds, animals and creeping things are separated from one another. They are differentiated, each according to its kind. The differentiation of humankind from animals and the earth belongs, then, to a pattern of separation that characterizes the entire creation. The pattern does not connote "over against," but it does set humankind apart. It frees humankind from the tyranny of nature and from the idolatry of nature, both marks of the *Enuma Elish*.

Yet in a turnaround, Genesis 1 also depicts humankind as a part of nature, within it and associated especially with the animals. Seven observations secure the point. (1) In 1:25–26, land animals and humankind are objects of the same verb, "make" (*'asah*), with God as subject.[53] (2) Earlier (1:21) the unique verb "create" (*bara*) described God's action in bringing about sea monsters and other aquatic animals as well as winged creatures. Similarly, in 1:27 *bara'* relates God's action in bringing about male and female. (3) God makes land animals and humankind on the same day, the sixth. (4) They inhabit the same space, namely "earth" (*'eres*). Like the animals, humankind is an earth creature. (5) God decrees that aerial and land animals and humankind eat the same food: "every plant yielding seed" and "every green plant (1:29–30). (6) God also decrees that both groups be "fruitful and multiply" (1:22, 28). Altogether, land animals and humankind share terminology, time, turf, table, and task. (7) Moreover, they share divine blessing (1:22, 28). As creatures within nature, they are not apart, though they are ranked.[54]

Both a part and apart: Hence, the distinction of having-dominion and subduing, reserved solely for humankind, perdures. In the structure of the liturgy as well as in the context and content of creation, the verbs *radah* and *kabas* belong to a hierarchy of harmony, with humankind at the climax of "day the six"— though not at the apex of creation itself. That position belongs to day seven, the day of divine rest. The concept of hierarchy helps to focus the meaning of the verbs.[55] It entails responsibility for promoting goodness, not for exercising domination and subjugation.

Throughout the liturgy runs the motif of responsibility. The firmament is responsible for controlling the waters. The greater light is responsible for ruling the day and the lesser light the night. The earth is responsible for producing vegetation and fruit. God charges both earth and water to "bring forth living creatures." At many levels, responsibility for the sake of order and harmony describes creation. Accordingly, this motif illuminates, even as it tempers, the power of having-dominion and subduing given to humankind. Neither absolute nor all encompassing, the power does not include, for example, control over the firmament and the lights. Nor does it permit humankind to kill and eat animal flesh (but cf. Gen. 9:3–4). Instead, the two verbs authorize humankind to represent God on earth. To designate the human status of representative and the human duty of responsibility, scholars propose various nouns with varying nuances: agent, avatar, caretaker, caregiver, plenipotentiary, royal vicar, surrogate, steward, shepherd, stand-in, trustee, viceroy, and vizier (but *not* "co-creator" or "partner in creation"). To have-dominion over animals and to subdue the earth is to be a caretaker (and caregiver) who protects, preserves, promotes, and provides for the earth and its inhabitants.[56]

Overall, context and text circumscribe the meanings of the two troubling verbs.[57] Within set limits, they commission humankind to do the work of God in the world: to image transcendent goodness, to live in harmony with the rest of creation, and to take responsibility for that harmony. Repeatedly, the context of Genesis 1 would disavow misuses of having-dominion and subjugating.

Summary

Assigning negative meanings to "have-dominion" and "subdue" in Genesis 1 based on the use of these words elsewhere in Scripture ignores, negates, or subverts their immediate context. This context connotes a positive hierarchical relationship of humankind and nature. It prohibits exploitation; it sanctions use; it censures abuse. The verbs themselves signify God's gift, not a human right. They assign responsibility to preserve and promote the goodness of God's creation.

The word "hierarchy" requires further comment. In certain circles across millennia, it has functioned negatively. It has been used (and so continues) to define and regulate sexual relationships, racial and ethnic identities, class status, ecclesiastical ranks, role assignments, and the like. For many people, it has acquired and absorbed a pernicious, even unredeemable, meaning.[58] As presented in Genesis 1, however, hierarchy does not pertain to the relationship between the sexes (or to the other relationships noted above, which are not even present). To the contrary, male and female (sexually differentiated but otherwise not defined) stand equal and mutual—both made in the image of God and both given dominion. Neither gender nor race, ethnicity, class, age, or position defines or describes them. Together they bear the environmental responsibility to preserve the goodness of creation. Caretakers, not destroyers, are they.

Although no direct line connects ancient priests to modern polluters, that judgment does not permit a triumphal ending to our reflections. As optimistic as Genesis 1 sounds, fragments, glimpses, and hints of chaos survive in it.[59] The watery abyss, present in the beginning before creation, does not disappear completely, but it is confined and controlled. The primeval darkness (*hoshek*) remains after the creation of light. Never called "good," it survives to become the night. Further, darkness maintains sequential priority in the formula that concludes each of days one through six: "there was evening and there was morning." Again, the repeated emphasis on "good" may harbor the suspicion that evil yet lurks. What is not said may be implicated in what is said. Why, for instance, is the word "good" absent in reference to day two, the making of the firmament (though the firmament is included in the overall judgment that "everything God created is very good")? Even if, for this question, the medieval rabbi Rashi (and others) offered an explanation, the larger issue endures.[60]

All in all, the magnificent, majestic, and mysterious environment portrayed throughout Genesis 1 moves away from the turbulent, tortuous, and torturous environment of the *Enuma Elish*. From Babylonian citizens to Judean exiles, from Marduk to Elohim, from slave to steward, from male to male and female, from bloody ground to green earth—the movement is decisive. And yet limits haunt biblical stories to come. Though God's creative work controls and transforms chaos, it does not eliminate it. The title of Jon Levenson's book makes the point: *Creation and the Persistence of Evil*.[61]

CONCLUSION: THE PERSISTENCE OF THE DILEMMA

That persistence endures. Three references—two biblical and one contemporary—suffice.

(1) In the Noah narratives, the priestly version of creation returns, but this time in negative form. "Now the earth was corrupt in God's sight and the earth was filled with violence" (Gen. 6:11). The flood of divine judgment follows. The chaotic waters return to destroy the earth and its inhabitants, human and animal. God spares only a remnant (Gen. 6:11–7:24) but through it renews earthy creation. Indeed, the priestly language of blessing in Genesis 1 reappears along with the command, "Be fruitful and multiply and fill the earth" (Gen. 9:1 NRSV). But this time permission to eat meat (9:3–6), though with limits, skews the relationship set forth with the animals in Genesis 1:29–30. In the end, to seal the renewal of creation after the flood, God establishes an everlasting covenant "with every living creature of all flesh that is on the earth" (Gen. 9:8–17 NRSV). In the renewal, with its echoes, allusions, and references to Genesis 1, the verbs *radah* and *kabas* do not appear. Nonetheless, the persistence of evil haunts the goodness of creation.

(2) When, in the seventh century BCE, the prophet Jeremiah meditated on these matters, he tied them to divine judgment upon a foolish and stupid people: a people lacking in understanding and refusing to do good; a people who have not preserved the goodness of the earth. Their failure led Jeremiah to envision the *un-writing* of Genesis 1: to foresee the destruction of the environment in a return to preexistent chaos. His poem disassembled the narrative of creation.

> I looked on the earth, and, lo, it was *tohu wabohu* [chaos and desolation];
>   and to the heavens, and they gave no light.
> I looked on the mountains, and lo, they were quaking,
>   and all the hills moved to and fro.
> I looked, and lo, there was no one at all,
>   and all the birds of the air had fled.
> I looked, and lo, the fruitful land was a desert,
>   and all its cities were laid in ruins
>   before the LORD, before his [God's] fierce anger.
>   (Jer. 4:23–26, NRSV, adapted)

(3) Transferred to the contemporary scene, this haunting and convicting poem evokes the ecological crisis in ways large and small.[62] It calls forth despair among observers who understand, if ironically, that abdicating dominion has contributed to the pollution and clutter of the earth.

> Clutter, clutter everywhere
>   Without an inch to spare
> Clutter, clutter everywhere
>   No room but to despair.
> Clutter, clutter everywhere
>   Without a space to breathe
> Clutter, clutter everywhere
> With ample room to grieve.[63]

A corollary of the predicament concerns the increasing power that humankind gives to technology, thereby forfeiting, in some instances, our God-given dominion to preserve and promote goodness. Accordingly, parodies of Scripture emerge:

> The word became digital and ruled among us.
> And we beheld its power,
>   the power as the begotten of the chaos monster,
>   full of fact and fear.
>
> Glory to technology in the highest
>   and servitude to its people on earth.[64]

Mutatis mutandis, this servitude may recall the "slave man" of the *Enuma Elish*, who works for warring gods. Abdicating human responsibility (dominion) for the sake of technological power (dominion) damages creation.[65]

Though abundantly blessed, the cosmos and all therein are not secure from the threat of chaos—a threat both endemic and acquired. In grappling with the latter, we, male and female created in the image of God, hold no small responsibility. Without commitment to stewardship, to caregiving for the sake of the heavens and the earth and all therein, without the exercise of human dominion rightly understood, creation may well revert to chaos. Looking around, how can we not see that the hour is late and we are not saved? The grass withers and the flower fades. The greening of the earth shrinks. The birds flee; the fish die.

Even the great whales, those creatures "of the fifth morning," cease "galloping out of darkness" and begin suffering unto death.[66] The polluting of the cosmos abounds; the environment weeps. Lo, all is not "very good," nor even "good."

Is the chaos dragon monster returning? If we continue in our misguided ways, what narrative will we tell? What ancient story will endure: a story of creation or destruction? of healing or hurt? of praise or fear? What poetry will we speak: words of lament, "I looked on the earth and, lo, it was *tohu wabohu*"? or words of celebration: ". . . the fields of glittering fire / where everything, even the great whale throbs with songs"?[67]

Mystery and majesty, misery and madness: the environment that holds us within its watery womb awaits our answer.

Notes

1. A definition of narrative: "An account in prose or verse of an actual or fictional event or a sequence of such events." See C. Hugh Holman, *A Handbook to Literature* (Indianapolis: Bobbs-Merrill Educational Publishing, 1980), 284.
2. For discussions and translations of the *Enuma Elish,* see, inter alia, "The Creation Story," trans. by E. A. Speiser in Isaac Mendelsohn, ed., *Religions of the Ancient Near East* (New York: The Liberal Arts Press, 1955), 17–46; Alexander Heidel, *The Babylonian Genesis* (Chicago: University of Chicago Press, 1963); Thorkild Jacobson, *The Treasures of Darkness: A History of Mesopotamian Religion* (New Haven, CT: Yale University Press, 1976), 165–91; Richard J. Clifford, *Creation Accounts in the Ancient Near East and in the Bible* (Washington, DC: The Catholic Biblical Quarterly Monograph Series, No. 26, 1994), esp. 82–93. This essay relies on Speiser's translation.
3. See Tikva Frymer-Kensky, *In the Wake of the Goddesses: Women, Culture, and the Biblical Transformation of Pagan Myth* (New York: The Free Press, 1992), 74–76.
4. Frymer-Kensky, *In the Wake of the Goddesses,* 78.
5. Cf. Clifford's description of the story as "a political cosmogony" (*Creation Accounts in the Ancient Near East and in the Bible,* 93).
6. For this phrase, see Jon D. Levenson, *Creation and the Persistence of Evil* (San Francisco: Harper & Row, 1985).
7. On the *Enuma Elish* and Gen. 1, see, e.g., Bernard F. Batto, *Slaying the Dragon: Mythmaking in the Biblical Tradition* (Louisville, KY: Westminster/John Knox Press, 1992), 33–39, 73–84; Kenton L. Sparks, "*Enuma Elish* and Priestly Mimesis: Elite Emulation in Nascent Judaism," *Journal of Biblical Literature* 126 (Winter 2007): 625–48. Scholars debate whether this creation account ends at Gen. 2:3 or 2:4a. For 2:4a (used in this essay) as the ending, either the original or an addition, see, e.g., E. A. Speiser, *Genesis,* The Anchor Bible (Garden City, NY: Doubleday & Company, Inc., 1964), 5–8; Gerhard von Rad, *Genesis* (Philadelphia: The Westminster Press, 1972), 46, 63; Claus Westermann, *Genesis 1–11: A Commentary,* trans. John J. Scullion, S.J. (Minneapolis: Augsburg Publishing House, 1984), 78–80; George W. Coats, *Genesis* (Grand Rapids: William B. Eerdmans Publishing Co., 1983), 42–48; Laurence A. Turner, *Genesis* (Sheffield: Sheffield Phoenix Press, 2009), 16. For 2:3 as the ending, with 2:4a as the heading or superscription or bridge to what follows (2:4b–3:24), see, e.g., Frank Moore Cross, *Canaanite Myth and Hebrew Epic* (Cambridge, MA: Harvard University Press, 1973), 301–2; Jon D. Levenson, *Creation and the*

Persistence of Evil, 66–68; Bernhard W. Anderson, *From Creation to New Creation* (Minneapolis: Fortress Press, 1994), 54; David M. Carr, *Reading the Fractures of Genesis* (Louisville, KY: Westminster John Knox Press, 1996), 74–75.

8. On dating the Priestly Source, see, e.g., Carr, *Reading the Fractures of Genesis*, 133–40. On the assignment of Gen. 1 to the P Source, with a thorough discussion of the passage, see Mark S. Smith, *The Priestly Vision of Genesis 1* (Minneapolis: Fortress Press, 2010). On questions about assigning Gen. 1 to the Priestly Source, cf. below note 39.

9. "Liturgy" as a set of forms used in public worship fits well Gen. 1:1–2:4a. Cf. its organization in seven days with repeated words, phrases, and sentences. Note also its use in the Jerusalem Temple after the Exile.

10. Numerous scholars have commented on the external design and internal structure of Gen. 1:1–2:4a. For views similar to the one presented here, views that span fifty years, see Claus Westermann, *The Genesis Accounts of Creation*, Facet Books (Philadelphia: Fortress Press, 1964), 6–22 and Ronald Hendel, *The Book of Genesis: A Biography* (Princeton: Princeton University Press, 2013), 32–38. For a recent, alternative structure, see Karl Loning and Erich Zenger, *To Begin with, God Created . . .: Biblical Theologies of Creation,* trans. Omar Kaste (Collegeville, MN: The Liturgical Press, 2000), 105–7. This alternative depicts Gen. 1:3–2:3 as a house. Days one, four, and seven, all concerned with the theme of time, form the framework for the paired days two and three, which set up the earth surrounded by the ocean, and the paired days five and six, in which living things are placed in earth and ocean.

11. See Anderson, *From Creation to New Creation*, 8. For comparisons of Marduk and Ea with Elohim, see David Toshio Tsumura, *The Earth and the Waters in Genesis 1 and 2: A Linguistic Investigation*, Journal for the Study of the Old Testament Supplement Series 83 (Sheffield: Sheffield Academic Press, 1989), 143–54; 166–67.

12. For differing translations, official and individual, cf., e.g., the King James Bible (1611), The Torah (1962); The Catholic Study Bible (1990); the New Revised Standard Version (1991); Everett Fox, *The Five Books of Moses* (New York: Schocken Books, 1995); Robert Alter, *The Five Books of Moses* (New York: W. W. Norton, 2004). For two recent choices, the first for the absolute and the second for the temporal clause, see Turner, *Genesis*, 11, and Edwin M. Good, *Genesis 1–11* (Stanford, CA: Stanford University Press, 2011), 10–12. Yet a third proposal, designed to avoid grammatical problems and to characterize a *sui generic* beginning, renders the opening word *beresit* as "to begin with" (Loning and Zenger, *To Begin with, God Created…,* 18–21). For an alternative translation of *bara'* as "separate," see Ellen van Wolde, "Why the Verb ברא Does Not Mean 'to Create' in Genesis 1:1–2:4a," *Journal for the Study of the Old Testament* 34 (September 2009): 3–23.

13. But see Tsumura, who holds that *tohu wabohu* means "emptiness," not chaos; that it means "bare" or "not yet productive"; that it is a positive, non-threatening phrase (*The Earth and the Waters in Genesis 1 and 2*, 17–43; 155–56; 162, 68). (Unless indicated otherwise, all biblical translations in this essay are my own).

14. Scholars disagree on whether the Hebrew word *tehom* (deep) echoes the name "Tiamat." For a linguistic affinity, see, e.g., von Rad, *Genesis*, 50; Sparks, "*Enuma Elish* and Priestly Mimesis," 630 n14; Susan Niditch, "Genesis," *Women's Bible Commentary; Revised and Updated* (Louisville, KY: Westminster John Knox Press, 2012), 30. For the opposite view, see, e.g., Tsumura, who holds that the word simply means "ocean" and is not related to Tiamat or any other dragon monster (*The Earth and the Waters in Genesis 1 and 2*, 156–59, 163–64.).

15. Cf. Theodore Hiebert, "Air, the First Sacred Thing: The Conception of רוח in the Hebrew Scriptures," *Exploring Ecological Hermeneutics*, ed. Norman C. Habel and Peter Trudinger (Atlanta: Society of Biblical Literature, 2008), 9–19.

16. See Victor P. Hamilton, *The Book of Genesis: Chapters 1–17* (Grand Rapids, MI: William B. Eerdmans Publishing Company, 1990), 103–17; Brevard Childs, *Myth and Reality in the Old Testament* (Naperville, IL: Alec R. Allenson, Inc., 1960), 30–42.

17. An observation regarding "greater and lesser" lights: the precise Hebrew words for "sun" and "moon" are not used because these words are also the names of ancient Near Eastern deities.

18. See, e.g., Levenson, *Creation and the Persistence of Evil*, 5–56; Terence E. Fretheim, "The Book of Genesis," *The New Interpreter's Bible*, vol. I (Nashville: Abingdon Press, 1994), 344–45. On Hebrew legends connecting the monster Leviathan and possibly Tiamat to the fifth day of creation, see Michael Bright, *Beasts of the Fields: The Revealing Natural History of Animals in the Bible* (London: Robson Books, 2006), 29–39.

19. These words open a hymn composed by Joseph Addison in 1712: hymn 148 in *Church Hymnary* (Norwich, UK: Canterbury Press, 2005).

20. See hymn 291, "All Things Bright and Beautiful," in *Voices United* (Canada: The United Church Publishing House, 1996). The words come from Cecil Frances Alexander (c. 1848); the music is adapted by Martin Shaw (1915) from a seventeenth-century English melody.

21. For the classic exposition of day seven, see Abraham Joshua Heschel, *The Sabbath: Its Meaning for Modern Man* (New York: Farrar, Straus and Giroux, 1951); cf. Loning and Zenger, *To Begin with, God Created . . .*, 113–16.

22. On heptadic structures throughout Genesis 1:1–2:4a, see U. Cassuto, *A Commentary on the Book of Genesis: Part I, From Adam to Noah* (Jerusalem: The Magnes Press, 1972), 12–15; Levenson, *Creation and the Persistence of Evil*, 66–77.

23. For an earth-oriented reading of day seven, see Howard N. Wallace, "Rest for the Earth? Another Look at Genesis 2:1–3," in *The Earth Story in Genesis*, ed. Norman C. Habel and Shirley Wurst (Sheffield: Sheffield Academic Press, 2000), 49–59.

24. For a classic study of the verb "bless," see Johannes Pedersen, *Israel: Its Life and Culture, I–II* (London: Oxford University Press, 1959), 182–212; cf. Josef Scharbert, "ברך *brk*," *Theological Dictionary of the Old Testament*, vol. 2, ed. G. Johannes Botterweck and Helmer Ringgren (Grand Rapids, MI: 1975), 279–308.

25. On this ending, see note 7 above.

26. Cf. Von Rad, *Genesis*, 52, 61.

27. See Timothy Polk, "In the Image: Aesthetics and Ethics through the Glass of Scripture," *Horizons in Biblical Theology* 8, no. 1 (June 1986): esp. 27–40; Claus Westermann, "Beauty in the Hebrew Bible," *A Feminist Companion to Reading the Bible*, ed. Athalya Brenner and Carole Fontaine (Sheffield: Sheffield Academic Press, 1997), esp. 586–89. Cf., e.g., Walter Brueggemann, *Genesis*, Interpretation Commentary Series (Atlanta: John Knox, 1982), 37; Anderson, *From Creation to New Creation*, 103–6; Shamai Gelander, *The Good Creator: Literature and Theology in Genesis 1–11* (Atlanta: Scholars Press, 1997), 96; Hamilton, *The Book of Genesis*, 120, 141. Cf. Sallie McFague, *A New Climate for Theology* (Minneapolis: Fortress Press, 2008), 74.

28. For a parallel use of *tob* as an aesthetic designation, yet on a much smaller scale, cf. the description of the baby yet to be named Moses in Exodus 2:2.

29. See, e.g., Good, *Genesis 1–11*, 8, 18; Gelander, *The Good Creator*, 101.

30. For a counter understanding of "good" (*tob*), which combines historical critical and postmodern perspectives, see Edward L. Greenstein, "Presenting Genesis 1, Constructively and Deconstructively," *Prooftexts* 21, no. 1 (Winter 2001): 1–22.

31. See Hymn 226, "For the Beauty of the Earth," in *Voices United.* The words were composed in 1864 by Folliett Sanford Pierpoint; the music was composed in 1927 by David Evans.

32. This confession was composed by Sarah Ryan and Phyllis Trible, reproduced by authors' permission.

33. On the phrase "of every kind" or "after every kind" for establishing the variety and "comprehensiveness" of God's creating, see Richard Neville, "Differentiation in Genesis 1: An Exegetical Creation *ex nihilo*," *Journal of Biblical Literature* 130 (2011): 209–26.

34. Comparing the phrase "image of God" to a reference in Ezek. 1:26, some scholars derive the meaning of "a physical resemblance" (so, e.g., Greenstein, "Presenting Genesis 1, Constructively and Deconstructively," 7). Other scholars find the meaning in human action rather than human nature; see Claus Westermann, *Genesis 1–11*, 147–67. On difference as well as similarity in the words "image" and "likeness," see Paul Niskanen, "The Poetics of Adam: The Creation of אדם in the Image of אלהים," *Journal of Biblical Literature* 128 (2009): 417–36.

35. Though the English verb "rule" may fit the Hebrew verb *radah*, in this essay we keep the traditional, familiar rendering "have-dominion." Cf., e.g., the KJV, NRSV, REB, and Fox, *The Five Books of Moses.* On "rule," cf. Smith, who uses it (*The Priestly Vision of Genesis 1*), and Alter, who rejects it for "hold sway" (*The Five Books of Moses*).

36. On the translation "it" rather than the traditional "him," cf. Fox, *The Five Books of Moses,* 15.

37. For an earlier discussion, see Phyllis Trible, *God and the Rhetoric of Sexuality* (Philadelphia: Fortress Press, 1978), 12–23.

38. Contra Phyllis A. Bird, "'Male and Female He Created Them': Gen. 1:27b in the Context of the Priestly Account of Creation," *Harvard Theological Review* 74 (1981): 129–59, who argues that the identity "male and female" relates only to fertility and not to the *imago Dei.* See also Niskanen, "The Poetics of Adam," 417–36.

39. Cf., e.g., the priestly writers of Leviticus whose male-centered theology subordinated female to male (Niditch, "Genesis," *Women's Bible Commentary*, 28, 30). The discrepancy between classical priestly theology regarding male and female and the proclamation of Gen. 1:27 is one reason, among others, that some scholars question the assignment of Gen. 1 to the Priestly Source. An alternative proposes that Gen. 1 is a document independent of all the established Pentateuchal sources. Another alternative proposes that Gen. 1 comes from a sub-branch of the Israelite priesthood, which did not support the view of male dominance and female subordination. On the priestly attribution, see above note 8.

40. See Helen Schungel-Straumann, "On the Creation of Man and Woman in Genesis 1–3: The History and Reception of the Texts Reconsidered," *A Feminist Companion to Genesis*, ed. Athalya Brenner (Sheffield: Sheffield Academic Press, 1993), 53–76.

41. Lynn White Jr., "The Historical Roots of Our Ecological Crisis," *Science* 155 (1967): 1203–7; reprinted in Frances A. Schaeffer, *Pollution and the Death of Man: The Christian View of Ecology* (Wheaton, IL: Tyndale House Publishers, 1970), 97–115; also in Garrett DeBell, *The Environmental Handbook* (New York: Ballantine, 1970), 12–26. For my earlier reflections on this article, see Phyllis Trible, "Ancient Priests and Modern Polluters," *Andover Newton Quarterly*, vol.

12 (November, 1971): 74–79. Cf. Rosemary Radford Ruether, who avers that White's "interpretation incorporates the Genesis language too directly into Christian and secular views of domination . . ." (*New Women New Earth* [New York: The Seabury Press, 1975], 187–96).

42. Cf., e.g., Anderson, *From Creation to New Creation*, 87, 112, 116, 132, 152; Gene M. Tucker, "Rain on a Land Where No One Lives: The Hebrew Bible on the Environment," *Journal of Biblical Literature* 116 (Spring 1997): 3–17; Jan Morgan, *Earth's Cry* (Melbourne, Australia: Uniting Academic Press, 2013), 97–106.

43. See Norman C. Habel, "Geophany: The Earth Story in Genesis 1," *The Earth Story in Genesis*, ed. Norman C. Habel and Shirley Wurst (Sheffield: Sheffield Academic Press, 2000), 34–38.

44. See also Norman C. Habel and Peter Trudinger, eds., *Exploring Ecological Hermeneutics* (Atlanta: Society of Biblical Literature, 2008), esp. Habel, "Introducing Ecological Hermeneutics," 1–8. For a theoretical analysis, see Elaine M. Wainwright, "Images, Words and Stories: Exploring their Transformative Power in Reading Biblical Texts Ecologically," *Biblical Interpretation* 20 (2012): 280–304.

45. To propose an "earth-oriented story" versus a "human story" skews the text both literarily and theologically. Throughout the entire liturgy, God alone (neither earth nor human) is the central character. Only God speaks. A progression of emphases emerges. The so-called "human story" belongs to the larger "earth-story"; the earth-story belongs to the all-embracing God-story; and the God-story belongs to the omnipotent narrator who controls the text from within and from beginning to end. Creation in Genesis 1 is perhaps more complex and more simple than we mortals can absorb.

46. For "negative overtones" of these two verbs in Gen. 1:26–28, see Toni Craven and Mary Jo Kaska, "The Legacy of Creation in the Hebrew Bible and Apocryphal/Deuterocanonical Books," *Spirit and Nature: The Study of Christian Spirituality in a Time of Ecological Urgency*, ed. Timothy Hessel-Robinson and Ray Maria McNamara, RSM (Eugene, OR: Pickwick Publications, 2011), esp. 22–23, 36–41.

47. See H.-J. Zobel, רדה *rada*, *Theological Dictionary of the Old Testament*, vol. 13, ed. G. Johannes Botterweck, Helmer Ringgren, and Heinz-Josef Fabry, trans. David E. Green (Grand Rapids, MI: William B. Eerdmans Publishing Co., 2004), 330–36.

48. See Brueggemann, *Genesis*, 32–33.

49. See S. Wagner, כבש *kabas*, *Theological Dictionary of the Old Testament*, vol. 12, ed. G. Johannes Botterweck, Helmer Ringgren, and Heinz-Josef Fabry, trans. David E. Green (Grand Rapids, MI: William B. Eerdmans Publishing Co., 1995), 52–57.

50. Craven and Kaska would discredit the context: "Arguably all is not 'very good' (*tob me'od*) for non-human beings and nature . . ." ("The Legacy of Creation in the Hebrew Bible and Apocryphal/Deuterocanonical Books," 22).

51. On the royal background of *radah* and *kabas*, plus the priestly background of *kabas*, with corresponding positive uses in Genesis 1, see Smith, *The Priestly Vision of Genesis 1*, 98–102.

52. On differentiation, see Neville, "Differentiation in Genesis 1," 209–26.

53. On the pairing of *bara'* (create) and *'asah*, see Anderson, *From Creation to New Creation*, 47–48.

54. Cf. the reported comment of the primatologist Jane Goodall, "who says that in a half century of observing chimps she saw many examples of compassion, altruism, calculation, communication, and even some form of conscious thought.

'There is no sharp line dividing us from the chimpanzee or from any of the great apes . . . .'" *The Week* 13, issue 629 (August 9, 2013): 9.

55. On the interrelation of hierarchy, dominion, and responsibility, see Michael Welker, *Creation and Reality* (Minneapolis: Fortress Press, 1999), esp. 70–73. Cf. Tucker who writes that Genesis 1 "plainly establishes a hierarchy," with, first, God transcendent over creation; second, God's "steward" (humankind); and, third, "the rest of the world" ("Rain on a Land Where No One Lives," 7). In contrast, Craven and Kaska adopt the concept "heterarchy," meaning "networked and interdependent." Quoting other writers, they "describe change from hierarchy to heterarchy as 'the rule by one to several rules by some'" ("The Legacy of Creation in the Bible and Apocryphal/Deuterocanonical Books," 26–27).

56. Welker develops beautifully the image of caretaker in *Creation and Reality*, 70–73. For the corresponding image of caregiver, see Fretheim, "Genesis," 346. On "human beings in the service of life," see Loning and Zenger, *To Begin with, God Created . . .*, 107–13. For viceroy and plenipotentiary, see Levenson, *Persistence of Evil*, 113–4. For avatar, see Tikva Frymer-Kensky, "Ecology in a Biblical Perspective," *Studies in Bible and Feminist Criticism* (Philadelphia: The Jewish Publication Society, 2006), 351–62, esp. 356. For theological discussion of steward, see Douglas John Hall, *Imaging God: Dominion as Stewardship* (Grand Rapids, MI: Wm. B. Eerdmans Publishing Co., 1986), esp. 68–75, 161–205; cf. also Hall's personal testimony in *Bound and Free: A Theologian's Journey* (Minneapolis: Fortress Press, 2005), 94–99. Cf. the remarks of Jane Goodall on Gen. 1:26: ". . . a more correct meaning [than dominion] is 'to rule over as a wise king rules over his subjects, with care and respect.' The [Hebrew] word implies a sense of responsibility and enlightened stewardship:" "Foreword," *Spots Before Your Eyes*, The Howard G. Buffet Foundation (Decatur, IL: Bioimages, 2003), 15.

57. In a forthcoming book, tentatively titled *Bible and Nature*, Richard Hiers offers, in chapter 4, other observations about the limits of Gen. 1:26–28: (1) Only the "aboriginal couple" was authorized to subdue the earth and have-dominion; nothing was said about their descendants. (2) This authorization precedes the flood of Gen. 6–9, after which the entire structure of life among human beings, other creatures, and God was "altered radically." (3) The words to "subdue the earth" and to "have dominion" are not repeated after Gen. 1:28; indeed, the Bible has "considerably more to say about nature and environmental issues" than the account in Genesis 1. On the last point, Hiers references Anderson, *From Creation to New Creation*, 152–71. See also Tucker, "Rain on a Land Where No One Lives," 3–17; Hiebert, "Re-Imaging Nature," 36–46; and Holmes Ralston III, "The Bible and Ecology," *Interpretation* 50 (January 1996): 16–26. A further observation: The natural world of the ancient Near East, which informs Genesis 1, is not the natural world of twentieth-first century America.

58. Despite valid and needed objections to the word "hierarchy" and its use in certain contexts (e.g., male power over female), the reality of the concept cannot be eliminated. Some hierarchies (whether permanent or temporary) persist, indeed are a given, without built-in negative features or consequences: e.g., hierarchies of expertise, of friendships, of parenting, and of diverse responsibilities (doctor and patient, pilot and passenger, teacher and student).

59. Cf. Levenson, *Creation and the Persistence of Evil*, 121–27.

60. Citing rabbinic sages and modern scholars, Cassuto proposes that the evaluation "good" is not appropriate for day two, "in as much as the work of water had not yet been completed." The completion comes on day three (*A Commentary on the Book of Genesis*, 34). Cf. Avivah Gottlieb Zornberg, *The Beginning of Desire* (Philadelphia: The Jewish Publication Society, 1995), 6–7.

61. For Levenson, see note 6 above. Cf. also Gregory Mobley, *The Return of the Chaos Monsters—and Other Backstories of the Bible* (Grand Rapids, MI: William B. Eerdmans Publishing Company, 2012), 1–33.
62. For a poignant, piercing, and prophetic meditation on Gen. 1:1–2:4a, which juxtaposes it to contemporary agonies and crimes on earth by male and female, see Luise Schottroff, "The Creation Narrative: Genesis 1:1–2:4a," *A Feminist Companion to Genesis*, ed. Athalya Brenner (Sheffield: Sheffield Academic Press, 1993), 24–38. For feminist theologians (as distinguished from feminist biblical theologians) who have explored issues of ecology in the Genesis creation accounts, see, e.g., Elizabeth A. Johnson, *Women, Earth, and Creator Spirit* (New York: Paulist Press, 1993); Sallie McFague, *The Body of God: An Ecological Theology* (London: SCM Press, 1993); *Super, Natural Christians: How We Should Love Nature* (Minneapolis: Fortress Press, 1997); *A New Climate for Theology: God, the World, and Global Warming* (Minneapolis: Fortress Press, 2008); Catherine Keller, "No More Sea: The Lost Chaos of the Eschaton" in *Christianity and Ecology: Seeking the Well-Being of Earth and Humans*, ed. Dieter T. Hessel and Rosemary Radford Ruether (Cambridge, MA: Harvard University Press, 2000); Rosemary Radford Ruether, *Gaia and God: An Ecofeminist Theology of Earth* (New York: HarperSanFrancisco, 1992); Mercedes Navarro Puerto, "Divine Image and Likeness: Women and Men in Genesis 1–3 as an Open System in the Context of Genesis 1–11," *Torah*, eds. Irmtraud Fischer *et al.* (Atlanta: Society of Biblical Literature, 2011), 193–249, esp. 196–216; Morgan, *Earth's Cry*, 97–106.
63. Phyllis Trible's "clutter" lines play on the poetry of Samuel Taylor Coleridge, "The Rime of the Ancient Mariner," lines 119–122, *The Norton Anthology of English Literature*, revised vol. 2 (New York: W. W. Norton & Company, Inc., 1968), 215–31.
64. Trible's parodies play on the Gospel of John 1:14 and the Gospel of Luke 2:14.
65. See, e.g., Neil Postman, *Technopoly* (New York: Vintage Books, 1993). Cf. reports on the dangers of big data: e.g., Steve Lohr, "Sizing Up Big Data," *The New York Times* (Thursday, June 30, 2013) F1, F10; William Falk, quoting Ray Kurzweil with the prediction that by 2045 "'there will be no distinction between man and machine'" (*The Week*, June 21, 2013). See also Eric Schmidt and Jared Cohen, *The New Digital Age: Reshaping the Future of People, Nations, and Business* (New York: Alfred A. Knopf, 2013), esp. 254–57. Even though Schmidt and Cohen write positively about the new digital age, they caution: (1) Technology is no panacea for the world's ills, but smart use of it can make a difference. (2) The virtual world will complicate the behaviors of existing world order. (3) Citizens will have more power, but with costs to privacy and security. (4) The technological transfer of power to individuals must come with the hope that they "will take it from there"—for the good. Though these authors do not engage theological matters, a biblical reader may well remember that the "very good" of Genesis 1 soon encounters the disobedience of male and female in Genesis 2:4b–3:24.
66. See the poem "Humpbacks" by Mary Oliver, *New and Selected Poems* (Boston: Beacon Press, 1992), 168–70. For a recent depiction of the inhumane treatment of whales, cf. the documentary "Blackfish" (2013). Regarding this documentary and related matters, see James Gorman, "Smart, Social, and Captive," Science Times, *The New York Times* (Tuesday, July 30, 2013): D1–2; Nicholas D. Kristof, "Can We See Our Hypocrisy to Animals?" *The New York Times*, Sunday Review (Sunday, July 28, 2013). See also Philip Hoare, *The Whale: In Search of the Giants of the Sea* (New York: HarperCollins, 2010).
67. Oliver, "Humpbacks," 170.

Chapter 3

From Pawn to Selfhood

The Character Leah

WILMA ANN BAILEY

In the book of Genesis, Leah, an Aramean, is the female ancestor of six of the Israelite tribes. Unlike many females in the Bible, whose characters are one dimensional, Leah changes and develops in the course of the narrative in which she appears. She moves from being a pawn in the schemes of men to a woman who is fully self-actualized. She distinguishes herself in part through the power of naming her children.[1]

SCHOLARS AND SOURCES

Commentators have not always been kind to Leah. Typically they seldom mention her while favoring, along with tradition, her sister Rachel.[2] Avivah Zornberg recounts midrashim that claim Leah was not meant to marry Jacob but rather his (guileless and open hearted)[3] twin brother, Esau. Another midrash blames her for deceiving Jacob that night in the marital bed in spite of the words of Jacob in the story in accuse Laban and not Leah of deceiving him.[4] Claus Westermann skips this story entirely in his introduction to Genesis.[5] Walter Brueggemann provides a brief analysis focused on Rachel and barrenness, concluding that the theological message is that "New Life is God's gift."[6] Even the feminist biblical commentary on Genesis barely mentions Leah. There she is identified only as Rachel's sister and co-wife, one among others who uses a servant as a surrogate and one whose eyes are an issue.[7]

The Leah stories in Genesis 29–30 derive from a combination of southern J and northern E sources with other material added. Three sons of Leah—Reuben, Simeon, and Judah (chap. 29)—are specifically connected to YHWH, the divine name used by the J source. Two sons whose birth stories are told in the following chapter, Issachar and Zebulun (chap. 30), are connected to Elohim, the divine name used by E. Ironically, Levi, the eponymous ancestor of the tribe of the priests, is not connected at his birth to either YHWH or Elohim. Moreover, neither Leah's daughter Dinah nor her two adopted children by her surrogate, Zilpah—Gad and Asher—are connected to any divine being. These differences hint at a complicated compositional history. This study will focus, however, on the character of Leah as she appears in the final form of the biblical text.

Leah is remembered primarily as the first of two sororal co-wives of the patriarch Jacob and the maternal ancestor of six of Israel's tribes including the two most significant: Judah, the tribe of the kings (and the ancestral tribe of modern day Jews), and Levi, the tribe of the priests. She is mentioned by name thirty-three times in Genesis, mostly in chapters 29 and 30. Outside of Genesis, she is mentioned only once, in the book of Ruth (4:11) where the townspeople of Bethlehem pronounce a blessing on Ruth that she may be like Rachel and Leah who "built the house of Israel." The blessing suggests that Leah's name became part of an ancient blessing formula in prenuptial rites.

Genesis 29:16 identifies Leah as the daughter of Laban and the sister of Rachel. In relation to Rachel, she is called *hagedolah*, which can mean the bigger or greater or more respected or older one. Usually translations choose the meaning "the older one,"[8] in contrast with Rachel, who is described as *haqetonah*, the smaller or less significant or younger one. But in 2 Kings 4:8 the term *hagedolah* is a synonym for a respected or respectable woman.[9] The term in Genesis may similarly suggest that Leah was the more significant or the more respected sister in the household and in society. Rachel is less significant, not because she is less worthy, but because of her place in the family and because she is still a child when Jacob first sees her.[10] When Laban explains why he exchanged Leah for Rachel, he uses different language. He says that it is not the custom to give *ha tse'irah*, the young[er] woman for *habekhirah*, the firstborn (Gen. 29:26). This language clearly refers to relative age.

After the introductions comes a physical description of Leah. Her eyes are said to be *rakot* (Gen. 29:17). Some English translations translate this word negatively, suggesting that she has poor or weak eyes,[11] but the NRSV and the NAB translate the word as "lovely" and the KJV as "tender." The meaning of the Hebrew word is uncertain. Leah is contrasted to her sister Rachel, who has a beautiful form and appearance.

Having nothing to offer Laban for bride wealth,[12] Jacob proposes that he work seven years for Rachel, the younger daughter. Initially Laban agrees. Later, reneging on his contract, Laban takes his older daughter Leah to Jacob to be his wife. Leah becomes a pawn in Laban's scheme to get an extra seven years of labor out of Jacob. Setting his daughter up for an unhappy marriage so that he can benefit financially fits his character. Since it is highly unlikely that Jacob is not aware that he is sleeping with the wrong woman, the story continues to expose Jacob as a less-than-honorable man. He is willing to use and then humiliate Leah before he attempts to straighten the matter out the next morning. Jacob never accuses Leah of being a willing participant in the scheme. He confronts Laban, not her. Leah's feelings about her situation as revealed in the birthing narrative that follows show her to be distressed. At first she tries to earn her husband's love by producing male children. When that plan is not effective, she sets her sights higher.

THE INITIATIVE OF LEAH

An unusual narrative ensues (Gen. 35:16–26). It does not follow the typical patriarchal pattern and focus on the male. Jacob recedes to the background. Leah and Rachel occupy the foreground. In a succinct way, the naming of the ancestors of Israel and their connection to Jacob and the women is repeated (Gen. 35:22c–26). The text thereby hints at a far more complicated story about the origins of the Israelite tribes in a matrilineal society quite different in social structure from later Israel, which was organized around patriarchy. Savina Teubal suggests that vestiges of matrilineal, matrilocal, and perhaps matriarchal social structures appear in the Hebrew Bible. She prefers to use the term "non-patriarchal."[13] Genesis 29–30 exhibits certain of these traits. Husband Jacob has left his family of origin to live with the family of his wives. In patriarchal societies, the typical pattern is the reverse: when women marry, they leave their family of origin to become part of their husband's family. In this story, however, women behave in unexpected ways. They name their babies and purchase the sexual services of a man, albeit their husband. Most likely, these disparate stories with origins in non-patriarchal cultures were edited to make sense in a patriarchal world. Accordingly, redactors connected Jacob to his sons.

YHWH—the God of the Abrahamic family (hence Jacob), but apparently not the God of the Laban family (Gen. 31:51–54)[14]—responds to Leah's plight. The narrative opens with YHWH noticing that Leah has no children. Yet Leah is not the only childless one. Jacob has no children; Rachel has no children; neither do Bilhah and Zilpah as far as the narrative reports. But that point is never made. If this narrative were primarily about the twelve tribes of Israel as they descend from Jacob, then Jacob's childlessness would have been the focus rather than Leah's.

The five opening verses of this story beginning with Gen. 29:31 are devoted solely to Leah and her babies. The structure of the birthing vignettes is similar to others in Genesis:

1. Leah (or "she") became pregnant and gave birth.
2. The child is a son.
3. She called his name X.
4. A reason is given for the name.

The fourfold pattern varies only in the order of its last two elements, which may be reversed. Sometimes the position of the son in the family is added (e.g., fifth or sixth). The statements surrounding the births of children to the servants Bilhah and Zilpah are shorter than those for Leah's children. Joan Ross-Burstall interprets Leah's statements as prayers of lament.[15] Although she is correct in identifying some elements of lament language, overall, with the exception of the birth of the first child, the naming rituals are not laments. They do not express complaint, sorrow, or grief.

Strikingly, none of the children receives a theophoric name even when YHWH or Elohim is credited with playing some role in the birth.[16] This fact suggests that the names existed as names prior to the connection to YHWH or Elohim as the God of the ancient Israelites. Yet scholars such as Martin Noth[17] and, more recently, Dana Pike have argued that "single element" names often result from shortening a longer name in Semitic languages.[18]

In this narrative, the naming of the child takes place, in every case, in direct speech by the mother or the woman culturally regarded as the mother. The servants, Bilhah and Zilpah, are not permitted to name their own children. The pattern first appears in the Bible when Eve names her son Seth (Gen. 4:25). Earlier, the narrator says that Eve bore Cain (Gen. 4:1–2). Eve then makes a statement that is a play on the name Cain: "I have acquired a man with YHWH" (Gen. 4:1). Though the text does not specifically say that she named Cain, it is strongly implied. The narrator reports that she bore his brother Abel without specifying who actually named him (Gen. 4:2). Genesis 4:25, however, attributes the naming of Seth to Eve, "She gave birth to a son and she called his name Seth," with the explanation that "*Elohim* has provided *for me* another son ...."[19] The language used is not "for us," that is, Adam and Eve, but "for me," similar to the language used by Leah and Rachel.

Other birth announcements in Genesis are more varied. For instance, a messenger from YHWH instructs Hagar to name her son "Ishmael," but the text indicates that Abram, not Hagar, gave him the name (Gen. 16:11, 15). The daughters of Lot, who are only referred to as the older one and the younger one, name their boys Moab and Benammi respectively (Gen. 19:37–38). The phrase "she called his name ..." is used. Yet the narrator, not the mothers themselves, provides the explanation for the names. This point is significant because the narrator interprets the names negatively. No mother in Genesis gives her child a name with negative connotations except for Rachel when she dies giving birth. Abraham names Isaac (Gen. 21:3). Esau is named by "they" and Jacob by "he" (Gen. 25:25–26). The "he" likely refers to Isaac. Leah names all of her children and the sons of Zilpah as well (Gen. 29–30). Rachel names her first son and the sons of Bilhah (Gen. 29–30). In another text, Rachel names her son Benoni (son of sorrow), but his father, Jacob, overrules her choice and changes his name to Benjamin (son of my right hand) (Gen. 35:18). Tamar gives birth, but the naming of her children is done by "he," the "he" presumably being Judah (Gen. 38:29–30). Joseph names his two sons, Manasseh and Ephraim (Gen. 41:51–52). Of all of these, Eve's naming of Seth most closely follows the formula found in the Leah and Rachel naming narratives, not only in the use of the phrase "she called his name," but in the connection made between the name, the child, and the mother. Eve, Leah, and Rachel all see the birth of a child as being something done for them as mothers, and they celebrate that experience in the name of the child.

Leah is the unloved wife of Jacob (the text reads "hated"). She is forced into a marriage not of her choice. Her husband is at least initially in love with her sister, Rachel.[20] YHWH conspires with Leah to have her give birth to a series of sons so that she may win her husband's love or at least attention. In narrative terminology, Leah is a round rather than a flat character. She changes in the course of the narrative and becomes more self-aware. Growth and change mark round characters in narratives. By contrast, flat characters play a role in carrying the story forward without themselves changing.[21]

In Genesis 29:31 the narrator comments, "YHWH saw that Leah was hated and he opened her womb."[22] Most contemporary translators soften "hated" to the milder "unloved" or "not loved."[23] That adjustment makes Jacob look better but does nothing for Leah. The phrase "he [YHWH] opened her womb" appears in only one other place in the Hebrew Bible, in Genesis 30:22 in relation to Rachel, though there it is not YHWH but Elohim who "opens her womb."[24] Rachel is called an *ishah akarah*, a phrase usually translated "barren woman" (Gen. 29:31). In English, in relation to humans, barren means sterile and is traditionally used to describe women only. Men are rarely described as barren.[25] The text never says that Leah is *akarah*.[26] So why is the phrase "he opened her womb" used for both Leah and Rachel?

The whole notion of the barren woman has probably been misunderstood. The writers of the Hebrew Bible seem to assume that human life, the seed, is carried by the man. What the woman contributes is a place for the seed to grow into a baby. In this way of thinking, if the womb is closed, as it is before a woman is able to receive the seed, a baby will not develop. Joan Cook provides an excellent brief study of the "barren woman" motif in her book, *Hannah's Desire, God's Design*. She notices that the phrase "YHWH closed her womb" is the reason given for Hannah's lack of children. The same phrase is used of the wives and enslaved women in Abimelech's household (Gen. 20:18).[27] The phrase "YHWH (or Elohim) opened the womb" means that the womb is prepared to receive the seed, which is why the phrase only occurs before the birth of the first child. A woman's womb may be said to be closed before puberty, after menopause, or by divine intervention in natural processes.

A structure in this narrative about Leah encompasses the birth/naming formula discussed above. It can be outlined as:

A. Reference to God

B. Birth and Naming of Son

　　1. Leah (or "she") became pregnant and gave birth.

　　2. The child is a son.

　　3. She called his name X.

　　4. A reason is given for the name.

C. Expected Result

The pattern is frequent but not uniform. Neither a role for God nor an expected result appears for each birth, but the tracing of the expected result shows Leah's character development.

The birth of Leah's first child begins a series of short vignettes. They picture a very intimate scene, mother and baby right after the birth. No one else is present. Only the child and God hear as Leah speaks the child's name, tells the child why she chose that name, and in some cases expresses what she hopes the outcome will be (Gen. 29:31–35).

Leah's first child is Reuben. She credits YHWH with having seen her pain. Naming the child Reuben, which means, "See, a son,"[28] she expresses the hope that "now, my husband will love me"[29] (Gen. 29:32). Presumably, at least nine months pass. Leah gives birth to a second son. She names him "Simeon," which is related to the word for "hear" (*shama*) because, she says, "YHWH has heard that I am hated" (Gen. 29:33). This expression suggests that the birth of Reuben had not brought about a change of heart in Jacob. When Leah's third son is born, she names him "Levi." Her assessment of her situation is changing. She no longer expresses a hope but a fact. "Now, by this time, my husband is joined to me" (Gen. 29:34). The name Levi is similar to the word "join" (*lawa*). Whether Jacob loves her or not, Leah correctly understands that she and he are joined by and through their three sons. When the fourth son is born, neither Leah nor the narrator credits YHWH or Elohim as playing a special role in the birth. Yet Leah names him Judah which means "he praises," because, she says, "This time, I will praise YHWH" (Gen. 29:35). Renita Weems treats this statement as a turning point in the narrative.[30] She and others interpret it as being an acknowledgement of God that had not previously occurred.[31] But Leah has previously acknowledged that YHWH had heard and seen her—adequate recognition of the deity's role. Although the character Leah is changing and growing, the naming of Judah is not a significant departure from her utterances earlier in the narrative.

After the birth of Judah, Leah takes a break from child bearing. Alice Ogden Bellis interprets the non-bearing interval to be a time when Jacob is not sleeping with Leah.[32] This explanation is reasonable and likely the intent of the narrative, though other explanations are possible, especially when one considers the taboos surrounding childbirth that are often practiced in many traditional societies that have the effect of giving women a break from childbearing.

THE INTERLUDE OF RACHEL

In the interlude, the text focuses on Rachel, who has not yet been heard from in the narrative (Gen. 30:1–8). Whereas the earlier Leah portion of the story opens with two characters, YHWH and Leah (29:31), the Rachel portion begins with no reference to either YHWH or Elohim. The narrator informs the reader that Rachel, noting that she is not bearing children, becomes jealous of her sister. The two initial characters are Rachel and Jacob. Their conversation is in the form of a quarrel. Rachel attempts to remedy the situation and her jealousy not by requesting divine intervention but by confronting her husband. She blames Jacob for her childless state. She claims that she will die if she does not have children. With sad irony, Rachel will later die not from an absence of children but in giving birth to a child (Gen. 35:16–20).

Rachel's accusation against Jacob is quite rational. As discussed above, in the Bible, men are always thought to carry the seed and women to be the soil into which the seed is planted by the man. When Rachel blames Jacob, she is simply indicating that she is unable to become pregnant because Jacob is either not sleeping with her or that he is unable to copulate with her. In the face of Rachel's challenge, Jacob himself blames God. Elohim, he claims, not he, "has withheld from you the fruit of the womb" (Gen. 30:2). Tellingly, Jacob says "from you" not "from us." There is no "us" in the Jacob and Rachel portion of the narrative. Jacob has four sons by Leah and producing children with Rachel does not appear to be a priority. A likely conclusion is that Jacob no longer loves Rachel, having found her to be difficult to live with. The narrative, after all, opens with her quarreling with him. Yet another interpretation holds that Rachel was prepubescent when they married and had not yet reached sexual maturity.[33]

THE ROLE OF FEMALE SERVANTS

Rachel finds her own solution to her childlessness.[34] She gives her servant Bilhah to Jacob and subsequently claims two of Bilhah's children as her own.[35] How Bilhah (and later, Zilpah) felt about being used as a surrogate the text does not say. The status of both women is, however, elevated despite the continued use of servant language as they become wives. At the birth of each servant's son, the narrator reports that she (Bilhah or Zilpah) bore *Jacob*, not Rachel or Leah, a son. Later references to Bilhah and Zilpah consider them to be the mothers of the sons named rather than surrogates for the other wives of Jacob. As Elizabeth Wyner Mark points out, according to Genesis 46, Zilpah has "more individual descendants and more generations of descendants" than Rachel, and yet contemporary interpreters of this text refuse to treat Bilhah and Zilpah as wives and matriarchs, unlike some Rabbinic traditions that preceded them.[36] Further, Mark argues convincingly that there was no real precedent for breeding and then adopting the children of servants as one's own. Her study of ancient documents reveals that the adoption situations described in them are not the same as those described for Leah and Rachel.[37]

Rachel names Bilhah's son Dan because she says "Elohim has judged me and has heard my voice and has given *me* a son" (Gen. 30:6b, c, d). The name Dan (*dan*) is similar to the phrase "he judged" (*dan*). In claiming the child for herself, Rachel disagrees with the narrator. The narrator reports that Bilhah bore a son for *Jacob*. As Bellis points out, the strong desire that Rachel has for a child is to fulfill both the need of self-worth and "economic security."[38]

Bilhah gives birth again, and again Rachel names Bilhah's son. She calls him Naphtali, a play on the word "wrestle" (*patal*). Does the name suggest that Rachel sees herself in a wrestling match with her sister? This suggestion is unexpected. Until this point, the narrative gives no hint that either Leah or Rachel sees herself in a competition with her *sister*. Jealousy was mentioned in Genesis 30:1, but jealousy is not quite the same thing as competition.

A RETURN TO LEAH AND ZILPAH

The story returns to Leah, who has not had a child since Judah was born (Gen. 30:9–13). She gives her servant Zilpah to Jacob as a wife. The narrator reports that Zilpah bore a son for Jacob, not for Leah. Leah names Zilpah's son Gad, suggesting fortune. Again, Leah gives Zilpah to Jacob, and she names Zilpah's second son, Asher, "he was happy." Leah, who has been focused on her husband and YHWH, now changes her orientation to the local women. "The women [lit. "daughters"] will be happy with me" (Gen. 30:13c). At this point, she seems no longer to care what her husband thinks. She has found a supportive community.

Yet the orientation toward other women may be in tension with the competition between the sisters suggested in the mandrake episode (Gen. 30:14–16). Leah's son Reuben finds mandrakes in the field. Though not edible, mandrakes were used in magical rituals and perhaps as an aphrodisiac[39] in the eastern Mediterranean world. Rachel wants some mandrakes. If mandrakes were used as an aphrodisiac, how ironic that Jacob does not need one to copulate with any of the other women but only with Rachel. Only here in the narrative does Leah express anger. She accuses Rachel, certainly unfairly, with having taken away her husband (Gen. 30:15). But Leah agrees to give her some of the mandrakes in exchange for the privilege of sleeping with their husband. Often in polygamous marriages the husband sleeps with each wife in rotation. Leah wants Rachel's night. When Leah approaches Jacob, she informs him that she has hired him (Gen. 30:16). In effect, Leah is treating Jacob, her husband, like a slave. She purchases his services from her sister, not directly from him. No longer the man that she is pining after, Jacob is now nothing more to her than a slave hired for his stud services. "He slept with her that night" (30:16c). In the course of the narrative, the character Jacob is diminished while Leah is elevated.

Leah gives birth to her fifth son, Issachar, after the narrator announces that *Elohim*, this time, had heard her (Gen. 30:17–18). Leah, however, credits Elohim with having provided her hire. The name Issachar appears to be related to the word for hire or wages (*sakar*; Gen. 30:18). Leah hires her husband for the night and then names her son "hire," or perhaps, "he is hired." It appears that two stories about how Issachar got his name are placed in tandem. One relates to Leah hiring Jacob for his services, the other to her receiving payment for giving her servant to Jacob as a wife. Subsequently, Leah gives birth to one last son, Zebulun (30:19–20). She credits Elohim with having gifted her with a good gift. She names that child, not "gift," as one would expect, but Zebulun, which may be related to a word that expresses the thought of being raised up, honored, or exalted (*zabal*). After the birth of her first son, Leah expresses the hope that her husband will change his attitude toward her, that he will love her. After the birth of her third son, she simply states that her husband is now joined to her. But with this last son, Leah has changed her expectations. She is no longer hoping for something but demanding something. When Zebulun is born, she says, "Now my husband will raise me up" (Gen. 30:20). The New Revised Standard Version translates, "Now my husband will honor me."[40] Leah cannot make her husband love her, but she can demand honor.

Isolating the expressions of Leah's hoped-for results from their contexts reveals a pattern of growth. The choice of punctuation below helps convey[41] my interpretation of her statements and show the changes in her character.

My husband will love me	Gen. 29:32
My husband is joined to me.	Gen. 29:34
My husband will honor me!	Gen. 30:20

In an honor and shame society, those social mechanisms may be employed even by women to force men to conform to societal norms. Jacob would be shamed if he did not honor his wife for what the community would recognize to be a significant achievement: giving birth to six sons who live to adulthood and in turn father the next generation. Leah's sense of self changes in the course of the narrative. She comes to understand the power that is in her hands.

THE LAST CHILDREN

Leah gives birth to one last child. This child does not appear on the lists of the stylized tribes of Israel. This child is a girl. The narrator does not claim this child for Jacob. Instead, the formulaic statement is shortened to "She gave birth to a daughter and she called her name Dinah" (Gen. 30:21). Leah names her daughter just as she named her sons. The pattern is consistent yet incomplete. No statement is offered of the meaning of the name.[42] Scholars who have noticed this omission assume that it reflects the lower status of girls. It is unlikely, however, that the name Dinah has no meaning in this narrative. Rachel names Bilhah's first son Dan, which means "he judged" because she says "Elohim has judged me" (Gen. 30:6). Dinah is a feminine form of the same name, which may be interpreted, "she judged."[43] That the same name as that of Rachel's (Bilhah's) son is chosen for Leah's daughter must be significant. The order in which the story is told may indicate that Leah is responding to her sister. Leah is suggesting that her female child will do the judging rather than Rachel's male child.

By the end of the narrative, Leah has grown. She controls her husband rather than he emotionally controlling her. She has used the social conventions of her own society to get the recognition that she craves. She is not content to simply accept her lot; she demands the respect that she has earned. Nonetheless, the narrative's ending returns to Rachel.

Finally, Elohim remembers Rachel and heeds her and opens her womb (30:22–24). She then gives birth to a son, Joseph, saying that "God has brought an end to my reproach." His name expresses the desire that YHWH (not Jacob), will *add* another son to her. The juxtaposition of the names Elohim and YHWH is of interest. If Rachel believes that Elohim assisted her in the birth of Joseph, why appeal to YHWH for the birth of a second son? Rachel has changed from being an angry, frustrated woman to one who takes control of her own destiny and achieves a measure of contentment. Strikingly, the narrator does not claim that Rachel bore Joseph for *Jacob*. Elohim and YHWH in every case where God is mentioned respond to the plight to the women, not Jacob. Jacob's wishes are not known at all.

The narrator specifically attaches Dan, Naphtali, Gad, Asher, Issachar, and Zebulon to Jacob. These children, the narrator claims, the women bear *for Jacob*. Reuben, Simeon, Levi, Judah, Joseph, and Dinah are not said to have been born *for Jacob*. It may be that the tribes listed second were the ones that had a secure position in Israel, whereas the first group's ancestry was not secure. Accordingly, the narrator wants to assure readers that these tribes have Israelite credentials.

ENDINGS WITH A FUTURE

Although Jacob initially was in love with Rachel, that relationship may have changed in the course of the narrative. Indeed, a coda to Leah's story at the end of Genesis suggests the change. When Jacob is dying (Gen. 49), he instructs his sons to take his body from Egypt and bury him in the cave in the field that Abraham bought from Ephron the Hittite. He says, "There they buried Abraham and his wife Sarah. There they buried Isaac and Rebekah. And there I buried Leah" (v. 31). In the end, he asks to be buried with Leah, not Rachel. This request may suggest that Jacob came to love the kind of woman whom Leah had become: self-aware, self-assured, strong and independent.

Before and after this series of births, Jacob holds the center of attention. The women are in the background. In the yearly Torah readings in Jewish synagogues, this text is set within the broader context of Genesis 28:10–32:3 under the title "Vayeitzei"[44] ("and he went out"), which nudges the reader to interpret the story with Jacob as the central character. Mainline Christian denominations that use the Revised Common Lectionary separate this text out from its broader context and list it for reading on a Saturday. The Sunday readings before and after, which are the only ones that most people will hear, focus on the Jacob narrative.

From a liberation standpoint, in this text, God notices the pain of those marginalized in society and works with them to remedy the situation within the constraints of the social structures of the time. The marginalization of the story itself within the interpretation of the Jacob narrative demonstrates that much work remains to be done in the recovery of lesser known biblical tales, especially those focused on women and the disenfranchised.

Notes

1. An earlier version of this article appeared in the *Proceedings of the Eastern Great Lakes Biblical Society* 29 (2009) under the title "Intimate Moments: A Study of Genesis 29:31–30:21." Reproduced by permission.
2. Gerald Janzen, *Genesis 12–50* (Grand Rapids: Eerdmans, 1993), 116.
3. Author's description.
4. Avivah Gottlieb Zornberg, *Genesis: The Beginning of Desire* (Philadelphia: The Jewish Publication Society, 1995), 211–12.
5. Claus Westermann, *Genesis: An Introduction* (Minneapolis: Fortress, 1992).
6. Walter Brueggemann, *Genesis*, Interpretation Commentary Series (Atlanta: John Knox, 1982), 255.
7. Athalya Brenner, ed., *Genesis: A Feminist Companion to the Bible* (Sheffield: Sheffield Academic Press, 1998), 174, 222–23.
8. See the NRSV.
9. The NRSV's "wealthy woman" is not tenable. Elisha as a prophet would have to stay with a respected and respectable woman or his own reputation would be sullied. The woman clearly is comfortable as she has a spare room built and furnished for Elisha, but wealth is not explicitly mentioned.
10. See Wilma Bailey, "Baby Becky, Menarche and Prepubescent Marriage in Ancient Israel," *Journal of the Interdenominational Theological Center* 37 (2011): 113–37. Rachel's childlike behavior is exhibited in Gen. 29:11 where she permits a stranger to kiss her before he introduces himself to her. The person later introduces himself as her cousin, Jacob, making the kiss respectable.
11. See JPS, NIV.

12. See T. M. Lemos, *Marriage Gifts and Social Change in Ancient Palestine* (New York: Cambridge University Press, 2010), 3. Bride wealth refers to assets given to the family of the bride but not the bride herself. Dowry, on the other hand, represents assets given to the bride by her own family of origin for her own use in the newly established household. In the case of Leah, she is given the maidservant, Zilpah. Lemos's research indicates that bride wealth is the primary marriage gift type in biblical stories.

13. Savina Teubal, "Examining the Non-Patriarchal Social System and Genealogy in Genesis," in *Sarah the Priestess: The First Matriarch of Genesis* (Athens, OH: Swallow Press, 1984), 53, 60–64.

14. See also the tradition alluded to in the Deuteronomistic History source Joshua 24:2.

15. Joan Ross-Burstall, "Leah and Rachel: A Tale of Two Sisters," *Word and World* 14, no. 2 (1994): 164.

16. Heriberto Haber in his article "Theophoric Names in the Bible" suggests that the name Judah is a combination of the syllable "YH" and a word for thank (*ydh*) where the "y" "became a vav and merged with the 'vav' of the Tetragrammaton." *Jewish Bible Quarterly*, 29, no. 1 (2001): 57.

17. Martin Noth, *Die israelitischen Personennamen im Rahmen der gemeinsemitischen Namengebung* (Stuttgart: Verlag Von W. Kohlhammer, 1925).

18. Dana M. Pike, "Names, Hypocoristic," in *The Anchor Bible Dictionary*, vol. 4 (New York: Doubleday, 1992), 1017. Most typically in these formulations, the theophoric element appears second, a position where it may drop out. Some tribal names appear in a longer form in the Bible with a theophoric element, as, for example, Dan and Daniel. It is certainly possible that some of the names may have been longer at one time. But others perhaps originated in cultures outside of ancient Israel as Martin Noth also suggests. See also Morris Jastrow Jr., "Hebrew Proper Names Compounded with YH and YHW," *Journal of Biblical Literature* 13 (1894): 101–27; 101–02.

19. All translations are the author's unless otherwise noted.

20. André LaCocque points out several places where love played a role in marriage in biblical narratives. See *The Feminine Unconventional* (Minneapolis: Fortress Press, 1990).

21. See Mark Allan Powell, *What Is Narrative Criticism?* (Minneapolis: Fortress Press, 1990).

22. Deuteronomy 21:15–17 speaks to a "hypothetical" situation where a man has two wives, one of which is hated and the other loved. If the firstborn son's mother is the hated one, he must still receive the status and benefits of being a firstborn son.

23. See the New Revised Standard Version, The New American Bible, New International Version ("not loved"), the Tanakh. Older Versions have "hated" (King James Bible) or "despised" (The Geneva Bible). Since the language refers to how Jacob felt about Leah, the softening of the language serves only to make Jacob look better.

24. In 1 Sam. 1:5–6 the narrator reports that YHWH had shut the womb of Hannah, the mother of Samuel. The NRSV interprets Isaiah 66:9 as "'Shall I open the womb and not deliver?' says the LORD?" The word "open," however, does not appear in Hebrew. Instead the word is *shebir*, a much stronger phrase meaning to sever or break open.

25. Deut. 7:14 contains a rare use of the masculine form of the word usually translated as barren.

26. Likely the phrase "barren women" as a genre title is inappropriate, given that many of the barren women do give birth, and usually to children beyond the one

where the text suggests divine intervention. See Joan E. Cook, *Hannah's Desire, God's Design: Early Interpretations of the Story of Hannah* (Sheffield: Sheffield Academic Press, 1999).

27. Cook, *Hannah's Desire, God's Design*, 11.

28. Etymologists have noted that the names are not necessarily derivations from the Hebrew words noted.

29. Ross-Burstall, in "Leah and Rachel," 169, interprets this statement as petition, but it is not structured as petition.

30. Renita Weems, "Leah's Epiphany," in *The Other Side* 32, no. 3 (1996): 8–11, 44–46.

31. James McKeown, *Genesis* (Grand Rapids: Eerdmans, 2008), 145.

32. Bellis, "A Sister Is a Forever Friend: Reflections on the Story of Rachel and Leah," *The Journal of Religious Thought*, 2, no. 1 (1999): 109–15; 112.

33. See discussion in Bailey, "Baby Becky, Menarche and Prepubescent Marriage in Ancient Israel."

34. The abrupt switch to Elohim from YHWH, which is sustained through the rest of the narrative except at the very end after the birth of Joseph, suggests a different source.

35. Rachel Havrelock claims that "in biblical narrative, birth is a moment of female collaboration when the boundaries of distinct bodies collapse, an occasion in which multiple female bodies operate in tandem"; in *The Torah: A Women's Commentary* (New York: Women of Reform Judaism and URJ Press, 2008), 166. There is nothing in biblical narrative to suggest this ideology. There is nothing in the text to suggest that Bilhah and Zilpah collaborated with Rachel and Leah to have their bodies used in this manner. Given the power differential between mistress and servant, it is impossible to propose anything except coercion. See Nahum M. Sarna, *The JPS Torah Commentary: Genesis* (New York: The Jewish Publication Society, 1989), 207, for the more traditional interpretation of the statement "she will bear on my knees."

36. Elizabeth Wyner Mark, "The Four Wives of Jacob: Matriarchs Seen and Unseen," *The Reconstructionist* 63, no. 1 (1998): 22–35; 22.

37. Ibid., 31.

38. Alice Ogden Bellis, "A Sister Is a Forever Friend," 111.

39. Samuel H. Dresner, "Rachel and Leah," *Judaism* 38, no. 2 (1989): 151–59; 154.

40. Tanakh, "exalt"; New American Bible, "my husband will offer me presents"; New International Version, "my husband will treat me with honor."

41. Biblical Hebrew did not originally use a system of punctuation. The punctuation in modern Bibles is a result of traditional and contemporary interpretation.

42. Speiser writes that the absence of explanation of the name Dinah may indicate that it is a later addition. E. A. Speiser, *Genesis* (New York: Doubleday, 1964), 231.

43. Norman J. Cohen also notices that Dan and Dinah are forms of the same name though he does not see Dinah as a response to Dan. See "Two That Are One: Sibling Rivalry in Genesis," *Judaism* 32, no. 3 (1983): 331–42; 341.

44. Tamara Cohn Eshkenazi, *The Torah: A Women's Bible Commentary*, 157.

Chapter 4

Folklore, Feminism, and the Ambiguity of Power

Women's Voice in Genesis?

SUSAN NIDITCH

The present piece builds on Phyllis Trible's pioneering work that has shaped the way that we think about women in the Hebrew Bible. I explore current inter-disciplinary scholarship on women's power and voice in the fields of folklore, women's studies, and cultural anthropology and through the lenses of work by several colleagues writing in these areas, with reference to Romanian, Afghan, and Chinese traditions. I review some previous scholarship on tales of women in Genesis and offer new suggestions in a comparative perspective. I also weave in work of my own on hair in the Israelite tradition, namely a study on the body, religion, and the Hebrew Bible that has implications for views of gender and other core aspects of Israelite identity.[1]

INTERDISCIPLINARY STUDIES OF WOMEN'S POWER

Margaret Beissinger works in the narrative traditions of Romanian and Roma or Gypsy cultures with special interests in women's studies, oral literatures, and epic. In a recent essay, Beissinger analyzes portrayals of various "Penelope"[2] fig-ures in Balkan tradition, women left behind the lines during the absence of their husbands or fiancés, who are off fighting a long war or sometimes imprisoned by their enemies, and whose return is always uncertain but awaited.[3] While the ideal is for the woman to remain faithful, no matter what, other more subversive accounts portray the woman as deciding to choose a new suitor and take her life into her hands, a decision that always goes punished, reinforcing, at least overtly, male control over females and the androcentric, patriarchal bent of the dominant culture. In looking at female heroines of these return songs and at Penelope, the West's archetypal waiting woman, Beissinger makes reference to two ways of defining "woman's experience" in such narratives from the perspectives of feminist criticism, and here she herself is influenced by the work of Lillian Doherty.[4]

Beissinger notes that "feminist criticism of literature frequently takes two forms: critical and utopian. Critical or 'closed' feminist readings show how women in literature reflect gender constraints . . . the ways in which male power is imposed on female society. . . . By contrast, utopian or 'open' feminist readings seek nuances within literature that allow for new affirmations of identity."[5] In Doherty's words, the latter approach attempts to "identify openings that undercut ostensible patterns of meaning."[6] Thus classicist John J. Winkler, another influence on Beissinger's work, suggests an understanding of Penelope that appreciates "the resourcefulness of women in cultures where they had hitherto been reported to be passive victims of male manipulation."[7]

In our own field, with reference to the women of Genesis, we might identify the thoughtful work of Esther Fuchs as critical and closed in orientation. Although the annunciations in Genesis, for example, do feature women and allow for their communication with the deity, they function, in Fuch's view, to propagandize for the very roles in society that demean and subjugate women.[8] J. Cheryl Exum, author of several other classic works on the women of Genesis, allows for more openness. She notes,

> Power is the ability to gain compliance with one's wishes and to achieve one's ends. Authority is culturally legitimated power, a power recognized by society and distributed according to a hierarchical chain of command and control. The matriarchs do not have authority; they are subordinate to their husbands. But they are not powerless . . . Sarah and Rebecca illustrate how women can have power in areas not normally accorded them by working through those in authority.[9]

Alternatively, as Exum notes, power can be achieved by the use of deception, a "subversive" means of getting one's way. Exum sees this backdoor means of achieving ends as "underhanded" and part of a "vicious cycle" whereby lack of authority forces the powerless to act in less than ethical ways.[10] I would suggest, to the contrary, that the narrators of Genesis love and respect tricksters, both male and female, and so in their view does the deity, a theme to which we will return.

The second folklorist whose fascinating research is relevant to the women of Genesis is Margaret Mills, a scholar who has explored Afghan traditional literature. Working in Afghanistan before the wars, with a variety of local storytellers, male and female, and more recently collecting and analyzing material from Tajikistan, Mills explores the ways in which the woman trickster operates as "a force for order."[11] And here we might draw a contrast with notions of the trickster as a somehow demeaned variety of protagonist. Like Beissinger, Mills is interested in how women caught in patriarchal cultures manage "to dance with chains on." She is also interested in the links between content, genre, and gender, providing important suggestions as we speculate about the possibility of women's voices or voices imitating those of women in Genesis. In Afghan culture, "men tend to tell stories about men, whereas women tell stories about men and women."[12] She finds it particularly interesting that women tend "not to masculinize" female heroines as she would expect them to if they "envied men's social options."[13] She asks if a kind of "hostage mentality makes them their own conceptual jailors," but concludes instead: "There is a second option which paradoxically inverts the envy hypothesis: it may be that Afghan women simply see options for action in traditional female roles . . . for Afghan women, the choice of meaningful dramas is wider within the feminine sphere."[14]

Mills notes that "women's stories with female protagonists are often centered on the domestic sphere and on the agonistic potential of kinship relations after marriage." Courtship is another favorite topic. "Women," she notes, "readily identify dramatic potential in the women's world."[15] (1991a: 72).

Even further afield from our own culture area and corpus, but I would argue just as relevant, is Dorothy Ko's controversial study of footbinding in sixteenth-through early nineteenth-century China. Ko's "revisionist" approach suggests that while, on the one hand, footbinding was a manifestation of male tyranny and domination, of "cruelty, violence, and the objectification" of women, on the other hand, such factors are "inadequate explanations for the longevity of the practice and the stubbornness with which women embraced it. At once beautiful and ugly, neither voluntary nor coerced, footbinding defies a black-and-white male-against-female and good-or-bad way of understanding the world."[16] As Foucault has noted, power is complex, having to do with "the tug and pull of relationships," what he calls a "plurality of resistances."[17] While Ko excuses none of the cruelty or the domination, she does provide a window on how women achieve some degree of self-expression, making their way in a man's world. She shows how they embrace traditional cultures and sometimes manipulate, subvert, or exploit to their own advantage the dominant world around them.

Beisssinger, Mills, and Ko thus emphasize certain themes in exploring tales and customs pertaining to women in traditional, male-dominated cultures. All three scholars point to the ways in which women in these cultures "dance with chains on" or with feet bound and describe how women find means of self-assertion, survival, promotion, creativity, and self-expression within certain circumscribed and potentially limiting gender boundaries. They ask, in particular, why women accept these boundaries and portray themselves as succeeding within them rather than overthrowing them. Mills notes further that women's stories in Afghanistan tend to be about their own world, a world of children, husbands, and home. Is any of this relevant to biblical material about women?

FEMALE TRICKSTERS: GENESIS 27 AND 38

Beissinger and Mills actually worked with female storytellers. They knew the originators of the stories and characterizations. Ko deals with interviews of women whose feet had been bound and has at her disposal a range of artifacts of material culture: footwear prepared by women for themselves. As biblical scholars, we face the always vexing questions about who wrote the Bible or any particular account. Whose story is it? We assume that the material was written down by men, elites of some kind who had access to writing, the capacity to preserve the tales, and a particular cultural and theological message they wished to preserve in the process. On the other hand, many of us would probably agree that the stories were not simply invented by these men. Indeed, if we move beyond ancient Israel and work comparatively, we find that tales of tricksters in Genesis 27 and 38 have counterparts throughout the world. That Israelite variants of such stories (oral and written) existed before, during, and after the setting down of the particular versions now found in Genesis is likely. Moreover, it is entirely possible that some of these variants were popular among women. The current content and message of the two trickster tales as preserved in Genesis 27 and 38 strongly indicate woman's interest and voice. Further, on some level, these are women's stories, sharing characteristics of the women's stories Mills collected in Afghanistan. If the writers are most likely men, these men have assumed a woman's voice. This voice emerges by contrasting Genesis 27 and 38 with Genesis 14 and 34:25–32 and by paying close attention to the motif of hair and lack of hair so important to the tale of Rebecca, Isaac, Jacob, and Esau in Genesis 27. Our study thus becomes partly about men's identification with the feminine in ancient Israelite tradition, the reasons for this identification, and the significance of it for Israelite worldview and the relationship with God.

Both Genesis 27 and Genesis 38 deal with precisely the sorts of "women's issues" that Mills notices in Afghan women's stories, in particular the concern with children: the concern with the success of the son, motherly devotion that intriguingly transcends loyalty to the husband and patriarch in the case of Rebecca, and the desire to give birth to a child and the place of a widowed, childless, in-marrying woman in the patriarchal clan in the case of Tamar. As underdogs, both women employ trickery to achieve their goals, working in behind-the-scenes ways to subvert men's business as usual. In Genesis 27, such custom would dictate that the elder son inherit according to the patriarch's wishes. In Genesis 38, the patriarch Judah seems to believe he can dispose of women of the clan at his whim, passing Tamar back from himself as father-in-law to her parents, after the exchange of the woman meant to bear his son's children goes awry. Further, both women, as tricksters, use particularly feminine means of achieving their goals. Rebecca creates and provides special clothing for Jacob's disguise and cooks delicacies to tempt and fool the old man Isaac. Tamar dresses as a prostitute to tempt Judah to have sex with her and provide her the offspring that would regularize her position in the clan.

The critical feminist readings described above would rightly suggest that on one level these acts of trickery merely reinforce oppressive realities and further serve to imprison the women in a certain androcentric situation. Indeed, so devoted is Rebecca to her son Jacob that she declares that Isaac's possible curse for their trickery should fall upon her rather than upon Jacob, and this is a world in which curses and blessings have real and visceral power to bring about misfortune or fortune. As for Tamar, what does she gain but an old, unpleasant husband and a place in his family? And we should recall that YHWH is behind their schemes and the success of their schemes. God is portrayed, as Fuchs would suggest, ultimately to reinforce traditional women's roles and attitudes in a man's world. These women are just falling into and reinforcing the same old oppressive trap. Where is the subversion here? And yet I would argue that in these tales of female tricksters, albeit within the contours of a traditional male social system and worldview, something more self-assertive by the women is going on, and it is something critical of the men.

First we notice that the men are dolts. Now perhaps male writers are being self-deprecating, but if so they do so in a way that adopts a female perspective. In Genesis 27, Isaac is pictured as a dotty old man who is blind in more ways than one. He loves Esau because Esau provides him with good eats. Esau is the elder, but we know that divine revelation to Rebecca has already indicated that the older will serve the younger, and Isaac is left out of the loop. The older son, like his father, is interested in immediate satisfaction of his desires rather than in delayed gratification, the more intelligent orientation to life. He hastily sells his birthright to Jacob in exchange for stew in order to satisfy hunger, a matter to which we will return in a moment. In Genesis 38, Judah is pictured to desire the immediate gratification of cheap sex. All too quickly, without inquiring into the matter, he is ready to burn to death the young widow, his daughter-in-law, who is accused of a capital crime of sexual impropriety when she is found out to be pregnant. He has already, by his own admission, been shown to be a laughingstock by the "prostitute," that is Tamar, who made off with the symbols of his identity and male leadership, his staff, his signet, and the cord that holds it. These items provide the wise woman with recognition tokens. Judah has to admit Tamar is in the right and that she deserves to bear a child in the name of his eldest son according to the very rules of the androcentric system to which they both belong. I see these tales as a put-down of men and examples of ways in which women do dance with chains on. Perhaps even more interesting, however, is the way Genesis 27 plays with the status of manliness to show a divine preference for the feminine or effeminate. This emerges through the motif of hair.

HAIR, GENDER, AND VOICE

In Hebrew Scriptures and ancient Israelite culture an important nexus between maleness, virility, warrior status, and special chosen status emerges in attitudes to hair. Examples of this nexus are provided by the Nazirism of Samson and Samuel, the pretensions of the would-be king/hero Absalom, and the poetic implications of Judges 5:2 and Deuteronomy 32:42. Hair is an entryway to Israelite identity, concepts of holiness, and attitudes to gender. It is integral to the ways in which biblical writers project and construct ideas of self-definition. While the growing of hair has critical meanings, the shaving or cutting of hair, whether self-imposed or externally imposed, is equally meaningful. Saul Olyan has seen the cutting of hair as related to patterns and processes of transformation.[18] Especially important for the present discussion is the involuntary, imposed cutting of hair, for it has to do with the loss of manhood and status. Relevant are certain biblical texts that employ the metaphor of shaving in the context of conquest and political humiliation. The tale of David's envoys to the Ammonites on the occasion of the death of the king provides an excellent example (2 Sam. 10:4–5). David's men are accused of being spies and sent back to him with robes ripped off up to their rear ends and beards shorn, half or whole, depending upon the manuscript tradition.

The motif of the ripped bottom of the robe (cf. Saul's encounter with David at 1 Sam. 24:4–7) and the imposed shaving of face hair both symbolize the loss of manly status and identity. Scholars have wisely cautioned that shaving hair against a person's will need not always connote a castration of sorts,[19] for the heads of women captives are shaved in Deuteronomy 21. As Olyan suggests, all of these instances have to do with some sort of alteration in status.[20] Given that beards are only grown by men, however, their loss in a culture which valorizes men's facial hair is a special affront with gendered connotations. Cynthia Chapman has discussed a comparable phenomenon in Assyrian portrayals, verbal and visual, of conquered enemies and the Assyrian conquerors, the former losing their beards or scraping them in the dust at the ruler's feet, while the virile, amply bearded ruler and his men lord over them.[21]

The bald cheek is a sign of having been bested in contest and made a woman. The narrator of the Samuel story implies as much. He observes about the envoys: "for the men were intensely shamed, and the king said, 'Return to Jericho until your beards grow back,' and they returned" (2 Sam. 10:5). They do not want to be seen. The action of the Ammonites incenses the Israelite king, for the emissaries are an extension of his person and his power, and in response to their attempts to humiliate the Israelites, he goes to war and roundly defeats them. The shaved beard and the ripped robe are potent symbols; the Israelites will not allow themselves to be unmanned or overpowered; that they are mere women is, on the other hand, precisely the message that the ill-fated Ammonites seek to send. The Ammonites clearly miscalculate; instead of putting the Israelites in their place, they commence a spiral of violence whereby visceral symbolic actions escalate to all-out war.

The men thus respond emotionally and viscerally to the forced removal of their hair, a response that the king fully understands and with which he identifies. The responses only make sense within a cultural context that equates male power with facial hair, the loss of the hair with loss of power. The Ammonites force the Israelite emissaries, who are substitutes for the king himself, to become walking symbols of defeat and humiliation and of the enemies' power.

This interpretation of the shaved cheek is reinforced by a brief image of conquest employed by the eighth century BCE prophet Isaiah. The language of shaving, razor, and reference to the body parts shaved creates a physical, bodily metaphor for consummate defeat and plays very overtly on erotic elements of manhood. The oracle predicts an invasion by the king of the superpower Assyria:

> On that day the Lord will shave with a razor,
> hired in "across the River," via the king of Assyria.
> The head, the pubic hair [lit. the hair of the "legs or feet"], and the beard,
> it will sweep away.
>
> (Isa. 7:20)

This brief oracular pronouncement draws upon the meanings of hair cutting, in particular the forced cutting of hair of the cheek and pubic areas, to create an image of subjugation and loss of power associated with the virility of the warrior.

In Genesis, another recurring visual contrast involving hair, one that more overtly and purposefully compares hair and the absence of hair, is drawn between the rival twin brothers, Jacob and Esau. An amusing British improv group of the 1960s, "Beyond the Fringe," produced a skit in which an Anglican pastor, speaking in an exaggerated parody of an upper class Oxbridge accent, delivers a sermon on the day's reading from Genesis that begins, "My brother Esau is an hairy man and I am an smooth man." The comedians and their modern audiences no doubt found this verse from sacred Scripture, taken out of context, to be incongruous, silly. What meaning can be derived from such an image? The ancestor hero of Israel, Jacob, father of the twelve tribes, whose name is later changed to Israel, is smooth whereas the founding father of the neighboring, related, Semitic-speaking people, the Edomites, is hairy. What images are projected and what sort of propaganda is implicit? Why is the preserved tradition comfortable with its less hairy founding father, given the strong links that exist in various biblical threads between hairiness, manliness, heroism, and charisma? Esau emerges first from the womb, and his hair is an immediate issue:

> And emerge did the first red
> all of him like a garment of hair.
> (Gen. 25:26)

The concept of Esau's chronological primacy is critical as are images of "redness," "garment, mantle, or cloak," and "hair." To be the firstborn within the social structure of a patrilineal society implies inheriting the father's status, lands, and clan leadership. This implicit leadership is accompanied by an appearance of ruddiness. The term for "red," *'edom*, is related to the term for the earth, a ruddy substance. The name of the first human, Adam, a term that can be translated humanity, also means earthling. Esau's redness is indeed related to the redness of the sandstone-rich land of the Edomites descended from him in the tradition and located to the east and south of Israel. Redness thus suggests earthiness, fecundity, and humanity. It is positive for a young man to be called ruddy. The handsomeness of the young hero David is equated with being *'admoni,* ruddy, the same form of the redness root that describes Esau.

In the prophets, the garment of hair is another loaded phrase. The prophets were known to wear hair mantles, as suggested by Zechariah (13:4). This postexilic biblical writer envisions a time when prophecy ceases or perhaps when the prophet seeks to hide his identity because so many previous prophecies have been proven wrong or deceptive. In any event, his hiding his identity as prophet is described in terms of his no longer wearing a "hairy mantle." Exactly what this cloak looked like we are not sure, perhaps some sort of cloak made of animal skins. Elijah is "a man of hair" (2 Kgs. 1:8), and his mantle appears to have special magical powers, a power inherited by the bald Elisha who inherits his master Elijah's cloak after the master's ascent in a fiery chariot. Whether the mantle of Elijah was a hairy mantle is not explicit in the text, but the associations presented in Zechariah are suggestive. Once again hair, the wearing of hair clothing, is positive, special. Perhaps like the redness, the hair mantle suggests closeness to the natural end of the nature/culture continuum, evoking an animal covered with hair. The deity himself appears to holy men on mountains, in the wilderness. When we add to these considerations the generally positive views of having lots of hair in the tales of the Hebrew Bible and especially the heroic, manly dimensions implied by tales of Samson (Judg. 13–16) and other hairy men, we must conclude that at the outset Esau looks like a promising patriarch. This view is reinforced by the description of Jacob's birth and the way the boys are as they grow up. Jacob emerges grasping the heel of his younger brother; he is second born. The older brother grows to be "a man knowledgeable in the hunt, a man of the open spaces" (Gen. 25:27). Imagery of nature, skill, and manly endeavors dominate.

Jacob grows up to be what the Hebrew calls *'ish tam,* one who dwells in tents (Gen. 25:27). The term *tam* comes from a root meaning "perfect" or "complete." As the Koehler-Baumgartner Lexicon (K-B) suggests, four nuances for this root are "healthy," "well-behaved," "quiet," and "upright/honest."[22] NRSV and JPS translations read "a quiet man." K-B also notes, however, that *tam* may mean perfect or complete in "a social sense," not roughhewn. Again, nuances of nature versus culture come to mind. They suggest translating "well-behaved" in the sense of civilized[23] as does Claus Westermann.[24] We might suggest "acculturated" or "domesticated." Instead of hunting, Jacob is pictured at the homestead making stew. The he-man Esau returns from the wilds hungry. Bigger than life, speaking in the language of heroic exaggeration, he declares he will die without food, and the younger brother sells him stew in exchange for the elder's birthright, a deal which the elder certainly does not take seriously. The serious, grasping younger brother does (Gen. 25:29–34).

Esau is Isaac's son. The storyteller declares that the father loves him because Esau provides him with game to eat (Gen. 25:28). Like son, like father. He likes his food, his wild caught food, and thinks in terms of immediate bodily rewards. He is a man of appetites, even when old and blind. Jacob, however, is his mother's favorite (Gen. 25:5). Had she not received a divine declaration that the older son would serve the younger? Jacob is "her son" (Gen. 27:6, 17), whereas Esau is Isaac's son (27:5). "Isaac loved Esau because he was food in his mouth, but Rebecca loved Jacob." It is the mother who loves her favorite boy, she who masterminds the plan whereby the younger takes Esau's blessing, a significant act of trickery in a world in which blessings and curses have the power to bring about what they predict. Mother and son are both tricksters and underdogs, the woman and the second (dare we say effeminate?) son, who use deception and roundabout means to further their goals. The son is ambitious; both he and his mother think of the future rather than of near-term gain; they are wily. And Jacob, the trickster, the younger, his mother's son, the domesticated man, is "a smooth man."

Rebecca discloses her plan for stealing the blessing, but Jacob worries that Isaac will recognize him and utter a curse rather than a blessing. He says, "Behold, Esau my brother is a man of hair, and I am a smooth man." The word for smooth is not necessarily a complimentary one. It connotes not only the absence of hair but also the slipperiness of the trickster. Wisdom literature warns of slippery men, not to be trusted. But Rebecca clothes him in a disguise of skins from the kid of a goat, placed on his arms and at his neck, and creates the illusion that he is Esau. The power to dress someone is an important indicator of who is in charge. The power is that of the mother, furthering the career of her favorite son. The clever deception convinces the blind father, Isaac, who "does not recognize him because his hands were like the hands of Esau his brother, hairy" (27:23). It's all about hair. Hair is identity or assumed identity, animal-like, thick, smelling of the fields. Strong contrasts in gender and gender bending are created by the imagery of hair, and all kinds of interesting stereotypes are at play.

The manly son is hairy, of the wild, makes guys' food, and is loved by his father. The second son is smooth, soft, lives in tents, cooks, and is beloved of his mother. He and she plan clever tricks together in secret while the father and son interact in a direct, up-front way. And yet, it is not the manly, firstborn who succeeds his father in this patrilineal and patriarchal world. In the tradition, the smooth son, Jacob/Israel, is father of the people Israel, and the Edomites, sons of Esau, the manly elder son, are relegated to lower status. The biblical writer seems to be rooting for Jacob, not Esau, for the writer describes a verbal theophany in which the deity reveals that Jacob is the deity's choice (Gen. 25:23). Rebecca is thus portrayed to know God's plan, one which overrides human laws concerning primogeniture. What are we then to conclude about the voice behind these tales in Genesis and about the use of hair as it relates to worldview and culture?

First we must ask if one can equate body hair with the hair of the head or beard in describing the particular biblical symbol system that associates manliness with hair. It would seem that in Genesis 25–27 the relationship between manliness and hairiness is even more obvious than in tales of Samson in which Delilah's shaving of the hero robs him of strength and status, turning him into the subjugated and weaker member of the couple, the female. Tales of Jacob and Esau do seem to partake of this interesting and gendered symbolic cluster. That being the case, might we suggest that the fact that the smooth, more effeminate hero is the one who obtains the status and the power implies the influence of a female voice, whether produced by a woman or assumed by a man?

The empowerment of smooth Jacob is thus an empowerment of women, albeit within the contours of an androcentric world. No woman warrior breaks free, no amazon overthrows the patriarchal system. Within that system, however, women and their surrogates succeed in behind-the-scenes ways through deception and trickery. The patriarch is blind and easily fooled; the manly, hairy son follows the rules and loses his position. The underdog in gender somehow prevails. Such stories portraying a loss of power to those who really hold the power in actual everyday life would certainly amuse women as all such stories amuse and psychologically liberate those without the power.

In its own way, Genesis 25–27 uses the equation between hair and identity quite subversively. Even if such stories and such a use of symbols may be rooted in women's stories and have to do with gender, something bigger is going on, for these stories are now part of the history of the people Israel and generations of male copyists, preservers, and composers saw them as fundamental expressions of Israelite origins and self-definition.

Who was comfortable with a smooth founding father and why? One possibility is suggested by Claus Westermann, who sees in Jacob's locus in the tent and Esau's in the wilderness a paradigm shift accompanying actual sociohistorical change from early times when people live off the land to more settled existence with domesticated flocks.[25] To accept fully Westermann's suggestion is to accept largely outdated and too simplistic views about the move from hunter/gatherer societies to nomadic existence to urban life as they pertain to the history of Israel. Along his lines, however, one might suggest that alternate paradigms of power are offered by the images of Esau and Jacob: one that valorizes brute force and simple thinking and another that valorizes sophisticated manipulation of the system and the use of brain rather than brawn. The latter might be expected to reflect urbane, sophisticated writers rather than country folk, although this too is to speculate. What we can say with certainty is that the writers of the Hebrew Bible, in various ways, love to portray the success of the disempowered who are aided by their ever present divine ally, the all-powerful YHWH. God loves the weak because their success is testimony to the realization that all power comes from God. In the views of androcentric writers, who is weaker than women? So Israel becomes the female in a relationship with her protector God.

Howard Eilberg-Schwartz has explored with creativity the implications of this situation in gender for Israelite men's views of themselves and their relationship with women on the one hand and God on the other.[26] Suffice it to say that given a long history of subjugation at the hands of ancient Near Eastern superpowers, the image of the underdog must have been a source of great identification for Israel throughout its history and tales of the success of tricksters a source of satisfaction. In Genesis 25 and 27, absence of hair becomes an important means of costuming the underdog appropriately. It is an image rooted in gender and richly endowed with sociological and theological implications. Israelite writers seem to be identifying purposefully with the less hairy man, and yet that identification has meaning ironically only in the context of a culture that values hair and sees hair in contexts of male leadership as a declaration of status and a source and symbol of power.

If Genesis 27, with its use of the hair motif, and Genesis 38 reveal something about women's story or men's assumption of the female voice and perspective, Genesis 14 offers an example of the male voice. This story places the patriarch Abraham in a heroic role, employing the same traditional pattern applied to David in 1 Samuel 30. Family members have been taken hostage in a warring context; the Israelite leader takes his retainers, goes to battle, and successfully liberates his kin from enemies. The context is military, the mode of confrontation is overt and direct, and the role is one of public leadership as the hero sallies forth to rescue his kinsmen: "Lot and his possession and the women and the rest of the people" (14:16). The type of content and the perspective differs from those of trickster stories in general and the tales of women tricksters in particular. If we are looking for a contrast in gender of voice, Genesis 14 would seem to provide a possible example of a story with a man's voice.

Another example of a tale dominated by a male voice might be provided by Genesis 32:25–32, the scene at the River Jabbok where Jacob wrestles with "a man" who turns out to be a manifestation of the divine, mysterious and unnamed. Much has been written about this scene, its psychoanalytical dimensions, the way in which it provides a transformation of the hero Jacob, a rite of passage whereby he becomes Israel, returns to the land, and reconciles with his brother Esau. Some have interpreted this scene of painful transformation as recompense or necessary penance for Jacob's having cheated his brother. It is above all a manly and heroic scene, for Jacob fights with beings divine and human and has prevailed (32:28). Could this manly passage in fact be compensation for or serve to balance the all too smooth and effeminate trickster, the son of his mother, describing victory in the male voice as a matter of physical combat, wounding, and the establishment of a relationship of respect between the two male combatants who recognize one another's power in direct physical terms? One thinks here of the way in which relationships are established between such manly men heroes as Gilgamesh and Enkidu, who emerge from their one-on-one combat as beloved brothers and constant companions.

Again, speaking about such contrasts in voice is not meant to imply male and female writers. Attention to gender within the framework provided by Mills, Beissinger, and Ko does, however, lead in some intriguing directions. Genesis 27 and 38 may reveal evidence of a female perspective. We have explored some of the ways in which female heroes are shown to "dance with chains on" and have grappled with the fact that those we assume to be male preservers and composers sometimes appear to identify with the feminine while other tales, such as the battle account of Genesis 14 and the scene at Jabbok in Genesis 32, seem to partake of a more overtly and fully masculine voice.

Notes

1. Susan Niditch, *"My Brother Esau Is a Hairy Man": Hair and Identity in Ancient Israel* (Oxford and New York: Oxford University Press, 2008).
2. In Homer's *Odyssey*, Penelope, wife of Odysseus, waits loyally for his return from war and long journey, virtuously fending off suitors as she waits.
3. Margaret Beissinger, "Gender and Power in the Balkan Return Song," *Slavic and East European Journal* 45, no. 3 (2001): 403–30.
4. Lillian Doherty, *Siren Songs: Gender, Audiences, and Narrators in the Odyssey* (Ann Arbor: University of Michigan Press, 1995).
5. Beissinger, "Gender and Power," 404.
6. Doherty, *Siren Songs*, 40.
7. John J. Winkler, *The Constraints of Desire: The Anthropology of Sex and Desire in Ancient Greece* (New York: Routledge, 1990), 139.
8. Esther Fuchs, "The Literary Characterization of Mothers and Sexual Politics in the Hebrew Bible," in *Feminist Perspectives on Biblical Scholarship*, ed. Adela Yarbro Collins (Chico, CA: Scholars Press, 1985), 117–36.
9. J. Cheryl Exum, *Fragmented Women: Feminist (sub)versions of Biblical Narratives* (Valley Forge, PA: Trinity Press International, 1993), 136–37. See also J. Cheryl Exum, "'Mother in Israel': A Familiar Figure Reconsidered," in *Feminist Interpretation of the Bible*, ed. Letty M. Russell (Philadelphia: Westminster, 1985), 73–85.
10. Exum, *Fragmented Women*, 139.
11. Margaret A. Mills, *Rhetorics and Politics in Afghan Traditional Storytelling* (Philadelphia: University of Pennsylvania Press, 1991), 301.
12. Margaret A. Mills, "Sex Role Reversals, Sex Changes, and Transvestite Disguise in the Oral Tradition of a Conservative Muslim Community in Afghanistan," in *Women's Folklore, Women's Culture*, ed. Rosan A. Jordan and Susan J. Kalčik (Philadelphia: University of Pennsylvania Press, 1985), 187–213; 188.
13. Ibid., 188.
14. Ibid., 189.
15. Mills, "Gender and Verbal Performance Style in Afghanistan," in *Gender, Genre, and Power in South Asian Expressive Traditions*, ed. Arjun Appadurai, Frank J. Korom, and Margaret A. Mills (Philadelphia: University of Pennsylvania Press, 1991), 56–77; 72. See also Margaret A. Mills, *Oral Narrative in Afghanistan: The Individual in Tradition* (New York and London: Garland, 1990).
16. Dorothy Ko, *Cinderella's Sisters: A Revisionist History of Footbinding* (Berkeley: University of California Press, 2005), 227.

17. Michel Foucault, *The History of Sexuality,* vol. 1, *An Introduction,* trans. Robert Hurley (New York: Vintage Press, 1980), 97.
18. Saul Olyan, "What Do Shaving Rites Accomplish and What Do They Signal in Biblical Ritual Contexts?" *Journal of Biblical Literature* 117 (1988): 611–22.
19. See C. R. Hallpike, "Social Hair," *Man* 4 (1969): 256–64.
20. Olyan, "What Do Shaving Rites Accomplish?" 611–22.
21. Cynthia R. Chapman, *The Gendered Language of Warfare in the Israelite-Assyrian Encounter,* Harvard Semitic Monographs 62 (Winona Lake, IN: Eisenbrauns, 2004).
22. Ludwig Koehler and Walter Baumgartner, *The Hebrew and Aramaic Lexicon of the Old Testament,* rev. by Walter Baumgartner and Johann Jakob Stamm, trans. M. E. J. Richardson, 7 vols. (Leiden: Brill, 1994).
23. Ibid., vol. 4, 1742.
24. Claus Westermann, *Genesis 12–36: A Commentary,* trans. John J. Scullion (Minneapolis: Augsburg Publishing House, 1985), 414–15.
25. Westermann, *Genesis 12–36.*
26. Howard Eilberg-Schwartz, *The Savage in Judaism: An Anthropology of Israelite Religion and Ancient Judaism* (Bloomington: Indiana University Press, 1990).

Chapter 5

The Journey of a Girl Who Talks Back

Mark's Syrophoenician Woman

HISAKO KINUKAWA

BORN TO BE A FEMINIST

My first nickname, given by my father, was "talking-back girl." I do not remember this because it was before I was three years old. My mother told me that I kept telling my parents, "No, no" and insisting on my own way to do things or to think. In addition, I had five siblings, born in eight years and growing up in close relationship, which naturally trained us in critical thinking to keep peace and practice fairness. I can say with the utmost confidence that I was born to be a feminist.

As an Asian feminist scholar of the New Testament, I have studied the reciprocally influential relationships between women and Jesus in the Gospel of Mark. Among the women in Mark, the Syrophoenician woman has held my special attention. She is the only woman in this Gospel who talks back to Jesus. As a talk-back girl, I have been drawn to her story and here turn to it with new questions and approaches. I will trace some parts of my own intellectual and faith journey, sketch some of the feminist theological voices and conversations in Asia, particularly Japan, and converse with other feminist exegetes as I revisit the Syrophoenician woman's story.

ENCOUNTERING FEMINIST EXEGESIS AND THEOLOGY

The first feminist exegesis on biblical texts I encountered was an article written by Phyllis Trible on Genesis 1–3. As I recall, it was in the 1980s. I felt as though I had been hit by lightning and was so excited that I could not move my eyes from it. Here was a feminist scholar who clearly spelled out what I had been struggling to express. At the same time I felt relieved and encouraged, as if I had met someone who affirmed me in thinking and writing as I did. No wonder I became more eager to expose myself to books written by feminist theologians from the West.

Around that time, my Japanese women friends who were frustrated with male-centered books written with a patriarchal mindset began translating books written by feminist theologians in Euro-American contexts. There were no feminist theologians' books produced in Japanese until then. As the result of our efforts, translated books finally began to appear in our markets. For example, in 1976, *Liberation Theology* by Rosemary Radford Ruether was translated and published.[1] In 1981, *The Church and the Second Sex* by Mary Daly and in 1982, *Womanspirit Rising: A Feminist Reader in Religion* edited by Carol Christ and Judith Plaskow were translated and published.[2] Elisabeth Moltmann-Wendel's *Ein eigener Mensch werden: Frauen um Jesus*, Letty M. Russell's *Human Liberation in a Feminist Perspective—A Theology*, and Phyllis Trible's *God and the Rhetoric of Sexuality* soon followed.[3]

MY EXPERIENCE WITH CHRISTIANITY IN JAPAN

My Christian faith was nurtured in a church movement called Non-Church. A Japanese man who had studied at a seminary in the United States of America returned to Japan and started this church independent of any established denominations or traditions. One characteristic of the church is reading the original texts of the Bible and applying the good news to contextual situations in Japan. I could have loved the practice if the interpretations and applications were not male-centered. But it was painful to stay in a pew with the uncomfortable feeling caused by heavily patriarchal interpretations of the Bible. My affiliation with this church began when I was a first-year college student. It was also my first commitment to the Christian faith. I am not a Christian by birth. Until then my life was happily spent in our multireligious and multicultural society, which has a mixture of Buddhism, Shintoism, Confucianism, and Christianity. My parents raised their children in these interdependently coexisting religious traditions and conventions.

As in most of the Asian countries, Christianity arrived in our country far later than other religions. Except in the Philippines, Christians have always been minority groups. In our country the number of Christians has never gone beyond 1 percent of the total population. None of the mainstream religions in

Japan is free from sexism. Women are often considered to be polluted. According to many religious traditions, by being subservient, obedient, and silent, women may gain honor.

ASIAN CHRISTIAN WOMEN'S FORUM

In 1979 the Christian Conference of Asia held the first Women's Forum in Penang, Malaysia, and about one hundred women from various countries in Asia participated. Aiko Carter, the only Japanese woman present, wrote, "It was obvious that communication was most difficult without a common language in Asia where colonialism and militarism had ruled in the past. Although women had similar experiences of oppressive social systems, we had difficulty sharing thoughts and wisdom. Women were afraid of talking about the deepest issue of the self in a group."[4]

Having no common language has always been a big issue among Asians. As the result of colonization as well as imperialism, we have been forced to choose English as our common language. I surmise that the reason the women did not raise their voices is found not only in the language problem, but also in shame/honor cultures that disciplined women to be subserviently quiet. In addition, for us Japanese, with our history of invading and colonizing other Asian countries, it has been more painful and harder to claim ourselves as Asian. We literally lose words among other Asians. Only around 1985 did women in Japan start raising their voices in church women's groups across denominational boundaries. More Christian women became aware of a patriarchal mindset and sexism hovering over churches. We questioned male-oriented sermons and sexist-colored Bible studies.

In Asia there are forty-eight countries, for whom I cannot speak because of their diverse social locations and complex situations. The same is probably true in talking about Asian feminist theologies generally. In this paper, therefore, I will concentrate on my experience in Japan, where it is hard to meet feminist theological scholars. Even Japanese women who have studied under feminist theologians in the United States or Europe hesitate to claim themselves to be feminist after they come back to Japan. They think that claiming to be feminist will exclude them from appropriate positions in academia. It is even harder to meet a woman in the biblical field.

I will turn to the story of the Syrophoenician woman because I have found few feminists have dealt with Mark's story in detail and because questions I raised a long time ago have still not been fully answered. I will compare interpretations by an American feminist biblical scholar, an Asian feminist from Sri Lanka, and me so that we may glimpse how I, as an Asian, interpret the story from my own social location. My interpretation has evolved through my own experience, through dialogue with the interpretations offered by these women, and through the challenge of new criticisms, especially postcolonial ones.

DOING FEMINIST BIBLICAL INTERPRETATION

In 1987, I published my first book in Japanese, *Feminism in the Bible*. I had already been practicing feminist exegesis, but in that book I realized my struggle with the texts was directly or indirectly related to sexism, classism, and issues of ethnicity, gender or sexual orientation as well as cultural, social, economic, and historical situations. It took a little while before I was more consciously able to engage the texts with a variety of exegetical methods, beginning with rhetorical and historical criticism and extending to postcolonial criticism. Because of my publications in books and journals, I was squeezed out of my non-church church and told that my theology was not appropriate. I decided to leave the church and became free to work ecumenically and beyond denominations. Soon after the incident, I left the country to do more study on feminist theology at the Graduate Theological Union in Berkeley affiliated with San Francisco Theological Seminary.

For my dissertation, from a Japanese feminist perspective, I attempted to elucidate the relationships between women and Jesus, including their reciprocal influence, as described in the Gospel of Mark. I searched for the identity and roles of women in the circle of Jesus' followers. I used historical and rhetorical reevaluation reflecting a feminist scale of values. Through the study I discovered women playing decisive roles in setting up stages so Jesus could become an active participant in egalitarian relationships by crossing the boundaries established by the patriarchal tradition. Convinced that this discovery would play an encouraging role for those still under the influence of patriarchy and sexism, I sought con-scientizing implications of this study for contemporary Japanese church women and men who are under the heavy influence of Japanese traditional cultural heritage and the oppressive patriarchal authority of the church.

MARK AND THE SYROPHOENICIAN WOMAN

Among the women in Mark, the Syrophoenician woman drew my special attention and interest. Few articles had then been written by feminist exegetes on the story of the Syrophoenician woman compared with its alternative version in Matthew, where she is called a Canaanite woman. The focus of the two stories is different. One article on the Matthean version, however, written by Gail R. O'Day, strengthened my exegetical stance. O'Day writes,

> Traditional form critical categories work from the assumption that Jesus is the protagonist of each story being studied, and seek to establish a taxonomy of Jesus' various functions. In our story, however, Jesus is not the protagonist; the Canaanite woman is. Traditional form critical investigation will therefore always come up empty, because it asks inappropriate questions of the text . . . . *[The text] tells an unconventional story with an unconventional protagonist.*[5]

Her interpretation supported my approach to the Syrophoenician woman, who dares to talk back to Jesus.

The story begins when Jesus "set out and went away to the region of Tyre" (Mark 7:24 NRSV). "Immediately" after a woman, a "Gentile, of Syrophoenician origin," hears of Jesus, she comes to him because she has a demon-possessed little daughter. The name Syrophoenicia, a colonial state of the Roman Empire, reflects the political situation of Jesus' day. The woman is racially Syrophoenician and politically and socioculturally a Greek/Gentile. Daring to cross the borders of culture and religion, she shows herself to be on the verge of a desperate situation with her demon-possessed daughter. She is determined to meet Jesus. Then "she begged him to cast the demon out of her daughter" (v. 26).

Jesus' two-clause response sounds harsh: (1) "Let the children be fed first," and (2) "for it is not fair to take the children's food and throw it to the dogs." Jews first and then Gentiles: Jews as children and Gentiles as dogs. Nevertheless, she is determined. She talks back to Jesus. Caught between life and death, she has to be assertive if she and her daughter are to survive. So she uses the same words that Jesus has used but in her own way. She answers, "Sir, even the dogs under the table eat the children's crumbs" (v. 28). Cleverly, she first affirms Jesus' saying and then makes full use of it to strike right back. She is intent on opening up the impasse she is facing.

As I read the text, I struggled with two particular issues: (1) why Jesus' answer to the woman is so offensive, exclusive, and harsh; (2) why his response to her plea is focused on food or table fellowship while her focus is on the healing of her sick child.

SHARON H. RINGE'S FEMINIST CHRISTOLOGICAL READING

In 1985, Sharon H. Ringe offered a feminist interpretation of this Markan story.[6] She reads the story from a gender perspective, mostly dialoguing with male exegetes, beginning her discussion with a shocking statement: "The church has trouble with uppity women"[7] The main question she wrestles with is why Jesus' response to the Syrophoenician woman's plea is so offensive (the first of my two questions). By pointing out that "it is Jesus who provides the hostile saying and the woman whose retort trips him up and corrects him,"[8] Ringe seems irritated that such a Christ be presented in any church. Then she grants the incident might have taken place *when even he was caught with his compassion down.* She then turns to the christological implication of the story, saying, "the story was originally remembered and retold in the community not for its ecclesiastical significance but *primarily because of its christological significance.*"[9] Through the Syrophoenician woman's tenacity, an act of trust, of engagement, risking everything, Jesus discerns a need to transform himself and cross the boundaries of ethnicity and gender that lie before him. The Christ that we see here reflects the genuinely human one in painful interaction with the woman. In conclusion Ringe says, "Here Jesus himself must learn about being that sort of Christ from one of the poorest of the poor and most despised of the outcasts—a Gentile woman on her own before God and humankind."[10]

Though she highly values the Syrophoenician woman's determined action as well as Jesus' sensitive transformation of himself, Ringe has not settled the question of why he uttered, or why Mark put in his mouth, such harsh words cast upon a woman who, according to Ringe, represents "the 'poor'—the economically poor and socially outcast, the sick, the oppressed, the rejected—who respond joyfully to the good news of God's reign."[11] Ringe suggests the christological significance of the story has had great impact upon the mission of the church. Yet I must wonder why the story, an incident which transformed even Jesus, has not more extensively influenced Christology within church history. Surely Christology, if interpreted according to this story, would differ from traditional teaching.

We cannot tell why Jesus answers so bluntly, but we do know that the Gentile woman hangs on tenaciously and refuses to be shaken off. After the seemingly strange conversation, Jesus says to her, "For saying that, you may go. The demon has left your daughter" (v. 29). Reading from an interactional perspective, the story may set forth who Jesus is to be as the life-giving Christ. By the end, Jesus is motivated to act, inviting the Gentile, the socially outcast, the materially poor, the sick, the oppressed, and the rejected into God's community.

RANJINI WICKRAMARATNE REBERA FROM THE PERSPECTIVE OF HER CULTURE IN SRI LANKA

Sri Lankan feminist theologian Ranjini Wickramaratne Rebera gives a cultural interpretation of the story. She tries to discern the meaning of the story in her own unstable society, which is in constant strife. Rebera begins her paper with a christological interpretation, as does Ringe. She further sees that the writer of the story uses this encounter to strengthen Jesus' messianic role. However, she suggests looking further.[12] She writes, "In South Asian cultures demon possession is an unacceptable phenomenon. Women who display signs of demon possession are considered to be either evil or unclean. . . . The search for healing is therefore also a search for cleansing."[13] She sees the pain of this woman reflected in "[t]he pain of mothers whose children have been killed in ethnic and racial war, permanently wounded through the effects of militarism, of drugs, or of substance abuse and of AIDS and HIV-related illnesses."[14] Seeing the fighting mothers in her homeland, Rebera asserts that the woman displays "*the power that rouses the weak* to action. . . . The Syrophoenician woman meets the power of the rabbi Jesus with the knowledge of her own sense of power. Her power is rooted in her protective strength, her capacity to care, and her commitment to the task she has set herself. She is an icon to women in today's church who are prevented from claiming the right to own their power and to use it for others, as this woman did."[15]

Living and struggling in her multicultural, multiethnic society, Rebera sees an interreligious encounter between the two. She conceives, "the challenge was done with intentions of trying to establish an understanding of each other's positions. . . . They worked towards the goal of being able to relate to each other rather than to dominate each other."[16] She calls it "mutual ministry." Rebera continues: "For Christian women in South Asia she stands tall as the sister who refused to take 'No' as the answer and who held her own until she achieved her goal. She invites us to find new and inclusive ways to dialogue as people of a multi-religious, intercultural South Asia."[17] By keeping her attention on the Syrophoenician woman and her demon-possessed daughter, Rebera sees the woman's strength in talking back to Jesus, whom she entrusts with her and her child's life, on the equal terrain of speech. For her, the story speaks of the power of the weak, their courage and tenacity. When her cultural interpretation is applied to the contemporary church in her country, the story seems to gain more life and strength.

SHARON RINGE'S SECOND ARTICLE

Sharon Ringe revisited the story of the Syrophoenician woman (and her interpreters) sixteen years after her first article and wrote another.[18] She repeats her point that within the structure of the story, "the woman's retort is the focal point."[19] This time she leads us into a first-century contextual reading of the text, which she calls an inductive exegetical approach. She looks at the social data underlying the author's interpretation of the woman and the literary devices at work in each character.

As resources for understanding the social-historical settings of the story Ringe consults both earlier and more recent scholars.[20] She traces the political and economic significance of Tyre throughout the first millennium BCE, including its influence as a center of trade and metallurgy. She understands the "region" or "environs" (*ta horia*) of Tyre to include surrounding agricultural lands and small communities near the border with Galilee.[21] Tyre, like other urban centers of trade, relied on these smaller farming communities and agricultural lands to feed the urban population. The reliance could become exploitative, Ringe notes. If harvests were poor and food was scarce, the requirements of the influential city dwellers could leave the poorer farmers and their communities facing hunger.[22] Ringe also points out that though the city would have been mostly Gentile, the "region," like most borderlands, would have been ethnically mixed, with both Jews and Gentiles.

Ringe then examines the social identity of the woman compared to Jesus: "The woman was one of the *city dwellers* separated from Jesus not only by religion and ethnicity, but also by economic loyalty. She is portrayed as part of the group in that region whose policies and lifestyle would have been a *source of suffering for her mostly poorer, rural, Jewish neighbors.*"[23]

That Mark calls her "Greek" suggests that she is educated and privileged. Ringe thinks the reason Jesus calls her "dog" is that she is one of the privileged ones in Tyre who exploit Galilean peasants. She then suggests that part of her discomfort with Jesus' contempt comes from her own identification with the urban, privileged woman from Tyre:

> The harshness of the language attributed to Jesus still offends me as a would-be follower of Jesus, but I understand *how fervent political commitment* (Mark's as well as, apparently, Jesus') un-tempers the tongue. As one of the world's "non-poor" I am uncomfortable with the picture of the privileged woman's acceptance of the subordinate posture 'under the table' as the price of her participation in the blessings Jesus offers, but that discomfort with the costliness of discipleship is appropriate.[24]

Ringe makes Jesus' harshness explicable by focusing on the woman's possible social and economic privilege. Yet she continues to consider her situation as a mother. Her subservient attitude, in this reading, comes from her destitute/desperate situation of having a demon-possessed child. She concludes, "*No one, regardless of other attributes of their lives, deserves such treatment at a time like that!* I am at a loss to understand what Mark is up to in crafting the story in this way, where it presents not general principles of social critique, but a specific individual case."[25]

Ringe offers provocative analysis of the social setting for Mark's story and raises fresh issues. Yet certain parts of her argument are not fully persuasive. In the Markan text, the setting of the story is clearly located in the region of Tyre, not explicitly the city. Therefore, it is more plausible to see the woman coming from a rural region mainly inhabited by peasants. Nevertheless, Ringe writes, "His words label her as contemptible, a 'dog', apparently (in this analysis) because she is part of the class of exploiters in the region."[26] Yet she ends her article with wavering on whether the woman is privileged, impoverished, or dowager. She is perplexed herself, wondering how to settle the ambiguity about the woman's social location.

Ringe's article offers key insights and invites fresh investigations of the story. Yet it seems to me she does not give a clear-cut answer to the two questions I raised. Why does Mark put in Jesus' mouth such harsh words for responding to the woman's plea? Why does Jesus then employ the language of bread/table community, even though her main concern is the healing of her sick child? That is, how does Mark relate the healing issue with that of food or table fellowship? Ringe's answer to the first is that Jesus' contempt in calling the woman a dog is because she is part of the class of exploiters in the region. To the second question, she does not make clear why Jesus used the language of table fellowship to defend himself and his compatriots, though she refers to ways farming communities in the ethnically mixed "region" were vulnerable to the city dwellers' needs and social influence.[27] Her interest seems to be more tilted toward questioning the woman's identity and her way of behaving. She feels uncomfortable with the woman's subservient attitude yet does not find a more positive significance in her talking back to Jesus.

Like Ringe, my interest is drawn to the social locations of the story and trying to uncover the power relationships at work that may cause the structure of dominant and subordinate relationships in the story, with particular insight from social science criticism and postcolonial criticism. Before returning to close exegesis of Mark's story, however, let me share a little more of my experience interpreting the Syrophoenician woman in an Asian context.

MY EXPERIENCE IN ASIAN CONTEXT

After my book *Women and Jesus in Mark from a Japanese Feminist Perspective* was published by Orbis Books in 1994, I became more engaged with Asian biblical scholars and theologians. When Sook Ja Chung from Korea and I had finished our doctoral work in 1992 at San Francisco Theological Seminary (SFTS), our earnest desire then was to see more Asian women have opportunities to expose themselves to feminist theological studies. It was the beginning of the birth of the International Feminist Theology Emphasis Group of the Doctor of Ministry (DMin) Program affiliated with SFTS. The first group met in Tokyo for a three-week intensive course. Letty Russell, Shannon Clarkson, and Katharine Sakenfeld were the teachers. The group had seven Korean, seven Japanese, and five Filipina women. Sook Ja and I coordinated the session. The program then was developed into a three-year DMin program and expanded to have more international women in the groups.

From 2000, as a part of the program, I started teaching a course on feminist hermeneutics of the New Testament at the SFTS summer session. Every woman who participated in the international feminist theology emphasis group came to SFTS for a summer program to finish her course requirement. Each time I met a different group of diverse women from all over the world. Every year we were enormously diverse in many ways. What I learned most is that even though we unanimously used "patriarchy/kyriarchy" as our heuristic key, each interpreter had a different connotation, content, or meaning in her own social, political, economic, and cultural context.

In my classroom, every woman struggled with the Syrophoenician/Canaanite woman. We read thirteen articles on the story written by feminist scholars, though they were mostly on the Matthean version. By the end of the course, all of us were transformed into women capable of talking back to Jesus as well as to the power in our churches and societies.

I have also been working on the board of the Asian Women's Resource Center (AWRC) for the last twenty years. Its journal, *In God's Image* (*IGI*), has been an excellent source to learn of feminist theologies practiced in Asia. Workshops, lectureships, and conferences have been great opportunities for Asian women to share our stories, pain and suffering and learn to be in solidarity with each other. As mentioned earlier, most Asian Christians are minorities in their country. Doing feminist theologies sometimes isolates us even from the church. Doing feminist theologies in Asia may mean talking back to our church, its tradition and teachings. Our endeavor to establish a strong stream of feminist theologians against the grain has still a long way to go.

Searching for Asian feminist theologies, I participated in the project of AWRC to publish four module books on introducing Asian feminist theologies. The current project is to evaluate the journey of feminist theologies described in *IGI* and to find out directions toward the future by looking back to see how far we have come. As a part of the project, I have been working on articles that dealt with texts in the New Testament. Among 120 biblical articles, a little more than half are related to NT texts. However, there are only three articles dealing with the Matthean version of the story of the Canaanite woman, and no analysis of Mark's Syrophoenician woman but my own. Even in Asia, Matthew's story is more popular than Mark's.

MY SECOND VISIT TO THE STORY
OF THE SYROPHOENICIAN WOMAN

As Sharon Ringe shows, the Syrophoenician woman's story invites analysis from social-historical, cultural, and postcolonial perspectives.[28] My interests and concerns now make me ask what kind of power relationships are at work in the story and what kind of powers are covertly working as hidden agenda beside the open agenda, which is easy to grasp. Dialogue with the story involves grappling with the political, social, economic, cultural, and religious situations of the ancient world where the story was born and recorded and where the people did not necessarily enjoy peace and justice.

To state my two questions more fully: (1) Why does Mark put in Jesus' mouth such harsh words responding to the woman's plea? Jesus says to her, "Let the children be fed first, for it is not fair to take the children's food and throw it to the dogs" (v. 27 NRSV). The children represent the Jews and the dogs represent foreigners, including the woman and her daughter. The expression is therefore Jesus' overt rejection of her plea. (2) Why does Jesus then employ the language of bread, even though he knows her main concern is the healing of her sick child? Why does Mark relate the healing issue to that of table fellowship?

Social Location of the Story

In the time of Jesus, both Galilee and Tyre were part of the territory occupied by the Roman Empire. Their cities and regions were under imperial control and oppressed by colonial politics. Despite the fact, the city of Tyre was one of the wealthiest and most important ports on the coast, well known for "its wealth based on metal work, the production of purple dye and an extensive trade with the whole Mediterranean region."[29] Because the city of Tyre had very little space for farming, it depended on importing agricultural products from Galilee and other places. "The Galilean hinterland and the rural territory belonging to the city (partly settled by Jews) were the 'breadbasket' of the metropolis of Tyre."[30]

In contrast, the residents of Galilee, mainly peasants and fisherfolk, suffered under a threefold oppression: (1) Roman imperialism; (2) the Herodean monarchy, which fawned on Rome; and (3) temple politics in Judea. Jonathan L. Reed notes that the city of Tyre was closer to Capernaum than Capernaum was to Jerusalem.[31] Tyre, then, especially its region, might not have sounded too foreign or distant to those residing in Galilee. Actually, villages inhabited by Jews could exist right next to villages inhabited by Syrophoenicians where the hinterland of Tyre intersected the hinterland of Galilee, with no clear borders separating the two. We can plausibly imagine that villages of different ethnic groups were intermingled in such areas, as Ringe also suggests. Galilean peasants must have been resentful when they saw their ruling class selling their produce to the highest bidders from urban Tyre. Agricultural crops produced by the peasants did not return to their daily table to satisfy their own basic need.

The Woman as a Greek

The woman is introduced as culturally Greek and ethnically Syrophoenician. The use of "Greek" may imply she would have known Greek and probably was thoroughly integrated in Hellenistic culture. Then her social status could have been of the upper class, as Ringe asserts in her second article. But the word may simply indicate that she was not a Jew, but a foreigner, which is consistent with usage of the term by almost all the New Testament writers.[32] Since Mark specifies that Jesus is in the "region of Tyre," it is more probable that the woman may be from one of the peripheral villages of Tyre, where people's lives were not as easy as the lives of those in the urban cities.

Impact of the Harsh Words Given by Jesus

Taking into consideration the bitter economic relationship between the affluent city of Tyre and exploited Galilee, we can see that Jesus' bitter words thrown to the woman would have had a powerful impact. The saying, which may appear so offensive to the woman, would reflect the humiliating power relationship that Galileans had to endure with respect to urban Tyrians. The words could mean: "First let the mouths of the poor people in Galilee be satisfied. For it is not good to take poor people's food and throw it to the rich Tyrians in the city." The words overtly express the reality of the destitute Galilean peasants and show their resistance against the power exercised by the urban people of Tyre. Jesus' reply could represent the common feeling of the Galilean peasants toward the wealthy Tyrians whom they viewed as rich and representing the Hellenistic culture of the elite. There is an obvious reason for him to use the language of bread/table fellowship.

The Woman as a Syrophoenician

Yet if the Syrophoenician woman in this story is from one of the villages in the hinterland of Tyre, which is very plausible, the village is surely peripheral from the perspective of the urban elite in the city of Tyre. Compared to them, the woman might not be rich or privileged. It is more plausible to say that the woman is from the hinterland with only limited access to the life of the urban rich and is socially ostracized because of her demon-possessed girl. Then it is easier for us to understand why she is not knocked down by Jesus' words. From her attitude we learn she does not identify herself with those at whom Jesus' harsh words are thrown and whom he criticizes. It is clear Jesus only sides with the Galilean destitute peasants and thus defends them over against the metropolitan Tyrians who benefit from the Galilean peasants.

The Woman's Religious Affiliation

Mary Ann Tolbert offers another view, suggesting, "His rebuff provides the opportunity for her faith to be fully revealed, for she takes his metaphor and turns it back on him."[33] However, her religious affiliation is not apparent from the representations given in the story. She may believe in the Tyrian God Melkart and other gods. Since we do not hear her own voice in this respect, it does not seem appropriate to ask about her religious identity. Although the story may imply that the woman has faith, the woman's response indicates that her interest is focused on her child's need to be cured. Kwok Pui-lan, supporting the woman's focus, says, "The woman, though denigrated by Jesus, speaks in a supportive and affirmative way, for she is concerned with maintaining the relationship."[34] Rebera gives the same interpretation as Kwok's, except Rebera sees the whole issue from her multireligious experience, which requires mutual patience as well as reception.[35]

Toward a Dialogical Interdependence

The woman does not succumb to Jesus' words that rebuff the populace of Tyre as a whole. In response, she says, "Yes, it is so, but, sir, even the dogs under the table eat the children's crumbs" (7:28; my literal translation). She acknowledges the primacy that the Galilean peasants ought to have. At the same time, if Jesus is more concerned about the Galileans with scarce food to live on, and if he critically reveals the dominant relationship of the Tyrians over the Galileans through his harsh words, she reminds Jesus of the fact that there are the other kinds of dogs (people of Tyre destitute like her and her child) that also need to be fed.

In this expression, we may see her raise a serious question to Jesus. Her words imply, "Can you totally ignore a sick child while talking about feeding the 'children' of yours?" If Jesus defends the children of Israel, the woman insists, she and her sick child should also be defended. She insists that Jesus' harsh words do not apply to her and her child. On the contrary, she and her child will be exploited by Jesus if he will not feed them, since they also are suffering. Therefore she does not give up. She is leading the dialogue toward an interdependent relationship for them.

Jesus' words emphasize that the woman is associated with a city noted for depriving even the smallest bits of food from Galilean peasants, who are forced to sell their produce to Tyre. On the other hand, her reply underscores that she and her daughter are also "Others" in the society of Tyre. Therefore she presses Jesus to expand his priority to the "Others" in Tyre and not to exclude her and her child from his table fellowship. She asks Jesus to be consistent in putting the primacy on the marginalized wherever they are and showing an egalitarian spirit toward those who are destitute. Had she not experienced being the Other in her society, she would not be able to be as confident as she is in asking Jesus' help. Her tenacity can be read as evidence that she is neither rich nor privileged. I disagree with Ringe in this respect.

Change in the Equilibrium of Power

Jesus responds to her with words that fully accept her request, "For your words, you may go . . . ." Jesus affirms her, as if he has learned a new lesson from her. In the first part of the encounter between Jesus and the woman, the equilibrium of power is apparently in favor of Jesus. Toward the end it becomes reversed. The last verse, "So she went home, found the child lying on the bed, and the demon gone" (NRSV), does not say anything about her faith, conversion, or religion. We must abstain from concluding she has become the first foreign woman follower of Jesus. The bread imagery in this story points not to Christian table fellowship but to the power relationships between Tyrian urban people and Galilean peasants over food production.

Conclusion

Two elements —the political and economic relationships between the regions of Tyre and Galilee and the oppressive power of Tyrians over Galilean peasants— provide a context for understanding why Jesus throws such bitter words at the woman. His words reveal a basic issue: the unfair distribution of food among rival colonies within the Roman Empire. The woman's words, however, demonstrate that she rejects being used as a foil in Jesus' conflict with the affluent urban Tyrians. Her words reveal that Tyrian society also is hierarchical and therefore Tyrian people are not monolithic. She identifies herself, instead, with the destitute Galilean peasants in the sense that she also is one of those whose needs must be met. When Jesus heals her daughter, he acknowledges her claim. In the same way, only after we see her need met may we begin talking about the story as encouraging a table fellowship inclusive of all those in need, wherever they are.

IMPLICATIONS FOR CHURCHES

Christian churches in Japan that claim to be advocating for the alienated in society are made aware that they themselves are a part of the affluent and dominant power over developing countries just like the city of Tyre over Galilee. We are also awakened to our mission of advocacy by exposing ourselves to the influx of migrant workers from the suffering parts of the world, much as the Syrophoenician woman reminded Jesus. This particular story reminds us of the complicated situation in which churches find themselves. To commit to be Jesus' disciples is not an easy task if churches stick to the middle class and individualistic faith that tend to keep their status quo in wealth and stability. This is a threatening story to most churches.

Since there are hardly any feminist biblical scholars in my country, sometimes I feel as if I am floating in a big ocean without knowing where I am headed. Once I called myself a panda, an animal so rarely seen in our country that it draws people's attention, but they then say "once is enough to see it." For the last two decades, Japanese society has made some progress in gender equality in the social and political spheres. Following the trend, more Christians have become interested in knowing what feminist theology is. Especially those who are marginalized in the society, those who are interested in seeking peace and justice, those who are stressed with male-centered messages preached in churches, and women are the most interested in the emancipatory messages given by feminist theologians. My struggle and talking back to power will have to continue.

Notes

1. Rosemary R. Ruether, *Liberation Theology* (New York: Paulist Press, 1972).
2. Mary Daly, *The Church and the Second Sex* (New York: Harper Colophon Books, 1975); *Womanspirit Rising: A Feminist Reader in Religion,* ed. Carol P. Christ and Judith Plaskow (New York: Harper and Row Publishers, 1979).
3. Elisabeth Moltmann-Wendel , *Ein eigener Mensch werden: Frauen um Jesus* (Gütersloh: Gütersloher Verlagshaus Gerd Mohn, 1980); Letty M. Russell, *Human Liberation in a Feminist Perspective—A Theology* (Philadelphia: The Westminster Press, 1974); Phyllis Trible, *God and the Rhetoric of Sexuality* (Philadelphia: Fortress Press, 1978).
4. Aiko Carter, "Journeying with Women Doing Theology," *In God's Image* 21, no. 4 (2002): 44.
5. Gail R. O'Day, "Surprised by Faith: Jesus and the Canaanite Woman," *Feminist Companion to Matthew,* ed. Amy-Jill Levine (Sheffield: Sheffield Academic Press, 2001), 114–25; 117; emphasis mine.
6. Sharon Ringe, "A Gentile Woman's Story," *Feminist Interpretation of the Bible,* ed. Letty M. Russell (Oxford and New York: Basil Blackwell, 1985), 65–72.

7. Ibid., 65.
8. Ibid., 67–68.
9. Ibid., 69–70, emphasis mine.
10. Ibid., 72.
11. Ibid.
12. Ranjini Wickramaratne Rebera, "The Syrophoenician Woman: A South Asian Feminist Perspective," *A Feminist Companion to Mark*, ed. Amy-Jill Levine (Sheffield: Sheffield Academic Press, 2001), 101.
13. Ibid., 102.
14. Ibid., 106.
15. Ibid., emphasis mine.
16. Ibid., 108.
17. Ibid., 110.
18. Sharon Ringe, "A Gentile Woman's Story, Revisited: Reading Mark 7:24–31a," *A Feminist Companion to Mark*, ed. Amy-Jill Levine (Sheffield: Sheffield Academic Press, 2001), 79–100.
19. Ibid., 83.
20. Thomas L. McClellan, "Tyre," *A Dictionary of the Bible*, ed. James Hastings, 5 vols. (New York: Charles Scribner's Sons, 1898–1904), 1101–2. Ringe also cites Josephus, Gerd Theissen, and a range of other Mark and Matthew scholars.
21. Ringe, "Revisited," 84.
22. Ibid.
23. Ibid., 86, emphasis mine.
24. Ibid., 97, emphasis mine.
25. Ibid., 97.
26. Ibid., 91, emphasis mine.
27. Ibid., 84–85.
28. Hisako Kinukawa, "Mark," *Global Bible Commentary*, ed. Daniel Patte (Nashville: Abingdon Press, 2004), 367–78.
29. Gerd Theissen, *The Gospels in Context: Social and Political History in the Synoptic Tradition*, trans. Linda M. Maloney (Minneapolis: Fortress Press, 1991), 73. "Its money was one of the most stable currencies in circulation at this period. This was certainly one reason why the temple treasury in Jerusalem was kept in Tyrian coin, even though this meant accepting the fact that the coins of Tyre depicted the god Melkart."
30. Ibid., 74.
31. Jonathan L. Reed, *Archaeology and the Galilean Jesus: A Re-examination of the Evidence* (Harrisburg, PA: Trinity Press International, 2000).
32. It is interesting to observe this is the only place where Mark uses the word "Greek" (*Hellēnis*, translated "Gentile" in NRSV) in his Gospel, and no other synoptic Gospel writer uses the word at all. In the whole New Testament, the word is used twenty-seven times. Half of them are found in Acts, and the other half are in Pauline letters, as easily expected. Exceptions are in John 7:35 and 12:20, and in Colossians 3:11. In almost all the cases the word is used to designate foreigners in contrast to the Jews.
33. Mary Ann Tolbert, *Sowing the Gospel: Mark's World in Literary-Historical Perspective* (Minneapolis: Fortress Press, 1989), 185.
34. Kwok Pui-lan, *Discovering the Bible in the Non-Biblical World* (Maryknoll, NY: Orbis Books, 1995), 74.
35. Rebera, "The Syrophoenician Woman," 107.

Chapter 6

Sacraments of Friendship

Embodied Love in the Gospel of John

GAIL R. O'DAY

For the Gospel of John, the defining category for telling the story of Jesus is the incarnation: "The Word became flesh and dwelt among us." These words from John 1:14 are the strongest affirmation of the incarnation—of the enfleshment, the embodiment of the Word—anywhere in the New Testament. Yet the significance of this affirmation is often overlooked in scholarly and popular interpretations and appropriations of the Gospel of John. John 3:16 ("God so loved the world"), not John 1:14, is the placard that is waved at sporting events, yet for John, the defining and decisive mark of that love is the embodiment of the Word. The ancient theologian Clement of Alexandria famously (infamously?) characterized John as a spiritual Gospel, an assessment that has been taken by centuries of readers and interpreters to mean that John values the spirit over the flesh, that John is primarily guided by a spirit/flesh dualism.[1] Yet the only way to maintain this perspective is to ignore the intensity of the claim for embodiment made by John 1:14. Perhaps most important, John's distinctive and central emphasis on the incarnation is often ignored in scholarly conversations about the locus of salvation in John. Jesus' life, even in a Gospel that begins with an affirmation of the enfleshment, embodiment of the word, is read as the means to a salvific end that is accomplished only through his death.[2]

When the incarnation is assumed as the backdrop of John's Gospel instead of read as determinative of everything in the Gospel, John's distinctive contributions to the New Testament story are overlooked, and the Gospel is thereby distorted. Not only is John's picture of Jesus distorted, but the ways Christian communities can participate in the life of Jesus are also distorted. In this essay, I want to restore the interpretive balance by focusing on the centrality of the incarnation and the body in John.

"AND THE WORD BECAME FLESH"

The Gospel of John opens with an eighteen verse prologue that signals to the reader what lies ahead. One helpful image for these opening verses is the overture to a musical or opera—the overture contains all the musical themes of the work that follows, but it is only as the opera or musical unfolds that the audience can recognize all the themes. The theme of the incarnation is clustered in the conclusion of the prologue (1:14, 16, and 18) so that—to continue the musical metaphor—a thematic crescendo propels the reader forward into the Gospel's story of Jesus.

The classic statement of 1:14 establishes the incarnation theme: "And the Word became flesh and made his home among us, and we have beheld his glory, glory as of the only begotten of the Father, full of grace and truth." It is further amplified by 1:16, "From his fullness we have all received grace upon grace," and 1:18, "No one has ever seen God. God the only Son, who is close to the Father's heart, has made God known."

These three verses are the necessary frame for understanding John's story of the revelation of God in Jesus. God is made known in the enfleshed life of the Word in the world, and that life is one of fullness and grace. This frame contrasts sharply with themes of sacrifice and emptying, common in other New Testament writings and later Christian traditions. John 1:14 could not be further removed from the kenotic perspective of Philippians 2:6–7, for example: "who though he was in the form of God, did not regard equality with God as something to be exploited, but emptied himself, taking the form of a slave, being born in human likeness" (NRSV). Both Paul and John begin from a pre-incarnational perspective, but they part ways at the moment of the incarnation. For Paul, the incarnation is a moment of emptying, of "giving up" that reaches its nadir in the death on the cross (Phil. 2:8). The low point of the death is then balanced by the high point of exaltation (Phil. 2:9). This perspective dominates most conversations, especially Protestant conversations, about the life and death of Jesus. But for John, the incarnation is not an emptying; rather, as 1:14 and 16 make abundantly clear, the incarnation is a moment of fullness.

To say that the Word becomes flesh, *sarx*, underscores the tangible presence of the incarnate Word in the world. Yet the radicality of this theological claim often is overlooked; first, because Christian tradition has become almost single-voiced in locating redemption and salvation in the death of Jesus in such a way that Jesus' life can become theologically irrelevant; and second, because John's use of flesh is subsumed under a reading of flesh shaped by Paul, Pauline scholars, and the ecclesial traditions (German Lutheran) that have dominated Pauline scholarship.[3] In John, quite distinct from Paul, for example, "flesh" is never identified with or used as a metaphor for the realm of human sin or even human brokenness. Instead, *sarx* is the coinage of human life and mortality. Whereas flesh is used as a metaphor in Paul, when *sarx* is used as a figure of speech in John, it is more synecdoche than metaphor. The part, flesh, stands for the whole, human life. We see this figure of speech in 1:13, when the Gospel describes human generation as resulting from "the will (or desire) of the flesh." The flesh is the realm of ordinary human existence, as it is also in John 3:6, "The one who is born of the flesh is flesh," and 17:2, "you have given him authority over all flesh." Flesh is where the action is—where the Word encounters and engages the world.[4]

When the Word becomes flesh, flesh is *at that moment* redeemed. Jesus redeems flesh by becoming flesh. Flesh is now the habitation of the holy. Human flesh is now the embodiment of God in the world.[5] The presence of God dwells in the flesh, not in the *skene* of the wilderness tabernacle or of the holy of holies. God can be seen and known in a human life and in the fullness of that life. The Word becomes flesh and dwells among us. The intimacy of this theological moment cannot be overemphasized. God is known because the Word, who dwells near the Father's heart (1:18), also dwells with human hearts. Indeed, the Word has a human heart. The incarnation places the most positive value possible on human life and on the human body.

That one of the central metaphors for naming the relationship between God and Jesus is that of a father and son also points to the importance of the incarnation and the body for the Gospel of John. John 1:18 speaks of Jesus as *monogenēs* (regularly translated as "the only begotten"). *Monogenēs* is an adjective formed by adding "*mono*" (single) to the verb *gennēthēnai* (as seen in 3:7), which importantly can mean both begotten and born or birthed. The English translator of *gennēthēnai* is forced to choose between a translation that favors the male procreative role (begotten—sired, to use an old-fashioned phrase) or the female role (birthed). Most translations favor the "begotten" side of that translation choice, yet given that the Fourth Gospel consistently favors and deploys words with double meanings, it is likely that the Fourth Evangelist wanted his Greek readers to imagine both aspects of *gennēthēnai* at play here.[6] The addition of the prefix "mono" names the distinctive relationship of the incarnate Word to God: the Son is the only begotten/birthed one of the Father. The use of this adjective with multiple meanings enables John to evoke in one word the full range of human birth and generation in describing the incarnation. Translations of this adjective as "unique" or "one and only" drop all links to the "birth" and "generation" root meanings and so miss the point of the adjective.

Monogenēs only occurs in one other place after the prologue, in Jesus' teachings in John 3:16 and 18. These second occurrences deepen the connections of the adjective with birth and embodiment since they are found in the conclusion to Jesus' teachings to Nicodemus about being born *anōthen* (3:3–8). The exchange between Jesus and Nicodemus centers on the meaning of birth and embodiment, expressed with two words with double meanings *gennēthēnai* and *anōthen* (which can equally be translated "anew" or "from above"). The most frequent translation choice for *anōthen*, "anew" or "again," privileges its temporal dimension and renders invisible its spatial or physical dimensions. The possible meanings in the combination of *gennēthēnai* and *anōthen* in 3:3–8 make the mind reel (born again, begotten again, born from above, begotten from above). No wonder Nicodemus is confused. "How is this possible?" is the last thing we hear Nicodemus say in this exchange (3:9).

Nicodemus has difficulty understanding the language of *anōthen* in part because he cannot hold the physical and the spiritual together: "How can anyone be born after having grown old? Can one enter a second time into the mother's womb and be born?" (3:4). Jesus tries to clarify Nicodemus's misunderstanding by restating the kind of birth he envisions with the phrase "born of water and Spirit." This phrase highlights the new life of which Jesus speaks, because "water" evokes the waters of physical birth and "spirit" points to a new birth from God. The physical birth and the spiritual rebirth go hand in hand here. They are not distinct options because flesh and spirit belong together in the new birth Jesus envisions. One is not reborn to a new life apart from the physical body; one is reborn to a new life within the physical body.

What Jesus offers Nicodemus is what Jesus himself embodies in the incarnation: God-made-present in the flesh. The promise of new life that Jesus extends here is a promise that will be experienced in the body of the believer and made possible by the body of Jesus. Jesus engages believers with his body—the living water that flows from his belly (or is it his womb, [*koilias*]?) (7:37–39); his body is bread, his blood, wine (6:53). Jesus' body is the temple (2:21).[7] Jesus' body is the place where God dwells, the place where God's presence can be found in the world (cf. also 1:51). Jesus' miracles are enacted in the realm of the body and its physical functions—a superabundance of wine, bread, and fish, healings, the raising of a man from the dead.[8] Jesus' incarnation, described by John as the fullness of God's grace, and the physical abundance of all of Jesus' miracles in John, center the Gospel of John on an image of God that creates new possibilities out of the stuff of human flesh, from love that dwells in the body.

"LOVE ONE ANOTHER AS I HAVE LOVED YOU"

Nicodemus's question, "How is this possible?," is a logical and indeed, legitimate question to pose in the face of Jesus' offer of a new birth. Since, as Nicodemus so appropriately points out, we cannot enter our mothers' wombs again, what will be the signs of this new birth, of this new life sustained not only by the waters of birth, but by the spirit, by that which comes from above? How is new birth and new life within the physical body possible?

One traditional answer to this question has been to eschew completely the physicality of the new birth and answer the question on the basis of a spirit/flesh dualism. This is a commonplace among Johannine scholars, who make this move without noticing how such a move undercuts the central claim of the incarnation around which the Gospel is constructed. If new life is to be found outside of, or apart from, our human bodies (often expressed as "in this life"), then the claim of the incarnation is unnecessary and worse, invalidated. A flesh/spirit dualism makes Nicodemus's question quite simple to answer—because our bodies are not involved in the new life—but the radical theological claim of the Fourth Gospel is lost.

Yet John itself presents an answer to Nicodemus's question that builds on, rather than negates, the centrality of the incarnation: that in the fullness of the life that Jesus lived, one sees the fullness of God, and the fullness of God is thereby available to believers. Fullness as a theological and christological category, as I noted earlier, is the exact opposite of the kenotic Christology that dominates Christian tradition and theology and that the weight of tradition regularly imposes on John. A kenotic Christology assumes that becoming human was an emptying, or even a debasement, and that this debasement is redeemed through Jesus' sacrificial death, which then returns him to glory. Ironically, such a kenotic reading itself inscribes a spirit/flesh dualism, because it generates a soteriology in which salvation is found in Jesus' sacrifice of the flesh.

By contrast, the radical claim of the incarnation in John means that Jesus' life encompasses all aspects of human flesh, and one of the defining marks of the flesh, of a human life, is mortality. By becoming flesh, the Word joins humanity in its mortality. It would not be the incarnation if there were no death, which is something that docetics and their opponents readily recognized. It borders on the tautological to say that Jesus is human because he dies and he dies because he is human, but such a near-tautology has real theological significance. Jesus' death is not a sacrifice of the flesh. Death is redeemed and redeeming because the Word-made-flesh lives a full life, embracing the inevitability of mortality. A Christology and soteriology grounded in the fullness of the incarnation finds the offer of salvation in the way that Jesus lived his life, up to and including his death.

John uses the language of love and friendship to describe how the Word-made-flesh lives.[9] In Greek, language of friendship is automatically language of love, since one of the main Greek roots for love—*philos*—is the Greek word for friend. Friendship is a theological category that renders a spirit/flesh dualism impossible, because human beings live and love as friends in our bodies, just as Jesus did.

To talk about friendship as a central theological category in the Fourth Gospel highlights a gap between the first century, in which John was written, and our time. Greek and Roman antiquity recognized the centrality of friendship as a moral category in a way that contemporary understandings of friendship do not. Today, friendship is the common currency of Facebook, greeting cards, and buddy movies rather than held up as the ideal for a good society to follow. But for John's readers, it would have been different. In antiquity, the category of friendship exemplified the mutual social obligation on which human society depended. The social relationship between friends, *philoi*, was a relationship between equals contributing together to the public ethos of citizenship and community.[10]

The ancient Greek philosopher Aristotle comments on the ideal conduct of a friend and illustrates the public and civic dimensions of friendship: "But it is also true the virtuous man's conduct is often guided by the interests of his friends and of his country, and that he will if necessary *lay down his life in their behalf.* . . . And this is doubtless the case with those who give their lives for others; thus they choose great nobility for themselves."[11]

Similarly, in the *Symposium*, Plato writes, "Only those who love wish to die for others."[12] These words of Aristotle and Plato—and similar sayings from later philosophers that carry this understanding of friendship into the period of the New Testament—sound remarkably like Jesus' words in the Gospel of John, "No one has greater love than this, to lay down one's life for one's friends" (15:13). The Gospel's first readers would recognize that with these words, Jesus is evoking a world in which the greatest moral good governs. For the first readers of John's Gospel, this cultural and philosophical link between friendship, love, and death in all likelihood meant that they did not understand Jesus' death as an act of emptying but as an expression of friendship, the fullest expression of love that one person can offer another. Jesus presents himself as the ultimate friend.

In 10:11a, Jesus says, "I am the good shepherd." The good shepherd "lays down his life for the sheep" (10:11b) and so puts care of the sheep above all else.[13] This act is in striking contrast to the hireling who would put the sheep in jeopardy rather than risk his own life (10:12–13). The contrast between the shepherd and the hireling is like that between the true and the false friend—the false friend will not be around in a time of crisis but the true friend will be. As one ancient storyteller writes, "Just so in calm weather a man cannot tell whether his sailing master is good; he will need a storm to determine that."[14]

When Jesus names himself as the good shepherd, he is saying that he is a true friend. He states this directly in 10:15, "I lay down my life for the sheep." The first-person language makes clear that Jesus is not speaking generally about the gift of one's life for others but rather that he is making a specific promise about his own life. Later verses in the good shepherd passage (John 10:17–18) resonate with the philosopher's teachings about the noble friend choosing to lay down his life, but Jesus' words are not generalized friendship teachings. They are about the conduct and promise of his life.

The inseparable connection between Jesus' love, life, and death is clearly expressed in John 13:1, "Having loved his own who were in the world, he loved them to the end." The translation in the NRSV, "to the end," is a perfectly legitimate rendering of the Greek phrase *eis to telos*, but it does not convey the full meaning of the phrase. This translation puts the emphasis on the temporal dimension of *telos* but overlooks the qualitative sense of that word. *Eis to telos* can also mean "fully" or, even better, "to perfection." So what John is saying about Jesus here is that Jesus' love for his disciples in his life and in his death is the same, and that this love was the full, perfect expression of love. To capture the full sense of the Greek, a better translation might be, "having loved his own who were in the world, he loved them to completion"—the completion of love, the completion of time. Jesus' death confirms what Jesus' life has already shown—that he loves, that he is a friend.

The connection between Jesus' offer of his life and the conventions of friendship is not often recognized when Christian theology and piety interpret the death of Jesus in John.[15] Perhaps it is feared that the resonance with the friendship conventions of John's time somehow diminishes the significance of Jesus' teaching about his own death or routinizes the death itself. Or that Jesus' death somehow becomes more ordinary if it is talked about as an act of friendship. Yet this reluctance to call Jesus' gift of his life an act of friendship minimizes the theological power of friendship and, ironically, eliminates one way of talking about Jesus' death that gives prominence to the incarnation and the realities of Jesus' life. Jesus gave his life to his friends as an act of love, an act that showed the full extent of his love.

It is also the case that friendship as an image of salvation is minimized because it sounds a different note from much other Christian language about salvation and redemption. The dominant models with which to talk about the saving effects of Jesus' death are those of vicarious suffering, sacrificial victim, or ransom for sins. The Gospel of John does not subscribe to any of those understandings of the death of Jesus, yet those perspectives so dominate most Christian theology and piety that the Johannine voice of friendship as the language of redemption is not easily heard.[16] For John, Jesus' death offers salvation because it is in fact an act of life-giving love. It is not an act in which something is taken away from Jesus, but it is an act that is about fullness, grace, and plenitude.[17] To see Jesus' death as an act of friendship enables Christians to experience the fullness of God's love in Jesus' act of embodied friendship.

Christian faith—and its theological articulations of the meaning of Jesus' death—is diminished both in terms of Christology and soteriology when the Johannine theology of friendship is overlooked. When the categories of law, sacrifice, and execution set the contours of the theological conversation, love and friendship disappear as means of redemption and salvation, and John's witness about the life and death of Jesus as friend is silenced.[18] Friendship is love in action, love in practice, and through John's witness we come to know that in embodied acts of friendship, one sees God.

Importantly for answering Nicodemus's question about how new life is possible in fully grown bodies, the life and love of friendship are not limited to Jesus. Jesus calls his disciples also to be ultimate friends: "This is my commandment, that you love one another as I have loved you. No one has greater love than this, to lay down one's life for one's friends" (15:12–13). The disciples therefore are not only on the receiving end of Jesus' love and friendship; they are invited to be active agents of love and friendship themselves. The invitation to love as Jesus loved is an invitation to love perfectly, to the completion of love.

"UNLESS I WASH YOU, YOU HAVE NO SHARE IN ME"

The commandment, "love one another as I have loved you," occurs twice in John (13:34–35 and 15:12–13), spoken by Jesus to his disciples during his last meal with them, on the evening of his arrest. The farewell meal in John differs dramatically from other accounts of this meal in Christian tradition, and this difference is crucial for understanding Jesus' commandment.

At the final meal in John 13, there is no narrative of the institution of the eucharistic meal, no deliberate, ritual sharing of bread and wine, and in fact, the traditional words of institution appear neither here nor anywhere else in John. John assumed, indeed counted on, his readers noticing that this key piece of the Jesus story was absent in its traditional form and location in this Gospel. The words of institution clearly were a well-known piece of oral tradition in early Christianity, as their presence apart from a narrative context in 1 Corinthians 11:23–26 attests. In telling the story of Jesus' last supper without these words, John simultaneously focuses the reader's attention on their absence at this point in the story and on what is present instead.

Yet the eucharistic traditions are not so much absent as reformed and relocated, retold in the feeding story and discourse of John 6. John has taken the eucharistic traditions out of the traditional chronological frame of the passion narrative and moved them forward into the narrative center of the recounting of Jesus' life and ministry. The relocation of the eucharistic traditions to the center of Jesus' life is consistent with a narrative technique John uses throughout the Gospel: traditions conventionally associated with the events leading up to the death of Jesus in the other canonical Gospels are moved out of the passion narrative and into the story of Jesus' life and ministry.[19]

Other traditions that are located within the passion narrative in the Synoptic Gospels and are placed before the account of Jesus' last days in John include the "cleansing" of the Temple (2:13–22); the Sanhedrin's decision to put Jesus to death (11:47–53); the anointing at Bethany (12:1–8), which takes place before the triumphal entry in John; and the "agony" in the garden of Gethsemane, which is refracted in 12:27–28. The integration of these "passion" traditions into Jesus' ministry coheres with the centrality of the incarnation for John, because their relocation emphasizes the seamless continuity of Jesus' life and death. Their relocation is not a result of John's ignorance of the traditions nor does it indicate that the Gospel had a careless editor. Rather, the incarnation so governs the Jesus story in John that the last days can only be understood as being part of every day. By moving traditions associated with Jesus' death into the beginning and middle of the story of Jesus' life, John asks his readers to incorporate the crucifixion, Jesus' death, into the larger story of the incarnation, his life. By dislodging the eucharistic traditions from the night of betrayal and death and moving them into the center of Jesus' life and ministry, these traditions help define Jesus' life, not distinctly his death.

Contained within the rich symbolism of the bread of life in John 6 are associations with the exodus manna tradition (e.g., John 6:32–34) and the wisdom tradition of the life-giving word of God (e.g., John 6:35). All these symbols and resonances shape the narrative and theological context in which John places the traditions about Jesus' flesh and blood (6:51–58). Exodus and Wisdom traditions, paired with "I am" sayings that mark Jesus' self-revelation throughout his life (6:35, 41, 48, 51), show that the gift of God that Jesus brings is not limited or demarcated by the events of the night of betrayal and death. The Gospel reader is not asked to choose among these meanings of bread, but to see them as expressions of the multiplicity of ways that Jesus' life makes life available to the believer.

The multiplicity of possibilities can be seen in Jesus' three affirmations of 6:51, [a] "I am the living bread that comes down from heaven. [b] Whoever eats of this bread will live forever; and [c] the bread that I will give is my flesh for the life of the world." Verse 6:51a draws on the exodus and manna allusions that informed the first part of the discourse. Verse 51b can be read as drawing on the wisdom traditions that shape much of vv. 35–40 (e.g., "Whoever comes to me will never be hungry, and whoever believes in me will never be thirsty"). Verse 51c, however, is the decisive theological lens that holds all the multiple images together. The phrase, with its vocabulary of flesh, give, world, and eternal life (live forever) recalls the earlier declarations: "and the Word became flesh" (1:14) and "God so loved the world that he gave his only Son so that whoever believes in him might not perish but have eternal life" (3:16).

Like John 1:14 and 3:16, John 6:51c speaks of the incarnation: the gift of the Word-made-flesh as a sign of God's love for the world. The use of flesh, *sarx*, in 6:51–58 locates this discourse solidly within the rhetoric of the incarnation. Jesus' words do look ahead also to his death, as there are clear resonances of the traditional eucharistic setting in much of John 6 (vv. 51–56 focus on eating and drinking the flesh and blood, for example). By refracting the eucharistic traditions through the primary lens of the incarnation, however, John reminds his readers that what is revealed in Jesus' death has already been revealed in the incarnation. Jesus' life is the life of the Word-made-flesh, already carrying in his flesh God's love for the world. Where the word *soma*, or body, appears in John, it always evokes the physicality of a human body (2:21; 19:31, 38 [2x], 40; 20:12). There is no symbolic use of *soma* in John, and no conventional eucharistic presentation in which Jesus, holding a piece of bread, says, "This is my *soma*" (Matt. 26:26; Mark 14:22; Luke 22:19; 1 Cor. 11:24). Jesus' death is a physical, tangible reality that belongs to the incarnation: the body in which God dwells is a human body that will experience death.[20] Jesus gives his flesh—meaning, he fully lives his life—for the life of the world.

By locating the eucharistic traditions in chapter 6, John theologically reconfigures the eucharist as the feast and sacrament of the living bread, not the feast and sacrament of betrayal and death. Jesus' life, not solely his death, is celebrated and experienced in the meal. The host of the eucharistic meal provides a superabundance of gifts that surpasses the needs and expectations of those who are present for the feeding. The radical interpretation of the eucharistic traditions that John works in chapter 6 presents the meal as a sacrament of the incarnation, a meal of Jesus' living presence for the community.

The dislocation of the Eucharistic meal into the story of Jesus' life creates a narrative opening for the institution at the farewell meal of a different sacrament, the foot washing. In the foot washing, Jesus makes the ultimate act of hospitality and friendship. He stands neither on ceremony nor on precedent but engages in an act that makes his love and grace visible. Foot washing was practiced in both Jewish and Greco-Roman contexts in the ancient Mediterranean world. The setting of the foot washing in John 13 fits the most common way that foot washing was practiced in antiquity, as an act of hospitality. Foot washing was a way of welcoming one's guests to one's home and one's table; after a journey, a person's feet would become dusty, and the host offered water so that guests could wash their feet. The foot washing was normally performed by the guests themselves, or in a wealthier household, by servants, but never by the host of the meal.

The opening verse positions the foot washing narrative as a symbolic enactment of the full extent of Jesus' love: "having loved his own who were in the world, he loved them completely" (John 13:1). To see the foot washing is to see the shape of Jesus' love. When Jesus washes his disciples' feet, he combines the role of servant and host. When Jesus wraps himself with the towel, he assumes the garb and position of the servant, but the act of hospitality that he offers is the initiative of a host. He then washes the disciples' feet and wipes them dry with a towel (13:5).

The verb used to describe Jesus' removal of his outer robe at 13:4 (*tithēmi*) is the same verb used earlier in John 10 to describe Jesus' laying down his life (10:15, 17–18). This verb choice signals the connection between the foot washing and Jesus' gift of his life—just as Jesus loves enough to "lay down" his life as an embodiment of the fullness of that love, so here he "lays down" his role as host to welcome his disciples completely into his home, and his life, that embodies love.

In the foot washing, Jesus and the disciples move from being servants and master, guests and host, to being friends. Later Jesus will name this transformation explicitly for the disciples: "I do not call you servants any longer, because the servant does not know what the master is doing; but I have called you friends, because I have made known to you everything that I have learned from the Father" (John 15:15). But already in the foot washing, he is enacting this transformation for them. In his embodied life, as the incarnate Word, he has led them into the mysteries of God by what he has said and done. Love is enfleshed in Jesus' actions here, because he institutes a ritual that is shaped by a communal embrace of life-giving love.[21]

Yet the significance of the foot washing is easily misunderstood, distorted away from being a sacrament of life and love to a sacrament of death and self-abnegating humility. Because Jesus' death, as distinct from his life, is so often the defining lens for understanding the Gospel, the foot washing is interpreted primarily as a sign, or even sacrament, of Jesus' death.[22] The weight of this reading can be seen in the fact that the verses in which Jesus interprets the foot washing as an example of service (13:12–15) are often treated as if they were the only interpretation. These verses, especially when read not in the context of John, but in the context of a kenotic Christology, turn the foot washing into a call for humiliation and self-sacrifice, like Jesus' humbling of himself on the cross. The problem with such an interpretation is that, as we have seen, there is no humbling and humiliation in Jesus' death in John.[23] Rather, in John, Jesus' death is an extension of his life, and he embraces his death as the fullness of love, not as an emptying.

That John does not understand service as humiliation but as an act of mutuality and reciprocity in love can be seen in Jesus' first description of the foot washing in 13:8–10, an interpretation that is largely silenced in popular and scholarly appropriations of this story. When Peter tries to stop Jesus from washing his feet, Jesus says to him, "Unless I wash you, you have no share in me." In the foot washing, Jesus gives the disciples something—a share with him—and that share with Jesus is what makes any subsequent acts of service and friendship possible for the disciples. Jesus has transformed the community through his embodiment of love so that they themselves can now embody love. Through the foot washing, the disciples share in Jesus' offer of his life. This share in and with Jesus is the backdrop to the language about service in 13:12–15 because the disciples' service to one another continues in their bodies what Jesus has done in his—to love one another fully. Service is not self-sacrificial; service is recognizing that the other is one's friend. A paraphrase of 13:8 in the language of friendship would be, "Unless I wash you, you are not my friend."

Seen in this way, the foot washing is a sacrament of friendship. Since John locates the foot washing at the last supper, and in effect replaces the Eucharist with this ritual, it is tempting to think that the sacramental dimension of friendship is exactly what John was trying to communicate through his storytelling. Jesus as the originator of the sacrament of friendship positions himself not simply as the model for what it means to be a friend but as the presence of God in the world through the act of friendship. And to the extent that we share in and embody Jesus' sacramental act of friendship, we, too, can be the presence of God in the world.

"THE HOUSE WAS FILLED WITH THE FRAGRANCE
OF THE PERFUME"

I want to close with a coda that underscores the centrality of the incarnation, the interconnectedness of Jesus' life and death, and the embodied sacrament of friendship in John.

The story of the foot washing in John 13 is not the first time that someone's feet have been washed and dried in the Gospel of John. In John 12:1–8, Mary anoints Jesus' feet and then wipes them dry with her hair. The verb "to wipe," *ekmasso*, used to describe Mary's actions, is the same verb used in 13:5 to describe Jesus' actions. This detail in the anointing story is regularly pointed to as being superfluous in this story, a stray element from the Lukan tradition of the anointing in which the woman wipes her tears from Jesus' feet with her hair (Luke 7:38). Yet this detail is far from superfluous. Rather, it serves as a marker for how to read John's anointing story. What Jesus at the foot washing will do for his disciples and will ask them to do for one another Mary has already done for him (12:3).

In telling the story of the anointing, John names both the quantity (a pound) and the quality ("costly," "pure nard") of the perfume, making clear that Mary holds nothing back in her anointing of Jesus. Mary's act of love toward Jesus is intensely embodied; she anoints him with an absurdly extravagant amount of perfume, its extravagance confirmed by the notation, "The house was filled with the fragrance of the perfume" (12:3). The fragrance that fills the house represents Mary's lavish and limitless love for Jesus. The perfume, like the water with which Jesus will soon wash his disciples' feet, is a sacramental element.

This reference to the perfume's fragrance may have additional significance. Still earlier, at 11:39, Martha, Mary's sister, attempted to stop Jesus from opening their brother Lazarus's tomb because of the stench that would come out of the tomb. Through Mary's act, the stench of death that once lingered over this household has been replaced by the fragrance of love and friendship. Moreover, Mary's act of love is offered in the growing shadow of Jesus' death. She does not greet Jesus' death with fear; she greets it with generosity, love, and devotion. For Mary, the reality of Jesus' impending death does not negate the need or possibility for an extravagant enactment of embodied love. Rather, her act underscores the inseparability of life and death. Mary does for Jesus' body in life what later will be done to his body in death (19:40).

Judas plays a major role in this story (12:4–6) and provides a contrasting image to Mary's embodied acts of friendship. Judas protests Mary's action as wasteful, suggesting that the money for the perfume could have been better spent on the poor (v. 5). Yet John carefully frames Judas's protest with a description of Judas that discredits anything that Judas says (vv. 4, 6). Not only is Judas the disciple who will betray Jesus (v. 4), but Judas is a thief (v. 6). The identification of Judas as thief (*kleptēs*) identifies Judas with those who undermine and undo the work of Jesus the good shepherd (10:1–18). Judas's protestation about the poor is mere pretense; he does not share with Jesus in the care of the flock. Judas's real protest is against a lavish display of love for Jesus. Unlike Mary, Judas does not respond to Jesus' life and the approach of Jesus' death with an act of love but with self-centered disdain. Judas's response leads to the destruction of the flock, whereas Mary's actions mirror back Jesus' own life of love.

In John, Jesus makes God and God's love known in a superabundance of embodied gifts—more good wine than any wedding feast needs, more bread than a crowd of five thousand can consume, the complete gift of his own life and body. Mary responds to that superabundance with her own embodied gift—a pound of pure nard, poured on Jesus' feet, wiped dry with her hair. Mary is born anew, living love fully in and with her body, sharing in the sacraments of friendship.

Notes

1. I would add that to read John solely as a "spiritual Gospel" also misreads what Eusebius says Clement says. Eusebius's full statement about Clement makes clear that Clement understands John to be supplementing, not replacing, the "facts": "Again, in the same books, Clement gives the tradition of the earliest presbyters, as to the order of the Gospels, in the following manner: The Gospels containing the genealogies, he says, were written first. The Gospel according to Mark had this occasion. As Peter had preached the Word publicly at Rome, and declared the Gospel by the Spirit, many who were present requested that Mark, who had followed him for a long time and remembered his sayings, should write them out. And having composed the Gospel he gave it to those who had requested it. When Peter learned of this, he neither directly forbade nor encouraged it. But, last of all, John, perceiving that the external facts had been made plain in the Gospel, being urged by his friends, and inspired by the Spirit, composed a spiritual Gospel. This is the account of Clement." Eusebius, *Church History*, VI 14.5–7. Alexander Roberts and James Donaldson, *The Nicene and Post-Nicene Fathers*, vol 1. At: http://www.newadvent.org/fathers/250106.htm.
2. See, for example, Craig Koester, "The Death of Jesus and the Human Condition: Exploring the Theology of John's Gospel," in *Life in Abundance: Studies of John's Gospel in Tribute to Raymond E. Brown*, ed. John R. Donahue (Collegeville, MN: Liturgical Press, 2005), 141–57.
3. The classic example of Pauline theology informing interpretation of *sarx* in John is Rudolf Bultmann, *Theology of the New Testament*, trans. Kendrick Grobel (Waco, TX: Baylor, 2007). (This reprint follows the pagination of the original, in two volumes, New York: Scribner, 1951–55).
4. See Gail R. O'Day, "The Love of God Incarnate: The Life of Jesus in the Gospel of John," in *Life in Abundance*, 158–67.
5. See Jennifer Glancy, "Torture: Flesh, Truth, and the Fourth Gospel," *Biblical Interpretation* 13 (2005): 2.
6. See Luise Schottroff's description of this as God's "asexuality" in "The Samaritan Woman and the Notion of Sexuality in the Fourth Gospel," in *What Is John? II: Literary and Social Readings of the Fourth Gospel*, ed. Fernando Segovia (Atlanta: Scholars Press, 1998), 157–81. Yet her proposed translation of "created" instead of "begotten" in this verse removes the incarnational dimensions of the verb.
7. Schottroff, "The Samaritan Woman and the Notion of Sexuality," 179–81.

8. Molly Haws, "'Put Your Finger Here': Resurrection and the Construction of the Body," *Theology and Sexuality* 13 (2007): 185.

9. See these studies of friendship and John: E. Puthenkandathil, *Philos: A Designation for the Jesus-Disciple Relationship: An Exegetico-Theological Investigation of the Term in the Fourth Gospel* (Frankfurt: Peter Lang, 1993); J. M. Ford, *Redeemer—Friend and Mother: Salvation in Antiquity and in the Gospel of John* (Minneapolis: Fortress, 1997); Sharon Ringe, *Wisdom's Friends: Community and Christology in the Fourth Gospel* (Louisville, KY: Westminster John Knox Press, 1999); Gail R. O'Day, "Jesus as Friend in the Gospel of John," *Interpretation* 58 (2004): 144–57; Barbara Reid, "The Cross and Cycles of Violence," *Interpretation* 58 (2004): 376–85. Interestingly, as long ago as 1981 Sandra Schneiders suggested the possible importance of friendship in the Fourth Gospel and that the Fourth Evangelist used the classic concept of friendship "in developing his unique presentation of love as the heart of the Christian experience"; "The Foot Washing (John 13:1–20): An Experiment in Hermeneutics," *Catholic Biblical Quarterly* 43 (1981): 86, fn. 30.

10. David Konstan, "Problems in the History of Christian Friendship," *Early Christian Studies* 4 (1996): 90. See, e.g., Martha Nussbaum, *The Fragility of Goodness: Luck and Ethics in Greek Tragedy and Philosophy* (Cambridge: Cambridge University Press, 1986); F. M. Schroeder, "Friendship in Aristotle and Some Peripatetic Philosophers," in *Greco-Roman Perspectives on Friendship* ed. John Fitzgerald (Atlanta: Scholars Press, 1997), 36; L. S. Pangle, *Aristotle and the Philosophy of Friendship* (Cambridge: Cambridge University Press, 2003).

11. Aristotle, *Nicomachean Ethics* 9.8.9 (H. Rackham, Loeb Classical Library).

12. Plato, *Symposium* 179B, also 208D. See also Aristotle, *Nicomachean Ethics* 9.8.9; Lucian, *Toxaris* 36; Epictetus, *Dissertations* 2.7.3; Seneca, *Epistles* 9.10. In the New Testament, see Rom. 5:6–8.

13. For an excellent discussion of "noble death" and its connections to John, see J. Neyrey, "The 'Noble Shepherd' in John 10: Cultural and Rhetorical Background," *Journal of Biblical Literature* 120 (2001): 267–91. Oddly, Neyrey never explicitly links the noble death motif with the motif of friendship, even though both John and Greco-Roman philosophers do.

14. Lucian, *Toxaris* 36 (A. M. Harmon, Loeb Classical Library).

15. Two important exceptions are Sandra Schneiders, "Foot Washing," and Barbara Reid, "The Cross and Cycles of Violence." Ford, *Redeemer—Friend and Mother*, attempts to reclaim friendship as a soteriological category for John. Her effort is not completely successful, however, because she tends to treat friend and mother as if they share the same set of social conventions, and so both terms lose their distinctiveness.

16. See O'Day, *John: Introduction, Commentary, and Reflections, The New Interpreter's Bible 9* (Nashville: Abingdon, 1995), 713–15.

17. So also Schneiders, "Foot Washing," 86–88.

18. So ibid., 86: "John describes God's salvific intention not in terms of sacrifice or retribution but in terms of self-gift: God so loved the world as to give God's only Son to save us."

19. This view was proposed by Wilhelm Wilkens in the 1950s but has received little attention. See Wilkens, "Das Abendmahlszeugnis im vierten Evangelium," *Evangelische Theologie* 18 (1958): 354–70 and *Die Entstehungsgeschichte des Vierten Evangeliums* (Zollikon: Evangelischer Verlag, 1958). Wilkens links this move with a redactional theory and carefully delineated anti-docetic purpose, but his sense of the ways in which John incorporates the "passion" into the

telling of the life story remains helpful. See also David Rensberger, *Johannine Faith and Liberating Community* (Philadelphia: Westminster, 1988), 71–77.

20. See O'Day, "The Love of God Incarnate," 163.

21. See O'Day, *John*, 722–28.

22. So, for example, R. Alan Culpepper, "The Johannine *Hypodeigma*: A Reading of John 13," *Semeia* 53 (1991): 133–52 and Francis J. Moloney, "A Sacramental Reading of John 13:1–38," *Catholic Biblical Quarterly* 53 (1991): 237–56.

23. Schneiders, "Foot Washing," 86.

PART 2
INTERRELIGIOUS VENTURES

Chapter 7

Learning in the Presence of the Other

Feminisms and the
Interreligious Encounter

MARY C. BOYS

The invitation to participate in the Phyllis Trible Lecture Series in 2008 and to revise my lecture for publication in 2013 provided occasion to juxtapose three dimensions of my life that I have seldom addressed together: the feminist theologian, the loyal critic of my Catholic tradition, and the experienced interreligious dialogue partner. Wrestling with these three dimensions enabled me to contemplate the complexities of "Interfaith Feminisms," the theme of the 2008 lectures in honor of my former Union colleague.

Interreligious encounter involves a pilgrimage to "thin" places and times. Here I evoke an aspect of the Celtic mythical landscape: sites where the veil between this world and the world beyond, between the temporal and the eternal, becomes thin, even translucent. Journalist Krista Tippett, reflecting on her interviews with a range of religious persons for her radio broadcast, "Speaking of Faith," writes: "Time and space become more generous when we explore ultimate truths in the presence of the other. 'Thin places' open up."[1]

At its best, sustained interaction between persons of different traditions of faith offers a glimpse of the Transcendent, an awareness of the Divine elusively present. Yet thin times and places require "thick" religiosity. Feminist theologies and serious interfaith involvement are ways of "thickening" one's religious understanding because they involve the demanding task of reweaving religious identity.

Accordingly, I propose we think about the encounter with the religious Other as including moments in which the veil between thin places and thick religiosity becomes both catalyst and consequence. This approach implies a threefold exploration: interfaith encounter and thin places, thick religiosity, and education for thick religiosity.

INTERFAITH ENCOUNTER AND THIN PLACES

Substantive conversation between persons of different religious traditions encompasses diverse purposes. It provides entrée into another tradition's beliefs and practices. It asks hard questions of traditional theologies. It demands discernment about the adequacy of longstanding formulations in light of new knowledge. It heightens awareness of ways in which one's own religious tradition has represented and misrepresented the "Other." The revelation of misrepresentation discloses the tribalism, racism, and xenophobia enmeshed in home traditions. Such a revelation, however painful, can intensify a desire for more capacious understandings of the Other. Moreover, enlarging the vision of the Other often provides a deepened grasp of one's own tradition.

Nevertheless, bringing knowledgeable religious peoples of good will together does not guarantee that such purposes will be fulfilled. *How interreligious dialogue happens is crucial.* Without thoughtfully calibrated strategies, attentiveness to tender scar tissue, and wise leadership, interreligious encounters may neither move beyond the superficial nor foster reconciliation. I have vivid memories of a gathering about twenty years ago, "Women of Faith," that brought together forty-five Muslim, Christian, and Jewish women for a two-day conference. The conveners asked us to participate in an exercise in which we were to gather in our "faith alike" groups and generate a list of five stereotypes of each of the other two traditions. This exercise immediately struck me as a bad idea—and it was. When the groups returned for the plenary session and began to read out their lists, fury broke out. As should have been anticipated, each stereotype elicited a vigorous defense as old (and not-so-old) wounds were opened up. The session poisoned the rest of the conference. The veil between the worlds seemed to solidify with each passing hour.

As this example illustrates, not every interreligious exchange takes us to thin places. The topics can be difficult, requiring exacting scholarship and technical mastery. Dialogue has its moments of drudgery and dullness. Much of the time nothing out of the ordinary seems to be happening—except that people from traditions that have warred with word and at times with weapons have come together in an honest attempt to understand one another. So perhaps on one level, every serious interfaith gathering is extraordinary. My sense, however, is that it is precisely the experience of thin places that makes perseverance possible during the quotidian times. Let me offer an extended example as a sort of case study.

For a number of years I have been involved in a project called "Exodus Conversations: How the Story of the Exodus Speaks to Jews, Christians, and Muslims: An Interfaith Commentary on the Passover Haggadah." Three of us are drawing upon a Haggadah—a Jewish text used at the Seder (the Passover ritual meal) to tell the story of deliverance from slavery in Egypt—as a framework to engage in and model how persons of the Abrahamic traditions might talk together about important issues.[2]

The Exodus is a common heritage in the Abrahamic traditions; so the fact that we are fashioning our commentary around a specifically Jewish text does not itself impose the perspective of one tradition on the other two. After many months of uncertainty about how to frame our project, we decided to work thematically. We identified some sixteen themes (e.g., blessing, experiencing the Divine, caring, struggling against oppression, recognizing women) and posed several questions for each of them. For example, for the theme, "recognizing women," we asked: (1) Where are women in the central narratives of your tradition? (2) What are some textual foundations for the role women have customarily played in your tradition? (3) What is the status of women in your tradition today? (4) What are your hopes for the role of women in your tradition? Mindful that our goal is to stimulate discussion rather than settle matters, we limited ourselves to about one hundred words in response to each question.

It has been a difficult project. We did not know one another, do not all live in proximity to one another, have no obvious model to follow, and are not equally knowledgeable about the two traditions outside our own. Moreover, each of us is conscious of the challenges of addressing difficult questions in brief, accessible prose; we are also mindful no one of us speaks for all in his or her tradition.

And yet, there are experiences of thin places. Let me give two examples.

In the early stages, I felt we were wandering in the desert without much clarity. I was also conflicted about staying with the project because of other commitments. I had gone out the door on one particular morning resolved to confess I just could not manage to stay involved. That February 2007 day we were working on the meaning of blessing in our three traditions. Each of us came, as we had agreed, with one hundred words of commentary on questions like "What does it mean for humans to bless God?" and "Does a blessing accomplish anything?" We also brought selected examples of blessings. As we shared ways in which our respective traditions formulate and use blessings, each of us recognized a wisdom and beauty in the others. Eyes lit up, the conversation sparkled, and energy filled the room. We ended that February session by writing a blessing our three traditions could pray. It is quite simple—

> Praise and blessing to you, O God,
> creator and sustainer of all,
> who has brought us together
> to know one another in peace.

I am not claiming a mountaintop experience. However momentarily, the veil thinned. Our bonds with one another strengthened, and the project suddenly seemed possible. In my Christian vocabulary, this experience seemed suspiciously like the breath of the Spirit.

Then in early October 2009, when we gathered in New York City after not seeing one another since the previous April, we keenly felt the absence of our convener, whose mother had died recently and whose younger sibling had developed serious cancer. Talk turned to one reality we all share: death. Again, the air grew thin. Truly, in Tippett's words, "Time and space become more generous when we explore ultimate truths in the presence of others." As we conversed, it became obvious that we should address how each of our traditions understands the meaning of death, how its rituals help to provide consolation for mourners, and how it speaks about life after death. Our conversation that day took us to a "thin" place.

As relationships grow across religious boundaries, a sense of the mysterious presence of the Divine hovers; there is the "trace of God who is always other and beyond all imaginings."[3]

THICK RELIGIOSITY

The term "thick religiosity" evokes Clifford Geertz's argument that anthropology requires "thick description."[4] Another way of imagining what I mean by "thick" is the poem "The Tree Says":

> The tree says: "How to love: put down strong roots.
> Be slow to rise. Study the turn of light
> before you ramify so that new shoots
> do not obscure old. Tolerate the flight
> of birds you welcomed. Deepen your old roots,
> match thick root to thick crown, down right, upright;
> in flood, that spread holds you, and in acute
> drought is within growing distance of some site
> of water. Cast seed too wide for dispute.
> Die into new usefulness—as perch, nest,
> locust house, grubhouse, wasp house, prop of vine."[5]

Like the tree, thick religiosity requires roots deeply planted: knowledge of sacred texts and the play of interpretations; commitment to the communal and transformative character of religion; awareness of the historical and cultural contexts in which the tradition originated and developed; sensitivity to the rich panoply of folk traditions, rituals, art, music, and devotions in which religion has been celebrated and communicated; and attentiveness to the contemplative dimension of life. Thick religiosity is requisite for interreligious learning, which "always starts from one's own convictions and tradition."[6]

Similarly, sustained interreligious dialogue nurtures and matures thick religiosity precisely because it requires understanding one's faith more clearly. Dialogue, claims philosopher of education Nicholas Burbules, is a "continuous, developmental communicative interchange through which we stand to gain a fuller apprehension of the world, ourselves, and one another."[7] The phrase, "a fuller apprehension of the world, ourselves, and one another" implies that without dialogue, one's understanding of religious tradition is inadequate, solipsistic. More simply put: "We not only need to understand one another, we need one another to understand ourselves."[8]

The contemplative attitude lying at the heart of dialogue contributes significantly to thick religiosity. Raimundo Panikkar calls this *intrapersonal dialogue*: "an inner dialogue within myself, an encounter in the depth of my personal religiousness, having met another religious experience on that very intimate level."[9] Such an interior dialogue is a process of letting the imagery, symbols, and basic concepts of another tradition *penetrate* one's being. It involves listening to the other in order to find one's own identity. It requires spiritual preparation: "Dialogue forces us—myself and the other—to find the ground of our common search in the Divine. Such dialogue demands commitment, honesty and openness to learn—qualities which are as difficult to sustain as the single-minded zeal which so much characterized the greatest of the old missionaries."[10]

All these elements speak to the importance of our own spiritual practices. In entering the realm of another religious tradition, profound differences emerge. In a globalized world that seems to grow ever more frightening and in which entrepreneurs of fear manipulate emotions, we may be tempted to hang on to what seem to be religious certitudes, confusing them with faith. Yet interior dialogue is a spiritual practice that sustains us in pondering our own faith tradition more intensely and enables us to live with a heightened sense of mystery and paradox—what Martin Buber termed "holy insecurity."[11]

Because dialogue is at heart the admission that one's perspective is not panoptic, it has a destabilizing dimension. Dialogue involves disequilibrium. Someone asks a question we have never thought of before. We try to explain in our best, if stumbling, way—and realize our own understanding is not as profound as we may have thought. Someone criticizes the hypocrisy or corruption that is part of our religious tradition. Most likely, the critique is not news to us, but to feel so exposed is difficult. In the face of the Other, one may experience dislocation and vulnerability.

The experience of disequilibrium in crossing religious borders may give rise to a defensive reaction to which Christians are especially prone: fitting the Other into some sort of theological scheme or overarching narrative. Christians also tend to fall prey to the temptation of shallow syncretism, borrowing rituals from other traditions without knowledge of their meaning and context. As a consequence, differences are elided. Yet interreligious dialogue depends upon exploring differences. It involves, as Michael Barnes says, an "encounter with the irreducible mystery of otherness," for which a sort of contemplative apophasis is necessary in the face of "limitation imposed by otherness of all kinds."[12] The question for a theology of dialogue, Barnes writes, is "not how the otherness revealed at the heart of selfhood can be synchronized into a more or less grand strategy, but how, more radically and yet more humbly, a certain passivity in the face of the other is to be recognized as *intrinsic* to the Christian vocation itself."[13] By passivity, I think Barnes means a contemplative stance vis-à-vis the Other: "A contemplative is a person who is willing to forget the self in order to offer attention to the other."[14]

The thick religiosity critical to interreligious education not only requires one to pursue more adequate understandings of one's home tradition but also leads to the questioning of conventional understandings, exposes the tradition's defects and injustices, and demystifies power arrangements—realizations familiar to those of us who are both feminists and church members. Not surprisingly, many religious authorities, at least in my experience, are at best wary of interreligious dialogue (if not hostile), as they are to feminism. Perhaps their suspicion is related to their roles. John Gager observes that those who hold positions of power "often define and defend themselves by emphasizing the difference between us and them." He concludes: "It is the additional factor of power and authority, I think, that turns competitors into enemies and insists on the conceptual nihilation of competing systems."[15]

Although Gager was speaking of the way in which early Christian literature on Judaism—produced by a literary elite holding leadership positions in the church—manifested hostility to Judaism, I believe his claim applies to the present as well. For example, in recent years in the Roman Catholic Church, scholars of the Christian-Jewish dialogue, particularly women, have been excluded from official dialogues with Jews. Meetings and conferences to which we were formerly invited are now closed to us. Similarly, in April 2012, the Vatican's Congregation for the Doctrine of the Faith (CDF) issued a mandate for episcopal (i.e., male bishops') oversight of the Leadership Conference of Women Religious (LCWR) because, in part, the CDF had detected "certain radical feminist themes incompatible with the Catholic faith" in the organization's programs and presentations.[16] In modifying feminism with "radical" while providing no criteria by which "radical feminism" is to be distinguished from other modes of feminist thought, the CDF (and the episcopacy more generally) signals its hostility to feminism. It is no coincidence that two of the most highly regarded Catholic feminist theologians, Elizabeth A. Johnson and Margaret Farley, have recently had their work denounced by high church officials.[17] Apparently, scholarship that challenges the formulations of the hierarchical church—whether in relation to scholarship on Christian-Jewish relations or feminist thought—is perceived as such a great threat that its premises must either be marginalized or denounced. The reaction of the hierarchical church in these instances aptly illustrates what Gager termed "the conceptual nihilation of competing systems."[18]

"Ecclesiastical dignitaries," writes Panikkar, "are bound to preserve tradition; they must consider the multitude of believers who follow that religion, for and to whom they are responsible. They are faced with practical and immediate problems; they must discover ways to tolerate, to collaborate, to understand. *But in general they cannot risk new solutions.*[19] The world, however, cries out for new solutions. The fate of the twenty-first century, Rabbi Jonathan Sacks claims, may turn on whether the world's religions can "make a space for those who are not its adherents, who sing a different song, hear a different music, tell a different story."[20]

Might not our inability fully to reconcile ancient claims of Christian faith with other religions lead us to greater humility about our tradition and draw us more deeply into the mystery of God? Might not our vulnerability in the face of otherness manifest the impossibility of speaking with a "panoptic" vision of God's actions in the world? Might it not lead us to aspire to, in the phrase of the fifteenth-century thinker Nicholas of Cusa, "learned ignorance": the "acknowledgment of religious believers that what they try to understand—namely, God, and the ways of God—constantly transcends their ability to grasp fully and articulate adequately what they have experienced."[21]

This encounter with mystery invites us to reflect upon our concepts of God. In her book, *Quest for the Living God*, Elizabeth Johnson reclaims the archaic term "Whither" to speak of God who is "gracious mystery, ever greater, ever nearer," the "boundless plenitude that is the vis-à-vis of the human spirit." God "cannot be situated within our system of coordinates but escapes all categories. Hence, to think rightly of God we must give up the drive to intellectual mastery and open up to the Whither of our spirit's hungry orientation." Quoting Karl Rahner, Johnson continues: "The concept 'God' is not a grasp of God by which a person masters the mystery; but it is the means by which one lets oneself be grasped by the mystery which is present yet ever distant." God is "incomprehensible holy mystery." [22]

Interreligious dialogue points beyond conventional images of God, thereby casting doubt on the tradition's system of coordinates and categories and inviting believers to imagine new horizons. Like feminism, interreligious dialogue invites us to reimagine ways of being in relationship with the Other. The art of reimagining requires great care, so I turn now to ways that thick religiosity develops.

EDUCATING FOR THICK RELIGIOSITY

In preparing my Trible lecture, I became intrigued with the interplay of thin places and thick religiosity, terms that I had not used before. Only later did I realize why I was so receptive to them. "Thick religiosity" is similar to "textured particularism," a term that arose out of the many years of dialogical work with Professor Sara S. Lee of Hebrew Union College, Los Angeles. For us this term means forming persons with a keen sense of the beliefs and practices of their own religious tradition as well as the finitude of that tradition. As we think of it, textured particularism is a prerequisite for a responsible religious pluralism.

A *textured* particularism differs from an *insular* particularism, which we see as synonymous with parochialism: superficial, provincial, and religion-centric, if relatively benign. *Insular* particularism seems all too prevalent; regrettably, many persons lack knowledge of religious traditions outside their own. This condition happens even within traditions themselves. For example, despite the ecumenical movement, many Christians are ignorant about other denominations. Without knowledge of the religious "other," persons tend to project categories and concepts from their home tradition on everyone else.

Adversarial particularism is a more dangerous form of particularism because it diminishes, caricatures, or even demonizes the Other. Ignorant of the Other, it gives rise to bigotry and legitimates discrimination (e.g., white supremacist groups, the Taliban). An adversarial particularism rightly gives religion a bad name—but it ought not to be confused with a textured particularism that is rooted in the rich images, practices, symbols, and stories of one's religious traditions.

Our experience suggests that a textured particularism is relatively rare. Even within our religious traditions, many people lack an experience of the tradition's profundity. And increasingly, it seems, religious identity is hybrid. It is not uncommon, even for seminary students, to have immediate family members from several traditions. I think of one student who listed Jews, Hindus, Christian Scientists, Presbyterians, Unitarian Universalists, pagans, and atheists among her family. This bricolage challenges theological educators to lead persons beyond superficial understandings and to question rigorously what "double belonging" might involve.[23]

A rich and receptive particularism offers greater possibility for developing a religious identity that is simultaneously rooted and adaptive, assured and ambiguous—that is, one that allows for engagement with the religious Other. A textured particularism is passionate. It implies deep, even visceral, connections to one's religious tradition. It requires a serious immersion in the community's life—in those symbol-rich moments in which the Divine Presence and the power of the faith community are experienced. At the same time, the requisite knowledge of one's tradition contributes to a profound humility about the tradition—the ways in which the community of faith has been unfaithful to its vision of God. Textured particularism, however, is relatively rare in our world.

In our time, a textured particularism must include knowing about the religious Other. This knowledge is especially important among the so-called Abrahamic religions, that is, Judaism, Christianity and Islam, which share profound commonalities and deep differences, as well as many tragic historical encounters. There are, of course, many religious "Others" to know, and the vast majority of us have neither the opportunity nor sufficient knowledge to engage all the religious traditions. Yet knowing just one other religious tradition beyond one's own offers a vast new horizon of understanding—not only of the tradition of the other, but also of one's own.

In our experience, interreligious learning makes significant contributions to the development of textured particularism. Professor Lee and I define this as "a form of interreligious dialogue emphasizing study in the presence of the religious other and encounter with the tradition the other embodies."[24] It involves fostering relationships *among* participants and *with* key practices, texts, and beliefs of the other's tradition.

When dialogue between religious persons is sustained over time and is done with seriousness, study, and commitment to relationships, it beckons us to move deeper in our own self-understanding. It calls us to draw upon the spiritual practices and discipline of our traditions so that what we talk about is also what we walk.

Interreligious encounter is an emotional experience and thus full of both promise and peril. It necessitates careful leadership in designing processes that enable persons to engage intensely with the religious Other. Participants (and leaders) arrive with their own insecurities, stereotypes, and agendas. History looms in the background—and frequently in the front of the room as well. Unanticipated questions arise, more complex understandings do not feel as comfortable as earlier ones, and the grasp of one's own faith may suddenly seem tenuous.

Of particular importance in interreligious learning is the opportunity for participants to share their deep connection to their own traditions, whether in talking about a personally meaningful text, ritual, or holy season. Preparing for such sessions involves participants in the "intra-religious dialogue" about which Panikkar has spoken. The challenge is to provide educational processes that enable participants to enter empathically into the Other's tradition and then to engage in sustained reflection about encounter with the Other.

Yet for all the emotional and affective elements in educating for dialogue, interreligious learning certainly requires intellectual engagement, even debate. Conversation, not argument, is the operative term because debate has one fatal weakness when it comes to dialogue: debate means that our listening tends to focus on refutation. Argument can all too easily focus on winning rather than on understanding. Argument, as philosopher of education Margret Buchmann points out, involves contestants. In contrast, conversation involves partners. She writes: "What makes conversation attractive is its reciprocal quality, breadth of subject matter, the room it gives to different voices, and the delightful turns it may take. Conversations have flexible rules of relevance and evidence. All manner of impressions, ideas, and experience can enter."[25] As Buchmann asserts, the ideals of flawless clarity and coherence are not as important in conversation as they are in argument. Thus "one may get answers to questions one never thought of asking (but ought to have asked) or have one's answers answered."[26] Yet conversation ought not be reduced to mere talk; it may well include argument and rest on logic.

Conversation is educative only when the conversation partners already know something—knowledge of self, as well as the subject at hand. Hence, the importance of stimulating the conversation with excellent resources and questions that demand thought. It is not the educator's job to control the conversation but to provide ample stimuli so discussants can speak with curiosity and candor, knowledge and insight, empathy and desire to know the Other.

Conversation between religious Others with a thick religiosity is the threshold to thin places. Like feminism, interreligious dialogue invites us to reimagine relationships:

> Praise and blessing to you, O God,
> creator and sustainer of all,
> who has brought us together
> to know one another in peace.

Notes

1. Krista Tippett, *Speaking of Faith: Why Religion Matters—and How to Talk about It* (New York: Penguin, 2008), 119. Tippett has renamed her radio program *On Being*; see www.onbeing.org.
2. Ruth Abram conceived bringing writers from the Abrahamic traditions together to create an interfaith Seder and has served as the coordinator of the project. The writers are Dr. David Arnow, Professor Muhammad Shafiq, and I. Our work is now available at http://www.exodusconversations.org.
3. Michael Barnes, S.J., *Theology and the Dialogue of Religions*, Cambridge Studies in Christian Doctrine (Cambridge: Cambridge University Press, 2002), 205.
4. Clifford Geertz, "Thick Description: Toward an Interpretive Theory of Culture," in *The Interpretation of Cultures: Selected Essays* (New York: Basic Books, 1973), 3–30.
5. Marie Ponsot, "The Tree Says," *Commonweal* 34/16 (Sept. 28, 2007): 14. Reproduced by permission of *Commonweal*.
6. Roger Burggraeve, "Alterity Makes the Difference," in *Interreligious Learning*, ed. Didier Pollefeyt (Leuven, Belgium: Leuven University Press and Peeters, 2007), 241.
7. Nicholas Burbules, *Dialogue in Teaching* (New York: Teachers College Press, 1993), 42.
8. Jean Halperin, cited in Diana Eck, *Encountering God: A Spiritual Journey from Bozeman to Banares* (Boston: Beacon, 1993), 189. Eck indicates that Professor Halperin made this remark at an interreligious consultation in Mauritius in 1983. For a report on this consultation, see Allan R. Brockway, "The Meaning of Life: A Multifaith Consultation in Preparation for the Sixth Assembly of the World Council of Churches," *Ecumenical Review* 35/3 (1983): 246–65. Brockway lists both Eck and Halperin as participants, but the Halperin quotation Eck uses was likely in her notes rather than in the official record of the consultation.
9. Raimundo Panikkar, *Intrapersonal Dialogue* (New York and Mahwah: Paulist Press, 1978), 40.
10. Michael Barnes, *Christian Identity and Religious Pluralism: Religions in Conversation* (Nashville: Abingdon, 1989), 115.
11. Martin Buber, *Daniel: Dialogues of Realization*, trans. Martin Friedman (New York: Holt, Rinehart, and Winston, 1964), 99. See also Sandra Lubarsky, "Dialogue: Holy Insecurity," *Religious Education* 91/4 (1996): 545.
12. Barnes, *Theology and the Dialogue of Religions*, 23.
13. Ibid., 129.

14. Robert Waldron, *Walking with Thomas Merton: Discovering His Poetry, Essays, and Journals* (New York: Paulist, 2002), xv.
15. John G. Gager, "The Partings of the Ways: A View from the Perspective of Early Christianity," in *Interwoven Destinies,* ed. Eugene Fisher et al. (New York and Mahwah: Paulist Press, 1993), 71–72.
16. "Doctrinal Assessment of the Leadership Conference of Women Religious," April 18, 2012. The full text may be accessed at http://www.usccb.org/loader. cfm?csModule=security/getfile&pageid=55544.
17. In March 2011 the American Bishops' Committee on Doctrine issued a harsh denunciation of Elizabeth A. Johnson's 2007 book, *The Quest for the Living God.* In June 2012, the CDF issued a "Notification" censoring Margaret Farley's 2006 book, *Just Love: A Framework for Christian Social Ethics.* Both Johnson and Farley are members of religious communities, so the ecclesiastical pronouncement may be interpreted as manifestations of the same mentality as the rebuke to the LCWR.
18. Gager, "The Partings of the Ways," 71–72.
19. Raimundo Panikkar, *Intrapersonal Dialogue,* 34–35.
20. Jonathan Sacks, *The Dignity of Difference: How to Avoid the Clash of Civilizations* (London: Continuum, 2002), 43.
21. *Learned Ignorance: Intellectual Humility among Jews, Christians, and Muslims,* ed. James L. Heft, Reuven Firestone, and Omid Safi (New York: Oxford University Press, 2011), 4
22. Elizabeth A. Johnson, *The Quest for the Living God: Mapping Frontiers in the Theology of God* (New York: Continuum, 2007), 35–37.
23. See Paul F. Knitter, *Without Buddha I Could Not Be a Christian* (Oxford: Oneworld Publications, 2009).
24. Mary C. Boys and Sara S. Lee, *Christians and Jews in Dialogue: Learning in the Presence of the Other* (Woodstock, VT: SkyLight Paths Publishing, 2006), 95.
25. Margret Buchmann, "Improving Education by Talking: Argument or Conversation," *Teachers College Record* 86/3 (Spring 1985): 441–53; citation, 451.
26. Ibid., 451.

Chapter 8

Speaking from Behind the Veil

Does Islamic Feminism Exist?

HIBBA ABUGIDEIRI

"Were you raised in the United States?" "Yes," I replied. "And your parents never forced you to wear the headscarf?" "No." I smiled. "And you received your doctorate from Georgetown?" "Yes," I answered, knowing full well what question would bear repeating: "And you *weren't* forced to wear the headscarf?" For the past decade, I have had this conversation—or some version of it—with several American women who, after hearing my public lecture on women in Islam, approached me, bewildered. To their credit, attending such events is an encouraging sign that increasingly Americans are interested in learning about Islam, especially from its adherents.

Still, as a Muslim woman academic, I am struck by the frequency and pre-dictability of such encounters and how they derive from a shared sense of unease and disbelief: that a highly educated Muslim woman, raised in the United States with feminist ideals of gender justice, would choose to wear the *hijab* (wom-en's Islamic dress) of her own accord. Indeed, for many Americans, the notion that an independent woman who is free to choose differently yet voluntarily adopts what is thought to be one of Islam's most pernicious practices against women is bewildering. The anomaly is based on the commonly held view that

Islam—more than (or unlike) its Jewish and Christian monotheistic counter-parts—has a long tradition of misogyny (e.g., veiling, seclusion, polygamy, etc.) that forecloses women from self-identifying with its beliefs and practices in any real and meaningful way. The God of Islam, put bluntly, hates women. Why then should women bother to love Him back? And if they do, their blinding faith must surely be the product of false consciousness.

Yet many do. Throughout Islamic history and across the diverse terrain of Muslim societies, Muslim women have expressed and continue to express their devotion to God (or not) in a myriad of forms. One contemporary expres-sion—noteworthy and certainly unexpected to many—is a movement increas-ingly identified as Islamic feminism. This essay demystifies the project of Islamic feminism by unveiling the movement's objectives and motivations as well as the strategies its proponents have employed to critique the hegemony of Islamic androcentrism. By reading and rereading foundational scriptural texts like the Quran, Islamic feminists generally seek to revive a more woman-inclusive ver-sion of Islam's sacred past in a broader struggle for gender justice. Their efforts have not been without consequence. Their critiques of historical interpreta-tions as well as their own reinterpreted scriptural views are having an impact on contemporary understandings of gender, especially on what it means to be, in Quranic terms, a "believing Muslim woman" today.

TAKING ON THE "F-WORD"

Islamic feminism appears to be an oxymoron. In the eyes of many Americans, feminism in any form seems nonexistent in Muslim-majority countries—a judg-ment typically demonstrated by, among other factors, the number of women who veil across the Muslim world. In fact, since the 1980s, young, urban, educated professional women are increasingly consenting to wear the *hijab* in what one scholar has recently called a "quiet revolution."[1] This trend is part of veiling's historical repertoire of complex meanings, multi-sited purposes, and diverse geographic manifestations. Yet in the West, the veil has been reduced to a symbol of Islam's degradation of women—one that presumably reflects the religious, not to mention coercive, nature of Muslim societies themselves. Furthermore, in the West, many assume that societies structured by religion preclude feminism. One of the prerequisites for feminism to emerge, at least in the Western experience, has been the privatization of religion.[2] Add to this the popular belief that while secular law may be more empowering for women, reli-gion and in particular Islamic law (Sharia) are inimical to gender equality, thus incompatible with feminism.[3] According to these views, then, women's faith in Islam would impede or retard the development of any *real* feminist conscious-ness. History, however, has proven otherwise.

Feminisms are more than a century old in some parts of the Muslim world.[4] In fact, in the Middle East, different feminisms have emerged in response to varied historical circumstances and have expressed themselves through discrete discursive frameworks. For example, at the turn of the twentieth century, when the region confronted declining Ottoman suzerainty, growing European imperialism, and socioeconomic and technological transformations, secular feminism emerged and drew on multiple discourses (including secular nationalist, Islamic modernist, human rights, and democratic). A century later, similarly responsive to global and regional developments, now in a postcolonial environment, Islamic feminism arose and was expressed in a religiously grounded discourse.[5] The first movement found its discursive framework and ethos of liberation within the nation-state (read: secularism), the second within the sacred text of the Quran (read: religion). While there is much to differentiate these ideological movements, both types of feminism organically (though not unproblematically) took root in response to real and dramatic politico-economic shifts linked to turn-of-the-century (twentieth then twenty-first) developments.

Misread, this argument could be understood as an attempt to create equivalence: because the Middle East experienced feminism, then the region is equal to or resembles the West. Yet equivalence is not the point. The argument, rather, is that the global effects of modernity have been experienced not along a bilateral East-West axis but in diverse societies. Muslim societies and the women that live within them have been no less subject to or impacted by global forces and dynamics of historical change related to modernity than have other societies. Like men, women in Muslim societies grapple with what it means to be a modern subject as they respond to societal changes, whether as self-professed feminists or otherwise. This would seem self-evident.

Yet too often, Muslim societies and their women have been portrayed in American media and scholarship as static and one-dimensional—a portrait that unreasonably places these societies outside of history, as residing in "anachronistic space: prehistoric, atavistic and irrational."[6] Such a view of a people with no historical agency reminds us that Edward Said's 1978 critique about ideology's central role in historically constructing Western understandings of Islam and Muslims remains trenchant.[7] A more fruitful approach to studying the emergence of diverse feminisms in Muslim societies is to place them, like any social movement, in their historical context. By historicizing feminism, we can attend to how and why particular women, and men, for that matter, have navigated and negotiated their collective identity-making within the exigencies of modern change, most notably by forming movements to affect their own kind of change.

To identify these movements as "feminist," however, is not without contention or debate. As with feminism in the United States, academics and activists interested in Middle Eastern secular or Islamic "feminisms" use the term in varied and contested ways.[8] Their challenge is one of nomenclature: What language and classificatory methods should be employed to study Muslim women who work to unseat patriarchal and misogynist structures of power? This question takes on greater significance when one considers the broader history of Western feminist scholarship and its problematic approaches to studying non-Western women, most certainly including Muslim women.[9]

Obstacles Posed by Western Feminist Scholarship

Postcolonial cultural theorists have offered complex critiques of Western feminist scholarship. By relying on assumptions of privilege and ethnocentric universality in their textual strategies, Western feminists have dehistoricized non-Western women by appropriating, or "colonizing," the complexities that make up their realities. In place of complexity, Western scholars have created a singular, cultural and ideological composite Other, the "third world woman" (read: ignorant, poor, uneducated, tradition-bound, domestic, family-oriented, and victimized).[10] This representation of the "third world woman" supplants the heterogeneous realities of non-Western women *as women*. Such a portrayal may help explain why feminisms in non-Western contexts are absent to the Western eye: the victim status of "third world women" in society renders them incapable of resisting oppression. Herein lies the problem: Western feminists have used their authorial power to define, suppress, or even erase the voices and experiences of Other women in order to privilege their own as the defining referent of legitimate feminist struggle. In so doing, Western feminist scholarship—like other types of scholarship— is not objective knowledge about a subject. Rather, scholarly production is inscribed in relations of power, "directly political and *discursive* practice in that it is purposeful and ideological."[11] There can be no apolitical scholarship.[12]

These sorts of critiques by postcolonial cultural theorists and cultural critics, along with their calls to historicize "third world feminisms," have pushed a dramatic rethinking of feminist scholarly frameworks and the privileged status of liberalism within them.[13] The West is no longer viewed as the locus from which all feminisms derive and against which they must be measured.[14] More and more, scholars understand feminism as meaning different things to different people in different contexts.[15] The term therefore has no fixed or fixable meanings since feminisms are produced in particular places and articulated in local terms.[16] "Feminism" is not bound to any one culture.[17]

Given this polyvocal nature, however, "it is hard to write about feminism."[18] Indeed, despite advancements, scholars continue to face challenges regarding language when qualifying and classifying feminism transnationally, not just in the Muslim world. Part of the problem is that "language is not helpful here."[19] If context—historical and of the moment—always matters, if feminisms must be located in their many differences and varieties, across time, geographical space, and culture, then feminism is always plural. To use "feminisms" yet refer to them as one risks writing of a homogenous politics. And if used in the plural, the term appears as many different kinds of feminism rather than their co-equal pluralism and singularity.[20] In other words, scholarly language and terminology regarding feminism—certainly including Islamic feminism—still struggle with situating difference and thus plurality.

Questions in Identifying "Feminists"

To the problem of language add the attendant question of how to classify activists. Should a scholar identify Muslim persons or groups under study as "feminist" if they themselves do not? Taking a self-identification approach would be safe: a person or project is feminist if she or they say they are feminist.[21] However, recent studies on Middle Eastern secular and Islamic feminisms have taken alternative approaches by using feminism descriptively or as an analytical tool, despite resistance from the women under study.[22] Margot Badran, for instance, uses the term, "not to impose a label of identity upon those who refuse it but simply as a way of *identifying* what it appears particular actors think and do."[23] After struggling to find synonyms for feminism, Miriam Cooke similarly applies the label to refer to "women who think and do something about changing expectations for women's social roles and responsibilities."[24] In fact, Cooke goes further by insisting on the word:

> I use [feminism] without apologies. . . . I want to keep the word because I believe in the power of naming, and feminism is a powerful name with historical resonance. . . . I am convinced that I will help to erase, in the words of the cultural critic Anne McClintock, "the long histories of women's resistance to local and imperialist patriarchies". . . . Feminism is much more than an ideology driving organized political movements. It is, above all, an epistemology. It is an attitude, a frame of mind that highlights the role of gender in understanding the organization of society. Feminism provides analytical tools . . . .[25]

As a feminist scholar, Cooke's goal is dually to decenter liberal feminism's hegemonic grip over feminist discourse, and thereby decolonize it, and to develop a more inclusive framework where diverse Muslim women can create transnational alliances by finding common ground in their shared quest for social justice and women's equality.[26] Framed as such, she feels justified in applying "Islamic feminist" to a broad and even disparate group of Muslim women who have traditionally been viewed as ideologically distinct. Mai Yamani, in an early work on the topic, takes a somewhat similar approach of grouping a broad array of women under the "Islamic feminist" banner, as does Elizabeth Fernea in her more recent anthropological "search for Islamic feminism."[27] While such accounts successfully convey the complex, lived realities and heterogeneous experiences of diverse Muslim women who seek to overturn the status quo (often through their own voices), the approaches and the positionality of the authors continue to draw scholarly critique.[28]

In sum, within a newly expanding body of scholarship on feminisms in the Muslim world, analytical questions and debates continue to be worked out.[29] In light of Western feminism's problematic legacy, scholarship written in the United States about women in the Middle East continues to grapple with the tricky question of "how best to deal with the political and theoretical complexities of speaking 'about' women while avoiding to speak 'for' *other* women."[30]

Roots of Muslim Ambivalence Toward Feminism

Beyond the scholarly challenges of studying Islamic feminism, the more pressing issue is why Muslims themselves have shown ambivalence, if not antipathy, toward feminism. Because of its ideological entanglements with European imperialism at the turn of the twentieth century and what many in the Middle East perceive to be American neoimperialism today, feminism carries largely negative historical associations that have polarized Muslims for much of the twentieth century. Feminist arguments were introduced in many parts of the Muslim world as part of the project of European imperialism. As Leila Ahmed passionately argues, to justify the colonial conquests of Muslim lands, European imperialists hypocritically appropriated feminist language to attack what were believed to be Islam's most misogynist customs and traditions, like veiling and polygamy, when often these same men were anti-suffragists while in Europe.[31] "Feminism on the home front and feminism directed against white men was to be resisted and suppressed; but taken abroad and directed against the cultures of colonized peoples, it could be promoted in ways that admirably served and furthered the project of the dominance of the white man."[32] "White men saving brown women from brown men," an expression attributed to the postcolonial theorist Gayatri Chakravorty Spivak, poignantly captures this imperialist phenomenon.[33] The significance of the phrase, however, goes much deeper.

The problem is not that white European men sought to "rescue" native women from the abuses of primitive traditions and the misogyny of religious laws imposed upon them by Hinduism, Islam, African paganism, and so on. Rather Spivak ultimately exposes how women—Hindu, Muslim, African, and others—problematically came to represent the ideological battleground between European colonial and native discourses. Through the colonial experience, woman became the quintessential signifier or symbol of ideological differences between "East" and "West." Feminism, then, was politically exploited by European men in the interests of empire (what Ahmed calls "colonial feminism"), putting colonized Muslim men on the defensive as they sought to preserve their cultural and religious traditions by protecting their women and families from the onslaught of the White Man's Burden.

More recently, while the actors and nature of the conflicts have changed, the ideological battleground between "Islam" and "the West" where women symbolize cultural and political fault lines remains intact. There is no better evidence of this than the "War on Terror" in the aftermath of the September 11 attacks. Lila Abu-Lughod eloquently asserts that American policymakers justified the 2001 intervention in Afghanistan in the name of liberating, or saving, Afghan women. Laura Bush's radio address on November 17, 2001, exemplifies how the plight of Muslim women was politically mobilized to rally Americans around the war cause. "Because of our recent military gains in much of Afghanistan, women are no longer imprisoned in their homes. They can listen to music and teach their daughters without fear of punishment. The fight against terrorism is also a fight for the rights and dignity of women."[34]

As deplorable as the conditions faced by Afghan women were under the Taliban regime, echoes Jasmin Zine, "the fact that their plight became strategically positioned as being 'prime-time worthy' only during the violent campaigns of the war on terror, reinforces their role as a political guise activated to engender sympathy for the military campaign as an act of 'liberating' oppressed Muslim women from fanatical Muslim men."[35] Afghan women were consequently reduced to tokens in a war against fundamentalism, erasing other important factors affecting their lives.[36]

Problematic, then, is that neat cultural icons like the Muslim woman have been conveniently employed, or deployed, in American political discourse to hide messy and complex historical and political dynamics and justify political undertakings.[37] "So extreme is the concern with Muslim women today," argues Cooke, that "women are no longer thought of as individuals: collectively they have become the Muslimwoman." The neologism Muslimwoman, she continues, "draws attention to the emergence of a new singular religious and gendered identification that overlays national, ethnic, cultural, historical, and even philosophical diversity."[38] Add to this that contemporary discourses of equality, freedom, and rights that have fueled American rhetoric of saving the Muslim woman resonate quite loudly—and problematically—with earlier colonial rhetoric.[39] The result is that "feminism [has] lost its legitimacy and moral authority in many quarters" of the Muslim world.[40]

No wonder many Islamic feminists refuse or eschew the label and in some cases have adopted alternative terminology, like "womanist" or "remakers of women" instead.[41] The problem is not necessarily ideological: many Islamic feminists have read and been influenced by liberal and transnational feminist writings, despite disagreements over certain premises.[42] The bigger issue is that, to many Muslims, feminism remains a tool of Western cultural hegemony and thus constitutes a corrupting pollutant that morally threatens the integrity of Islam's traditional gender norms and family structure.

Take the view of Sayyid Mawlana Maududi, one of the most influential Muslim thinkers and Quranic commentators of the mid to late twentieth century. In his widely read book on women in Islam, popular in the 1970s and 80s (at a time of rising conflicts between the United States and Middle East and their entanglements in the Arab-Israeli conflict), Maududi defends the primacy of women's traditional roles within the Muslim family as the cornerstone of a strong and healthy Islamic society, in contrast to what was thought of as the West's deteriorating societal malaise and rampant "sexual anarchy."[43] Like many other Muslim thinkers, then and now, Maududi focuses on the deleterious effects of "women's lib" on Western women (they live unnaturally as men) and consequently on the Western family and society (the West has therefore failed to become a "righteous civilization").

> The world of today, even in this 20th century, falls far short of this Islamic standard. . . . Whatever rights the woman has been granted in the West have been granted her not for her own sake but as if she was the man. The woman is still inferior in the Western eyes as she was in the past ages of ignorance. In the West a real genuine woman has yet to have respect. . . . The so-called respect that she enjoys today is in fact for her being the he-woman or she-man who is physiologically a woman, but mentally a man, and who pursues masculine activities in life. Obviously, this respect is for manhood, not for womanhood.[44]

With these cultural binaries as the backdrop, Islamic feminists are forced into an ideological minefield. If their goal is to establish gender justice based on a reenvisioned set of Islamic gender norms, and thus unsettle Muslims' longstanding normative view of Muslim family life, then adopting the "feminist" label could discredit, and typically has discredited, their work and opened them to accusations of corrupting Islam. They also risk alienating themselves and their activism from the Muslim communities of which they are a part and which they seek to reform.

The legacy of feminism in Muslim lands clearly carries complex political baggage, which, as demonstrated here, must be unpacked before one can appreciate the contextual and textual dynamics that have constituted the making of Islamic feminism. Far from having no history, feminism in the Middle East has had, among its diverse effects, a long, contentious history that in many ways mirrors and refracts the ongoing political conflicts and ideological battles between "Islam and the West." This mired history forms the backdrop against which Islamic feminism emerged and with which it continually contends.

DISAGGREGATING THE PROJECT OF ISLAMIC FEMINISM

In the 1990s, scholars on the Middle East increasingly identified Islamic feminism as a new movement spreading across the region, but most noticeably in Iran and Egypt, where Islamist movements had first appeared in the 1970s. In fact, Margot Badran has demonstrated that Islamic feminism emerged out of, and as a contestation to, the Islamist movement, with the Egyptian case proving exemplary.

> Islamic feminism appeared at a moment of late postcoloniality and a time of deep disaffection over the inability of Middle Eastern nation-states to deliver democracy and foster broad economic prosperity. . . . In the final third of the twentieth century, new groups and classes—mainly the recently urbanized entering the middle class—experiencing the pushes and pulls of modernity (expressed in uneven access to new opportunities and

uncertain benefits) and an accompanying cultural anomie, were attracted to Islamism.[45]

As the discourse of democracy became globally dominant, women were as dissatisfied as Islamists were with the authoritarianism that characterized many Muslim postcolonial states and the attendant problems of social stratification. Over time, however, as Islamist discourses increasingly propagated a more conservative view of gender as a return of women to a "purer" and more "authentic" domestic life away from the public scene, women grew more concerned about this conservative reading of Islam and found the need to respond.[46]

Val Moghadam and Ziba Mir-Hosseini draw parallel arguments about the rise of Islamic feminism within the context of Iran in 1979. Both analyze ensuing developments into the 1990s that spurred Iranian women to become disillusioned with the Islamic Republic's official discourse on women and undertake their own movement for change.[47] In fact, Mir-Hosseini calls Islamic feminism "the 'unwanted child' of political Islam," which emerged, not because Islamists offered an egalitarian vision of gender relations, but because political Islam gave activist women the language to sustain a critique of the gender biases in ways that were previously impossible. This ultimately "opened a space, an arena, for an internal critique of patriarchal readings of the Shari'a that was unprecedented in Muslim history."[48]

Aside from Islamism, another catalyst for Islamic feminism—arguably more crucial not only in the Middle East but globally—has been the increase in female literacy (including some women becoming experts in the religious sciences). Growth in literacy has coincided with the spread of information through cyberspace: local knowledge and global knowledge can now be produced almost simultaneously.[49] As a result, Muslim women have been uniting in a "shared culture, diffused by electronic media, education, literacy, urbanization, and modernization" as they have become aware of connections among their experiences and those of Muslim women elsewhere—whether in Pakistan, Afghanistan, Saudi Arabia, Indonesia, Palestine, or America.[50] Indeed, women's personal experiences themselves mobilized the movement, as their spirituality, scholarship, and activism came together.[51] This would certainly explain the rise of American-Muslim "scholar-activists"[52] whose Islamic feminist scholarship has circulated within the United States (especially within university settings) in explosive numbers since the 1990s but that has also been accessed overseas, often instantaneously, through the Internet.[53] Intellectually and technologically equipped, Muslim women have been thinking for themselves and answering, with their own Islamic voice, the conservatism of Islamists.[54]

Of course, Islamic feminists do not speak with a single voice: their views reflect local, diverse, multiple, and evolving positions.[55] This makes it nearly impossible to graph the movement's global incarnations or identify its diverse cast of international actors here. Nevertheless, as a representative sample, this study emphasizes the work of a number of American scholar-activists (Riffat

Hassan, Amina Wadud, Asma Barlas, Azizah al-Hibri, Ziba Mir-Hosseini, among others) who arguably are becoming the face, or voice, of Islamic feminism in the United States and abroad (despite many of them avoiding or contesting the label). Feminisms do speak to each other, whether in agreement or disagreement.[56] While important differences exist among Islamic feminisms' global articulations, one can still discern a set of core characteristics and the general contours defining this expansive movement. These characteristics include the primacy of the Quran as *the* single source of liberation, a critique of Islamic patriarchy as exclusionary and misogynist, and the right of *ijtihad* (scriptural reinterpretation) within a broader female-inclusive scriptural approach to redress gender injustices.

The Primacy of the Quran

Islamic feminism anchors its calls for women's liberation and gender reform within an Islamic, and more specifically Quranic, framework. The movement frames the issues of gender and women's rights within a larger quest for social justice as determined by the Quran—a kind of Islamic liberation theology. The centrality of the Quran in constituting an ethos of liberation cannot be overstated. Some may deem it illogical that Muslim women would look to the very scriptural source that presumably oppresses them. A cynical view would see this reliance on the Quran as simply strategic, as a method of assuring legitimacy. Yet this group of women, but also men,[57] foreground their claims for gender equality and social justice on a real and unwavering belief in the Quran's divine guidance as the perfect and preserved Word of God. As Divine Discourse, argues Barlas, "the Qur'an is inviolate, inerrant, and incontrovertible; it is both the source of Truth and the quintessential source and language of the faith."[58] As divine guidance, moreover, it presents a promissory vision that makes self-actualization possible: "I come away from the Qur'an," writes Wadud, "with the sense that all the questions I have asked can be clarified therein. Not literally 'answered,' as some would say, implying that the Qur'an has the (only) Truth, or that all Truth is in it. Rather, the Qur'an establishes a true vision of the world and beyond, with meanings and possibilities of self that lead to certainty and peace."[59] The Quran's truth-claims, in a word, speak to women in ways that move them to action in their pursuit of sacred "meanings and possibilities of self."

In fact, the Quran offers Islamic feminists an inimitable discursive framework for female self-determination. It holds human equality as a sacred principle and presents justice as essential to the divine order of the universe.[60] Its liberatory potential, then, resides in its precepts and promise of divine justice.[61] In fact, Islamic feminist activism can largely be explained by an unequivocal belief in the Quran's egalitarian ethos—a belief that has mobilized activists to address the injustices that women have been forced to endure as a result of Muslims' failure to realize this potential. Riffat Hassan's push into feminist activism is in many ways representative:

> The more I saw the justice and compassion of God reflected in the Qur'anic teachings regarding women, the more anguished and angry I became seeing the injustice and inhumanity in which Muslim women in general are subjected in actual life. I began to feel strongly that it was my duty—as a part of the microscopic minority of educated Muslim women—to do as much consciousness-raising regarding the situation of Muslim women that I could.[62]

Armed with the Quran, feminists locate their work of transforming practices of gender asymmetry within a broader quest for social justice.

So, what exactly is the problem? If equality and justice are foundational Quranic precepts, how did Muslim women get into this mess? And more importantly, why not simply reform Islamic law today according to the Quran's egalitarian ethos? The single most critical obstacle to an Islamic reformation of Muslim identity based on gender justice—and therefore the single most articulated (and unifying) critique by Islamic feminists—is Islam's patriarchal tradition of silencing. Silencing is a form of exclusion. Women's exclusion from Islam's historical development has been most evident in textual, and thus legal, production and troubling in its gender(ed) effects.

The Critique of Patriarchal Exegesis

The critique may be summarized succinctly. Men have historically arrogated for themselves the authority of scriptural interpretation, and therefore lawmaking, during foundational moments of Islam's formation. Women's experiences and voices—oral and written—were therefore excluded from the interpretive process and from formulating the very canons of Islamic orthodoxy and jurisprudence. Feminist scholars widely agree that the tenth century, during the time of the Abbasid Empire, was a defining period in constituting foundational paradigms for understanding the Quran, Prophetic Tradition (Sunna), and law (through *tafasir* or exegetical commentaries; *tafsir*, singular).[63] Not coincidentally, misogynist attitudes and praxis were commonplace in the period. Feminist scholars therefore emphasize the tenth century as the period when women became excluded from the production of religious discourse.

Yet exclusion has not always been the case. Muslims readily point out that women actively participated in the creation of religious knowledge at the time of Muhammad.[64] Islamic feminists identify this historical precedent as strong evidence of Islam's egalitarian practices (not to mention justification for their own activism), while their critiques isolate the canonization of Sharia law against the backdrop of Arabia's tenth-century "tradition of misogyny" as the primary cause of women's legal subordination.[65] Ahmed references this shift as the muting of Islam's "stubbornly egalitarian voice"; Azizah al-Hibri initially calls it "the patriarchal takeover of Islam," but later terms it more provocatively as "the result of Satanic logic infiltrating Muslim laws and distorting Muslim beliefs."[66] For Khaled Abou El Fadl, women's exclusion resulted from men "misusing and abusing God's authority in order to impose a suffocating patriarchy."[67] As the makers and overseers of theology and law, men deemed themselves the sole interpretive authorities of Islam, despite the existence of qualified women scholars.

Herein lies the single most powerful critique Islamic feminists have leveled against Islamic patriarchy: historically, male exegetes wrote their misogynist biases about women's roles and nature into exegetical works on the Quran (*tafasir*), yet these interpretations came to be associated with the Quran itself.

> In other words, it was the secondary religious texts that enabled the "textualization of misogyny" in Islam. These texts have come to eclipse the Quran's influence in most Muslim societies today, exemplifying the triumph not only of some texts over others in Muslim religious discourse but also of history, politics, and culture over the sacred text.[68]

Islamic feminists frame exegesis as the subjective product of the fragilities and fallibilities of human memory—and therefore as contestable artifacts of Islamic history.[69] Other Muslims, however, have granted sacred status to Islamic exegesis, holding that traditional scholars were able to replicate Muhammad's own methodology due to their proximity in real time to him and to the first Muslim community.[70] This commonly held belief has rendered the *tafasir* timeless, normative, and ultimately irrefutable (since it is believed that these exegetes got it right).

This belief, retorts Barlas, is problematic for its "denial of historicity": "Belief in the 'theoretical infallibility' of these scholars and the idea that the knowledge they produced transcends its own historicity arises in, and also gives rise to, a view of imaginary time that serves to draw Muslims close to what is distant from us in real time and to distance us from that which, in real time, is close to us.[71]

The central problem is less the specific interpretations of exegetes (though they certainly require redress) than the ahistorical interpretive *approach* they employ to derive scriptural meanings. Hermeneutics, not revelation, is the issue. For Islamic feminists, no method of Quranic exegesis can be fully objective; each exegete makes some subjective choices. Subjectivity becomes problematic to the interpretive process, however: "When one individual reader with a particular world-view and specific prior text asserts that his or her reading is the only possible or permissible one, it prevents readers in different contexts to come to terms with their own relationship to the text."[72] The failure to make a hermeneutical distinction between the Quran and interpretation, between divine speech and human speech, has allowed interpreters to assign culturally specific meanings to the Quran while also endowing those meanings with timeless relevance. The Quran, consequently, becomes confused with its *tafsir* and Islam with patriarchy.[73]

The "textualization of misogyny" was not possible without women's exclusion from the founding paradigms of Islamic knowledge production: women were foreclosed from refuting, contesting, condoning, or nuancing male interpretations or offering alternative readings of their own. With male interpreters exclusively formulating law, with male subjectivities and experiences acting as the sole referent of Muslim religious experience, and with women's subjectivities, knowledge, perspectives, experiences, and desires excluded, ultimately male worldviews became imposed on Quranic meanings and then mistaken for the Quran itself.

The result of the hermeneutical silencing of women, most critically, is the historical production of misogynist gender laws in the name of the Quran. These laws problematically form the basis of Sharia and consequently of Muslim state laws. This "patriarchal jurisprudence"[74] has meant that men, not women, have defined and set the ontological, spiritual, mental, biological, and legal terms of what it means to be a "believing Muslim woman." Silenced, women's voices have been replaced by male exegetes who have spoken, and continue to speak, in their name. Yet male legal definitions of Islamic womanhood are deficient at best and anti-Quranic at worst: deficient, because they dismiss the very possibility that women can speak and act on their own behalf as creations, or trustees [khilafa], of God; and anti-Quranic, because their formulations fall egregiously short of divine justice, particularly when considering today's failing family laws concerning marriage and divorce. "The near-total exclusion of women from the process whereby law was formulated is partly to blame for the fact that women's basic rights are often sacrificed when dominant modes of argument press claims into their extreme form…. But had women been conversation partners, such doctrines would likely have looked very different."[75]

Indeed, if women's voices had been included in Islam's foundational texts, arguably Muslims today would be engaging a very different Islamic past based on a more equitable set of gender norms and laws.[76]

The Right of *Ijtihad*—Scriptural Interpretation

Kecia Ali argues that "women's participation in the pleasures of the text is an important route to women's participation in the pleasures of life."[77] When free to interpret a text, to formulate and ascribe its textual meanings, women have the autonomy to "consent" to the practices that derive from those meanings. This conviction forms the cornerstone of Islamic feminist activism and the premise of their calls for a female-inclusive reinterpretation of the Quran. After all, if the central problem of *tafasir* is that male interpreters read patriarchy into the Quran, or "textualized misogyny," then the solution, according to Barlas and Wadud, is for women to "*unread*" patriarchal interpretations of the Quran" by *rereading* the Quran directly. Indeed, Islamic feminists, like other feminists, have come to understand textual reappropriation as a fundamental strategy of empowerment.[78]

To decenter "male epistemic privilege," and thereby challenge traditional male exegetes and their interpretive strategies,[79] Islamic feminists have reappropriated the terms of Quranic engagement by demanding the inclusion of women interpreters and a gender-critical hermeneutics that can recuperate

Islam's "stubbornly egalitarian voice." But to interpret the Quran, Islamic feminists have had to contend with the question of authority. They have done so by
claiming the right of *ijtihad*, or scriptural reinterpretation—a right historically
reserved for men—on the basis that they are answering the Quran's many calls
to believers, men and women, to use their intellect and knowledge to read it.[80]
In other words, they retrieve their interpretive authority from the Quran itself.
Their push for greater inclusion constitutes a call for equality, a corrective to a
history of textual "voicelessness," and a crucial act to fortify women's identity in
Islam and the Islamic authenticity of their claims for reform.[81]

Not only are Islamic feminists calling for fresh rereadings of the Quran
inclusive of women, they are undertaking these projects themselves. To do
so, they have formulated pioneering gender-critical hermeneutics that guide
their interpretive approaches and new interpretations of Islamic womanhood
and gender rights. Expectedly, the Quran, and by extension a Quranic worldview based on God's Oneness (*tawhid*)—what Wadud calls a "tawhidic paradigm"—grounds their hermeneutical claims.[82] Indeed, Quranic concepts like
tawhid (unicity or absolute monotheism), *khalifa* (trusteeship; agency), and
taqwa (moral consciousness in the trustee of God)—which are conceptually
unrelated to issues of gender—are brought together to form a moral framework, a hermeneutical guide, based on the ethical treatment between humans.
When applied to issues of gender, these concepts make possible more just and
equitable laws.[83] In this reading, humans, as God's representatives on earth
(*khilafa*), are called to match God's absolute oneness (*tawhid*) in their just
treatment of each other (*taqwa*) as equal representatives of God, with the same
human dignity and without regard for any socially constructed markers of difference (race, gender, religion, class, etc.).[84] Women, then, would be endowed
with a moral agency that ensures their full humanity and their capacity for
self-determination. In such a view, patriarchy is antithetical to *khilafa*, for by
eradicating women's moral agency, patriarchy negates the possibility of true
surrender to God.[85]

Unlike traditional Muslim exegetes, Islamic feminists envisage Muslim identity, as women and men, not within a social system based on a body-centered
method of understanding gender rights and social roles, as demonstrated by
Maududi's view earlier. Rather, they see Muslim identity as deriving from a
spiritual paradigm of equal moral agency first; this agency, in turn, lays the
foundation for a hermeneutical approach, and by implication a just legal system, that allows women and men to freely realize their full and equal status as
God's trustees. Until woman's nature is understood in spiritual terms first, and
flesh second, women will continue to face injustices within a legal system that
understands their ontological value in strictly biological (read: maternal) terms.
This work, then, like the work of other feminist movements, is "fundamentally
about reordering the way 'natural' is seen, spoken, and lived."[86] For them, as the
Quran constitutes the sole and primary reference in defining what "natural" is
and is not, central Quranic concepts like *khilafa* must be prioritized in defining

humanity's intrinsic nature, and precedence must be given to human spirituality over a constructed biological providence.

UNITY WITHIN PLURALITY

In addition to foregrounding a moral framework of human agency, the doctrine of, and belief in, *tawhid* as Islam's most central concept provides Islamic feminists with a way of understanding the Quran as a holistic and coherent text whose logic and larger *Weltanschauung* (worldview) cannot contradict God's self-ascribed attributes, such as Unity, Justice, and Incomparability. "Given the unity of Divine Ontology and Divine Discourse," argues Barlas, "we need to begin our reading of God's Speech by connecting it to God. Thus, God's Self-Disclosure needs to become intrinsic to any project of Qur'anic hermeneutics."[87] If God, as Unity, cannot reveal a contradictory or disconnected message, or, as Justice and Incomparability, cannot be anthropomorphized as oppressive, patriarchal, or misogynist, then how can God's Speech? This methodological criterion underpins Islamic feminists' textual strategy of "interpreting the Quran with the Quran," that is, decoding the meanings of Quranic verses based on, among other things, the Quran's context, worldview, overriding principles, and language (semantics, syntax, reoccurrences, etc.).[88]

This self-referential approach does not, however, preclude the possibility of deriving multiple understandings of God's revelation. By emphasizing the Quran's textual polysemy, Islamic feminists show how the Quran can be read in multiple modes, including egalitarian ones.[89] Indeed, key to an effective liberatory hermeneutics is that interpretation must itself be an open process, one that no single vision can conclude since "the activity of discerning the divine discourse is forever incomplete."[90] Rather than restrict Quranic meanings, then, Islamic feminists invite Muslim communities, in their diverse settings, to read the Scripture anew in the attempt at generating new sacred meanings reflective of their lived realities and ethical standards of conduct. "A pluralism of readings, the multiplicity of interpretive interests, and the Qur'an's own polysemy do not mean, however, that the Qur'an itself is variant."[91] What changes, argues Wadud, is not the Quran but "the capacity and particularity of the understanding and reflection of the principles of the text within a community."[92] This, concludes Barlas, is why in Islam "hermeneutics aspires not to erase the distinction between the Qur'an and its exegesis but to bridge it ever more scrupulously."[93]

In conclusion, like many scriptural reformist movements, Islamic feminists see hermeneutics as key to unlocking the great potentialities and possibilities of divine speech in redressing Islamic patriarchy and its "tradition of misogyny." By using a "critical faith-centered approach," one that locates the struggles of their faith-based feminism in anti-patriarchal readings of the Quran and new understandings of Islamic gender justice, Islamic feminists are able to redirect the potency of religion and spirituality, not merely as problematic sources of oppression, but as powerful sites of resistance.[94] Their activism and their schol-arly works—indeed, their life's work—reflect a dedication not simply to gen-der justice, but to a profound and deep-seated belief in God as revealed in the Quran. Their activism reminds us "that the current struggle to recover the voice of women is crucial to no less than a recovery of Islam itself."[95] Articulated more poignantly by Barlas: "To accept the authority of any group and then to resign oneself to its misreading of Islam not only makes one complicit in the continued abuse of Islam and the abuse of women in the name of Islam, but it also means losing the battle over meaning without even fighting it."[96] And fight they must.

Notes

1. See Leila Ahmed, *A Quiet Revolution: The Veil's Resurgence, from the Middle East to America* (New Haven, CT: Yale University Press, 2012). For other works on this movement, also see Sherifa Zuhur, *Revealing Reveiling: Islamist Gender Ideol-ogy in Contemporary Egypt* (New York: SUNY Press, 1992); Nilufer Gole, *The Forbidden Modern: Civilization and Veiling* (Ann Arbor: University of Michi-gan Press, 1996); Fadwa El Guindi, *Veil: Modesty, Privacy, and Resistance* (New York: Berg Publishers, 1999).
2. Ziba Mir-Hosseini, "Beyond 'Islam' vs. 'Feminism,'" *IDS Bulletin*, vol. 42, no. 1 (2011): 2.
3. See Haideh Moghissi, *Feminism and Islamic Fundamentalism: The Limits of Post-modern Analysis* (London: Zed Books, 1999). In contrast, for discussion of ways that Islamic laws benefit women more than secular law, see Asifa Quraishi-Landes, "Secular Is Not Always Better: A Closer Look at Some Woman-Empowering Features of Islamic Law," Institute for Social Policy and Understanding, Policy Brief #61 (June 2013).
4. Margot Badran, "Between Secular and Islamic Feminism/s: Reflections on the Middle East and Beyond," *Journal of Middle East Women's Studies* 1 no. 1 (2005): 6.
5. Ibid., 8.
6. Anne McClintock, *Imperial Leather: Race, Gender, and Sexuality in the Colonial Conquest* (New York: Routledge, 1995), 40.
7. See Edward W. Said, *Orientalism* (New York: Vintage Books, 1979).
8. For different uses of "feminism" to discuss women's movements in the Muslim world, see, for example, Margot Badran, *Feminists, Islam, and Nation: Gender and the Making of Modern Egypt* (New Jersey: Princeton University Press, 1995); Elizabeth Warnock Fernea, *In Search of Islamic Feminism: One Woman's Global Journey* (New York: Doubleday, 1998); Valentine M. Moghadam, "Islamic Feminism and Its Discontents: Toward a Resolution of the Debate," *Signs: Jour-nal of Women in Culture and Society,* 27 no. 4 (2002); Miriam Cooke, *Women Claim Islam* (New York: Routledge, 2001); Ziba Mir-Hosseini, "Beyond 'Islam' vs. 'Feminism.'"
9. Chandra Talpade Mohanty, "Under Western Eyes: Feminist Scholarship and Colonial Discourses," in *Third World Women and the Politics of Feminism*, ed. Chandra Mohanty, Ann Russo, and Lourdes Torres (Bloomington: Indiana University Press, 1991), 53.
10. Mohanty, "Under Western Eyes," 51–52, 56.
11. Ibid., 53. Also see Anne McClintock, *Imperial Leather.*
12. Mohanty, "Under Western Eyes," 53.

13. Zilla Eisenstein, *Against Empire: Feminisms, Racism, and the West* (London: Zed Books Ltd., 2004).
14. Badran, "Between Secular and Islamic Feminism/s," 12.
15. Mir-Hosseini, "Beyond 'Islam' vs. 'Feminism,'" 1.
16. Margot Badran, "Islamic Feminism, What's in a Name?" *Al-Ahram Weekly* 17 (January 2002).
17. Cooke, *Women Claim Islam*, x.
18. Eisenstein, *Against Empire*, 181.
19. Ibid.
20. Ibid.
21. Sylvia Walby, *The Future of Feminism* (Cambridge: Polity Press, 2011), 5.
22. See Margot Badran, *Feminists, Islam, and Nation*; Elizabeth Warnock Fernea, *In Search of Islamic Feminism*; Miriam Cooke, *Women Claim Islam*; Margot Badran, "Between Secular and Islamic Feminism/s."
23. Badran, "Between Secular and Islamic Feminism/s," 15.
24. Cooke, *Women Claim Islam*, ix.
25. Ibid.
26. Jasmin Zine, Review of *Women Claim Islam*, by Miriam Cooke, *American Journal of Islamic Social Sciences* 19, no. 4 (2002): 112, 114.
27. Mai Yamani, "Introduction," in *Feminism and Islam: Legal and Literary Perspectives*, ed. Mai Yamani (New York: New York University Press, 1996), 1; Fernea, *In Search of Islamic Feminism*, 415.
28. About Miriam Cooke's book, Jasmin Zine, for example, argues that she lacks critical self-reflexivity since she does not locate or question her own social position in relation to her research among Muslim women and thus leaves open the question of whether she may be complicit in maintaining dominant hegemonic control over Muslim women's discourses. Zine, Review of *Women Claim Islam*, 112. Zine offers a more elaborate critique of Cooke's positionality in Jasmin Zine, "Lost in Translation: Writing Back from the Margins; Roundtable Discussion: Religion, Gender, and the Muslimwoman," *Journal of Feminist Studies in Religion* 24, no. 1 (2008): 110–16. Nadje Ali claims that Badran's broad analytical category of feminism ultimately conceals two types of feminisms. See Nadje Sadig Al-Ali, Review of *Feminists, Islam, and Nation: Gender and the Making of Modern Egypt*, by Margot Badran, *Bulletin of the School of Oriental and African Studies*, University of London 60, no. 2 (1997): 363–64. Lila Abu-Lughod also critiques Badran for being so over-eager to defend her subjects as "genuine feminists" in her study that she dismisses important questions—such as how we should situate women whose feminism was supported by some Europeans and developed in response to colonial definitions of backwardness of the East—that would help us think through the complexities of third world feminisms. See Lila Abu-Lughod, "Before Post-Colonialism," *The Women's Review of Books* 12, no. 6 (1995): 13–14.
29. To see how the label "Islamic feminist" is imposed on a scholar-activist who ultimately refutes it, see Valentine M. Moghadam, "Islamic Feminism and Its Discontents"; Ziba Mir-Hosseini, "Beyond 'Islam' vs. 'Feminism.'"
30. Azam Torab, Review of *Feminism and Islamic Fundamentalism: The Limits of Postmodern Analysis*, by Haideh Moghissi, *American Journal of Sociology* 106, no. 4 (2001): 1208 (emphasis added).
31. Leila Ahmed, *Women and Gender in Islam* (New Haven: Yale University Press, 1992), 152.
32. Ibid., 153.

33. See Gayatri Chakravorty Spivak, "Can the Subaltern Speak?," in *Colonial Discourse and Postcolonial Theory: A Reader,* ed. Patrick Williams and Laura Chrisman (Hertfordshire: Harvester Wheatsheaf, 1994).

34. Lila Abu-Lughod, "Do Muslim Women Really Need Saving? Anthropological Reflections on Cultural Relativism and Its Others," *American Anthropologist* 104, no. 3 (2002): 784.

35. Zine, "Between Orientalism and Fundamentalism: The Politics of Muslim Women's Feminist Engagement," *Muslim World Journal of Human Rights* 3, no. 1 (2006): 9.

36. Ibid.

37. For a critique of American political discourse's appropriation of the plight of Afghan women, see Eisenstein, *Against Empire,* 162–65.

38. Miriam Cooke, "Deploying the Muslimwoman, Roundtable Discussion: Religion, Gender, and the Muslimwoman," *Journal of Feminist Studies in Religion* 24, no. 1 (2008): 91.

39. Abu-Lughod, "Do Muslim Women," 783; Mir-Hosseini, "Beyond 'Islam' vs. 'Feminism,'" 6.

40. Mir-Hosseini, "Beyond 'Islam' vs. 'Feminism,'" 6.

41. Cooke, *Women Claim Islam,* ix.

42. Moghadam, "Islamic Feminism and Its Discontents," 1164. Importantly, the Iranian women that Mir-Hosseini interviewed did not have a problem with the "Islamic feminist" label more than they did with feminism's premise of gender equality. Mir-Hosseini, "Beyond 'Islam' vs. 'Feminism,'" 4.

43. See S. Abul Ala Maududi, *Purdah and the Status of Woman in Islam* (Lahore: Islamic Publications Ltd., 1972).

44. Ibid., 160.

45. Badran, "Between Secular and Islamic Feminism/s," 8.

46. Ibid., 9.

47. Mir-Hosseini, "Beyond 'Islam' vs. 'Feminism,'" 4; Moghadam, "Islamic Feminism and Its Discontents," 1143.

48. Mir-Hosseini, "Beyond 'Islam' vs. 'Feminism,'" 6.

49. Badran, "Between Secular and Islamic Feminism/s," 9, 14.

50. Cooke, "Deploying the Muslimwoman," 98–99.

51. Roxanne D. Marcotte, "Muslim Women's Scholarship and the New Gender Jihad," in *Women and Islam,* ed. Zayn R. Kassam (Denver: Praeger, 2010), 131.

52. Gisela Webb, "Introduction: May Muslim Women Speak for Themselves, Please?" in *Windows of Faith,* ed. Gisela Webb (New York: Syracuse University Press, 2000), ix.

53. Amina Wadud's *Qur'an and Woman,* and its many translations for audiences overseas, is a good illustrative example. See Amina Wadud, *Qur'an and Woman: Rereading the Sacred Text from a Woman's Perspective* (New York: Oxford University Press, 1999).

54. Badran, "Between Secular and Islamic Feminism/s," 9.

55. Mir-Hosseini, "Beyond 'Islam' vs. 'Feminism,'" 5.

56. Badran, "Between Secular and Islamic Feminism/s," 13.

57. There are a number of men who identify with the movement who contributed chapters or are written about in *A Jihad for Justice: Honoring the Work and Life of Amina Wadud,* eds. Kecia Ali, Juliane Hammer, and Laury Silvers (U.S.A.: www.48HrBooks.com). See, for example, Abdennur Prado, "Qur'anic Feminism: The Makers of Textual Meaning"; Amanullah De Sondy, "Why Masculinity Matters in the Study of Islam and Muslims"; and Michael Muhammad Knight, "Building and Destroying." In *Women in Islam Reflections on Historical*

and Contemporary Research, ed. Terence Lovat (New York: Springer, 2012) see Terence Lovat, "The 'Women's Movement' in Modern Islam: Reflections on the Revival of Islam's Oldest Issue," and Kelly al-Dakkak, "Reconciling Traditional Islamic Methods with Liberal Feminism: Reflections from Tunisia by Mohamed Talbi." Many scholars add Khaled Abou El Fadl to this group, though he refuses this affiliation. See Khaled Abou El Fadl, *Speaking in God's Name: Islamic Law, Authority and Women* (Oxford: Oneworld, 2001).

58. Asma Barlas, "Believing Women" in *Islam: Unreading Patriarchal Interpretations of the Qur'an* (Austin: University of Texas Press, 2002), 32–33.

59. Amina Wadud, *Inside the Gender Jihad: Women's Reform in Islam* (Oxford: Oneworld Publications, 2006), 9.

60. Wadud, *Gender Jihad*, 10.

61. Barlas, "Believing Women," 15.

62. Riffat Hassan, "The Issue of Woman-Man Equality in the Islamic Tradition," in *Women's and Men's Liberation Testimonies of Spirit,* ed. Leonard Grob, Riffat Hassan, and Haim Gordon (New York: Greenwood Press, 1991), 66. Also see Barlas, "Believing Women," 209–210; Wadud, *Gender Jihad*, 9–10.

63. Most feminist scholars cite Leila Ahmed's work on gender and Islam as pioneering in making this argument. See Ahmed, *Women and Gender in Islam.*

64. Barlas, "Believing Women," 9.

65. Ahmed, *Women and Gender in Islam,* see the chapter titled "Elaboration of the Founding Discourses," 79–101.

66. Azizah al-Hibri, "A study of Islamic Herstory: Or How Did We Ever Get into This Mess?," *Women's Studies International Forum* 5, no. 1 (1982): 215. Hibri, "Introduction," 54.

67. Abou El Fadl, *Speaking in God's Name,* x.

68. Barlas, "Believing Women," 9.

69. Hibba Abugideiri, "Revisiting the Islamic Past, Deconstructing Male Authority: The Project of Islamic Feminism," *Religion and Literature* 42, no. 1 (2010): 3.

70. Barlas, "Believing Women," 53.

71. Ibid., 24.

72. Wadud, *Qur'an and Woman,* 5.

73. Barlas, "Believing Women," 9; Wadud, *Qur'an and Woman,* 1.

74. Azizah Y. Al-Hibri, "An Introduction to Muslim Women's Rights," in *Windows of Faith,* ed. Gisela Webb (New York: Syracuse University Press, 2000), 54.

75. Kecia Ali, "Just Say Yes: Law, Consent, and Muslim Feminist Epistemologies," in *A Jihad for Justice,* 133.

76. Abugideiri, "Revisiting the Islamic Past," 2.

77. Ali, "Just Say Yes,"133.

78. Wadud, *Gender Jihad*, 8.

79. Barlas, "Believing Women," 5, 209.

80. Ibid., 210.

81. Wadud, *Gender Jihad*, 8; Wadud, *Qur'an and Woman,* 2.

82. See, for example, Wadud, *Gender Jihad*, 24–32; Barlas, "Believing Women," 13–15; al-Hibri, "Introduction," 51–54.

83. Wadud, *Gender Jihad*, 32–33; Barlas, "Believing Women," 106–7.

84. Knight, "Building and Destroying," 33.

85. Khaled Abou El Fadl, "Foreword," in Amina Wadud, *Gender Jihad*, xii; Wadud, *Gender Jihad*, 35–37.

86. Eisenstein, *Against Empire*, 182.

87. Barlas, "Believing Women," 13.

88. Wadud, *Qur'an and Woman,* 5.

89. Barlas, "Believing Women," 4–5.
90. Ibid., 35.
91. Ibid.
92. Wadud, *Qur'an and Woman*, 5.
93. Barlas, "Believing Women," 37.
94. Zine, "Between Orientalism and Fundamentalism," 15, 17, 18.
95. Lovat, "The 'Women's Movement' in Modern Islam: Reflections on the Revival of Islam's Oldest Issue," 1.
96. Barlas, "Believing Women," xi.

Chapter 9

The Emergence of Muslim American Feminisms

YVONNE YAZBECK HADDAD

Arab and Muslim feminisms have been initiated in response to a Western project that, across several centuries, has persistently sought to transform Muslim women into replicas of Western women. Muslim societies have been constrained to respond to perceptions that deem the women of the Muslim world to be deficient, not measuring up to the standards of Western women. As a growing number of Muslims began to make America their home, post 1965, they found themselves objects of derision by the public and the media, who depicted them as coming from a culture dominated by violent men who oppress their women. Every decade since, new generations of Arab and Muslim Americans have had to face a heightened emphasis on the need to save Muslim women, an emphasis generated by various sectors of American society: governments, missionaries, and feminists, often in response to the media and public reactions to a series of crises overseas.[1]

Each generation's struggle has required contesting the dominant negative narrative that depicts Arabs and Muslims as backward and violent people who can only be "civilized" by violent means. Each generation has attempted to counter disinformation, affirm Muslim humanity, defend the faith, and incorporate its discourse into American mainstream values. Each generation appears to believe that the root of prejudice is ignorance and that if only Americans knew the truth, they would cease to treat Arab and Muslim American citizens as "other."[2]

Arab and Muslim feminists in fact may share many concerns that American feminists have about oppressive patriarchal systems and the goals of improving life for women. Nonetheless, they continue to feel that American feminists, even when standing in solidarity, tend to dictate what Arabs and Muslims should seek and feel. "I used to feel, and still do sometimes, . . . like an outsider in feminist circles," said one Arab woman. This "outsider" feeling stemmed from the fact that the "white" feminists, unable to relate to Muslims outside of the stereotypical space in which Western feminists boxed them, always came back to the questions of female genital mutilation and honor killing.[3]

This essay highlights the efforts of several generations to fit into and respond to the culture of the United States, despite their experiences of prejudice and persistent questions about their ability ever to measure up to the values and standards American feminists present as applicable to all women. While many Muslim women in the United States have attained professional status in such fields as medicine, engineering, law, and academic scholarship, many continue to feel judged as somehow "lacking" or "not feminist enough." Each generation of Arab and Muslim women has expressed feelings of rejection, "otherness," and judgment that somehow they are not qualified to be "real Americans." The essay discusses how Arab and Muslim women have responded to the prevailing American racist and sexist images into which they have been cast. In writing and in social engagement, various cohort groups have struggled to create a place for an authentic Arab and Muslim American existence free of judgments about their inferior status and dismissal of their choices as complicity in their own oppression.

Feminists among the initial immigrant Muslims argued from an analysis of Islamic texts that Islam was actually a pioneer in liberating women. They affirmed that Islam grants women "broad social, political and economic rights, education and training rights and work opportunity rights," including the right to independent ownership, the right to inherit, the right to keep one's own identity, the right to respect, the right to marry whomever one likes and to end an unsuccessful marriage, and the right to education.[4] Islam also affirms the right to sexual pleasure.[5] Muslim feminists have since argued that Muslim women can be elected to political offices and participate in public affairs. Under the leadership of the prophet Muhammad, Islam gave women a bill of rights that endows them with the freedom to develop their individuality, to engage in shaping their society, and to participate effectively in public religious life. At the time of the prophet Muhammad women were allowed to pray with the men in congregational prayers at the mosque and to act as imams for women (and sometimes for both sexes in their household). Women participated in military campaigns and could devote themselves to the study of religious sciences, theology, the Qur'an, and the traditions.[6]

Beginning in the 1990s, several Muslim feminists focused specifically on the Qur'an, seeking to transform the patriarchal interpretations of the text. Despite the growth of radical Islamic groups overseas, these women challenged the dominant interpretation in *fiqh* (Islamic jurisprudence). Their primary focus was fashioning a new interpretation rather than criticizing male misogynist Muslim scholars in the manner of Western feminists. The essay explores efforts to "negotiate gender through the Qur'an." Since 9/11 and the subsequent "war on terrorism," a virtual industry of Islamophobia has promoted suspicion and hatred of Muslims, putting a special spotlight on Muslim women, questioning their choice to remain faithful to a religion that is often depicted as misogynist. Muslim feminist responses to American culture since 9/11 have varied strikingly: from progressive to pietistic, from "Fundo Chic" to "Native Informers." The last section of the essay argues that a decade after 9/11, new Muslim American feminisms are gaining ground among the millennial generation, evident not just in scholarship, but in clothing, literature, public service, journalism, film, and television.

ENCOUNTERING AMERICA

Understanding the complexities of Muslim American feminisms requires recognition of the long history of European and American prejudice, reaching back to the eighteenth and early nineteenth centuries. When in the nineteenth century French and British forces built up their colonies in Muslim lands, they emphasized the trope of the passive "Muslim woman" in need of European rescue. Mohja Kahf demonstrates that colonial powers had a vested interest in portraying the Muslim woman as oppressed at the same time that their policies were serving that oppression.[7] In the United States, the first foreign military engagement was with the Barbary States (1801–1805). The propaganda for that war framed the Muslim woman as seeking rescue from the clutches of brutal Muslim men, part of the essentialist interpretation that posits the Muslim as the quintessential Other who is shaped both personally and culturally by a religion viewed as the opposite of Christianity.[8] Other events furthered the image of Islam as a religion that subjugates women. In 1842 the American Oriental Society was formed, helping to institutionalize the Orient and its people for the academy, producing literature that imagined "Islam as the antithesis of both the religious and political systems of the new American nation."[9] Reports written by Christian missionaries who sought to convert the Muslim world to Christianity promoted a world divided into cultural polarities: Christian and Muslim. Both Catholic and Protestant missionaries decided that the best way to penetrate Muslim societies and modernize them was through the education of women. Muslim women were depicted appealing to Christian women for help to be liberated from seclusion, ignorance, polygamy, and the veil.[10]

Such images continued to be perpetuated in the twentieth century. The majority of Muslims immigrated to the United States after 1965. They encountered a nation undergoing convulsions that threatened its self-perceived identity as the dominant virtuous nation in the world. The Republic was being challenged by headlines heralding the "Death of God" and the triumph of secularism. Challenges also came from those not yet incorporated in its melting pot. The loss of the war in Vietnam spawned demands for alternate identities. American exceptionalism was being challenged by rebellious youth experimenting with drugs and Eastern religions, as well as by Black power, the feminist movement, and gay rights. New Muslim immigrants watched with disbelief the radical "bra burning" feminists of the United States and Europe denouncing their own cultures. At this time, overseas, Islamists sought to keep Muslim women from emulating Western gender paradigms. Instead, a model of Islamic womanhood was propagated as a necessary precondition for the emancipation of society from foreign cultural domination. International Islamic movements were centered on the social preservation of Islamic society with a special call for the transformation of women into an Islamic model: a Muslima (the Arabic feminine form for "Muslim").

FEMINIST SCHOLARS AND ACTIVISTS POISED BETWEEN AMERICA AND OTHER NATIONS

Other international events in the late twentieth century had a strong impact on Arab and Muslim Americans. The Arab Israeli wars of 1967 and 1973 and the Israeli invasion of Lebanon in 1982 were followed by America's identification with Israeli victories. Some Muslim and Arab women had previously sought solidarity with American feminists. After these events, however, Arab Americans, both Christian and Muslim, concluded such solidarity was not forthcoming, primarily because of persistent corrosive racism and the apparent intolerance of American women for different perspectives. American feminists demonstrated no empathy for the suffering of Lebanese and Palestinian women and children who were casualties of the 1982 war. The rejection was a traumatic experience, felt as a betrayal by their American "sisters." One Arab American feminist, who prefers not to be named, referred to the rejection as the "unveiling of the racist edifice of Western feminism." Accordingly, Arab American feminists withdrew from the National Organization of Women (NOW) and formed their own groups. Disenchanted with the American feminist magazine *Signs*, which they felt to be racist, a secularist group among them began publishing their own journal called *Mizna*. Aziza Y. al-Hibri of the University of Richmond founded KARAMAH, an organization dedicated to training Muslim women to advocate for their rights as guaranteed in the Qur'an.

A small number of Arab and Muslim women scholars, mostly secular in orientation, began to explore the status of women in Islam. That the role and condition of women in the Arab and Muslim world did not measure up to the American standard needed no argument; so they focused on the causes of the prevailing conditions. Afaf Lutfi al-Sayyed Marsot of the University of California at

Los Angeles argued that the condition of women in Muslim societies is not due to the teachings of Islam because the Qur'an has injunctions protecting women's economic rights. Marsot laid the blame on family customs and social traditions that impeded the progress of women. Leila Ahmed of Harvard Divinity School passionately criticized Orientalist depictions of Muslim women, blaming Muslim males for creating restrictions that bind Muslim women.[11] Amira Sonbol of Georgetown University set out to explore women's agency through an examination of Egyptian court records. She noted that Muslim women, far from being oppressed weaklings confined to the home, have been prominent in the public square, running their own businesses and initiating litigation before judges. The legal rights guaranteed by Islam have been severely constrained by modern laws imported from Europe and imposed by colonial powers.[12]

The fall of the Shah of Iran in 1979 precipitated a new emigration from that country. A group of émigré Iranian scholars who were opposed to the subsequent Khomeini regime addressed women's issues, challenging the policies and ideology of the Islamic Republic. Among them was Mahnaz Afkhami, who had served as Iran's Minister of State for Women's Affairs from 1976 to 1978. For five years she headed The Sisterhood Is Global Institute, an international non-governmental organization (NGO) with consultative status to the United Nations. Founded in 1984, the Institute attempted to facilitate strategies to address women's rights, freedoms, and power. Since coming to America, Afkhami has concentrated her efforts on working for justice for Muslim women and has written extensively on women's human rights, the politics of participation, and global feminism from a Muslim perspective.[13] Other Iranian-American scholars, including Shahla Haeri, have produced accurate sociological, economic, and political information and also analyses about women in Muslim nations.[14] Their research aims to improve the prevailing conditions for Muslim women in a variety of cultural contexts.

Pakistani, Egyptian, Palestinian, and other women located in the United States also study the situations of women in their home countries. These scholars focus on family life, including mate selection, marriage, sexuality, and divorce, and on issues of religious, ethnic, and national identity. They also research issues of culture conflict, youth, feminism, and the veil. Through teaching, writing and public presentations they provide important voices in the articulation of what it means to be a Muslim woman in the North American context. For example, Shahnaz Khan, a Canadian Muslim of Pakistani origin, identifies issues used by Western feminists to essentialize Muslim women or issues coopted by Orientalist discourse. Khan reframes them in non-Orientalist terms. She reexamines practices that have been classified or discussed in purely religious terms—such as women's punishment in Pakistan for *zina* (adultery)—and demonstrates that such matters are in fact products of economic, political, and patriarchal conditions unrelated to religion.[15]

By the 1990s, Islamization was beginning to take hold overseas. Many of the newest immigrants to the United States seeking economic opportunities or political or religious asylum had been socialized on its ideology. Secular feminist scholars who had been battling misogynist and patriarchal teachings about women overseas began to address the new challenge in the United States. Fatima Mernissi, one of the most popular secular feminists in the 1980s, advocated studying the traditions of Islam in order to focus feminist efforts on transforming the discourse from within. She became the fore-mother of a wave of Muslim women, both in the Muslim world and in diaspora, convinced that to engage with the Islamists, women must participate in creating Islamic knowledge.[16] Islamic knowledge should not, they believed, be the exclusive domain of male scholars.

Islamic feminism is one manifestation of the struggle for women's rights, including the right to work, initiate divorce, and have custody of their children. Initially ridiculed by Muslims as well as by some Westerners, the term Islamic feminism was coined in the 1990s in preparation for the United Nations' Fourth World Conference on Women in Beijing, titled "Women's Rights Are Human Rights."[17] Traditionalists and Islamists, however, challenged the slogan as a renewed Western agenda to undermine Islamic societies by promoting such "abominations" as premarital sex, abortion, and homosexuality.

Globalization and the communications revolution helped facilitate the creation of activist Islamic feminist networks that collaborate on various projects and provide international support for aspiring feminists. These include national organizations such as Sisters in Islam (SIS) in Malaysia[18] and BAOBAB for Women's Human Rights in Nigeria,[19] both of which came into existence in response to the re-Islamization policies of the 1990s that increased segregation in society. These feminist organizations provided counterarguments to impede policies that attempted to roll back liberalized legislation benefitting women. A transnational organization called Women Living Under Muslim Laws (WLUML)[20] focused its energies on the project of reforming the laws of Muslim states in order to make them accord with the "spirit of the Qur'an." The Junta Islámica Catalana of Barcelona brought various Muslim feminists from around the world including a contingent of Muslim American feminists.[21] During their first meeting, participants reaffirmed a Muslim woman's right to reflect and strategize as well as to access the mosque freely.[22]

ISLAMIC FEMINIST INTERPRETERS: NEGOTIATING GENDER THROUGH THE QUR'AN

The work of many Islamic feminist scholars, sometimes referred to as "gender jihad," consists of a reexamination of the Qur'anic text, a search for passages to be promoted as models of liberation.[23] Most of this scholarship reinterprets Qur'anic verses that have been used by traditional scholars to formulate laws that discriminate against women, particularly relating to the marriage context. This work grounds women's rights in the immutable Qur'an.

Pioneering this line of study was Pakistani American scholar Riffat Hassan, who argued that the Qur'an affirms the equality of women. If one holds to the basic principles that the Qur'an is the word of God and that God is just, it is logically impossible that the Qur'an would support the unjust (and unequal) treatment of women. Hassan argued that religion as interpreted by males is used as an instrument to oppress women rather than to free them from unjust legal and social systems. Consequently, most Muslims find it obvious that women are unequal to men and do not challenge this supposition. Hassan sees men's alleged superiority to be based on three theological assumptions that have been dramatically and incorrectly interpreted. These are (1) that God's primary creation is man (not in the generic sense) and that woman came from man's rib; (2) that woman is primarily responsible for the "fall" and expulsion from the garden of Eden; and (3) that not only was woman created "from" man, but that her existence is "for" man and not of significance in itself. In contrast, Hassan avers that a careful study of the Qur'anic text reveals (1) that man and woman are created from one soul and that the rib story is an extra-Qur'anic tradition copied from Jewish literature; (2) that Adam and Eve were equally responsible for the fall; (3) and that men and women were created from one soul to be mates to each other and that woman was not made to serve her husband.[24]

Another scholar of the Qur'an, African American Amina Wadud, has inspired a generation of young American Muslim women. In *Qur'an and Woman*, Wadud severely criticized neo-traditionalist strategies as conservative and reactionary. At the same time, she dismissed secularist interpretations by Muslim women because they were antitraditional, pro-Western, and ignorant of the importance of Islam and Islamic spirituality as a dimension of identity for women. For her, Islam is not a historical phenomenon that happened once and for all but a dynamic process constantly being created in accord with the cosmic order God established. Wadud noted that women have traditionally been voiceless, not engaged in interpreting the Qur'an. A major gap in understanding resulted, one that cannot be closed by simply repeating that the Qur'an promotes equality. Therefore, a new exegetical understanding is needed. It requires an alternative *ijtihad* (engagement in interpretation of the text) that must include radically rethinking the text of the Qur'an.[25] In 2005, Wadud attracted further controversy when she led the Friday prayer for a mixed-gender congregation in the United States.

Following in Wadud's footsteps, a number of African American Muslim women have become involved in the study of the Qur'an. Caroline Rouse refers to their activities as "negotiating gender" through exegesis, allowing men and women to come to a mutual understanding and new Muslims to become familiar with the text and its emerging interpretations.[26] Rouse refers to the efforts by women to redefine the duties specified in the Qur'an as "engaged surrender"—not to their husbands, but to the text itself. The Qur'an gives women not only affirmation as women but also empowerment as African Americans.

Islamic scholar Asma Afsaruddin challenges the common but simplistic assumption that public space belongs to men while private space belongs to women. This division is "meaningless," she says and ignores "the specificities of gender, culture, class, race, ethnicity, and historical time."[27] She posits that the application of a public-private dichotomy to the Islamic world reflects the spirit of Orientalism.[28] She writes about women's traversal of public space and the process of negotiation of their gendered identities and "exploration of avenues that enable self-empowerment."[29] By this she means carving out space for women's discourse, which in some instances results from establishing solid connections between the private and the public spheres. Afsaruddin also addresses the "discourse of the veil," which from the Western feminist or modernist points of view has been deemed a symbol of "female subjugation." She argues that early, medieval, and modern Islamic histories show this assessment to be a simplistic and reductive understanding of religious matters. For some Muslim women, the contemporary adoption of the veil is a vital marker of empowerment and greater political activism.

In the post 9/11 period, some Muslim women scholars on American campuses have continued the pursuit of the gender jihad model, providing fresh interpretation of the Qur'an, the *hadith* (traditional authoritative texts about Muhammad and his companions), and *fiqh* (Islamic jurisprudence). Addressing the challenge set by Amina Wadud, Asma Barlas of Ithaca College (former member of the Zia al-Haqq's government in Pakistan) reiterates that recovering the scriptural basis of sexual equality in Islam is vital. She argues that a politics of sexual differentiation privileged males by transforming biological sex into politicized gender with which male interpreters analyzed the entire Qur'an. Acknowledging that the Scripture was revealed in the context of a traditional patriarchy, she sets out to discover whether the text itself supports patriarchal exegesis. She poses two sets of questions: whether the Qur'an is a patriarchal or misogynist text that supports sexual inequality or the oppression of women and whether the Qur'an permits and even encourages liberation for women. Recognizing that Muslims have read and continue to read the Qur'an in more than one way, she concludes that the answers to the two questions are, respectively, a resounding no and yes.[30] Barlas demonstrates a number of features about the Qur'an which she sees as crucial to understanding the text as not sexist. While the Qur'an addresses patriarchy, it does not condone it. The Qur'an does not represent God as male and does not present men as ontologically superior to women (God created humans from a single self). The Qur'an notes some distinctions between men and women but does not establish sexual and gender inequality. Male interpreters, says Barlas, have impeded Muslims from seeing the Qur'an as a basically anti-patriarchal text.

Persuaded that English translations of the Qur'an available in the United States perpetuate a patriarchal interpretation of the social structure of Muslim society, Laleh Bakhtiar has provided a new English translation of the text. She is especially concerned with the potentially troublesome passage Q 4:34, which seems to allow men to beat (*idrib*) those wives that are (contrarian) *nushuz*. Bakhtiar believes that by following an intertextual method of interpretation (*tafsir al-qur'an bi'l-quran*), one can see that the rights given to women by God in the Qur'an would preclude men having the right to beat women.[31] For Bakhtiar, to come to an understanding of this verse one must turn to the example of the Prophet of Islam, who never beat or struck his wives under any circumstances. She insists that "it is not a personal interpretation but one that calls for a return to the Sunnah."[32] According to Bakhtiar, "it is not the Quran that misrepresents things but the manner in which the commentators have understood this verse. This means that everyone has the right to come to a realization about what they know to be the truth no matter what their level of Quranic knowledge may be. All have a right to weigh in on the issue based on what they know to be Reality."[33]

Other scholars have focused less on the Qur'an itself and more on the content of Islamic law. Asifa Quraishi, professor of law at the University of Wisconsin Law School, is a founding member of both the National Association of Muslim Lawyers (NAML) and American Muslims Intent on Learning and Activism (AMILA). She has served as a member of the Muslim Women's League and has been a member of the board and then president of KARAMAH. Quraishi has been actively fighting against misinterpretations of the Qur'an and sharia that are used by religious leaders who, fixated on the idealized image of Muslims, ignore the needs of individuals and communities. She notes that while Qur'anic verses and *fiqh* rulings are supposed to be protecting women, in fact they are being skewed to work against them in extremely unjust ways. This skewing is especially true in countries like Nigeria and Pakistan, where issues of domestic violence, child custody, and lack of access to education, employment, and maternity are glossed over.[34]

THE IMPACT OF 9/11 AND THE GLOBAL WAR ON TERRORISM

As a response to the attacks of 9/11, the Global War on Terrorism, with its military offensives against Afghanistan and Iraq, was also promoted as a war to liberate the oppressed women of Islam. The consequences of American interventions, however, have been problematic. Prior to the initiation of the war, Iraq boasted the highest literacy rate among women in the Arab world, and women were integrated into the work force. The war and its aftermath have been a major setback for Iraqi women; yet the American administration of George W. Bush described the war as liberating the Iraqi women. "The women of Iraq . . . bring skills and knowledge that will be vital to restoring Iraq to its rightful place in the region and in the world. The U.S. will engage with Iraqi women to secure and advance the gains that they have achieved so far."[35] The same theme carried over into the Obama administration. Discussing possible troop withdrawal from Afghanistan, President Barak Obama lamented its effect on women, again assigning America the role of defender of women. "We don't believe it is in the interests of the United States or the world to create a safe haven for terrorists and stand by and watch women's rights be abused."[36]

The American administration also responded to the 9/11 attacks by launching a global project to create moderate Islam, a significant part of which focused on the empowerment of Muslim women. On December of 2002, President Bush launched the Middle East Partnership Initiative (MEPI) with the goal of "advancing freedom in the Arab world" and specifically focusing on the political, economic, educational, and health disparities of women in the region.[37] Since 2002, MEPI has invested "over $480 million in reformers' efforts to overcome these obstacles," giving the majority of its funding to nongovernmental organizations "with innovative ideas for accelerating progress in the region."[38] MEPI and its partners have established over 450 programs in sixteen Middle Eastern and North African countries and the Palestinian Territories.[39] MEPI is also aimed at raising awareness of women's rights and educating women on politics and the democratic process.

Within the United States, immediately after the attacks on New York and Washington, D.C., security measures placed the Muslim population and its institutions under virtual internment conditions. As Muslim men targeted by American security agencies became less visible on the American scene, women became the spokespeople for their religion, thus opening up new avenues of leadership and service. In the post-9/11 environment Muslim women in the West found themselves propelled into the limelight as the representatives of an Islam that by then was reviled and maligned.

Since 2002 some Muslim organizations in the United States, such as the Islamic Society of North America (ISNA) and the Islamic Circle of North America (ICNA), have also undergone changes that significantly affect women. They have become more open to including women in their public programming, providing women's input into deliberations as well as creating a space for their reflections. They have even begun to publish pictures of women on their websites and publications. Gender segregation during communal prayer in mosques is still standard. Yet in many mosques, some customs that had made the mosque an exclusively male area of life have been relaxed as more comfortable space is being cultivated. An increasing number of organizations have expanded the areas of women's activities and are including women in their executive committees.[40]

Some professional women have decided to don a *hijab* (headscarf) and to begin attending mosque functions. Study groups for women have been set up to reflect on Islam in the modern world, including how it can be presented to fellow Americans. Several Islamic organizations have issued guidelines to their constituents on how to engage women in their activities, such as the online booklet *Women Friendly Mosques and Community Centers Working Together to Reclaim Our Heritage.*[41] Prominent Muslim feminists who have emerged since 9/11 are diverse in their social analyses and their approaches to the Qur'an and to Islam.

Progressive Voices

Among the feminists who gained prominence after 9/11 are those who self-iden-
tified as "Progressive Muslims."[42] While proclaiming their allegiance to Islam
they have also insisted that they share American values and want to participate in
building a better American future. Some have been reluctant to call themselves
feminist because of the baggage associated with the term. They are confident
and comfortable operating in a public square, proudly defending their faith and
community through writing, reflecting, and publishing as authentic voices of
Muslim Americans. Sometimes they have felt caught among family traditions
that frown on their freedom, religious conservatives who have created models of
ideal Muslim womanhood into which they are expected to fit, and an American
culture that does not recognize them for who they are as rational human beings
who choose to be Muslim.

Islamic scholar and Professor Kecia Ali—a self-proclaimed "Progressive
Muslim"—attempted a critical study of the role of women as it appears in the
Qur'an and *fiqh* with special focus on sex and gender equality in marriage and
the rights of LGBT Muslims.[43] She notes a discrepancy between doctrine and
practice, especially since the American context is so different from the forma-
tive period of Islamic jurisprudence.[44] She writes that ideas of sex and gender in
the Qur'an and Islamic jurisprudence are fundamentally patriarchal and hierarchical. Injustice and oppression do not come from God; rather, people bring
it upon themselves. Consequently, humans are responsible for making moral
judgments.[45] Specifically, Ali argues that it is incumbent on Muslims who are
interested in gender equality to consider a restructuring of marriage. A new paradigm is necessary if Muslims want marriage to be egalitarian; this shift requires
identifying and, if necessary, redefining, licit sex in Islam.[46]

Ali believes that "Muslim feminists have become part of the [Muslim] intellectual tradition and, in doing so, have begun to push the boundaries and
reshape its contours."[47] It is important to be honest and recognize the challenges
presented by the Qur'an to those committed to gender and social justice. This
task involves avoiding "selective" presentations of the scriptural material and
confronting verses that do not necessarily sit comfortably with the sentiments of
a modern reader.[48] For Ali, the Islamic revelation set in motion a transformation
for a given historical time and place. To stay "relevant," Muslim understanding
must shift to confront modern time and space. In other words, Islam is meant
to be lived in history, and human beings have, for better or worse, taken on the
role of earthly vice-regents. That role cannot be fulfilled by merely carrying out
orders, but it must involve the exercise of initiative, judgment, and conscience.[49]

Azizah Y. al-Hibri has focused most of her efforts on legal reform, particularly on women's rights, domestic violence, and developing an equitable marriage contract. She has written and lectured on the Qur'an, carefully examining
Qur'anic verses relating to women and justice.[50] Al-Hibri uses the historical context of the Qur'an to defend women's rights. As noted earlier, she is the founder

of KARAMAH—Muslim Women Lawyers for Human Rights—through which she has trained hundreds of women to reexamine the reasons behind Islamic law. KARAMAH caters particularly to individuals who want to become community activists, illustrating the shift many Muslim feminists are making from a focus on the individual to community concerns.

Al-Hibri rejects "forcibly imposed" definitions of women's rights and calls for the establishment of an International Muslim Women's Human Rights Commission.[51] She proposes that a "Satanic logic" has undermined Qur'anic interpretation and has produced chauvinistic interpretations placing one creature (man) above another (woman). Noting that the domination of women by men is contradictory to the assurance of the Qur'an and that "domination is contrary to piety," she insists that the Qur'an is a text that eliminated hierarchy in human society. The Qur'an is internally consistent because it "repeatedly describes the relationship between husband and wife as one of tranquility, affection and mercy"; therefore, hierarchical, patriarchal, and oppressive interpretations are incorrect.[52]

Pietistic Voices

Other American Muslim women have found a comfort zone outside the arena of textual or historical analysis in varied expressions of pietistic spirituality or personal engagement with the divine. This approach liberates them from doing daily battle with a society that rejects and demonizes Islam in the public square. Such Muslims maintain their Islamic identity in a more quietistic and serene life. Women can engage with the divine on a level where all creatures are equal and where issues of gender equality are not given prominence of place.

One such author who has gained a following among Muslims on college campuses is Yasmin Mogahed. She has identified the problem of Western feminists as their focus on man as the standard, having "erased God from the scene." She notes that what "we often forget is that God has honored the woman by giving her value in relation to Himself—not in relation to man."[53] What Western feminists miss is "that God dignifies both men and women in their distinctiveness—not in their sameness."[54] Women will never be liberated, she says, until they stop trying to be like men and value their God-given distinctiveness. She criticizes Western women for becoming slaves to the demands of capitalist society: "Be thin. Be sexy. Be attractive. Or . . . be nothing."[55] She notes that some Western women are beginning to see the value of choosing to stay home and have children. "It took women in the West almost a century of experimentation to realize a privilege given to Muslim women 1400 years ago."[56]

A *Salafi* Response

Apart from such pietistic voices, so far we have looked primarily at Muslim feminist scholars who have struggled within the confines of the Qur'an and tradition to determine how the theme of equality for women can be developed. Pakistani Canadian author and speaker Farhat Hashmi complicates the definition of a Muslim feminist in the post 9/11 era. She preaches that "A wife should comply with her husband's wishes . . . he is her divinely appointed imam."[57] Hashmi is not a traditionally trained jurist but holds a PhD in Islamic Studies from Glasgow University in Scotland. Her work is mostly in Urdu. She has wide appeal among middle and upper middle class Pakistani women in diaspora and in Pakistan, where her lectures may be attended by as many as ten thousand women. Her tapes, CDs, and lectures are available on the Internet. Hashmi founded the Al-Huda International Institute in Pakistan with a teaching mission of instilling "pure Islamic morals and attitudes." Two branches of Al-Huda are operating in North America, in Houston and Toronto. Her students can graduate with a diploma after a year and are considered qualified to teach Islam and interpret the Qur'an. Hashmi resides in Toronto and has advocated for the implementation of the sharia in Canada.[58]

Hashmi appeals to those who seek unqualified answers that give comfort and assurance of divine sanction for their "choice." She empowers women from the educated and privileged class to cope with the humdrum of life, providing emotional strength cheerfully to accept their fate and arrive at a peaceful resolution of turmoil. Her focus is on individual transformation leading to equanimity and peace. Acceptance of one's fate may even include the husband marrying a second wife in the unstable circumstances of war. Hashmi also initiates women into the worldwide sisterhood of Islam, helping them learn to be patient as their societies and religion are being "assaulted." She preaches anticonsumerism and modesty and rails against American culture. Not surprisingly, Hashmi has many harsh critics. Her devotees are accused by detractors of indulging in Western culture, wearing Western dress, holding coffee klatches for women who are now "ready for Islam." Among the many epithets she has earned are "Fundo Chic" (posited as squarely opposite to what was in the 1970s called "radical chic"),[59] "Wahhabi," "Internet Evangelist," and the "Rich man's preacher."[60]

Native Informers

A few Muslim women have spoken what they call "the truth" about Islam to Western audiences who are eager to hear apparently "Muslim" denunciations that support Western prejudices. These women are deemed feminists by Westerners because they have divested themselves of the cultural trappings of Islam. The Islamophobia industry, backed by millions of dollars, has created venues for native informers to attack Islam, in the process becoming rich and sought-after celebrities. They are featured as experts with insider knowledge on talk shows and appear at churches and synagogues as "representatives" of Islam and Muslim women. They generally reinforce the stereotypes held by Westerners and call on Muslims to shed their chains to tradition.

Among the first and most prominent of the so-called native informers is Irshad Manji, a Canadian journalist who seeks recourse to secular ideas in her critique of Islam. She is the author of two books: *The Trouble with Islam Today*[61] and *Allah, Liberty and Love*.[62] She has received international recognition and has appeared on numerous television shows attacking Islamic teachings about women. She has also received several prizes and was named a "Young Global Leader" by the World Economic Forum and a "Feminist for the 21st Century" by *Ms.* Magazine.

Asra Nomani, to cite another example, is an Indian American Muslim journalist who worked for the *Wall Street Journal* and *Salon* Magazine. She has no formal Islamic education and admits to never having been a part of the Muslim community in her hometown until she became pregnant out of wedlock and began considering performing hajj.[63] The kidnapping and murder of her friend, the journalist Daniel Pearl, inspired her to write *Standing Alone in Mecca: An American Woman's Struggle for the Soul of Islam*.[64] She became an activist for "reclaiming women's rights and principles of tolerance in the Muslim world."[65] Nomani's lack of traditional knowledge often makes her seem like an outsider looking in at Islam.[66] Emphasizing her "Americanness," she demands to take part fully in her religion as an educated, independent, American Muslim woman. [67] In her effort to reclaim everything in Islam that honors and respects women, she wants to do away with patriarchal and backward ideas that have become a part of the tradition. She calls for a new paradigm that recognizes gender equality and an end to rigidity in religious practice.[68] Nomani has received more notoriety for her "Islamic Bill of Rights for Women in the Mosque" and "Islamic Bill of Rights for Women in the Bedroom." She does not back up any of her claims with reference to the Qur'an, hadith, or other Islamic sources. She is against anything that does not provide an appropriate space for women in Islam, including the rule against extramarital sex,[69] gender segregation in mosques,[70] and other issues such as non-Muslims not being allowed in Mecca, Saudi Arabia.[71]

Other women who have become darlings of the press and of the Islamophobia industry include Ayaan Hirsi Ali and Wafa Sultan. Western audiences celebrate them as "Muslim feminists" despite the fact that Hirsi Ali describes herself as an atheist and Wafa Sultan participated in 2009 in forming "Former Muslims United." Both were listed among the one hundred most influential people of the world by *Time* magazine: Ayaan Hirsi Ali in the April 18, 2005, issue, and Wafa Sultan in the February 24, 2006, issue. They had meteoric rises because they were adopted by anti-Muslim organizations that used their statements to promote anti-Muslim sentiments. Ali is a Somali-Dutch-American, author of *Infidel*[72] and *Nomad: From Islam to American—A Personal Journey through the Clash of Civilizations*.[73] She claimed that the Prophet Muhammad would be considered a pedophile in today's world. She has received numerous international prizes including "European of the Year." Wafa Sultan gained notoriety by taking on an Islamic leader from al-Azhar on international television, accusing the prophet Muhammad of being a false prophet and Islam of producing nothing valuable to world civilization. In her book *A God Who Hates: The Courageous Woman Who Inflamed the Muslim World Speaks Out against the Evils of Islam*,[74] she makes such inflammatory statements as: "America re-formed me, armed me with knowledge, clarified my vision, and helped me outline my plan to save those victims. I decided to bring 'Allah' to justice on criminal charges."[75]

The Millennial Generation

In addition to raising Islamophobic reactions in the United States, the attacks on the World Trade Center and the Pentagon engendered a level of support for Muslims on the part of some Americans. This perspective was most obvious in the concern for Muslim women. Some people, for example, offered to escort Muslim women to medical appointments and on grocery shopping trips. At the University of Michigan an event called "Hijab Days" was held as non-Muslim women donned a *hijab* for the day in solidarity with Muslim women. Similar solidarity events took place at several other universities, including the Universities of Chicago, Wisconsin, Texas, and New Mexico. Many Muslim women who never covered before began to wear the veil as a sign of allegiance to the faith. More than ever the *hijab* became a visible symbol of Islam, and young Muslim women tried to determine whether or not to wear Islamic dress and in what appropriate styles. Young American Muslim women continue to explore their identities and contribute to society and the public good in varied ways.

Islamic Dress

Islamic dress has become both the symbol of women's identification with their religion and the target of more Western derision. While the press tends to depict the veil as the symbol of oppression, many Muslim American women have adopted it as a symbol of confidence, a way to witness to their identification with a faith that they believe is revealed by God. Islamic dress has also become a means of communication. Through their dress Muslim women state proudly that despite what the general public thinks of their faith, they bear witness to an Islam that stands for equality, peace, and justice. For some it serves as an invitation to the observer to join in a conversation and learn how putting on a scarf or other form of Islamic dress can be liberating.

Nousheen Yousuf-Sadiq, an aspiring scholar in religion who seeks to "bridge the gap" between Muslim and non-Muslim Americans, reflects on her reasoning for wearing the headscarf: "In this size-obsessed world, I took quite a while to become comfortable with my own body. . . . The secret lay in my decision to wear *hijab*, the Islamic headscarf—a feminist strategy I used to become comfortable in my own skin and to master the delicate mix of my American and Muslim identities." Yousuf-Sadiq is quite critical of America's obsession with looks and appearances, particularly the pressure, "the frontal assault," created by fashion magazines. She reports that she was reluctant to wear the headscarf fearing the effect it would have on her future. While the initial period involved self-consciousness and discomfort, with time the headscarf became more comfortable and even empowering. "When following the Islamic dress code, I had control over who did and didn't look at me, who did and didn't touch me. I had a greater sense of authority over how people viewed me because for the first time, people were not seeing my outer appearance—they were seeing *me*."[76]

Along with increased wearing of Islamic dress has come the commodification of the Muslim wear industry. Nadia Rayan and Nora Ghaneian, for example, are sisters who founded a company called RAYAN focused on creating stylish clothing that fits within the parameters of Islam and conservative dress. Their work features bold colors, feminine details, and accessories in order to create a line that is "totally customizable" for women, no matter what their style. The sisters draw their inspiration from their community, considering what clothing their friends and others would wear. RAYAN now participates in the Fashion Fighting Famine runway show and donates a percentage of their profits to the needy.[77] This company represents a rapidly expanding Muslim dress industry aimed at both female and male customers.

Literature and Art

Muslim women are also gaining cultural prominence as writers, particularly novelists. Egyptian-born Samia Serageldin, who emigrated with her family to the United States in 1980, is perhaps best known for her novel *The Cairo House*, which traces three decades of political developments in Egypt including the assassination of President Sadat and the rise of Islamic feminism.[78] In a 2000 article for the *North Carolina Writers' Network Newsletter* she describes her life in a "happily hybrid culture" of Egyptian cuisine and French governesses, the repression of the Nasser regime, and her own move to the United States where she saw her sons playing soccer in North Carolina. "There was no room in this brave new world for my memories of jasmine and dust," she writes. "I locked away my photograph albums of Egypt in the attic and blended into my new environment like a perfect chameleon."[79] It was her effort to recover her lost voice, to reconcile her present with her past that engendered *The Cairo House*. She confesses that the only way she could overcome her natural reticence was to hide behind "the fig leaf of fiction." Serageldin has helped forward the cause of Arab and Muslim American women writers in numerous articles and contributions to anthologies.

In two autobiographical books, widely-read American Muslim writer Asma Gull Hasan describes for Americans the experience of growing up in a "liberal" Muslim family. She refers to herself as a "Muslim Feminist Cowgirl" who grew up in a Pakistani family in Colorado. In her first book, *American Muslims: The New Generation*,[80] she attempts to illustrate that one can be a believing Muslim without veiling, following strict regulations, or being a stay-at-home woman.

Hasan has published in a variety of newspapers and journals and made appearances on CNN, Fresh Air, Morning Edition, Fox News, and many other radio and TV programs. Her second book, *Why I Am a Muslim* (2004),[81] is partly a personal memoir and partly an effort to describe an Islam that is tolerant, diverse, and affirming of women's rights. Being Muslim, she insists, has allowed her to be a better American.

In *Muslim American Youth*, Selcuk R. Sirin and Michelle Fine provide autobiographical sketches of Muslim women and their adjustment to the post 9/11 atmosphere in the United States. One story captures the thoughts and feelings of a fourteen-year-old American Muslima: her aspirations, her enjoyment of studying, and her religious life. Although at times she does not always "follow the rules," she talks about her experience after her decision to wear the *hijab*. Some of her friends began to act awkwardly; she eventually lost friendships over this decision. When she tells her parents that she wants to study genetics at Stanford, her mother's reply is, "Aisha, just go to Brooklyn College . . . because you are going to get married anyway."[82] In another sketch Sirin and Fine present a young Palestinian American Muslima named Sahar who proudly boasts about having friends from a diverse array of cultural backgrounds. She is also proud to wear the *hijab* and very much enjoys answering inquisitive questions about her culture and her religion.[83]

Sirin and Fine also relate the story of a young Turkish woman who wears the *hijab* and describes herself as a "Caucasian/white/Euro-American." She reports that she often "gets into fights" when people make her uncomfortable and stare at her. Indeed, she takes pride in opportunities to educate others about Islam and says that she is not intimidated by others but lives a very active life. Her advice to young Muslim women who don the headscarf is "not to be scared of anybody, to show and to be proud."[84] Another interviewee, Sabreeha, describes a similar experience and the anger she felt at this "ignorance." People ask her where she comes from, and she is keen to say that she was born and raised in Long Island. She is frustrated with people who think that she is a foreigner just because she wears traditional Islamic styled clothing (*jilbabs* and *hijabs*).[85] For most of these women, wearing a scarf provides a teachable moment.

Exposing the various ways in which Americans have both ridiculed and criticized Muslim men and women, and in particular the veil, Hadia Mubarak wrote the following about her claim to Islamic identity and dress, called "Shockproof Rag":

> I've never walked ten steps behind a man. Nor have I hid behind a veil of
> oppression.
> I'm not ashamed of my body, nor the thick silky locks of hair concealed from
> your eyes.
>
> Rag head, camel jock, terrorist, I dodge stereotypes like missiles fired from F-16 jets
> That explode before my eyes, deafening my ears, shattering my dreams,
> creating of me an image that I cannot recognize.

Glimpses of Hollywood movies with veiled women scurrying like a bundled
   package
Of subordination, Arab men blowing up planes, headlines that scream terrorism,
Circumcised women venting on Oprah, is all they see in me.

Eyes glued to a piece of cloth on my head, they gawk and shake their heads.
Don't give me pity, I call this freedom of choice. Call modesty your enemy,
But it is my liberation from succumbing to conformity.

Mubarak's poem has been broadly featured in the media and on the Internet.[86]

Some organized efforts have begun to support and encourage contemporary Muslim writers in their work. For example, in January 2004, a group of Muslim women dedicated to presenting and promoting "positive Islamic fiction and nonfiction reading materials" formally established the Islamic Writers' Alliance to help new writers find publishers, to increase public awareness of works by Muslim women writers, and to promote creative fictional Islamic works for Muslim children.

Presence in the Public Service

Some women in the post 9/11 era have made their mark in national Muslim institutions by assuming leadership positions. Ingrid Mattson was the first woman elected president of the Islamic Society of North America (2006–2010), and Hadia Mubarak (author of the poem above) was the first woman elected National President of the Muslim Student Association (2004). Other women are choosing to participate in the public square in different ways. They are not confined against their will as the media tends to depict them; they are not hidden, not oppressed, and not silenced. They have assumed the role of Muslima, visible, vocal, and present, contributing to the Muslim community by witnessing to the faith and its mission of liberation while contributing to the American society of which they are an integral part.

While some immigrant parents initially shied away from involvement in American politics and did not begin to take part in elections until the 2000 presidential election, some of their children's generation are more comfortable working within the American political system. One public figure who has attracted some critical press because of her faith commitment is Huma Abedin, who has worked with Hillary Clinton, first in the White House and later as Deputy Chief of Staff for the Secretary of State. She was included in *Time* magazine's "40 under 40" (October 14, 2010). Another prominent Muslim woman, Dalia Mogahed, was a Senior Analyst and Executive Director of the Gallup Center for Muslim Studies. In April 2009, she was appointed by President Obama to the Advisory Council on Faith-Based and Neighborhood Partnerships.

Scores of other Muslim American women are engaged in the public sphere. A brief survey suggests the scope of their influence and service. At the time of this writing, Egyptian-American Rudy Gharib is the Deputy Director for Digital Communications for the U.S. Agency for International Development

(USAID).[87] Reema Dodin is Floor Director for the majority whip, Senator Richard Durbin.[88] Shirin Tahir Khel previously served as special assistant to the President and Senior Director for democracy, human rights, and international operations of the National Security Council.[89] Zeenat Rahman is currently serving as Special Adviser on Global Youth Issues to Secretary of State John Kerry and as the Director of the Office of Global Youth Issues.[90] She has created and managed more than a dozen international youth programs and often speaks about the importance of youth involvement in dialogue to create understanding and peace among diverse communities. Zayneb Shaikley serves as the Associate Counsel and Initiative Liaison for the William J. Clinton Foundation.[91] Other Muslim women advocate indigenizing Islam into American society. Human rights attorney Engy Abdelkader specializes in the defense of civil liberties for Muslims, both domestically and internationally.[92] Farhana Khera is currently the president and executive director of Muslim Advocates, a national legal agency that works to promote "freedom, justice and equality for all, regardless of faith."[93]

Raised in Tennessee by Egyptian parents who espoused a traditional view of the role of woman as mother and housewife, Hebab Ahmed considers herself a Muslim feminist. She recalls, "I confronted the contradictions in my upbringing, searching for my true identity and role as a Muslim woman." She even engaged in arguments with her father about his understanding of women's roles and admits that finding her identity was a great "struggle."[94] After 9/11 she decided not only to wear the *hijab* but also to don the *niqab*. She has founded two nonprofit organizations: Daughters of Eve, a youth club, and Muslim Women's Outreach, which engages in interfaith dialogue and educates non-Muslims about Women in Islam.

Yusra Tekbali, an American Muslima of Libyan descent, has worked as a staff assistant for the United States House of Representatives, volunteered with the Arab American Institute, served as an elected member of the American-Arab Anti-Discrimination Committee, and reported and blogged on issues related to Libya. In a piece she wrote titled "Hill Diaries," she says, "When I walk through the halls of the Capitol building, in the footsteps of white, Christian men, I'm reminded of the Declaration of Independence and the values America was founded on. I feel patriotic because I believe in those principles, in justice and equality for all."[95]

Journalism and Filmmaking

Muslim American women are also contributing in the fields of journalism, television, and film. Malika Bilal is the digital producer and cohost of *The Stream*, a social media community television show on Al-Jazeera English. She has also worked as an editor and writer for the channel, as well as writing for a Tribune Company newspaper and working for Voice of America. Another Al-Jazeera writer and producer, Laila al-Arian, has also reported for prestigious news outlets[96] and is the coauthor of *Collateral Damage: America's War against Iraqi Civilians.*[97] Fatemeh Fakhraie, an author and a blogger, has written on issues such as Islamic feminism, Islam, politics, and race. She is the founder and editor-in-chief of Muslimah Media Watch.[98]

Other Muslim women are starting to make their mark on the creation and production of films. Farah Nousheen, for example, is the winner of the National Association of Muslim Women's Best Film Producer of 2003 award for her film *Nazrah: A Muslim Woman's Perspective. Nazrah* (Arabic for "perspective") depicts a diverse group of Muslim women living in the Pacific Northwest who are engaged in an open dialogue about Islam, stereotypes, and current political events. The film conveys diverse views on the lives of Muslims at a time when Islam is in the international spotlight.

Another Muslim woman, Mara Brock Akil, is a Hollywood producer and writer known primarily for her TV series *Girlfriends* and *The Game*, which have been screened on UPN, the CW Network, and BET. She and her husband, director/producer Salim Akil, are among the most successful African American producers in Hollywood. They coproduced a very popular remake of the film *Sparkle.* In a male-dominated business, she quickly earned her place for her ability to represent women's viewpoints more accurately than her male counterparts. The screenplays she has written tackle sensitive topics, including the stereotypes of race, class, gender, and sexuality. So far, none of her characters has been Muslim, but she does not rule that possibility out.[99]

CONCLUSION

The long history of encounters between Islam and the West, reaching back to colonialism and the formation of the American Republic, continues to play an important part both in the ways in which Muslims are viewed and in the current processes of formulating Muslim self-identification. Western colonizers of Islamic territories, accompanied by contingents of Christian men and women on a mission to spread modernization and salvation through the gospel, justified their actions by proclaiming a mission of virtuous intent. Their goal was an extension of Western values, providing enlightenment to inferior and backward Islamic cultures. The conquest of Muslim territories, including the plundering of their resources, was justified as part of a "civilizing mission" to redeem the world. Colonizers focused particularly on what they depicted as the "miserable and pathetic status" of Muslim women, who were envisioned as segregated, ignorant, and swathed. Once liberated, the women were to become the cornerstone of the reenvisioned Muslim world rebuilt on Western ethical and cultural foundations. Muslim women in the West—whether religious or secular, immigrant or American born, African American or white or Latina convert, and regardless of color, nationality, ethnicity and religious or ideological commitment—have been generally seen as monolithic by Western government bureaucrats, orientalists, intellectuals, journalists, and propagandists, and also too often by Western feminists. This image is changing, however, as a new generation of Muslim women comes into its own. Many in this new generation who appropriate a Muslim American feminist identity endow it with a new meaning. They reject the anti-male bias of traditional Western feminism. Engaged and assertive, the new Muslim identity may appear an "in your face" feminism. Its members do not hesitate to cover their hair if they so choose; nor do they apologize for such a choice. Rejecting a constraining dogmatic adherence to traditionalism, they have developed a comfortable feminist lifestyle that is at once modern and Islamically validated. Islam is viewed as a dynamic and inherently flexible faith, valid for all times and summoning its believers to reinterpret its teachings for the historical moment and in the context in which they live. Muslim American feminists, believing that the Qur'an, unlike other scriptures, pioneered the liberation of women, deeply resent that many Western women appear to have declared a war on Islamic cultural values.

Contemporary Muslim feminist publications address both Muslims and non-Muslims not in apologetic tones, nor with reinterpretations to appease the enemies of Islam in the West. Rather they seek to recapture the essence of the revelation to the prophet Muhammad as implemented by the fathers and mothers of the faith under his guidance. Muslim feminists insist that the Qur'an is open to reinterpretation by each generation as it responds to the challenges of the time. Their interpretation proceeds from the understanding of the Qur'anic message as "a mercy to humanity" rather than a fixed text that constrains human development.

While Muslim feminist activists in each decade of the last half century have found new ways to channel their passion, their attempts to reinterpret the Qur'an, the teachings of the Prophet, and the law are aimed at promoting gender equality and justice. Their work has not necessarily gained acceptance among all the male leaders of Islamic umbrella organizations in the United States or the recognized authorities of the faith. Yet these feminists are popular among their peers and the younger generations who read their writings. Increasingly, a few leaders of the older generation of the mosque movement have noted their popularity and have invited them to address plenary sessions at national meetings and Muslim conventions in order to attract the youth.

Islamic feminist discourse has been carefully calibrated in the light of Western norms while being grounded in the Qur'an and the hadith. It is the product of a long, painful encounter with European colonialism, American hegemony, Judeo-Christian exceptionalism, and the projection into the international context of universal models of womanhood as developed by Western feminists. Muslim feminists point with pride at the achievements of Muslim women who have been heads of state, including Tansu Ciller in Turkey, Benazir Bhutto in Pakistan, Khalida Zia and Shaikh Hasina in Bangladesh, and Megawati Sukarnoputri in Indonesia. Recognizing and calling attention to the many examples of Western exploitation of women's bodies, they make clear that they believe women are better served by the gender justice provided in the Qur'an.

Notes

1. Lila Abu-Lughod, *Do Muslim Women Need Saving?* (Cambridge: Harvard University Press, 2013).
2. Helen Hatab Samhan, "Politics and Exclusion: The Arab American Experience," *Journal of Palestine Studies* 16, no. 2 (1987): 11–28.
3. Zeina Zaatari, "In the Belly of the Beast," in *Arab and Arab American Feminism: Gender, Violence, and Belonging*, ed. Rabab Abdulhadi, Evelyn Alsultany, and Nadine Naber (Syracuse, NY: Syracuse University Press, 2011), 72.
4. Haifaa A. Jawad, *The Rights of Women in Islam: An Authentic Approach* (London: The Macmillan Press, Ltd., 1998), 7–9.
5. The prophet Muhammad is reported to have taught: "When one of you copulates with his wife, let him not rush away from her, having attained his own climax, until she is satisfied." Ibid., 10.
6. Ibid., 14.
7. Ibid., 4.
8. Robert J. Allison, *The Crescent Obscured: The United States and the Muslim World 1776–1815* (New York: Oxford University Press, 1995). For critical overviews of Western depictions of women under Islam, see Linda Steet, *Veils and Daggers: A Century of National Geographic's Representation of the Arab World* (Philadelphia: Temple University Press, 1998); Mohja Kahf, *Western Representations of the Muslim Woman: From Termagant to Odalisque* (Austin: University of Texas Press, 1999); Rana Kabbani, *Imperial Fictions—Europe's Myths of the Orient* (Bloomington: Indiana University Press, 1994); and Lamia Ben Youssef Zayzafoon, *The Production of the Muslim Woman: Negotiating Text, History, and Ideology* (Lanham: Lexington Books, 2005).
9. Fuad Sha'ban, *Islam and Arabs in Early American Thought: The Roots of Orientalism in America* (Durham, NC: The Acorn Press, 1991), 195.
10. Annie Van Sommer and Samuel Marinus Zwemer, *Our Moslem Sisters: A Cry of Need from the Lands of Darkness Interpreted by Those Who Heard It* (New York: Fleming H. Revell Co., 1907), 15. See also Mary Taylor Huber and Nancy C. Lutkehaus, eds., *Gendered Missions* (Ann Arbor: University of Michigan Press, 1999); Samuel Zwemer and Mrs. Samuel Zwemer, *Moslem Women* (The Central Committee on the United Study of Foreign Missions, 1926; repr. Piscataway, NJ: Gorgias Press, 2009).
11. Leila Ahmed, *Women and Gender in Islam: Historical Roots of a Modern Debate* (New Haven: Yale University Press, 1993).
12. Amira El-Azhary Sonbol, *Beyond the Exotic: Women's Histories in Islamic Societies* (Syracuse, NY: Syracuse University Press, 2005); Sonbol, "Rethinking Women and Islam," in *Daughters of Abraham: Feminist Thought in Judaism, Christianity, and Islam*, ed. Yvonne Yazbeck Haddad and John L. Esposito (Gainesville: The University Press of Florida, 2002), 108–46.
13. Mahnaz Afkhami, "Claiming Our Rights: A Manual for Women's Human Rights Education in Muslim Societies," in *Muslim Women and the Politics of Participation: Implementing the Beijing Platform*, ed. Mahnaz Afkhami and Erika Friedl (Syracuse, NY: Syracuse University Press, 1997), 109–20; Afkhami, "Gender Apartheid and the Discourse of Relativity of Rights in Muslim Societies," in *Religious Fundamentalisms and the Human Rights of Women*, ed. Courtney W. Howland (New York: St. Martin's Press, 1999), 67–77; Afkhami, "Promoting

Women's Rights in the Muslim World," *Journal of Democracy* 8, no. 1 (1997): 157–67; Afkhami, *Women in Exile* (Charlottesville: University Press of Virginia, 1994); Afkhami, ed., *Faith and Freedom: Women's Human Rights in the Muslim World* (London: Tauris, 1995).

14. See, for example, the extensive writings of Shahla Haeri, Afsaneh Najmabadi, Guity Nashat, Nayereh Tohidi, Haideh Moghissi, and Nesta Ramazani.

15. Shahnaz Khan, *Muslim Women: Crafting a North American Identity in Diaspora* (Gainesville: University of Florida Press, 2000).

16. Fatima Mernissi, *Women and Islam*, trans. M. J. Lakeland (Oxford: Basil Blackwell Ltd., 1991).

17. Described at the UN Women website, "Beijing and Its Follow-up," http://www.un.org/womenwatch/daw/beijing/.

18. Sisters in Islam website, sistersinislam.org.my.

19. BAOBAB women website, baobabwomen.org.

20. Women Living Under Muslim Laws website, wluml.org.

21. Junta Islámica website, juntaislamica.org/presentacion/.

22. New women's organizations providing services have come to the fore including American Muslim Women's Association (amwaaz.org); The Sisters' Wing of the Islamic Circle of North America (ICNA), founded 1978 (icna.org/icna-sisters-wing); International League of Muslim Women, 1984 (tilmwinc.org); Muslim Women United (Richmond, Virginia), 1989 (muslimwomenunited.org/); Muslim Women's League, 1992 (mwlusa.org); Women in Islam, 1992 (womeninislam.org); Rahima Foundation, 1993 (rahima.org); Karamah: Muslim Women Lawyers for Human Rights, 1993 (karamah.org); Peaceful Families Project, 2000 (peacefulfamilies.org); Muslim Women Resource Center (Illinois), 2001 (mwrcnfp.org); Muslim Advocates, 2005 (muslimadvocates.org); Women's Islamic Initiative in Spirituality and Equality (WISE), 2006 (wisemuslimwomen.org).

23. Hibba Abugideiri, "Hagar: A Historical Model for 'Gender Jihad,'" in *Daughters of Abraham*, 81–107.

24. Riffat Hassan, "The Issue of Woman-Man Equality in the Islamic Tradition," in *Women's and Men's Liberation: Testimonies of Spirit*, ed. Leonard Grob, Riffat Hassan, and Haim Gordin (New York: Greenwood Press, 1991), 68–82. See also Hassan's "On Human Rights and the Qur'anic Perspective," in *Human Rights in Religious Traditions*, ed. Arlene Swidler (New York: Pilgrim Press, 1982); Hassan, "Muslim Feminist Hermeneutics," in *In Our Own Voices*, ed. Rosemary Skinner Keller and Rosemary Radford Reuther (San Francisco: Harper, 1995), 455–59; Hassan, "Human Rights in the Qur'anic Perspective," in *Windows of Faith: Muslim Women Scholar-Activists in North America,* ed. Gisela Webb (Syracuse, NY: Syracuse University Press, 2000), 241–48; Hassan, "Islamic Hagar and Her Family," in *Hagar, Sarah, and Their Children: Jewish, Christian, and Muslim Perspectives*, ed. Phyllis Trible and Letty M. Russell (Louisville, KY: Westminster John Knox Press, 2006), 149–67. See also Nimat Hafez Barazangi, *Woman's Identity and the Qur'an: A New Reading* (Gainesville: University Press of Florida, 2004).

25. Amina Wadud, *Qur'an and Woman: Reading the Sacred Text from a Woman's Perspective*, 2nd ed. (New York: Oxford University Press, 1999).

26. Caroline M. Rouse, *Engaged Surrender: African American Women and Islam* (Berkeley: University of California Press, 2004).

27. Asma Afsaruddin, "The Hermeneutics of Gendered Space and Discourse," in *Hermeneutics and Honor*, ed. Asma Afsaruddin (Cambridge, MA: Harvard University Press, 1999), 1–28; 1.

28. Ibid., 3.

29. Ibid., 5–6; 7–9.
30. Asma Barlas, *"Believing Women" in Islam: Understanding Patriarchal Interpretations of the Qur'an* (Austin: University of Texas Press, 2002); Barlas, "The Qur'an and Hermeneutics: Reading the Qur'an's Opposition to Patriarchy," *Journal of Qur'anic Studies*, 2 (2001): 15–38; Barlas, "Women's Readings of the Qur'an," in *The Cambridge Companion to the Qur'an*, ed. Jane McAuliffe (Cambridge: Cambridge University Press, 2006), 255–72.
31. Laleh Bakhtiar, "Introduction," in *The Sublime Quran* (Chicago: Kazi Publications, 2009), xxii.
32. Ibid., xxiv.
33. Ibid.
34. Asifa Quraishi, "Her Honor: An Islamic Critique of the Rape Laws of Pakistan from a Woman-Sensitive Perspective," *Michigan Journal of International Law* 18 (1997).
35. Coalition Provisional Authority and Iraqi Governing Council, the November 15 Agreement: Timeline to a Sovereign, Democratic and Secure Iraq, available online at: http://iraqcoalition.org/government/AgreementNov15.pdf.
36. Amanda Terkel, "George W. Bush Warns against Withdrawal from Afghanistan: 'Women Would Suffer,'" *The Huffington Post*, Apr. 1, 2011, http://www.huffingtonpost.com/2011/04/01/bush-withdrawal-afghanistan-women-suffer_n_843537.html.
37. "U.S. Commitment to Women in the Middle East," Office of the Senior Coordinator for International Women's Issues, Sept. 6, 2005. Available at U.S. Department of State Archives, http://2001-2009.state.gov/g/wi/rls/52487.htm. Accessed Nov. 13, 2013.
38. The U.S. Middle East Partnership Initiatives, U.S. Department of State, mepi.state.gov. http://2001-2009.state.gov/documents/organization/109470.pdf.
39. U.S. Middle East Partnership Initiatives, http://2001-2009.state.gov/documents/organization/109470.pdf.
40. Sarah Sayeed, "The American Mosque 2011: Women and the American Mosque," available at http://www.hartfordinstitute.org/The-American-Mosque-Report-3.pdf .
41. *Women Friendly Mosques and Community Centers: Working Together to Reclaim our Heritage*, http://www.islamawareness.net/Mosque/WomenAndMosquesBooklet.pdf.
42. Omid Safi, *Progressive Muslims: On Justice, Gender, and Pluralism* (Oxford, UK: One World, 2003).
43. Kecia Ali, *Sexual Ethics and Islam: Feminist Reflections on Qur'an, Hadith and Jurisprudence* (London: Oneworld, 2006), 13–21, 95.
44. Ibid., xix, xxii, 37–38.
45. Ibid., 149–50.
46. Ibid., 95, 151–52.
47. Ibid., 153.
48. Ibid., 153–54.
49. Ibid., 156–57.
50. Azizah Y. al-Hibri, "An Introduction to Muslim Women's Rights," in *Windows of Faith: Muslim Women Scholar-Activists in North America*, ed. Gisela Webb (Syracuse, NY: Syracuse University Press, 2000), 12–16.
51. Ibid., 53–55, 71.
52. Ibid., 11–12.
53. Yasmin Mogahed, *Reclaim Your Heart: Personal Insights on Breaking Free from Life's Shackles* (San Clemente, CA: FB Publishing, 2012), 120.

54. Ibid., 121.
55. Ibid., 122.
56. Ibid., 128.
57. "Farhat Hashmi Operating in Canada," *Daily Times,* May 6, 2005, http://archives .dailytimes.com.pk/national/06-May-2005/farhat-hashmi-operating-in-canada.
58. "Editorial: 'Pakistani Factor' in Canadian Terrorism," *Daily Times,* June 5, 2006, http://archives.dailytimes.com.pk/editorial/05-Jun-2006/editorial-pakistani -factor-in-canada-terrorism.
59. Nadeem F. Paracha, "The Fundo Chic? The joke's on us!" On *Orkut* social net-working site, January 6, 2007.
60. "Editorial: 'Pakistani Factor' in Canadian Terrorism," *Daily Times,* June 5, 2006.
61. Irshad Manji, *The Trouble with Islam Today: A Muslim's Call to Reform in Her Faith* (New York: St. Martin's Press, 2005).
62. Irshad Manji, *Allah, Liberty and Love: The Courage to Reconcile Faith and Free-dom* (New York: Free Press, 2011).
63. Asra Q. Nomani, *Standing Alone: An American Woman's Struggle for the Soul of Islam* (San Francisco: HarperCollins, 2006), 22, 36, 195.
64. Ibid., 48.
65. "Biography: Asra Nomani," at asranomani.com.
66. Nomani, *Standing Alone,* 35, 40, 59.
67. Ibid., 20, 53, 196.
68. Ibid., 196, 293, 295.
69. Ibid., 10–11, 20.
70. Ibid., 197–213.
71. Ibid., 48.
72. Ayyan Hirsi Ali, *Infidel: My Life* (New York: Free Press, 2007).
73. Ayaan Hirsi Ali, *Nomad: From Islam to American—A Personal Journey through the Clash of Civilizations* (New York: Free Press, 2010).
74. Wafa Sultan, *A God who Hates: The Courageous Woman who Inflamed the Muslim World Speaks Out against the Evils of Islam* (New York: St. Martin's Press, 2009).
75. Ibid., 109.
76. Nousheen Yousuf-Sadiq, "Half and Half," in *I Speak for Myself: American Women on Being Muslim,* ed. Maria M. Ebrahimji and Zahra T. Zuratwala (White Cloud Press, 2011), 18–21.
77. Designer Spotlight: RAYAN, Fashion Fighting Famine website, http://www .fashionfightingfamine.com/2/post/2013/01/designer-spotlight-rayan.html.
78. Samia Serageldin, *The Cairo House* (Syracuse: Syracuse University Press, 2003).
79. Samia Serageldin, "Live in Interesting Times," *NC Writers' Network Newsletter,* Sept./Oct. 2000.
80. Asma Gull Hasan, *American Muslims: The New Generation* (New York: Con-tinuum International Publishing Group, 2001).
81. Asma Gull Hasan, *Why I Am a Muslim* (Element Books Ltd., 2004).
82. Selcuk R. Sirin and Michelle Fine, *Muslim American Youth: Understanding Hyphenated Identities through Multiple Methods* (New York: New York Univer-sity Press, 2008), 26–28.
83. Ibid., 54–57.
84. Ibid., 81–3.
85. Ibid., 161–62.
86. Hadia Mubarak, "Shockproof Rag," reproduced by permission of the author; performed at http://www.youtube.com/watch?v=xCjOZcByspA. See also "Muslimah Speaks" website, http://muslimahspeaks.com/poetry/shockproof -rag-hadia-mubarak-spoken-word-poetry/.

87. Gharib has also worked as Advisor and in the U.S. Department of State as both a Digital Media Specialist and the Senior Public Diplomacy Officer. Her work focuses on social engagement, development in the Middle East, and creating understanding between Americans and Muslims, http://blog.usaid.gov/author/ rudy-gharib/; http://calstate.fullerton.edu/news/2005/214_gharib.html.
88. Dodin previously served as Floor Counsel as well as Research Director in the Office of the Assistant Majority leader. A professional profile is available at linkedin .com.
89. Khel was the senior advisor and chief interlocutor on U.N. reform to Condoleezza Rice and served as special assistant to the President and Senior Director for Democracy, human rights, and international operations of the National Security Council.
90. Rahman has previously worked for USAID as the Deputy Director for Faith Based and Neighborhood Initiatives and as Director of Policy for the Interfaith Youth Core, in which she worked closely with the White House and federal agencies to "advance programs related to youth, religious identity, interreligious engagement and interfaith service." A professional profile is available at linkedin .com and at http://www.state.gov/r/pa/ei/biog/194928.htm.
91. Shaikley has previously worked as an Orfalea Fellow in the Legal and Domestic Policy Departments with the same foundation and has experience in legal research, writing, and mediation as well as corporate and employment law. A professional profile is available at linkedin.com.
92. Abdelkader is a Legal Fellow with the Institute for Social Policy and Understanding (ISPU) and is frequently featured in the *Huffington Post* where she "explores the intersection of law, religion, race, gender and politics" and provides commentary on global and domestic issues faced by Muslims around the world. A professional profile is available at http://karamah.org/authors/engy-abdelkader.
93. Khera has served as counsel to the U.S. Senate Judiciary Committee, Subcommittee on the Constitution, and worked as an advisor for Senator Russell D. Feingold, Chairman of the Constitution Subcommittee, on difficult civil rights and liberties issues that arose as a result of the government's antiterrorism policies after September 11, 2001. She is the recipient of many honors and awards for her work in American Muslim's civil rights, the racial and religious profiling of American Muslims, American Muslim charities, and national security as they affect American Muslims. See profile at http://www.huffingtonpost.com/ farhana-khera.
94. Hebab Ahmed, "The Muslim Feminist," in *I Speak for Myself,* 32–33.
95. Yusra Tekbali, "Hill Diaries," in *I Speak for Myself,* 1–6.
96. Including *The Nation,* Alternet, *The Independent, The Guardian, The Australian,* United Press International, and the *Washington Report on Middle East Affairs.*
97. See professional profile for Al-Arian at http://www.huffingtonpost.com/ laila-alarian/.
98. Fatemeh Fakhraie, "Roots," in *I Speak for Myself,* 13.
99. Neda Ulaby, "Mara Brock Akil on Playing 'The Game' in Hollywood," Jan. 10, 2012, npr.org, http://www.npr.org/2012/01/10/144949335/tv-producer -profile; Kim Masters, "Hollywood's Undercover Hit Makers: Salim and Mara Brock Akil," *Hollywood Reporter,* August 9, 2012. http://www.hollywoodreporter .com/news/sparkle-whitney-houston-salim-mara-brock-akil-359947. A professional profile for Akil is also available at http://www.imdb.com/name/ nm0015327/bio.

Chapter 10

Sarah and Hagar

A Feminist European Perspective on Actual Controversies

ULRIKE BECHMANN

During my study of theology in the eighties, I came across the name of Phyllis Trible. Feminist theology was new, and we were taking up exciting studies on women in the Bible and theology. As an Old Testament scholar, I was especially interested in the Bible and women's issues, as I am today. We organized groups to read feminist studies, and the German versions[1] of Phyllis Trible's *Texts of Terror* and *God and the Rhetoric of Sexuality* were among them. These texts were not part of the curricula at that time. So it was an exciting journey on new roads, opening up the possibilities of my own feminist studies. Feminist theology has extended since then in all subjects of theology, but especially in biblical studies.

Sarah and Hagar provided the theme for the Phyllis Trible lectures in 2004, with a volume based on the series published in 2006.[2] I will not repeat the exegesis provided in that book, but I will rely on it as I take up this topic again with a new and extended focus. After a short look at the main points of feminist exegesis on Abraham, Sarah, and Hagar, I will consider the symbolic meaning of Sarah and Hagar in the European religious context and the dangerous reception of the *difference* between these women when it comes to anti-Semitism, to Islamophobia, and to the reception of the Israeli-Palestinian conflict. Then I will ask, What do we do with a text that is considered to be holy *and* is a text of terror? What kind of critical biblical hermeneutic is required? Last but not least I introduce two different approaches to interreligious dialogue in Europe: the institutional male-dominated dialogue related to Abraham with a biblical hermeneutic of acceptance; and the feminist dialogue related to Sarah and Hagar with a biblical hermeneutic of protest.

SARAH AND HAGAR—STORIES OF TERROR AND STORIES OF LIBERATION

After centuries with only the patriarchs Abraham, Isaac, Ishmael, Esau, and Jacob as the focus of theological interest, feminist scholars put the matriarchs and their theological relevance in the center of study. Today we have an extensive body of feminist research on the stories about Sarah and Hagar, their sons Isaac and Ishmael, as well as the other women of Abraham's extended family. The new perspectives on the Sarah-Hagar stories reveal that these texts are both texts of terror and texts of liberation.[3]

The terror: Both Sarah and Hagar are depicted as mothers with special concerns that many women even today have in life. Sarah, Abraham's wife (Gen. 11:27), was endangered twice by Abraham (Gen. 12:10–20; 20). Her barrenness put her on the margin of the family, and she had to fight for a son by any means. Hagar, the Egyptian, lived as a slave woman and was forced to provide the son for Sarah. But when she had conceived, Sarah afflicted her so that she decided to flee, away from Sarah's face and out of Sarah's eyes (Gen. 16). The words used for "afflict" (*anah*) and for "flee" (*barach*) are used later in the story of the exodus of Israel. Also the names for Hagar's way to Egypt (Shur, Kadesh, Barnea) indicate that she uses the same route that Israel will take later. Hagar is the first person to practice an exodus: away from the slave house of Abraham and Sarah to Egypt as Israel later left the slave house of Egypt.[4] Being sent back to Sarah by the angel of God, Hagar was cast out with her son a second time. She finds herself in the desert with only a little bit of water and bread and is near death (Gen. 21).

Abraham's wives live in a patriarchal system. Both are victims of this system; both are endangered twice and judged to have value only if they have born a son. But within this system they live in rivalry. Sarah uses her dominating status to oppress Hagar. She seeks to gain from this system. She uses Hagar, who as a surrogate mother has no control over her body, and finally casts Hagar and Ishmael out of her house.

The liberating side: Both women play a different but central role for narrated biblical history as well as for theology. Their actions and fates are the driving force to bring the stories forward.[5] Both women's needs and cries are heard by God.

The fate of Hagar, the probably black slave from Egypt, has been taken up by African American womanist theologians such as Delores Williams[6] and Renita Weems[7] and also by African women theologians.[8] They relate her story to the fate of black women and others who have experienced slavery, with no rights of their own. Hagar's encounter is exceptional in the Bible. She is the first and only woman to reveal and name God out of her own experience. Fleeing abuse from Sarah, Hagar sees God as God has seen her. "Have I really seen God and remained alive after seeing him?" (Gen. 16:13 NRSV). Hagar is the only person in the Bible who uses this name, "El-Roi." Her experience of a God "who looked after her" was preserved in the name of the well Beer-lahai-roi. Hagar is found by an angel at the well, sent back, but showered with promises for a better future for her progeny (Gen. 16). Cast out after the birth of Isaac, she is again blessed and saved by God. Hagar is even paralleled to Abraham.[9] The sons of both are blessed to be a great nation. Indeed, both Hagar and Sarah receive a revelation from God and, through their sons, a future to build up their house (Gen. 16:2; 21:13).

Without exploring the depths of these women's individual characters, one may consider *their relationship*. Sarah and Hagar have been viewed as models of struggle and rivalry between women. But their conflicts arise through a patriarchal background. In the Old Testament the women never talk directly to each other and, after Hagar's expulsion, they never meet again. The text separates them forever. Hagar with her offspring through Ishmael belongs to Egypt and the Arabian South (Gen. 25:12–18), Sarah with her offspring through Isaac to Judah and Hebron, where she is buried (Gen. 23). This dichotomy has influenced the reception of the Sarah and Hagar stories, especially in Paul's enraged identification of Hagar with law and slavery and Sarah with freedom and liberty (Gal 4:21–31).[10] As the conflict of the women extends to their sons Isaac and Ishmael, the antagonism and stereotype of conflict lasts to this day.

SARAH AND HAGAR: FEMINIST PERSPECTIVES ON ACTUAL EUROPEAN CONTROVERSIES TOWARDS JUDAISM AND ISLAM

Sarah: Ambivalent Symbol of Judaism in the European Context from Anti-Semitism to Christian-Jewish Dialogue

Despite certain theological traditions that "integrated" Sarah into Christian history as the mother of the church,[11] Sarah is known as the mother of Isaac (and grandmother of Jacob/Israel) and therefore stands for Judaism. In Europe, Judaism was not only the former but "the other" religion, and as such was rejected. Any relation was thought of as difference and—less neutrally—conflict. For many centuries Christians used this difference not only to oppress Jewish people but to persecute and cast them out of their homes, villages, and towns. The fate of the Jewish people in Europe is only too well known as a history of persecution despite times of living together.[12] During the twentieth century growing European anti-Semitism culminated in the Shoah through the Nazi regime. And it was not coincidental that in 1938 the Nazis forced Jewish women by law to attach the name Sarah as second name to their given first name.[13] Men had to add the name "Israel." This law was one of many to put Jews at the margin of the society and one of many steps toward the goal of expelling or killing all European Jews.[14]

Longstanding theological anti-Jewish traditions[15] had nourished the ideas of anti-Semitism. Parts of the churches deepened the cut between Christianity and Judaism through an explicit new anti-Jewish theology.[16] After the Second World War many people were shocked and ashamed about these traditions. Bilateral Christian-Jewish dialogue began. It was the Americans in Germany who started to look for persons in society as well as in the churches who were not involved in the Shoah or who had been actively working to save Jewish people. They installed the first Christian-Jewish societies ("Gesellschaften für christlich-jüdische Zusammenarbeit") similar to such societies in other countries.[17] The Protestant Church of Germany formulated the "Stuttgarter Schuldbekenntnis."[18] Later the churches also began to rework and reflect upon their part in the catastrophe of the Shoah. They tried to redefine theological traditions: reframing Pauline theology, relying more on Romans 9–11 instead of Galatians 3–4; reconstructing the historical background of Jesus and his followers as a Jewish movement within a pluralistic Judaism; and reclaiming the Old Testament as a normative basis for Christian theology. Last but not least, a "theology after Auschwitz" (Johann Baptist Metz[19]) asked what could be said of God in the face of Auschwitz. Dialogue between Christian and Jewish women also challenged Western European feminist theology concerning its anti-Jewish tradition and brought changes even within European feminist theology.[20]

For years more and more Jewish people have been returning to Europe, including to Germany. Synagogues have been rebuilt. In Potsdam, near Berlin, the Abraham Geiger College was established in 1999 to qualify rabbis.[21] The first female rabbi, Alina Treiger, was ordained in Germany in 2010, and the second, Anja Deusel, was ordained in 2011 at the synagogue in Bamberg. Nevertheless, antagonist attitudes have not vanished completely. Many synagogues and Jewish museums are in need of security measures. The danger is not daily, but right-wing and even Nazi-affiliated groups are a reality that should not be underestimated.

Hagar: Ambivalent Symbol of Islam in the European Context of Islamophobia

Hagar and her son Ishmael are understood to be the ancestors of Arab people. Today they are symbols of Islam. They are connected through the hadith[22] to the hajj, the pilgrimage to Mecca, and Hagar's grave is venerated in Mecca. For more than twenty years there has been dispute over the public representation of Islam.[23]

Problems of Islamophobia in Europe are growing but differ depending on context. No one "European" Islam exists. Each European country has a very different history of how Muslims came to live there and from what part of the world they have come.[24] Their culture, their religious or secular attitude, and their enculturation differ very much. The colonial history of some European countries plays an important role for immigration. In Great Britain the majority of Muslims came from Pakistan, in the Netherlands from Indonesia or Surinam, and in France from North Africa.[25] Muslims from Bosnia fled to Austria in the nineties during the war in former Yugoslavia; the Bosnians have been part of the Austrian monarchy since the end of the nineteenth century.[26]

Another source for the Muslim presence in Europe is the active policy of inviting migrant workers to come. Germany asked Turkish people to come for jobs during the 1960s and 1970s. They were called "Gastarbeiter" ("guest-workers") who were expected to leave after some time.[27] And this arrangement is what the workers themselves anticipated. They wanted to earn good money and enough to take it home. But instead, many of these people stayed, and they brought their families. During the first years all of them were perceived as Turks, Yugoslavians, Pakistanis, Iranians, Indonesians—but not as Muslims. Needless to say, not all migrants were Muslims. Differences of culture and traditions were evident, and groups were not labeled all together by only one characteristic. Religion did not serve as the key identifier. But slowly the perception changed, a change that has roots in the breakdown of the "Ostblock" and East-West conflict in 1989. Soon a new conflict was prophesied, the "clash of civilizations,"[28] taking "the West" and "Islam," each viewed as a single and homogeneous culture, as not being able to live together in peace. Further political developments (too numerous and complex to explore here) combined with reactions to the terror of 9/11. As a result, "Muslim" became the main and at times the only identity marker of people who are in fact quite diverse in terms of culture, tradition, and religion. Now, too often, all "Muslims" are perceived to be a unity. Any cultural, regional, or other form of diversity is ignored and negated. This perception creates problems when, for example, political representatives require one single institution to represent and speak for the Muslim population.

Today about twenty million Muslims live in Europe, and 4.7 percent of the population are Muslims with immigrant backgrounds. Many more belong to the second or third generation born in Europe; they are French, Swiss, Austrian, German, or British. This Muslim presence challenges the debate about European identity, which is in full swing. The main question in the center of all these debates becomes: Is European identity multicultural and multireligious, or is European identity solely or predominantly Christian? Despite the long history of a hostile relation to Judaism, Jewish-Christian European roots and values are conjured up as a common heritage contradictory to Islam. The discussion implies that Islam has different values and even a different ethic from Europe and that there is no such thing as a European Islam.[29]

Muslim Women as a Target from Right-Wing Groups and Secular Feminism

For years now the question of European identity has been bound to public Muslim representation in Europe. Muslims are considered to be "the Other," much as Jews were depicted as "the Other" in former times. Certain symbols of Islam are tackled as being "foreign" and therefore not allowed or not well accepted in Europe. One symbol is the mosque, especially the minaret. In Switzerland the majority decided in a plebiscite that no minarets are allowed—a country that has only four minarets on mosques![30] Another symbol connects exclusively with women: the symbol of women's clothing, especially the headscarf in all variations. Of course a majority of Muslim women in Europe are secular and live according to Western standards, including clothing. They are not visible as *Muslim* women. What sometimes causes tensions, however, is the headscarf.[31] The *visibility of this Muslim female symbol* has provoked a new anti-Muslim attitude, often together with misogyny. Muslim women wearing traditional clothes are looked at not only as oppressed and male-dominated persons but also as foreign, not integrated, not belonging to this part of Europe. Sometimes they face open hostility in the streets. These Muslim women are under a double stigma: as Muslims and as women. Unfortunately, right-wing groups use these perceptions not to liberate women but to foster Islamophobia.[32] That there is no one "Islam" but thousands of contextual variations is a differentiation these groups are not willing to recognize.[33]

But there is also an antagonistic view from parts of the secular feminist movement. For example, the editor of the first German secular feminist magazine, titled *Emma*, is Alice Schwarzer. She has fought for women's rights for three decades. Schwarzer is now one of the main antagonists toward Islam, especially against Muslim women who are wearing traditional clothes.[34] She holds that Islam (if not any religion) oppresses women, forces them into unwanted marriages, and even allows killing young independent women in the name of family honor. Muslim women who contradict these assumptions, who are proud of a liberating understanding of Islam, are attacked. Schwarzer is supported by some Muslim women who have written books about their fates of being married, beaten, or threatened.[35] These attitudes of violence toward women do exist—no doubt about that. Even in Germany there have been cases of the murder of young women who seemed to violate the honor of the family because of their relation to men. Violence against women exists all over the world. But is its cause Islam? Or is it culture? Or is it patriarchy? All three elements are intertwined and cannot be separated easily. Patriarchy is an underlying structure beyond any one single religion or culture. Women who accept certain rules in clothing and a certain family-bound role in society are also found in other religious groups, for example, in ultra-orthodox Jewish groups. And more could be named.

No doubt, pressure on Muslim women has to be fought against, and Muslim women who need protection must receive it. What is problematic in these campaigns is the lack of differentiation of Islamic contexts. For Muslim women in Europe there seems to be only one way to live, and those who want to take their freedom to wear a headscarf are dismissed. Secular women do not accept the decision of other women to live and to dress their way, not out of pressure but out of a free and self-defined interpretation of what their religion requires from them and what they are willing to do. Muslim women have various reasons to choose traditional clothing. Elderly women of the first generation of migrants may wear their clothing out of tradition and/or religious motives, as a way to retain their identity. Many younger women decide to wear a headscarf in order to stand up against the pressure on them not to wear it. As Muslim women, they want to send a signal to society. And some young women decide to wear the Muslim head scarf even if it was not traditional within their family or community.[36] Bosnian Muslim women in Austria are one example.

During the war in former Yugoslavia many Bosnian Muslims came to Austria. Bosnians understand themselves as an indigenous European Islam.[37] Many people there did not practice Islam in the Communist era, and women did not wear special clothes or a headscarf. But the war changed the situation. "It was the war that brought back the scarf," a female student told me. She took on a scarf against the will of her mother. She and others demonstrate their identity as proud Muslim women not only in the context of Austria, but also in the context of war and post-war in Bosnia where Muslims were attacked. Young women of the second and third generation, born in other European countries, are also expressing their identity through different types of Muslim clothing. A label "style islam"[38] tries to combine fashion and Islamic clothing. The phenomenon is discussed as hybrid identity, which combines formerly contradictory meanings and attitudes, as, for example, being a modern woman and wearing traditional clothing.[39]

Muslim women rely on their own self-defined interpretation of Scripture and tradition. This reliance is true for women who deny the religious necessity to dress according to a tradition outside of Europe and who declare the European tradition is their native context. This self-definition is also true for women who define a certain dress code, including a scarf, as part of their religious identity. Secular feminism as well as the traditional patriarchal view allow only one choice. This stance is a form of patriarchy, or let us say matriarchy in this case, because it demands surrender under a certain perception of feminism or tradition. Muslim women in Europe are no longer willing to accept definitions other than their own.[40]

The Conflictive Relation Between Sarah and Hagar as Hermeneutical Perception on the Israel-Palestine Conflict

These different and conflictive interpretations of Sarah and Hagar also influence the European context regarding the political attitude toward the Israeli-Palestinian conflict. Often the conflict is explained with or interpreted in the light of the ancient story: this has been a fight between Isaac and Ishmael since the times of the forefathers and foremothers and will last forever. This way of reading the Bible implies a hermeneutic that *follows* the conflicting structures of the biblical text and therefore is not able to overcome them.[41] After the Second World War and the catastrophe for Jewish people, the new European paradigm of cooperation, acknowledgment, and support for Israel has had an important impact, especially on German's policy in the Middle East. The problems of the Arab-Israeli war in 1967 and the occupation of the Palestinian land since then have not been tackled effectively. This view is supported in Christian churches partly through the identification of Hagar/Ishmael with Muslims and the new antagonist attitude toward Muslims in Europe. The identification is projected on the Palestinian side—Palestinians seem to be foreign, not part of the European culture, hostile toward Judaism from ancient times. This perception is tragic for the Israel-Palestinian conflict—which is not primarily rooted in religion but in politics. The struggle is about land. And it is not a conflict between Jews and Muslims but one between the Israelis and the Palestinians. Both societies are multireligious and pluralistic in various respects. This view also ignores the Arab Palestinian Christians[42] in this conflict and their views on the political situation.

The recent statement of the Arab Palestinian Christians has been published as "Kairos Palestine. A Moment of Truth."[43] The church leaders of the Kairos document call to end the perception of a biblical conflict between Isaac and Ishmael with a one-sided Isaac-Israel solidarity:

> Furthermore, we know that certain theologians in the West try to attach a biblical and theological legitimacy to the infringement of our rights. Thus, the promises, according to their interpretation, have become a menace to our very existence. The "good news" in the Gospel itself has become "a harbinger of death" for us. We call on these theologians to deepen their reflection on the Word of God and to rectify their interpretations so that they might see in the Word of God a source of life for all peoples.[44]

Analyzing the situation in the light of the Bible without a concise and differentiated analysis of the context deepens the conflict and hinders finding a political way of living together that is based on justice for both. In such a reading, Abraham and Sarah, both buried in Hebron, have no power to bring the parties together or to create the feeling of unity or family.[45]

A CRITICAL BIBLICAL HERMENEUTIC: THE BIBLE— SOMETIMES NOT FOR IMITATION BUT DISSENT

The Biblical Text Is Not Innocent

Sarah and Isaac are cut off from Hagar and Ishmael not just by *interpretations* of the biblical text. The Bible itself gives reason for the violence and the gap between both women and their sons. The *text* separates them and sets the conflict—if not Genesis alone, then the interpretation of Paul in Galatians 4.[46] Of course, there are many relevant biblical texts that are not burdened by problems of violence. Others can be defused by careful exegesis and historical positioning. And yet, the whole Bible as we have it has been canonized as Holy Scripture, which means that the text is taken to be sacred in its entirety. The biblical texts are thus meant to be read as absolutely relevant texts, not as arbitrary ones. This applies to the violent biblical texts as well, but in what way?

How, then, should we handle Holy Scripture if some of its contents are far from holy and actually run counter to both principles of humanity and core theological insights? How should we handle "texts of terror" in the Holy Scripture[47] that seem to legitimize violence and oppression? Texts in either Testament which accept slavery, oppress women, murder rivals, segregate Others, prescribe the killing of a conquered people?[48] Women's history is packed with biblical justification of oppressing women. Therefore feminist, womanist, and liberation theology—just to name some—have questioned traditional hermeneutics and developed a different approach to *texts of terror*.[49] Holy texts about conflicts, war, discrimination, and violence are dangerous if their literality is taken normatively, as is obvious in the interpretation of Sarah and Hagar and of Isaac and Ishmael in regard to the Israeli-Palestinian or other conflicts.

What Does Normativity of the Bible Mean for Texts of Terror?

What does "normativity" mean in these cases? Generally it is taken to mean that the texts are relevant by all means. Often "relevance" suggests that they have to be followed and their value (based on a literal reading) is given. Normativity in this understanding requires taking up the perspective of the narrating voice of the text. Obviously, this understanding of normativity of a biblical text causes problems. When, for example, Sarah and Hagar are taken to represent Judaism and Islam, or when Isaac and Ishmael stand for Israel and Palestine, then following Sarah's perspective means casting out Hagar and Ishmael. Such an understanding supports Islamophobia, hatred, and—in Israel and Palestine— occupation and war. What is needed, therefore, is a differentiated access to the different biblical texts. We need a hermeneutic that allows interpretations that take reflexive account of the way we handle the often very contradictory biblical texts while also paying attention to our distance from the texts in time. They are plural in themselves, therefore not finally or inevitably patriarchal in their intratextual collocation. Often this plurality is at first sight abnormal and surprising.

Differentiated Hermeneutics Beyond the Biblical Perspective

The Bible presents not *a* theology, but several theologies. The discipline of exegesis may unravel the diverse interpretive threads and trace the various texts back to their originating situation, including political, social, and religious backdrop of the time. Exegetical analysis can also illuminate what perspectives and interests were brought to bear on the material as it was handed down and how in the Bible itself the normativity of reception—including the historical concerns and constraints, sufferings, and hopes—impacts the normativity of tradition. By helping to give a text a profile, exegesis makes available important information for non-exegetical ways of relating to the biblical texts, that is, for appropriating readings.

Reading the Bible today also requires bringing a new context in dialogue with biblical texts. Two interpretive processes must go hand in hand: identifying one's own situation in the light of the biblical texts and perceiving the texts in the light of a specific substantive interest. Both processes are mutually dependent. Therefore it is crucial to realize that there are a variety of modes of normativity apart from simple acceptance. Normativity can refer to the ability of the multi-faceted texts to elicit a variety of different responses. The Bible narrates what oppression means for the victims; it shows what patriarchy does to women. The stories provoke perception and reaction through the art of the narrative. A change of perspectives is possible: to see through Abraham's eyes, through Sarah's eyes, through Hagar's eyes, through God's eyes. The texts demand that we take a stance! They call on us to relate them to current events and promote theological debate. They teach us how violence is used and what violence does to victims. They provoke us to say: No! We must not repeat such violence, but learn from it, resist and correct it.

So the relevance or normativity of texts of terror is that they provoke *rejection*! But how to resist? The texts offer opportunity for reflection on evil, and they teach which examples *not* to follow![50] They invite readers to find texts that are in solidarity with contemporary values of human rights—against the violent text.

ABRAHAM VERSUS SARAH-HAGAR: TWO CONTRADICTORY EXAMPLES OF INTERRELIGIOUS DIALOGUES

The Male-Dominated Abrahamic Dialogue: The Interpretation of One's Own Situation in the Light of the Biblical Texts

After the Second World War, Europe was in a state of catastrophe by any measure. Churches were shocked to realize not only the enormous scale of violence and destruction but also the inadequacy and even guilt of their own theology. In order to prevent conflicts that could extend to wars, interreligious dialogue seemed and seems today the only alternative. But where could common ground be found? As one of many other shared religious figures Abraham is assumed to be a common basis for interreligious dialogue: Was not Abraham called the "father" to all nations (Gen. 12:3)? And Paul's "our father Abraham" (Rom. 4:12) was taken up for Christians as for Jews. Only at the end of the sixties if not in the seventies did the Muslim community come into focus as a European religious community. Bilateral Christian-Muslim dialogues started, and Abraham seemed to be the ideal bridge among the three monotheistic religions. The fact that Ibrahim plays a central role in Islam (e.g., Sura 2.231–44) encouraged extending interreligious studies also to Islam. Abraham, one hoped, could bridge all three monotheistic religions.[51]

The Practice of Abrahamic Dialogue

Most initiatives for dialogue have a common biblical hermeneutic regarding Abraham. Not only the Second Vatican Council but also many other institutions and scholars took the biblical figure of Abraham as the founding father for Jews, Christians, and Muslims.[52] The dialogue of the three religions was called trialogue—claiming that we all are children of Abraham. Hans Küng, former professor in Tübingen, Germany, founded the international program of a "World Ethos," starting with the "Abrahamic religions" that Karl-Josef Kuschel, also part of the World Ethos institution, related to the common father Abraham.[53] Of course differences are noted but not valued as crucial. From one of the numerous publications comes an example: "As the 'father of many nations' Abraham gives his believing seed a unity that transcends the diversity of the human family—gender, race, nationalism, and generations. Diversity is good and of God, but diversity falls under the shadow of the arching unity provided by Abraham's seed, our Lord Jesus Christ . . . . Finally Christians can best discover that they are of Abraham in the words of the writer to the Hebrews: 'By faith, Abraham . . . obeyed.'"[54]

The hermeneutical process within these dialogue programs was that of identification of one's own situation in the light of the biblical texts. The situation is torn, so one looks for a tool of unity in the Bible that may be the base for a unity to be built. The identification is direct: The religious communities (and their leaders) are children of the "purified" Abraham, the model of faith, according to Genesis 12:1–3, Genesis 15:6, and Paul's "our father" in Romans 4:12. The Islamic tradition sees Abraham without these distortions as the main figure in the line of the prophets. These "Abrahamic" dialogue initiatives are not questioning "Abraham" as a common and therefore uniting figure from the religious traditions. Abraham is used in a context of torn relations and is proposed as the new common basis.

A Feminist Perspective on the Abrahamic Dialogue and Its Biblical Hermeneutic

From a feminist perspective, this male perspective in the official dialogues holds important implications.

1. The identification with Abraham is not easily possible for women. It is a one-sided identification that is not surprising given the fact that these officially

held interreligious dialogues are done by official bodies of churches and other religions. Their patriarchal structures are reflected in the participants as well as in the themes. Men hold the majority of positions in official religious bodies and chairs at the universities. A minority position is something women share, along with the common ground of finding patriarchal structures within religious bodies.[55] Women are not included in representative numbers in these dialogues nor are the topics gender-based.[56]

2. Abraham as a common basis for unity is a very selective biblical hermeneutic. In general, it ignores Hagar, Sarah, and the female perspective on the figure of Abraham. He is a conflicted character: lacking confidence in God and endangering both women as well as his two sons. It was Paul who combined Genesis 15:6 with Genesis 12:3 in order to praise the belief of "our father Abraham" (Rom. 4:12), and Paul guides the continuing reception of Abraham.

3. A focus on Abrahamic dialogue is not only a selective biblical hermeneutic but a patriarchal one. The model of faith, Abraham, demands submission. Abraham "is" our father—and there is no protest heard, no critique welcome that says "No" to this Abraham, who endangered his whole family. The freedom for an alternative is missing. Because the text is "holy," no reaction other than surrender is possible. Holiness and surrender seem inseparable.

4. What is more, this reception of the "common father" ignores that Abraham has a very different meaning for all three so-called Abrahamic traditions. Christians especially tend to focus on Abraham as the common father and to propose him as the uniting bond. For Jews Abraham is vital as the father of Jewish people because of the circumcision and God's promises for a great future (Gen. 17). For Muslims, Ibrahim is vital as the father for the Arabs; Ibrahim is closely related to the Muslim ritual of the hajj, to the Kaaba, to the ritual prayer, and the main topics of the Islamic belief (cf. Qur'an 2,122–34). He is the one who recognized the one God in the midst of polytheism (Qur'an 19,41–48; 26,69–89). But different from Judaism and Islam, in Christianity, Abraham is not the center of belief. No ritual, no credo, no sacraments are connected to Abraham. Christians have nothing to lose offering Abraham as common basis. Their basis is Christ, not Abraham. This difference brings forth an imbalance among the three religions when it comes to interreligious dialogue.

5. The *practice* of Abrahamic dialogues *on a local level* does seem to contradict these critical remarks. Many interreligious initiatives name themselves "Abrahamic" or take Abraham as a basis for their programs, and they are working efficiently.[57] And of course women are involved. For most of the participants in these initiatives, interreligious dialogue as such and the longing for a pluralistic society in respect of each tradition is important. They are working toward these aims under the label Abraham but probably not because of Abraham. Rather, the interest in contact, in mutual understanding, and in tolerance leads to a peaceful living together. Success derives from the *attitude* of respect for other people, respect for their lives and their "Otherness." Therefore even without the figure of Abraham, there would be other figures or theological ideas to support

these activities. The practice overtakes the ideology, and Abraham is used as a brand name but not the spiritual basis for the activities.

6. This tension might be clear if one puts the commitment to "Abraham" to the test. What if fierce conflicts with very different social interests are dominating the society? Will Abraham last as a basis in order to minimize the conflict? Who or what religious community would take a stand maybe even against its own interests in favor of the Others because of Abraham? The example of Hebron with the fierce conflict between the Israeli settlers and the Palestinian inhabitants nourishes doubts that Abraham is of any help if the basic attitude of respect is missing, ignored, or even openly rejected. Abraham could support the opposite too. Settlers in Hebron use Abraham and the patriarchs as reason for oppression.[58]

7. In Europe, practical interreligious initiatives rely often on Abraham, especially on the themes of hospitality (Gen. 18), faith (Gen. 15), and common father. And there are also international initiatives that have taken up "Abraham" in order to characterize their dialogue project. It is like a brand name but seldom the spiritual *reason* for the initiatives. And the conflict in Hebron demonstrates that Abraham as such has not the necessary might to end violence or even war.

In sum, to rely on Abraham in interreligious dialogues ignores wide parts of the Abraham narrative, including the women's stories and fates, along with feminist biblical research on them. The official dialogues do not include women in representative numbers or focus on women's agendas and topics. Abraham as model requires obedience, and an Abrahamic model emphasizes common ground even where differences are dominant. Such a biblical hermeneutic requires surrender under a certain version of the story of Abraham and his family, under the texts of terror.

The Feminist Sarah-Hagar Dialogue: The Interpretation of the Biblical Texts in the Light of One's Own Situation

A Different Practice of Women

Even if women are not adequately represented in a significant number among the "main players" of interreligious dialogue, women were and are very active with respect to initiatives for dialogue. Throughout the decades, women have engaged in interreligious and intercultural dialogues on different levels. Women from different religions and faith communities are increasingly interacting in order to share their experiences and develop strategies for reform and empowerment. This approach is necessarily contextual, problem-oriented, and pragmatic. It works on living together, not only speaking together. But these activities and practical initiatives of women are often not known or not acknowledged as interreligious or intercultural dialogue. Women's experiences are not expected to contribute to a theoretical conception of interreligious dialogue or intercultural dialogue, despite the fact that women work on the praxis of living together.

The majority of these dialogues are self-initiated and contextually rooted. They are organized on three main structures: by regions, by themes, or by groups (e.g., women theologians). The women's focus is often on concrete matters such as reducing violence, sharing resources, and living together in multireligious and intercultural societies.[59] Of particular interest is that some of these women's interreligious dialogues begin with Sarah and Hagar, not Abraham. And this orientation implies a different biblical hermeneutic. Two European interreligious initiatives that rely on Sarah and Hagar provide examples of these feminist dialogues.

Switzerland—Interreligious Think Tank of Women

Women of diverse faiths in Switzerland advocate interreligious dialogue—and especially women's interreligious dialogue. The Swiss theologian Doris Strahm published texts of Jewish, Muslim, and Christian women about interreligious dialogue with the title "Damit es anders wird zwischen uns" (*That it may be different between us*).[60] In contrast to official dialogues, the women are referring to Sarah and Hagar. Strahm also founded an "Interreligious Think Tank" in Switzerland[61] in 2008 with Jewish, Christian, and Muslim women. Their common goals are to advance religious freedom and to use the potential of religions to strengthen justice. These women are working together to strengthen their own identity—not to find a unity that ignores differences. They want to strengthen solidarity and to work on the subject of feminism and religion. Their manifesto says, "Freedom of women and religion are not contradictory. Manifesto for a differentiated debate of religion and the rights of women." They seek to make an impact on the growing Islamophobia and the right-wing activities in Switzerland. From a feminist religious standpoint they try to differentiate themselves from the feminist secular women who argue against religion as oppressing women.

Germany: Sarah-and-Hagar Initiative

In Germany in 2001 about thirty women from different cultural, national, and religious backgrounds founded an interreligious initiative ("Arbeitskreis für frauenpolitische Fragen der jüdischen, christlichen und islamischen Religionsgemeinschaften"),[62] calling themselves the "Sarah-and-Hagar Initiative." They met on a regular basis. Themes of the meetings included mutual respect for religious tradition and visions for justice and peace, brought together with actual politics and gender issues. In five years the women discussed their common interests in social politics like integration, gender mainstreaming, and the rules of antidiscrimination of the European Union. Education, family, and employment were identified for common political and gender mainstreaming activities. In 2006 the initiative published a paper on impulses for a gender-biased social policy on the basis of Jewish, Christian, and Muslim traditions.[63] They pointed out the double discrimination of women: as part of a minority as well as part of a culture and religion that is depicted as "foreign"—a fate of women in patriarchal structures. Groups in different regions of Germany were established.

A Critical Biblical Hermeneutic within the Practice
of the Feminist Interreligious Dialogue

What biblical hermeneutics are implied when these groups relate themselves to Sarah and Hagar? Feminist women in interreligious dialogue take another path relating their situation to the Bible. They interpret the biblical texts in the light of the women's situation, reversing the Abrahamic dialogue. They are challenged by the given problems. The situation needs healing, urgently! And the feminist European women's dialogue is based on human rights: equality, freedom of religion, peace. So, what to do with and what to learn from the biblical texts that speak of separation and conflict?

With Sarah and Hagar the women choose a text about women living with different status in a hierarchical system and with a very different fate. They acknowledge a gap if not a contradiction between their own options and attitudes and the biblical text. Using Sarah and Hagar to name interreligious dialogue contradicts the biblical story. Never do these women talk directly to each other. They live on two sides of their society, and Sarah uses her status to cast Hagar out. As women in dialogue refer to these texts, their use implies a hermeneutic of protest against the biblical text. The women are building up a reality that contradicts the biblical background they rely on. Their dialogue starts with life that is conflictive. The light of the situation darkens the given shadow of the biblical narratives and makes the terror obvious. And the light of the situation requires saying "No" to the biblical "solution" of casting out the "Other" and finding a way to come together with the "Other." This does not mean that this dialogue has no conflicting themes. But the dialogues of the women start not with unity but with difference, and they take the Bible as a tool to learn what is *not* to be done! They use the Bible to imagine clearly the outcome of conflict and to use the texts as a warning not to go the same way.

This dialogue implies first talking to "Other" women on the same level with an analysis of the difference in society. From there one can work on the goals: No top-down dialogue. No patriarchal attitude to Others. No top-down relation of texts over us. No patriarchal imperative about how women have to understand their faith. Women are subjects of their own spirituality. And no to political trends, parties, and rhetoric that use difference to establish different rights or even expulsion of people. The right-wing movement is growing, and we have seen in Germany that some of them are even ready to murder people just for being Muslims.

Both dialogues, the Abrahamic and the Sarah-Hagar initiatives, are aiming at the same goal: a society of respect and equality. But the way toward these aims differs in reference to biblical hermeneutics. The Abrahamic dialogue assumes a unity of religions through Abraham and works on that basis; the Sarah-Hagar dialogue starts with the difference and conflict and uses this as a tool for social analysis and as a warning in order to find a different way. Feminist European interreligious dialogues go beyond the male structures and put in the center women and their perspectives on their situation, accepting differences among people as well as in texts. The difference in approach aims not at separation but at solidarity with women so that they will enjoy human rights within Europe.

CONCLUSION

Let me conclude with an outlook on another text. The only opportunity where the sons of Sarah and Hagar meet again is in Genesis 25. Both sons come together to bury their father, Abraham. God blesses Isaac (Gen. 25:11). This blessing is parallel to that God gave Ishmael and Hagar in Genesis 21: Ishmael shall be a great nation. Now both sons hold a blessing, and Ishmael's progeny is named in Genesis 25:12–18. But in verse 18 we read, "They dwelt from Hav'ilah to Shur, which is opposite Egypt in the direction of Assyria; he settled over against all his people." This is not the perspective of a peaceful living together. Burying their father Abraham together is also burying the only common basis they have. From now on, both rely on their own identity, and conflict is part of them. The feminist women in Europe who rely on Sarah and Hagar know this—and they also buried Abraham, the link between the two women. Interreligious dialogue means to bury the ideology of unity and to embrace difference and identity, but in solidarity!

Notes

1. Phyllis Trible, *Mein Gott, warum hast Du mich vergessen? Frauenschicksale im Alten Testament* (Gütersloh: Gütersloher Verlagshaus Mohn, 1990); *Gott und Sexualität im Alten Testament* (Gütersloh: Gütersloher Verlagshaus Mohn, 1993).
2. Phyllis Trible and Letty Russell, eds., *Hagar, Sarah, and Their Children: Jewish, Christian, and Muslim Perspectives* (Louisville, KY: Westminster John Knox Press, 2005).
3. Phyllis Trible, "Ominous Beginnings for a Promise of Blessings," in Trible and Russell, *Hagar, Sarah, and Their Children*, 33; Trible, *Texts of Terror: Literary Feminist Readings of Biblical Narratives* (Philadelphia: Fortress Press, 1985), 4; Moumita Biswas, "Various Identities of Hagar," *Student World* 1 (2005): 96–107.
4. This was presented by Jürgen Ebach in a Bible Study during the *Deutscher Evangelischer Kirchentag* May 20–24, 2009, see: Jürgen Ebach, Bibelarbeit zu 1, Mose 16,1–16: Wo kommst du her, und wo willst du hin?, http://www .kirchentag2009.de/presse/dokumente/dateien/BAB_46_1651.pdf.
5. Irmtraud Fischer, "On the Significance of the 'Women Texts' in the Ancestral Narratives," in *Torah: The Bible and Women: An Encyclopedia of Exegesis and Cultural History,* Bible and Women Series, vol. 1.1, ed. Irmtraud Fischer, Mercedes Navarro Puerto, and Andrea Taschl-Erber (Atlanta: Society of Biblical Literature, 2010), 251–94.
6. Delores S. Williams, *Sisters in the Wilderness: the Challenge of Womanist God-Talk* (Maryknoll, NY: Orbis Books, 1993); John W. Waters, "Who Was Hagar?" in

Stony the Road We Trod: African American Biblical Interpretation, ed. Cain H. Felder (Minneapolis: Fortress Press, 1991), 187–205.

7. Renita J. Weems, *Just a Sister Away: A Womanist Vision of Women's Relationships in the Bible* (Philadelphia: Innisfree Press, 1988).

8. See for example Constance Ambasa-Shisanya, "A Reflection on the Hagar Narratives in Genesis through the Eyes of a Kenyan Women," in *Interpreting the Old Testament in Africa*, ed. Mary N. Getui, Knut Holter, and Victor Zinkuratire (New York: Peter Lang, 2001), 147–51; see also Waters, "Who Was Hagar?," 187–205; Alan Cooper, "Hagar in and out of Context," *Union Seminary Quarterly Review* 55, 2001: 35–46.

9. Irmtraud Fischer, *Die Erzeltern Israels. Feministisch-theologische Studien zu Genesis 12–36* (Beihefte zur Zeitschrift für die alttestamentliche Wissenschaft 222; Berlin: de Gruyter, 1994); Irmtraud Fischer, *Women Who Wrestled with God: Biblical Stories of Israel's Beginnings*, trans. Linda M. Maloney (Collegeville, MN: Liturgical Press, 2005).

10. See Ulrike Bechmann, "Rhetorische Figuren der Entgrenzung. Abraham, Sara und Hagar bei Paulus," *Bibel und Kirche* 66, 2011: 9–14; Angelika Magnes, "Different Mothers, Births and Inheritances, Die Rede von zwei Frauen in Gal 4,21–31," in *Geschlechterverhältnisse und Macht. Lebensformen in der Zeit des frühen Christentums, Exegese in unserer Zeit 21*, ed. Irmtraud Fischer and Christoph Heil (Wien: LIT-Verlag, 2010), 110–27.

11. The discussion about anti-Judaism refers to the "integration" and therefore estrangement of Sarah from Judaism; see Rainer Kampling, "Und Sara weint . . . ," in *Sara lacht . . . Eine Erzmutter und ihre Geschichte. Zur Interpretation und Rezeption der Sara-Erzählung*, ed. Rainer Kampling (Paderborn: Schöningh, 2004), 253–60.

12. See Jeremy Cohen, ed., *Rethinking European Jewish History*, Littman Library of Jewish Civilization (New York: Oxford University Press, 2009).

13. See Landeszentrale für politische Bildung, ed., *Die Nacht, als die Synagogen brannten. Texte und Materialien zum Novemberpogrom 1938* (Stuttgart: Landeszentrale für politische Bildung Württemberg, 1998).

14. David Bankier and Israel Gutman, eds., *Nazi Europe and the Final Solution* (Jerusalem: Yad Vashem, The Holocaust Martyrs' and Heroes' Remembrance Authority; The International Institute for Holocaust Research, 2003, 2nd ed., 2009).

15. See Walter Dietrich, ed., *Antijudaismus—christliche Erblast* (Stuttgart: Kohlhammer, 1999).

16. Susannah Heschel, *The Aryan Jesus: Christian Theologians and the Bible in Nazi Germany* (Princeton, NJ: Princeton University Press, 2008).

17. See Josef Foschepoth, *Im Schatten der Vergangenheit. Die Anfänge der Gesellschaften für Christlich-Jüdische Zusammenarbeit* (Göttingen: Vandenhoek & Ruprecht, 1993).

18. Erklärung des Rates der Evangelischen Kirche in Deutschland gegenüber den Vertretern des Ökumenischen Rates der Kirchen vom 19. Oktober 1945 (Stuttgarter Schuldbekenntnis), http://www.hdg.de/lemo/html/dokumente/Nachkriegsjahre_erklaerungStuttgarterSchuldbekenntnis/index.html.

19. See Gregory Baum, *Christian Theology after Auschwitz* (London: Council of Christian and Jews, 1976); Günther Bernd Ginzel, *Auschwitz als Herausforderung für Juden und Christen* (Heidelberg: Schneider, 1980); Ekkehard Schuster, *Trotzdem hoffen. Mit Johann Baptist Metz und Elie Wiesel im Gespräch* (Mainz: Matthias-Grünewald-Verlag, 1993); Paul Petzel, *Christ sein im Angesicht der Juden: zu Fragen einer Theologie nach Auschwitz* (Münster: LIT, 2008); Gerhard

Langer and Gregor Maria Hoff, eds., *Der Ort des Jüdischen in der katholischen Theologie* (Göttingen: Vandenhoeck & Ruprecht, 2009).

20. See Leonore Siegele-Wenschkewitz, ed., *Verdrängte Vergangenheit, die uns bedrängt. Feministische Theologie in der Verantwortung vor der Geschichte* (München: Kaiser, 1988); Britta Jüngst, *Auf der Seite des Todes das Leben. Auf dem Weg zu einer christlich-feministischen Theologie nach der Shoah* (Gütersloh: Kaiser, 1996).

21. http://www.abraham-geiger-kolleg.de/.

22. Hadith or ahadith (the Arabic plural) are post-Qur'anic authoritative traditions about deeds and sayings of Mohammed and his companions.

23. Stefano Allievi, "Islam in the Public Spaces: Social Networks, Media and Neo-communities," in *Muslim Networks and Transnational Communities in and across Europe*, ed. Stefano Allievi and Jorgen Nielsen (Leiden/Boston: Brill, 2003), 1–27; Martin Baumann, "Religion und umstrittener öffentlicher Raum. Gesellschaftspolitische Konflikte um religiöse Symbole und Stätten im gegenwärtigen Europa," *Zeitschrift für Religionswissenschaft* 7, no. 2 (1999): 187–204.

24. Nina Clara Tiesler, *Muslime in Europa. Religion und Identitätspolitiken unter veränderten gesellschaftlichen Verhältnissen* (Politik & Kultur 8; Berlin: LIT, 2006).

25. See Stephane Lathion, "Muslims in Switzerland: Is Citizenship Really Incompatible with Muslim Identity?" *Journal of Muslim Minority Affairs* 28, no. 1, (2008): 53–60; Muhammad Anwar, "Muslims in Western States: The British Experience and the Way Forward," *Journal of Muslim Minority Affairs* 28, no. 1 (2008): 125–37.

26. See Hugh Poulton, ed., *Muslim Identity and the Balkan State* (London: Hurst, 1997).

27. Heino Henkel, "Turkish Islam in Germany: A Problematic Tradition or the Fifth Project of Constitutional Patriotism?" *Journal of Muslim Minority Affairs* 28, no. 1 (2008): 113–23; Monika Mattes, *"Gastarbeiterinnen" in der Bundesrepublik, Anwerbepolitik, Migration und Geschlecht in den 50er bis 70er Jahren*, Geschichte und Geschlechter 48 (Frankfurt: Campus-Verlag, 2005).

28. Unfortunately Samuel Huntington's thesis got too much attention and influence—even with the false perception of "Islam" and "West" each as one culture, ignoring the diversity in Islam and "the West" itself. See Samuel Huntington, *The Clash of Civilizations? The Debate* (New York: Council on Foreign Affairs, 1993); for the critique see Chiara Bottici and Benoît Challand, *The Myth of the Clash of Civilizations* (London: Routledge, 2010).

29. Nezer Al Sayyad and Manuel Castells, eds., *Muslim Europe or Euro-Islam. Politics, Culture, and Citizenship in the Age of Globalization* (Lanham: Lexington Books, 2002); Tariq Ramadan is one of the prominent exponents to promote a European Islam. See Jacques Neirynck and Tariq Ramadan, *Peut-on vivre avec l'islam?* (Lausanne: Favre, 1999).

30. See Matthias Tanner, ed., *Der Streit um das Minarett. Zusammenleben in der religiös pluralistischen Gesellschaft* (Beiträge zu einer Theologie der Religionen 8), (Zurich: Theologischer Verlag, 2009); Jörg Hüttermann, *Das Minarett: zur politischen Kultur des Konflikts um islamische Symbole* (Weinheim: Juventa, 2006).

31. See Georg Tafner, "Das islamische Kopftuch: Brennpunkt des verschleierten Kampfes um die europäische Identität; eine europapädagogische Kurzbetrachtung," *Österreichisches Archiv für Recht & Religion* (2010): 98–119; Christian Joppke, *Veil: Mirror of Identity* (Cambridge: Polity Press, 2009); John Richard Bowen, *Why the French Don't Like Headscarves. Islam, the State, and Public Space* (Princeton, NJ: Princeton University Press, 2007).

32. Klaus Hödl, "Islamophobia in Austria. The Recent Emergence of Anti-Muslim Sentiments in the Country," *Journal of Muslim Minority Affairs* 30 (2010): 443–56. Hödl argues that in Austria, Islamophobia is part of Judeophobia.
33. Leila Ahmed, *The Quiet Revolution: The Veil's Resurgence, From the Middle East to America* (New Haven, CT: Yale University Press, 2011); Amina Wadud, *Inside the Gender Jihad: Women's Reform in Islam* (Oxford: Oneworld, 2007).
34. Alice Schwarzer, *Die große Verschleierung. Für Integration, gegen Islamismus* (Köln: Kiepenheuer & Witsch, 2010).
35. See Necla Kelek, *Himmelsreise: mein Streit mit den Wächtern des Islam* (Köln: Kiepenheuer & Witsch, 2010).
36. "Positionierungen im islamischen Diskursfeld: religiöses Selbstverständnis junger Musliminnen im Spannungsfeld von Identitätspolitik und multiplen Identitätskonstruktionen," ed. Mechthild Rumpf, Ute Gerhard, Mechthild M. Jansen, *Facetten islamischer Welten. Geschlechterordnungen, Frauen- und Menschenrechte in der Diskussion* (Bielefeld: transcript Verl., 2003), 195–218.
37. See Hugh Poulton, ed., *Muslim Identity and the Balkan State* (London: Hurst, 1997); Hansjörg Schmid, "Muslime in Europa zwischen Globalisierung und Lokalisierung. Gesellschaftspolitische und theologische Perspektiven im Anschluss an Enes Karić und Tariq Ramadan," *Cibedo* 2007, H.4, 8–16.
38. See www.styleislam.com.
39. See Keri E. Iyall Smith and Patricia Leavy, eds., *Hybrid Identities. Theoretical and Empirical Examination* (Leiden: Brill, 2008). For a critical questioning of the term "Hybrid Identity" see Toni Sandset, "Some Thoughts on Hybrid Identity," "Hybrid Identity: Dictionaries, Identities," and "Are We All Hybrids?" in *New Narratives. Multicultural Literature at the University of Oslo*, http://newnarratives.wordpress.com/issue-1-hybrid-identity/some-thoughts-on-hybrid-identity/.
40. See Hilal Sezgin, ed., *Manifest der Vielen. Deutschland erfindet sich neu* (Berlin: Blumenbar Verlag, 2011); Annelies Moors and Ruba Salih, "'Muslim Women' in Europe. Secular Normativities, Bodily Performances and Multiple Publics," *Social Anthropology* 17 (2009): 375–78.
41. For a concept to overcome these narrative distortions today see Kristen I. Urban, "Isaac and Ishmael: Opportunities for Peace within Religious Narrative," *Journal of Religion, Conflict, and Peace* 2, no. 2 (2009), http://www.religionconflictpeace.org/node/51; Rosemary Radford Ruether, *Nächstenliebe und Brudermord* (München, 1978).
42. See Ulrike Bechmann and Mitri Raheb, eds., *Verwurzelt im Heiligen Land. Eine Einführung in das palästinensische Christentum* (Frankfurt: Knecht, 1995); Harald Suermann, "Arabische Christen in Israel und palästinensische Christen," in *Sur les pas des Araméens chrétiens. Mélanges offerts à Alain Desreumaux* (Paris: Greuthner, 2010), 433-445.
43. See the declaration "Kairos Palestine. A Moment of Truth," http://www.kairospalestine.ps/ that complains that many churches and theologians ignore Palestinian issues out of a theological identification of the biblical Israel with the political state of Israel.
44. Kairos Document 2.3.3.
45. See Ulrike Bechmann, *Gestörte Grabesruhe. Idealität und Realität des interreligiösen Dialogs am Beispiel von Hebron / al-Khalil* (AphorismA - Reihe Kleine Texte 24; Berlin, 2007); Nazmi al-Jubeh, *Hebron (al-Halil). Kontinuität und Interpretationskraft einer islamisch-arabischen Stadt* (Tübingen: Diss,1991).
46. For a differentiated view that Genesis does not only opt for conflict see Thomas Naumann, "Das Erhörungsmotiv im Namen Ismaels und seine narrativen Variationen," in *Berührungspunkte. Studien zur Sozial- und Religionsgeschichte Israels*

und seiner Umwelt. Festschrift für Rainer Albertz zu seinem 65, Geburtstag, ed. Ingo Kottsieper (Münster: Ugarit-Verlag, 2008), 21–38; Thomas Naumann, "The Common Basis of the Covenant and the Distinction between Isaac and Ishmael in Gen 17: The Case of Ishmael and the Non-Israelite Descendants of Abraham in the Priestly Source," in *The Foreigner and the Law: Perspectives from the Hebrew Bible and the Ancient Near East,* ed. Reinhard Achenbach, Rainer Albertz, and Jakob Wöhrle (Alter Orient und Altes Testament 350; Wiesbaden: Harrassowitz Verlag, 2011), 89–109; Jakob Wöhrle, "Isaak und Ismael: zum Verhältnis der beiden Abrahamsöhne nach Genesis 17 und Galater 4,21–31," *Evangelische Theologie* 71 (2011): 115–32.

47. An extended understanding of "Holy texts" is discussed in vol. 3 of the periodical *Concilium* 3, no. 34 (1998) (Title: *Die heiligen Schriften der Frauen/Holy Scriptures of Women*).

48. See Rosemary Radford Ruether, *Faith and Fratricide: The Theoretical Roots of Anti-Semitism* (New York: Seabury Press, 1974); Erika Meijers, "White Brothers—Black Strangers: Dutch Calvinist Churches and Apartheid in South-Africa," *Exchange* 38 (2009): 365–80; Richard Elphick, "Dutch Reformed Missions and the Roots of the Apartheid Ideology," in *Mission und Macht im Wandel politischer Orientierungen. Europäische Missionsgesellschaften in politischen Spannungsfeldern in Afrika und Asien zwischen 1800 und 1945,* ed. Ulrich van der Heyden (Missionsgeschichtliches Archiv 10; Stuttgart: Steiner, 2005), 563–75.

49. See Gerlinde Baumann, *Gottesbilder der Gewalt im Alten Testament verstehen* (Darmstadt: Wissenschaftliche Buchgesellschaft, 2006); see also Eric A. Seibert, *The Violence of Scripture: Overcoming the Old Testament's Troubling Legacy* (Minneapolis: Augsburg Fortress Publishers, 2012).

50. See Ottmar Fuchs, "Kriterien gegen den Missbrauch der Bibel," *Jahrbuch Biblische Theologie* 12 (1997): 243-74; Ottmar Fuchs, *Praktische Hermeneutik der Heiligen Schrift* (Stuttgart: Kohlhammer, 2004).

51. The Second Vatican Council envisioned Abraham as the uniting figure of Judaism, Christianity, and Islam in the Declaration *Nostra Aetate.* See Ulrike Bechmann, "Aggiornamento, Vatican II, and Dialogue," *Theology Digest* 53 (2006): 225–28; Roman Siebenrock, "Theologischer Kommentar zur Erklärung über die Haltung der Kirche zu den nichtchristlichen Religionen Nostra aetate," in *Herders Theologischer Kommentar zum Zweiten Vatikanischen Konzil,* Bd. 3, ed. Peter Hünermann and Jochen Hilberath (Freiburg: Herder, 2005), 591–693.

52. See David B. Burrell, "The Abrahamic Faiths in Their New Context," in *Essays in Memory of David A. Kerr,* vol. 2, ed. Stephen R. Goodwin (London: Continuum, 2009), 84–95. For a critical view see Ulrike Bechmann, "Abraham und Ibrāhīm. Die Grenzen des Abraham-Paradigmas im interreligiösen Dialog," *Münchener Theologische Zeitschrift* 58 (2007): 110–26.

53. See Hans Küng, *Projekt Weltethos* (München, Zürich: Piper, 1990); Hans Küng, *Dokumentation zum Weltethos* (München, Zürich: Piper, 2002); Karl-Josef Kuschel, *A Symbol of Hope for Jews, Christians and Muslims,* trans. John Bowden (New York: Continuum Publishing Company, 1995); Karl-Josef Kuschel, "One in Abraham? The Significance of Abraham for Jews, Christians, and Muslims Today," in *Memory and History in Christianity and Judaism,* ed. Michael A. Signer (Notre Dame, 2001), 183–203.

54. Kenneth A. Matthews, *Genesis 11:27–50:26. An Exegetical and Theological Exposition of Holy Scripture,* Vol. 1B, (The New American Commentary; Nashville: Broadman & Holman Publishers, 2005), 97.

55. See Marie-Theres Wacker, Susan Ross, and Hille Haker, eds., "Andere Stimmen—Frauen in den Weltreligionen," *Concilium* 42 (2006), a volume that

collects voices of women describing their perspectives and situations within different religious traditions from the northern and the southern regions.

56. See Ursula King, "Feminism: The Missing Dimension in the Dialogue of Religions," in *Pluralism and the Religions: The Theological and Political Dimensions*, ed. John D'Arcy May (London: Cassell Academic, 1998), 40–55; Ruth Tetlow, "The Missing Dimension: Women and Interfaith Encounter in Birmingham," *Current Dialogue* 46 (2005), http://wcc-coe.org/wcc /what/interreligious/cd46 -10.html.

57. Here are some examples of initiatives in Europe that name themselves "Abrahamic": The Christian-Islamic Initiative Region Stuttgart celebrates the "Abrahamfest" (feast of Abraham); a play "Abraham today" was written and performed together; a project "Haus Abraham" (house of Abraham) was founded in order to promote dialogue, respect, tolerance and hospitality. In Munich an association of Jews, Muslims, and Christians was founded as "Freunde Abrahams" (friends of Abraham); there are "Abrahamitische Teams" (Abrahamic teams), qualified people of all three religions who go as a team to schools or communities in order to discuss interreligious topics or lead training groups for interreligious competence.

58. See Tamara Neumann, "Religious Nationalism, Violence, and the Israeli State: Accommodation and Conflict in the Jewish Settlement of Kiryat Arba," in *Religion und Nation—Nation und Religion. Beiträge zu einer unbewältigten Geschichte*, ed. Michael Geyer and Hartmut Lehmann (Göttingen: Wallstein, 2004), 99–115.

59. For the German context see Ottmar Fuchs, "Caritaseinrichtungen als Orte interreligiöser Praxis," *Theologische Quartalschrift* 189 (2009): 262–72.

60. See Doris Strahm and Manuela Kalsky, eds., *Damit es anders wird zwischen uns. Interreligiöser Dialog aus der Sicht von Frauen* (Ostfildern, 2006).

61. www.interrelthinktank.ch.

62. http://www.gender-kirche-gelsenkirchen.de/de/interreligioeser-dialog/sarah -hagar-initiative/.

63. "Impulse für eine geschlechtergerechte Sozialpolitik auf der Basis jüdischer, christlicher und muslimischer Traditionen" in *epd-Dokumentationen* 30, no. 1 (2006), http://www.gender-kirche-gelsenkirchen.de/de/interreligioeser-dialog/ sarah-hagar-initiative/.

Chapter 11

The Woman of Jericho

Dramatization as Feminist Hermeneutics

ULRIKE BECHMANN

The story of Sarah and Hagar provides hermeneutical guides for current European, feminist, interreligious dialogue (as I analyze in chapter 10), and shows that we must position ourselves and our context carefully in relation to the biblical stories—in other words, that we must engage in critical hermeneutics. A differentiated hermeneutics requires recognizing the complexity of the Bible. Texts from the distant past and from disparate backgrounds have been handed on as God's word in human words and preserved as a normative, collective memory for faith communities. The Bible came into being through a process of continuation and commentary that allowed for a variety of views. What is needed, therefore, is a differentiated access to the biblical texts.

In womanist theology, African American and African women identified with Hagar's life and fate and drew fresh strength and hope against their oppression. How, then, might a reader approach texts in which God does not side with the victims, but with the winners? This alliance with winners against victims is evident in Joshua 6, the battle of Jericho. This text, like the Abraham narratives, is often related to the Israeli-Palestinian conflict and the promise of the Land.[1] The more-than-well-known story recounts how Joshua and the people of Israel come to Jericho, the fortified town. With trumpets and God's will the walls come down and Jericho is conquered (Josh. 6:1–21). Bringing Jericho down is God's message and God's deed. The final verses read, "So the people shouted, and the trumpets were blown. As soon as the people heard the sound of the trumpets, they raised a great shout, and the wall fell down flat; so the people charged straight ahead into the city and captured it. Then they devoted to destruction by the edge of the sword all in the city, both men and women, young and old, oxen, sheep, and donkeys" (Josh. 6:20–21 NRSV). These verses convey the narrative perspective of the biblical text. Did not God directly destroy Jericho? Yet this perspective is not the only one possible. Even with God presented as being solely on the side of Joshua, the text offers an occasion to illustrate a hermeneutic of protest through identification with other characters in the narrative.

An exegetical analysis provides a starting point. Historical analysis shows that the conquest story is entirely fictional and that Jericho was never conquered by the Israelites under Joshua.[2] The story was composed during the exile to teach that during the time of the kingdoms Israel had not had the necessary trust in God to be able to maintain the land. The redaction of the text even incorporated military critical elements and strategies to instruct ancient communities not to imitate the book of Joshua. That is, the stories of conquering the land with God's help themselves communicate that these elements are not to be repeated! Not even in the time of the Exile.[3] But the reception of Joshua today is different; usually European or American readers tend to associate Joshua with the perspective of Israel; politically the story is used to explain the Israeli-Palestinian political conflict, especially the occupation of the West Bank since 1967.

The most popular way of recalling this story may be the African American traditional spiritual of the first half of the nineteenth century, "Joshua fits the battle of Jericho." The spiritual stems from a context where oppressed people needed walls to come down. Some situations are so difficult that no other solution is possible than to hope for a Joshua to come in order to obtain freedom. These people were far from being military conquerors. Today, however, many church people sing the spiritual. The problem starts when people identify themselves wrongly, when the strong side takes up this story to confirm that they are the ones to emulate Joshua. When one with military power identifies himself or herself with Joshua, violence and readiness to kill may be inevitable. For application, however, situations must be comparable and fit contextually in the sense that they correspond in their social structure. The Bible has a different message for the strong and the weak, the rich and the poor, the aggressors and the victims.

Even Joshua 6, however, in all its brutality may offer the chance to take a different stance. The story mentions persons that have no word on their own but who are present, like the women of Jericho. Women are named as those who are killed (v. 21). The victims are present in the text and invite readers to see through their eyes. So imagine one woman of Jericho and her perspective.

The Jericho Woman
(to be performed following a reading of the biblical text)

Hello. You don't know me, but we met already in the story. I'm a woman of Jericho. You don't know me by name—by the way, my name is Nachla—I'm one of the forgotten ones.

But I'm there in the text, in the last verse you just heard: ". . . men and women, oxen, sheep and donkeys." You see—I'm one of these women. I want to meet you. You are going with Joshua?

Well, still the wall of Jericho is there and the gate is open. I'll show you around a bit if you like. You know, we live in a nice city. There is a spring that never dries up, not even in the summer. This spring is important, because Jericho can be hot, especially in summer. Because of the water we have all this greenery here! You can see a lot of fruit trees all around the city. And palms; there are plenty of them. Some call Jericho the "City of Palm Trees."

Look at the wall and the big gate. It is necessary to have it and to protect it well. We are a rich city! Many travelers and merchants are coming to our city. And sometimes also enemies.

Come with me down our main street; I'll show you our temple. Isn't it a fabulous building? Perhaps you can get a glimpse through the open door of all the silver and gold vessels that are in there! We are really very thankful to our goddesses and gods to live in such a good place.

But come to my house. You must be thirsty. I can offer some milk and some fruits. Here is my house.

Look, these are my children. I have three of them. Here, my daughter is twelve years old. Isn't she a beauty? And I can tell she is bright, too! I really have to find a good man for her who likes her. Oh, here comes my youngest child. He is three years old. He likes to play around with our donkey. And you know, we sometimes think that the donkey likes him best too.

But look at the sun; time is running out. You have to hurry to join Joshua again. You must leave before the gate is closed. If the gate is closed, nobody can go out or in. So hurry up to go back.

Tomorrow, when the sun rises, the wall will fall down. The city will be burnt. Joshua will take all the silver and gold for his God. You know, the God of Joshua has no mercy at all, not even for the old ones or the children.

So go now, and tomorrow, when the walls come down, we will meet again—and then you will kill me.

Interpretation that presents not only the winners but also the victims enables us to see and hear differently. It offers the chance to think anew. What would be necessary to overcome war and destruction?

In 2005 I introduced the "Woman of Jericho" during a conference in Bethlehem. The ecumenical music group "Cross Culture" (Chicago) responded—and they proposed to sing the well-known spiritual instead as: "Listen to the woman

of Jericho . . . ."⁴ Whoever is listening to the woman of Jericho is resisting the
violence of a text of terror. Perhaps this woman may also point the way back to
other contemporary contexts and current interreligious dialogues. The woman
of Jericho invites readers to explore imaginatively and ethically the importance of
gendered biblical hermeneutics. Her perspective sheds light on the dark side of
stories of victory and triumph. Exploring such stories with gendered biblical
hermeneutics may also allow one to see the "Other" in actual controversies with
potential solutions.

Notes

1. The World Council of Churches in Hofgeismar in 2012 held a conference on the
   use of the book of Joshua and subsequently issued "Message from the Conference
   in Hofgeismar," 27 February 2012, http://www.oikoumene.org/en/resources/
   documents/wcc-programmes/public-witness-addressing-power-affirming-peace/
   middle-east-peace/message-from-conference-in-hofgeismar-germany.
2. See Klaus Bieberstein, "Joshua—Jordan—Jericho" (Orbis Biblicus et Orientalis
   143), (Fribourg: Vandenhoeck & Ruprecht, 1995); Kort van Bekkum, *From
   Conquest to Coexistence: Ideology and Antiquarian Intent in the Historiography of
   Israel's Settlement in Canaan* (Leiden: Brill, 2011).
3. See Norbert Lohfink, "Landeroberung und Heimkehr. Hermeneutik zum heuti-
   gen Umgang mit dem Josuabuch," *Jahrbuch Biblische Theologie* 12 (1997): 3–24.
4. The text was first published in Esther Epp-Tiessen, "People Dispossessed of the
   Land," in *Under Vine and Fig Tree: Biblical Theologies of Land and the Palestin-
   ian-Israeli Conflict*, ed. Alain Epp Weaver (Telford, PA: Cascadia Publishing
   House, 2007), 75–82.

PART 3
THEOLOGY AND ETHICS

Chapter 12

Ecological Theology in Women's Voices

ELIZABETH A. JOHNSON

THE CONTEXT: FORGETTING CREATION

In our day, awareness of the magnificence of Earth as a small planet hospitable to life is growing among peoples everywhere. It is an ecological awareness, ecological from the Greek word *oikos*, meaning household or home. This living planet, with its thin spherical shell of land, water, and breathable air, is home for human beings, our only home in the vast universe. It is also home to a wondrous diversity of species that interrelate to form networks of living ecosystems. Perhaps life exists in some form on other planets (Mars?) or moons (Europa?) of the solar system or on extrasolar planets in the Milky Way galaxy. Definite knowledge one way or the other lies in the future. At this moment, Earth, this jewel of a blue marble floating in a black sea of space, is the only place we know of in the vast universe where life abundant abides.

Ecological awareness has arisen against a paradoxical background. On the one hand, we stand in wonder at modern scientific discoveries about the enormous age, size, interrelatedness, and ongoing dynamism of the universe of which life on Earth is a part. On the other hand, we are struck with the terrible knowledge that we humans are inflicting deadly damage on our planet, ravaging its identity as a dwelling place for life. Practices of consumption, exploitation of resources, and pollution of a growing human population are dealing a sucker punch to life-supporting systems on land, sea, and air, making for nightmare headlines: global warming, melting ice caps, rising sea levels, rain forests logged and burned, ruined wetlands, garbage-filled oceans, polluted water, sickening air, poisoned soils. The widespread destruction of habitats has as its flipside the extinction of plant and animal species that dwell in them. By a conservative estimate, in the last quarter of the twentieth century 10 percent of all living species went extinct. The dying off has only become more rapid in the twenty-first century. The behavior of the human species is killing birth itself, shutting down the future of our fellow creatures who took millions of years to evolve. In the blunt language of the World Council of Churches, "The stark sign of our times is a planet in peril at our hands."[1]

At first glance, it seems odd that the natural world does not have a place of honor in theology. The belief that God created this world, not just human beings but the whole natural world, is a central pillar of Christian teaching. The Bible itself opens with a magnificent mythic poem detailing how God utters the world into being, with all its various habitats and fecund creatures, and delights in it on the Sabbath day (Gen. 1:1–2:4a); the Bible closes with a vision of a transformed heaven and earth awash in the glory of God (Rev. 21:1–4). In less picturesque fashion all the creeds of the church include the natural world in their confessions of faith. Among them, the Nicene Creed confesses the church's belief "in one God, the Father almighty, Maker of heaven and earth, of all things visible and invisible"; and in Jesus Christ "through whom all things were made," and who became incarnate, suffered, died, and rose again; and "in the Holy Spirit, the Lord and Giver of life" who awakens hope for "the resurrection of the dead and the life of the world to come." There is no catechism that does not make the doctrine of creation a central teaching. This faith in God the Creator of all things has as its corollary the intrinsically worthy quality of what has been created: "and God saw that it was good" (Gen. 1:10).

Over the centuries, however, for a variety of reasons theology narrowed its interests to focus on human beings almost exclusively. Our special capacities, roles, sinfulness, and need for salvation became the all-consuming interest. The result was a powerful anthropocentric paradigm that shaped every aspect of endeavor. It cast Christology, for example, in its mold. The good news of the gospel flowing from the death and resurrection of Christ offered hope to human beings while the great biblical theme of cosmic redemption flew by in silence. Every area of theology can be charted making similar moves. Even theology of creation, once it gave due play to the appropriate truths, became a backdrop for the human drama. The natural world was simply there as something God created for human use.

This sketch is incomplete because there were always exceptions. In an influential study, *The Travail of Nature*, Paul Santmire points out how Irenaeus and the mature Augustine, among some few others, included the natural world in their understanding of salvation history.[2] Other historical studies find the ecological motif showing up in some of the early desert Fathers and Mothers, in first millennium Celtic saints like Bridget and Ciaran, and in medieval thinkers such as Hildegard of Bingen, Meister Eckhart, and Julian of Norwich; appearing around the edges of scholastic theologians like Thomas Aquinas and Reformers Martin Luther and John Calvin; surfacing in the sensitivities of the Wesley brothers, John and Charles, and in Teilhard de Chardin; and blossoming in Eastern Orthodox theologies. By every account Francis of Assisi stands out for his extravagant love and blessing of fellow creatures. This subterranean stream of creation theology shows Christianity is not an inherently anti-ecological faith. Yet in the overall voice of theology, the voice heard in universities, seminaries, and pulpits until the latter part of the twentieth century, the natural world as a subject of religious interest had largely slipped from view.

Without losing valuable insights into the grandeur, misery, and redemption of the human condition, theology in our ecological era must broaden its anthropocentric focus for its own adequacy. It must reclaim the natural world as an essential element both in theory and in practice or risk missing one of the great, if not the greatest, religious issues of our age. It is not a matter of either-or, of either human importance or the value of all other life. The ecological crisis makes clear that human populations and the natural world will flourish or collapse together. Given the long eclipse of interest in nature, however, the mandate now is to bring the buzzing, blooming world of life back into theological focus.

At this juncture in the history of theology, women have joined the public conversation for the first time. Their voices make distinctive contributions to this life or death project.

WOMEN'S VOICES

The first Earth Day was celebrated in 1970. This event coincided with the period when the second wave of feminism in the United States resulted in biblical and theological study being opened to women on a wide scale. In short order, women began to teach and publish in a scholarly vein. Almost from the beginning some saw the connection between sexism and ecological harm. Rosemary Radford Ruether's first book, *New Woman/New Earth* (1973), argued that there can be no liberation for women and no solution to the ecological crisis within a society whose fundamental model of relationship is one of patriarchal domination, for this pattern of control is at the core of the oppression of both women and the earth.[3] Mary Daly's groundbreaking work *Beyond God the Father* (1973) connected women's struggle with the struggle of all earth's inhabitants to participate, against high odds, in a vibrant community of life. Forging a cosmic covenant of sisterhood would change our culture from one of environmental degradation to a culture of reciprocity, she wrote, because we are all siblings, and "one does not rape a sister."[4] The analysis grew richer as women of color and of different ethnic groups in the United States and women on different continents brought their own contexts into the conversation. Early on *Inheriting Our Mothers' Gardens* (1988), edited by Letty Russell, Kwok Pui-lan, Ada María Isasi-Díaz, and Katie Geneva Cannon, struck chords of connection between women, nature, racial oppression, poverty, struggle, and the beauty that women create on and with the earth.[5] By now, in the twenty-first century, women of all races on every continent have generated a treasury of important ideas that are contributing to the "greening" of religious discourse. The following three areas of theology provide a sampler.

Christian Anthropology

Classical theology dealt with the meaning of being human under the rubrics of the person being created body and soul in the image of God, being sinful yet redeemed by Christ and sanctified by the Holy Spirit, and being destined for eternal glory. Within this overarching picture, the significance of being male and female found its place. What is a woman? What is a man? What role does difference play within and between the genders? And who gets to decide?

Women's analysis casts suspicion on the customary answers, which for centuries have been shaped by the paradigm of hierarchical dualism. Drawn originally from Hellenistic philosophy, this thought pattern divides reality into two separate spheres, spirit and matter, and ranks them as being of greater and lesser value, respectively. On the one hand, spirit is a transcendent principle expressed in act, autonomy, reason, the soul, in what is light, permanent, infinite. Matter, on the other hand, is an inferior principle manifested in passivity, dependence, emotions, the body, in what is dark, transitory, finite.

For the human person as a generic individual, this dualism meant the body was less valuable than the soul, which was meant to rule over the recalcitrant flesh. When applied to gendered human beings, hierarchical dualism identifies men with spirit, capable of acting with rational vigor and obviously closer to the divine. Women embody the lower, material principle, existing with a natural inferiority for which there is no remedy. Translated into social structures, this worldview requires the headship of rational man over emotional woman, whose reproductive powers and life skills he needs but whom he must control for her own good. The dualism also elevates human beings as a whole, blessed with rational souls, over Earth's other living creatures, which are allied with matter and thus of lesser worth. The spirituality typically associated with this thought pattern by and large devalued the earth as a decaying present reality over against heaven, an eternal spiritual reality. Progress along a path of holiness was propelled by the metaphor of ascent: one must flee the material world and rise to the spiritual sphere where the light of divinity dwells. Even when the natural world was granted a certain value, this judgment was based on its usefulness for human beings, not its own merit. The framework of thought had no room for nature's intrinsic worth.

Culturally and symbolically, women have long been associated with "Mother Earth," both bringing forth life and nurturing it out of their own bodies. In a dualistic framework, both are placed on the underside of the dualistic relation. While both are necessary to maintain man's life, man rightfully masters and commands them, for he is superior in the ontological hierarchy of being. The oppression of woman thus becomes symbolically the oldest archetype of the connection between social dominance and the domination of nature, both defined and controlled by patriarchal systems.

Ruether was the first to extend this analysis beyond women and nature to include the oppression of race and class, whereby one privileged group defines and subjugates another.[6] Elisabeth Schüssler Fiorenza coined the word *kyriarchy*, or the rule of the lord, to denote this interlocked complex of oppressions that is broader than *patriarchy*, or simply the rule of men over women.[7] Kwok Pui-lan has gathered voices that broaden the critique further to include colonialism, one nation assuming it has the right to invade and occupy another to profit from its resources while ignoring the devastating effect on indigenous cultures and their natural environment.[8] In all these instances violence is always present, implicitly or explicitly, as an essential instrument for kyriarchal control.

In the face of this powerful tradition of subordination, women's intellectual and practical efforts to develop mutual relations of partnership between the sexes and between human beings and the earth make clear that it is not enough just to mention them—add women and stir, or add creation and stir. The taproot of hierarchical dualism goes so deep that no matter how we superficially trim the branches, the tree will continue to grow distorted and unjust relationships. The taproot must be uprooted and a new vision of wholeness be put down in its place.

With this imperative women labor to give new religious valence to the body, reaffirming the sacrality of matter by seeing the life-giving powers of women's bodies and of nature linked to divine creative activity itself. Moving away from gender essentialism, they develop the idea of women that highlights and respects difference. Criticizing the abstract concept of the isolated individual, they construct a relational notion of the self constituted in community. In place of hierarchical relations they work to develop the idea of reciprocal relations between women and men that prize mutuality. In these and other ways women's theological work of self-definition over against the traditional dualistic paradigm has direct implications for greening religious discourse. As women to men, so the natural world to humanity: both relations in need of profound healing. Deconstructing the pyramid of privilege in favor of the circle of the community of life, all networked in different but mutual relations, women's work in theological anthropology—still a work in progress—points a way forward to a holistic theology of nature.[9]

Theology of God

Modern theology, undertaken with the rational tools of the Enlightenment, generally arrived at the existence of a deity by rational inference, modeled him on a ruling monarch, and placed him at the very peak of the hierarchy of being. "He," for the dualistically superior male was always the prime model for this construction, dwelt beyond the world, uncontaminated by its messiness. Even when this Supreme Being was portrayed with a benevolent attitude (which the best of theology did), "He" was still essentially remote, breaking in periodically to reveal and save, to work miracles or punish. This notion is still current in popular culture as captured in the description of disaster as "an act of God" for which one can be remunerated by an insurance policy. Doing justice to neither the transcendence of God, who is not a being among other beings acting in this world, nor to divine immanence, the Spirit of God indwelling and empowering all reality, this type of theology forgot that everything abides *in* God, in whom "we live and move and have our being" (Acts 17:28) and who in turn encompasses all things, being "above all and through all and in all" (Eph. 4:6).

Women's work in this area goes far beyond simply retrieving female and cosmic images of God from Scripture and historical tradition. These retrievals are important, and their power to disrupt patriarchal discourse about a male-inflected God who justifies male authority on earth cannot be underestimated. More profoundly, theology in women's voices uses these images as windows to a new vision of the ineffable Holy One who relates to the world intimately and differently from the ways of a patriarchal monarch. In her beautiful essay on the biblical use of womb imagery, for example, Phyllis Trible traces what she calls the semantic journey of a metaphor "from the wombs of women to the compassion of God."[10] In all complexity this journey unveils the God who, more than any mother possibly could, loves without limit. Other women have explored the Wisdom tradition, discovering in the female figure of Sophia the God who is forever active in the world, creating, liberating, showing the path to life. Still others track the biblical *ruah* to uncover divine immanence in every blessed or broken situation; or to draw out themes of divine maternity, from pregnancy and giving birth to nursing and carrying, all of which connote aspects of salvific love.[11]

Among those who see that expanding the image of God has significant import for the natural world, Sallie McFague makes an intriguing contribution.[12] In place of the monarchical model, she proposes a thought experiment that would imagine God as Mother, Lover, and Friend of the world, which is God's body. As she works out this insight systematically, it becomes clear that a powerful ethic motivates her theology. Not only does she restore what is physical, the earth itself, to prime theological value. But aware of the suffering that bodiliness entails, she also construes faith so that believers *must act* responsibly on behalf of the whole community of life to protect and restore its flourishing.

Consider McFague's theology of God as Mother. Mothers do three things: they give birth, rejoicing that the new life exists; they feed and protect their young; and they work to ensure that the young grow and are fulfilled. So too with God the Creator. Like a mother she brings forth the world, humans and all other species alike; she cares for the most basic needs of life; and she wants all to grow and thrive. Far from sentimental stereotypes of maternal softness, the female experience of gestation, birth, and lactation engenders vigorous protective instincts. Thus, one implication of this maternal model is an ethic of justice. God as mother wants all the children to be fed; she angrily judges those who hog the table to the detriment of others who starve; restoring food to all in the community of life is absolutely essential. "The mother-God as creator is involved in economics, the management of the household of the universe, to ensure the just distribution of goods to *all*."[13]

As with anthropology, women's theological work on God has far-reaching impact on greening religious discourse.[14] At this point we have left far behind a universe of body-spirit dualism presided over by a distant king. In its place, what is coming into view is a holistic model of an interdependent community of life, created and indwelt by a generative Mother-Lover-Friend in saving communion with all creatures. For believers, an ethic of ecological care follows with compelling logic.

Ethics

As the women's movement has spread globally, a chorus of culturally diverse voices adds its own challenging, inspiring music. One relevant theme repeats in virtually every developing nation, namely, the connection between women and earth and the poverty that devastates both. Ivone Gebara in Brazil and women of the *Con-spirando* Collective in Chile; Aruna Gnanadason and Astrid Lobo Gajiwala in India; Virginia Fabella in the Philippines and Marianne Katoppo in Indonesia; Mercy Amba Oduyoye of Ghana and Teresia Hinga of Kenya— these are but a few whose writings forge an ethical link that theology ignores at the risk of its own integrity.[15]

From economic, political, and cultural perspectives, ecological ethics casts a strongly critical light on the current depletion of Earth, its resources, and the living creatures that call it home. The way human beings consume, exploit, and pollute is literally ruining other species in the community of life. From a religious perspective, this ongoing destruction of life is a deeply sinful desecration, fully warranting the coinage of new terms such as ecocide, biocide, geocide to describe them; all are forms of murder. Unfortunately, some ethicists tend to concentrate on the ecological crisis in isolation, to the exclusion of human beings suffering from injustice; some even pit these concerns against each other. But such women as named above will not let us forget the deep-seated connection between ecological devastation and social injustice. Poor people suffer disproportionately from environmental damage; ravaging of people and ravaging of the land on which they depend go hand in hand.

In the Amazon basin, for example, lack of just distribution of land pushes dispossessed rural families to the edges of the rain forest, where, in order to stay alive, they practice slash-and-burn agriculture, in the process destroying pristine habitat, killing rare animals, and displacing indigenous peoples. In the United States, major companies export work to factories across the Mexican border (*maquiladoras*) that cheaply employ thousands of young, rural women to make high quality consumer goods for export while they live in unhealthy squalor in an environment spoiled by toxic waste. Again, the economically well-off can choose to live amid acres of green while poor people are housed near factories, refineries, or waste-processing plants that heavily pollute the environment. The bitterness of this situation is exacerbated by racial prejudice, as environmental racism pressures people of color to dwell in these neighborhoods.

Feminist analysis clarifies in particular how the plight of the poor becomes intensified in poor women whose own biological abilities to give birth are compromised by depleted environments and whose nurturing of children is hampered at every turn by lack of clean water, food, and fuel. Women-initiated projects such as the Chipko movement in India, where village women literally hug the forest trees to prevent lumber interests from cutting them down, and the Green Belt movement started by Nobel Peace Prize winner Wangari Maathai in Kenya, where women plant millions of trees and receive a small income for nurturing them, show how restoring the Earth interweaves intrinsically with the flourishing of poor women and their communities. Women's ethical reflection pioneers the way theology must widen attention beyond humanity and recenter vigorous moral consideration on the whole community of life in order to do justice even to needy human beings.

Theological anthropology, theology of God, ethics: such are but a few of the sub-disciplines in which women have contributed to the growing field of ecological theology. Many superb thinkers have not been named, among them Karen Baker Fletcher, Chung Hyun Kyung, Anne Clifford, Celia Deane-Drummond, Gabriele Dietrich, Mary Grey, Grace Jantzen, Catherine Keller, Sun Ai Lee-Park, Diane Neu, Anne Primavesi, Mary Evelyn Tucker, and Delores Williams. In vastly different, creative ways, each has consulted the experience of women's struggle for human dignity and parlayed this experience into incisive wisdom about ecological theology and ethics. (Not all women have done this work, though I think every responsible theologian today should, women and men alike.) Grateful for all this theological work and indebted to its wisdom, I began to wonder about an area not yet discussed very often in ecological theology, namely Christology. Christian faith pivots on the gospel with its good news of salvation centered in the life, death, and resurrection of Jesus Christ. Is there any connection with our theme? Or is concern with the ecological well-being of the earth just an add-on to teaching about Christ? My own research has surfaced profound connections, presented here as one more woman's voice exploring the ecological meaning of Jesus' ministry, death/resurrection, and connection with the flesh as expressed in incarnation.[16]

JESUS CHRIST AND THE EARTH

As depicted in the Gospels, Jesus of Nazareth's ministry was a brief burst of joyful light. Centered on the coming reign of God, his teaching in parables, healings, and table practices conveyed the compassion of the Holy One for all people, especially for the lost and marginalized. Having inherited the creation faith of Jewish tradition, his vision encompassed all creatures in hope of the coming blessing. Hellenistic dualism had no part in this way of thinking. McFague has drawn the discrete Gospel episodes together into a usable idea she calls the "christic paradigm" that functions as a kind of shorthand that illuminates what the Gospels in their various ways are all about. In a word, "liberating, healing, and inclusive love is the meaning of it all."[17] Those who believe in Christ make a wager that love as Jesus enfleshed it in a human way reveals the ineffable compassion of God. It is the meaning encoded at the core of human life and at the heart of the universe itself. Write the signature of the christic paradigm, drawn from gospel mercy, across the evolving world. Then it becomes clear that Jesus' proclamation of the reign of God in word and deed reveals that plenitude of life for all—not just for one species or an elite group in that species but for all, including poor human beings and all living creatures—is God's original and ultimate intent. It is not just souls that are important. Physical bodies, gifted with dignity, also matter to God: all bodies, not only those beautiful and full of life but also those damaged, violated, starving, dying, bodies of humankind and otherkind alike. Jesus' ministry grounds compassion for all the bodies in creation. With evolutionary awareness, we observe the christic paradigm take on an ecological dimension.

The end of Jesus' life provides another avenue for a positive reprise of the natural world. No exception to perhaps the only ironclad rule in all of nature, Jesus died, his life bleeding out in a spasm of state violence. This disastrous event has always been at the center of christological interpretation. Contemporary theology is rich in reflections on the power of Christ's death to disclose the self-emptying, compassionate nature of divine love, which suffers in solidarity with human beings in order to redeem. Jürgen Moltmann's influential book *The Crucified God* makes this telling point: the dying Jesus' experience of abandonment, reflected in his prayer, "My God, my God, why have you forsaken me?" and the horrific loud cry that ended his life (Matt. 27:46, 50) show that he descended into the very depths of godforsakenness. Thereby the incarnate Son of God ensures that no one will ever again have to die godforsaken, for divine presence will be there.[18] It is as if by inhabiting the inside of the isolating shell of death, Christ crucified brings divine life into closest contact with disaster, setting up a gleam of light for all others who suffer that darkness.

Is this solidarity limited to human beings? Or does it extend to the whole community of life of which human beings are a part? All creatures come to an end. Those with nervous systems know pain and suffering: "the whole creation has been groaning in labor pains until now" (Rom. 8:22), waiting with eager longing to be set free from its bondage to decay. There is strong warrant for extending divine compassion to embrace the suffering groans and the silence of death of all creatures. This unfathomable divine presence means they are not alone but accompanied in their anguish and dying with a love that does not snap off just because they are in trouble. In relation to the natural world, the death of Christ then becomes an icon of God's redemptive co-suffering with all conscious animal life as well as with the human victims of natural and social competition. Calvary reveals that the one God whose presence fills the earth is a God of suffering love, in solidarity with all creatures' living and dying through endless millennia of evolution, from the extinction of species to every sparrow that falls to the ground. Biologically speaking, new life continuously comes from death, over time. Theologically speaking, without diluting the affliction by a facile hope, we dare to think that the presence of the living God in the midst of pain bears creation forward with an unimaginable promise. This conviction does not solve the problem of suffering in a neat systematic way. It does make a supreme difference in what might come next.

For Christian faith, the cross does not have the last word. It blossoms as the tree of life: "He is risen, Alleluia." Starting with a humiliated body laid in a tomb, the resurrection tells of the creative power of divine love triumphing over the crucifying power of evil and the burying power of death. Thanks to its original context in Jewish eschatological expectation, this Easter news has always involved bodiliness as an essential element. Far from the Greek dualism that envisioned the human being composed of separable body and soul, Hebrew anthropology knew only of the body-person, dust of the earth and breath of God in unbreakable unity. Hence, it is not Jesus' soul alone that is saved from death, but his whole body-person-self.

For Jesus personally, the abiding, redeemed validity of his human historical existence was brought to life in God's presence forever. The joy that breaks out at Easter, however, comes from the realization that his blessed destiny is not meant for himself alone, but for everyone who dies. Paul uses a terrific metaphor when he refers to Christ as "the first fruits of those who have died" (1 Cor. 15:20). If you have ever grown tomatoes, you know the joy of picking the first ripe one. But there are more ripening on the vine, and their day of harvest will come. Christ, the first fruits of those who have fallen asleep, the first tomato! Death, then, does not mean annihilation. Rather, the risen Christ awakens hope for transformation of our whole body-person-self, dust and breath together, into the glory of God.

Does this hope apply to other species? Biologically, the human species is interwoven with all life on this planet and its cosmic matrix, from which we cannot be separated. Hence the resurrection gives assurance that the evolving world of life, all of matter in its endless permutations, will not be left behind but will likewise be transfigured by the creative power of God. This assurance would not hold if Easter marked simply the spiritual survival of the crucified one after death. But Christ rose again in his *body*, and lives united with the flesh forever.

So the risen Christ is to be found at the very heart of creation as the gracious and effective promise that creation is indeed going somewhere. Realizing this connection, in the fifth century Ambrose of Milan could preach, "In Christ's resurrection the earth itself arose."[19] Realizing this connection, in the twentieth century Karl Rahner could preach that Christ's "resurrection is like the first eruption of a volcano which shows that in the interior of the world God's fire is already burning, and this will bring everything to blessed ardor in its light. He has risen to show that this has already begun."[20] Easter is the feast of the future of the Earth.

In a beautiful synergy of visual and verbal poetry, the Roman Catholic liturgy of the Easter vigil symbolizes this hope with cosmic symbols of darkness and new fire, light spreading from candle to candle, and earthy symbols of flowers and greenery, water and oil, bread and wine. The first reading is the creation story from Genesis 1. At a climactic moment the *Exsultet*, sung once a year on this night, shouts: "Exult, all creation, around God's throne," for Jesus Christ is risen! The proclamation continues:

> Rejoice, O earth, in shining splendor,
> radiant in the brightness of your King!
> Christ has conquered! Glory fills you!
> Darkness vanishes forever!

The moment passes quickly, but it is nevertheless stunning. At the most magnificent liturgy of the year, the church is singing to the Earth! It, too, needs to hear the good news, because the risen Christ embodies the ultimate hope of all creation. The coming final transformation of history will be the salvation of everything, including the evolving community of life and the whole cosmos itself, brought into communion with the God of life. Because the living God who creates and empowers the evolutionary world also joins the fray, personally drinking the cup of suffering and going down into the nothingness of death, affliction even at its worst does not have the last word.

Before the end of the first century Christians came to believe that in dealing with Jesus of Nazareth, they were dealing with one who is Emmanuel, God with us in the flesh. Odd as it might sound, they developed the radical notion that the one transcendent God who creates and empowers the world freely chooses to save the world not as a kindly onlooker from afar, but by joining this world in the flesh. This insight found influential expression in the prologue of John's Gospel, which declares at its climax: "and the Word became flesh and lived among us" (John 1:14). The original Greek of the Gospel does not speak of the Word becoming human (*anthropos*), or man (*aner*), but flesh (*sarx*), a broader reality. *Sarx* in the New Testament connotes the finite quality of the material world which is fragile, vulnerable, prone to trouble, perishable, the opposite of divine majesty. Taking the powerful biblical theme of God's dwelling among the people of Israel a step further, John's Gospel affirms that in a new and saving event the Word of God *became* flesh, entered personally into the sphere of the material to shed light on all from within.

In truth, the configuration of *sarx* that the Word became was precisely human. *Homo sapiens*, however, does not stand alone as a species. In our day scientific knowledge is repositioning the human species as an intrinsically related part of the evolutionary network of life on our planet, which in turn is a part of the solar system, which itself came into being as a later chapter of cosmic history. The current consensus about cosmology holds that the universe originated about 13.7 billion years ago in a primordial explosion rather inelegantly named the Big Bang. Under pressure of gravity, the original gasses that spewed out combined to form stars, and billions of stars together formed galaxies. Roughly five billion years ago, in one corner of one spiral galaxy, giant clouds of debris were spewed out by ancient first-generation stars exploding in their death-throes. These clouds of dust and gas coalesced to form our star, the sun, and the planets of our solar system. Evolutionary biology indicates that 3.5 billion years ago on our own planet, the third rock from the sun, another momentous change took place when chemicals and minerals combined in such a way that they formed creatures that could reproduce: the advent of life. Then like a branching tree, life evolved from sea to land to air; from plant to animal life; and on that branch from primates to human beings, we mammals whose brains are so richly textured that we experience self-reflective consciousness and freedom, or in philosophical terms, mind and will.

These discoveries make clear, very concretely, that everything is connected with everything else; nothing conceivable is isolated. What makes our blood red? Iron. Where does it come from? Drawing on the universe story, Arthur Peacocke explains, "Every atom of iron in our blood would not be there had it not been produced in some galactic explosion billions of years ago and eventually condensed to form the iron in the crust of the earth from which we have emerged."[21] Quite literally, human beings are made of stardust, as are all other living creatures on this planet. In addition, our descent from life that started in the ancient seas means that we humans share with all living creatures on earth a common genetic ancestry. Trace the great branching tree of life back through time and you come to a shared trunk and the same deep root. Bacteria, pine trees, blueberries, horses, the great wild Atlantic tuna—we are all kin in *one* community of life.

The landscape of our imagination expands when we realize that the flesh of humanity itself is part of the vast body of the cosmos. In this context, the *sarx* of John 1:14 reaches beyond Jesus and beyond all other human beings to encompass the whole biological world of living creatures and the cosmic dust of which we are composed. The incarnation has cosmic significance. Rather than being a barrier that distances us from the divine, the matter of this world can function as a mediation to the immediacy of God. Hence by carrying out our creative responsibilities in and to the world of matter, to the natural world and all its inhabitants, to species in their current struggle to survive, we set out on the path of discipleship. Interpreting Christology this way roots an ethic of earthkeeping in the deepest core of Christian faith. Ethically, it impels us all to seek ways of living with other species on the tree of life, treating them with respect and vigorous care and being proactive in their protection. We share with them a common origin, a common history, and a hope-filled common goal; they are our kin.

An ecological Christology reveals at least this much.

CONCLUSION

Androcentric theology is passé. So too is anthropocentric theology. Women's work in its multifaceted difference is helping to grow theology into a broader, more generous enterprise. A flourishing humanity on a thriving earth in an evolving universe, all together filled with the glory of God: such is the global vision theology is being called to in this critical time of Earth's distress. Ignoring this vision will keep churches locked into irrelevance as today's terribly real drama of life and death is being played out in the natural world. But rediscovering the religious value of the natural world sets us off on a great spiritual adventure. Instead of living as thoughtless or greedy exploiters, we become empowered to live as sisters and brothers, friends and lovers, kin of the natural world that God so loves.

Notes

1. World Council of Churches, Canberra Assembly, "Giver of Life—Sustain Your Creation!" in *Signs of the Spirit*, ed. Michael Kinnamon (Grand Rapids: Eerdmans, 1991), 55.
2. Paul Santmire, *The Travail of Nature: The Ambiguous Ecological Promise of Christian Theology* (Minneapolis: Fortress, 1985), chaps. 3 and 4; see also the resource compiled by Jame Schaefer, *Theological Foundations for Environmental Ethics: Reconstructing Patristic and Medieval Concepts* (Washington, DC: Georgetown University Press, 2009).
3. Rosemary Radford Ruether, *New Woman/New Earth* (New York: Seabury, 1973).
4. Mary Daly, *Beyond God the Father* (Boston: Beacon, 1973), 178.
5. Letty Russell, Kwok Pui-lan, Ada María Isasi-Díaz, and Katie Geneva Cannon, eds., *Inheriting Our Mothers' Gardens: Feminist Theology in Third World Perspective* (Louisville, KY: Westminster, 1988).
6. Rosemary Radford Ruether, *Sexism and God-Talk* (Boston: Beacon, 1983) and her *Gaia and God: An Ecofeminist Theology of Earth Healing* (San Francisco: Harper, 1993).
7. Elisabeth Schüssler Fiorenza, *But SHE Said: Feminist Practices of Biblical Interpretation* (Boston: Beacon, 1992).
8. Kwok Pui-lan, ed., *Hope Abundant: Third World and Indigenous Women's Theology* (Maryknoll, NY: Orbis, 2010).
9. Heather Eaton, *Introducing Feminist Theologies* (London: T&T Clark, 2005) offers one fine overview; see also Mary Heather MacKinnon and Moni McIntyre, *Readings in Ecology and Feminist Theology* (Kansas City, MO: Sheed and

Ward, 1995); and Agnes Brazal and Andre Lizares Si, eds., *Body and Sexuality: Theological-Pastoral Perspectives of Women in Asia* (Manila: Ateneo de Manila University Press, 2007).
10. Phyllis Trible, *God and the Rhetoric of Sexuality* (Philadelphia: Fortress, 1978), 31–59.
11. See Elizabeth A. Johnson, *She Who Is: The Mystery of God in Feminist Theological Discourse* (New York: Crossroad, 1992).
12. Sallie McFague, *Models of God: Theology for an Ecological, Nuclear Age* (Philadelphia: Fortress, 1987).
13. Ibid., 116–23.
14. Carol Adams, ed., *Ecofeminism and the Sacred* (New York: Continuum, 1993) collects an amazing array of feminist and womanist ecological perspectives.
15. Ivone Gebara, *Longing for Running Water: Ecofeminism and Liberation* (Minneapolis: Fortress, 1999); Mary Judith Ress, *Ecofeminism in Latin America* (Maryknoll, NY: Orbis, 2006); and Rosemary Radford Ruether, ed., *Women Healing Earth: Third World Women on Ecology, Feminism, and Religion* (Maryknoll, NY: Orbis, 1996).
16. Elizabeth A. Johnson, *Ask the Beasts: Darwin and the God of Love* (London: Bloomsbury, 2014).
17. Sallie McFague, *The Body of God: An Ecological Theology* (Minneapolis: Fortress, 1993), 161.
18. Jürgen Moltmann, *The Crucified God* (New York: Harper and Row, 1974), 242–46.
19. Ambrose of Milan, Patrologia Latina, 16:1354.
20. Karl Rahner, "Easter: A Faith that Loves the Earth," *The Great Church Year: The Best of Karl Rahner's Homilies, Sermons, and Meditations*, ed. Albert Raffelt (New York: Crossroad, 1993), 194–95.
21. Arthur Peacocke, "Theology and Science Today," in *Cosmos as Creation*, ed. Ted Peters (Nashville: Abingdon Press, 1989), 32.

Chapter 13

Daily Life Challenges as the Criterion for Biblical and Feminist Theological Hermeneutics

IVONE GEBARA

INTRODUCTION

Since the last century we have observed a separation among different fields of study that reflect on religion and the living out of religion in daily life, with all the limits, challenges, and wisdom present in it. The gap between scientific research and religious experiences is wide, despite various scholars' publications in newspapers, books, or on the Internet. In the same vein, most religious authorities seem to ignore new challenges and new approaches. They continue to repeat the same theological content of the past and reinforce the power of cultural hierarchical models.

In the last ten years, I have felt deeply challenged by the complex movement of human religious beliefs, particularly in some institutional churches. Throughout this time I have been trying to identify aspects of this moving puzzle. In my personal view it is not an ordinary puzzle where we can slowly adjust the various pieces and see the previous picture or the stamp. It is a puzzle where there is not a fixed picture in advance, in spite of some pieces with defined colors and forms. Each person and each group moves as a piece in her, his, or its direction. The result could be a mixture of harmony and clashes. From the perspective of this moving puzzle, to have faith, have a religion, be a believer or not a believer, worship the Bible, the Qur'an, or any other sacred text is to follow the heavy flow of the traffic of new ideas melded with old ones.

To be clearer about my reflections, I must say that in Latin America reading and interpreting the Bible are linked to a Christian church that itself provides the ways to understand the texts. Inside and among the churches, we can find a multiplicity of interpretations and conflicts. A secular reading of the Bible as a literary book is not widespread on our continent.

My reflection develops aspects of this complex and challenging situation. A provisional and limited analysis, it offers a view of the present context of Latin America, particularly Brazil. As a scholar and feminist activist, my aim is to build bridges of mutual learning and to make connections between different cultural worlds in our present history in order to help us to live with dignity.

In my way of perceiving the problem, there is sometimes a gap between an analytical way of reflecting about religious subjects, including biblical studies and feminist religious studies, and what common believers experience as their faith in different situations. Similarly, we observe a distance between some new anthropological and theological research since the last century and the continuity and spread of patriarchal theologies linked to past cultures and past philosophies. Advanced religious studies and theological research seem to be cultural products offered and accepted by a very small elite. Such studies and research modify quite minimally traditional religious practices without offering new alternatives of worship or simple new theological teachings more adjusted to the current challenges of our living together.

One can ask why this gap is present, particularly in Latin America where liberation theology, ecumenical biblical studies, and feminist theology from the perspective of the poor introduced, more than thirty years ago, a qualitative difference in the understanding of Christian tradition.[1] Why have we not been able to continue this liberationist movement? Why are we so far from a democratic sharing of knowledge, especially in certain areas of human sciences? And why are the authorities of Christian churches so resistant to the new winds blowing in our time?

In my understanding this gap reveals different anthropological aspects frequently hidden from our common perception on religious issues. I want to stress some of them, which I have perceived personally from living throughout these years, in order to suggest why most institutional Christian churches are still reproducing theologies that do not help the present challenges of our world, especially regarding women's issues. Further, I want to share some reasons why feminist theology is not strongly present in Christian communities, particularly in the lives of poor women believers in Latin America.

TWO SIDES OF THE SAME COIN AND PERHAPS MORE

I propose the image of a coin spinning, in some moments showing one face and in other moments the other side. But one face depends on the other, and the movement sometimes provokes confusion between the two faces and expresses the complex movement of human history. Given this complexity, the description of each face is limited. It allows us to have an idea about what is happening, though not in totality.

On the one hand, scholars in religious fields, theologians, and philosophers of religion frequently treat the complex phenomena of religion only as an object of study. They study religion, but they are not necessarily believers in a religion, in spite of their personal interest. This observation is not a judgment but an important point to help us understand what is going on in the daily life of many scholars and of many believers. In a sense I can say that scholars treat religion as an *object*, from the outside: observing, studying, and comparing different sources, texts, contexts, methods, and interpretations. They submit religious beliefs to one model of rationality present in our time, and they critically affirm these beliefs according to their personal anthropological, political, and ethical choices, and scientific hypotheses. It is a kind of rationalistic analysis and sometimes a reduction of religion to their perspective or to an ethical and political perspective without considering what is going on in the diverse community of believers with their diverse experiences, contexts, cosmo-visions, personal problems, and emotional aspects. For some scholars, these aspects seem contradictory to rational scientific affirmations and new religious insights. This last observation does not reduce the value of religious investigation or theoretical hypotheses or different scientific approaches, but it invites us to reflect more on these issues from pluralistic and interconnected perspectives.

On the other hand, believers—particularly poor people, and among them most women—are living religion from the inside. From their necessity, from their sufferings, from their unanswered questions they live religion and seek answers. The inside is connected to their external living situation, to the sorrows, sufferings and hopes of the moment. That is, the interior responses they claim are connected to the exterior realities of their daily life—always demanding relationships of help, of consolation, of justice and freedom. Who is supplying these needs? What are institutional religions doing to answer some of these human necessities?

In Latin American life today, Big Temples—an expression of a new Pentecostal tradition—are full of people searching for some transcendent help, particularly deliverance from diseases or other problems that afflict their lives. Men lead most of the Temples. In Roman Catholicism, processions to different sanctuaries are still full of people, particularly women, walking with big candles or carrying stones in their hands or on their heads to pay promises or to ask for deliverance. Most of them feel guilty because of what they call their sins, which sometimes are connected with sexual issues. Exorcisms as well as traditional devotions of the nineteenth century are back again. It means that our lives, in spite of the present high technology and science, deal with more than a rational program, more than human rights struggles, and more than scientific perceptions of human history. From a popular religious perspective, daily life is full of destructive possessions called the devil, and some people believe that this possession is a real entity that takes their lives and destroys them.[2] They can live this destruction in their poor lives, especially when the lack of housing, food, jobs, and other necessities are present in their daily lives. Even within technological rationality, for most people something beyond themselves is at work in their everyday life.

To be clearer, I am introducing a distinction between living religion and thinking religion from a rational and methodological perspective. I am also affirming that there are at least two logics to deal with religion, even while recognizing their possible connections: one from the inside and the other from the outside. Sometimes they can be integrated, but frequently an existential and theoretical gap persists.

Scholars and other intellectuals develop a special rationality about the events of daily life. They are trained to develop a rational logic quite different from the logic of most believers.[3] For numerous believers, forces beyond their possibilities of understanding move history and can intervene in life and change what *perhaps* is not expected to change. The living of daily life is more or less understandable despite the many daily surprises. Believers have capacity for reflection and analysis, but at the same time they know that there is much more to living. For most, theoretical reasoning has limits, evident by observing daily life events. Again, other reasons, other logics, and other unknown powers make up what is known. For these people, life is not moved only by precise rational thought or by laws that can be controlled by human beings but by an unknown and mysterious reality that is feared and that we are called to praise and thank. This mysterious reality, called God or the spirits, knows more about us and our destiny than any of us do. The spirits or the almighty God act frequently in hierarchical and powerful ways. Finally we have to submit to them and accept that they overcome our own limits. Simply put, from this mental organization of human life patriarchal beliefs are founded. The possibility to change our history depends more on the forces above us than on ourselves. Because of these beliefs, it is difficult to move deeply and change together some behaviors that could be beneficial for all.

Most believers do not engage in a critical analysis about the construction of these hierarchies and their power over us. Such discussion is not integrated in their daily culture. For most of them what happens in our history has to do with the decision of the spirits, who are able to judge us, to help us, and also to punish us following their mysterious will.

Scholars discuss these hierarchies in an abstract way and frequently without any connection to a community of believers. The gap between them and the group of religious believers is clearly present.

FEMINIST THEOLOGY AND POPULAR BELIEFS

Feminist theology in Latin America began in the 1980s with the concern and responsibility to be linked to the most important struggles for women's dignity, and with a particular option for poor women.[4] Quickly, however, for different reasons feminist theology took another direction, not from a theoretical approach but from a practical one.

Feminist theology in Latin America also reproduces the split characterized by the distance between living religions, controlled by traditional hierarchical power, and thinking religions. We must be aware that while our theological reflections have yielded benefits, our research remains distant from the living faith of common people. Most people do not want to be bound by a group of religious thinkers who invite them to be critical and to change. They prefer to keep traditional expressions. Let me share, for example, some ideas or images developed by feminist theologies and some of their impacts:

- Beginning with the criticism of a monotheistic image of God the Father that reflects men's domination, we introduce a *re-flexion,* a distance, a suspicion, a doubt, a different way of looking at the experience of God. We also introduce new emotional experiences and new language. These critiques identify a division inside us, an evident distance from our traditional beliefs and a change from what is the official belief in our culture. We learn that *God is good and powerful and has a male image.* While new images are spread in small feminist circles, most people inside the churches are using and believing in the same patriarchal image of God, the same prayers, the same symbols in the expression of their public beliefs. Feminist theologians have small entry into such religious circles. Personally, they mostly feel far removed from these traditional expressions of faith.
- The inclusive idea of the *Jesus Movement* rather than the centrality of the person of Jesus is rejected by traditional christological belief. Most poor and middle class people cannot live from their deep beliefs without this centrality, particularly within themselves. They need to find a subject, a personal energy, and a name with whom to relate. They are used to being inhabited by the centrality of God, the father, and Jesus, the only son. They find it hard to deal with a movement inside themselves. I am sure that there are lots of misunderstandings in the way in which these ideas were explained to simple people. What we have to preserve or remember is that the psychological and emotional aspect present in these patriarchal religious experiences is relevant to the development of new ideas and propositions from feminist perspectives. Being aware of that situation encourages us to find new ways to spread new ideas and methodologies and to stay close to simple people searching for meaning and help in their lives.

A new way of reading the Bible stresses the wisdom and also the contradictions and cruelty present in the book.[5] For most young and adult believers this new way causes insecurity regarding what they learned to be the Word of

God. The proposed new experience seems to limit the authority of the sacred book, give it another place in their lives, another interpretation, and reduce its importance. Insecurity surfaces regarding their relationship with the book and with what is called the Word of God. Accordingly, most people prefer to put these new insights in parentheses or forget them and go back to their traditional patriarchal ways of reading, celebration, and prayer. These old ways are more adjusted to the cultural and political background still strongly present in our countries in spite of the varnish of modernity and democracy.

In spite of this insecure situation present in church circles and basic community celebrations, some people are able to welcome with joy and freedom all these critical ways of reading and understanding Christian tradition. We know how much the new perspectives helped some women particularly to introduce issues such as reproductive rights, sexual orientation, rights for choice and pleasure, struggle against domestic violence and sexual violence—all in a different and more open perspective.[6] Further, these new perspectives helped most women to rethink how to deal in daily life with situations where life is threatened by all sorts of diseases and unfair situations. New women's organizations, designed particularly to struggle for justice, developed from these new theologies and biblical hermeneutics.

What impresses me is that most of these women touched by feminist perspectives do not share this new meaning publicly in their communities. Consequently, we can observe again the split between the new paradigms and their public expression in daily life and faith. Fewer feminist women use a communitarian reference to share their faith and to worship with others in ways consistent with their new insights. They live new forms of sisterhood struggling for laws to protect women, also denouncing daily life injustices inside some churches, but without a community, a regular presence, and a regular worship. In regard to this question, I note that the last census in Brazil (2010) shows that women, in larger numbers than men, are leaving the Roman Catholic Church. The split is reinforced because religious authorities do not value the new struggles and choices of women as Christian struggles for dignity. As we know, feminist theologians do not have the opportunity to introduce an alternative Christian interpretation and formation inside Christian communities, particularly in the Roman Catholic tradition. For this tradition there is only one church and one Master, Jesus the Unique Son of God, represented by the power of the male clergy. Women still deal with the problem of recognition by church authorities while trying to communicate women's choices and expectations. Women's authority in monotheistic religions is still not recognized. In addition, civil and political authorities of different countries recognize as religious authorities only those who are invested by an institutional religious power. The lack of religious power among women remains stark.

In different places of our continent, cultural changes from a patriarchal background are still in their beginnings. We must also admit that for some people, the wisdom of traditional religions has been more or less abandoned and replaced by a new religion of consumerism or by other alternatives that can give them some support or immediate meaning. The emptiness of religious references is not remedied but discarded in the present rush of life. Again, we are invited to think about what religious references mean today, how they can help us, and how we can deal with past/present new references.

BELIEVING FROM THE INSIDE

From the inside most people from Latin America who inherited colonial Christian tradition believe in the patriarchal God and look at Scripture as a justification of their sufferings or source of consolation within the insecurity and difficulties that they are living. This view does not mean that they know or read the Bible. They listen to some texts and some comments; they develop some local traditions; they have some ideas and references from their churches or from their families that enable them to receive the sacraments and affirm their Christian identity. In some places religious identity remains very important in spite of the new challenges of our time.

From this simple cultural and educational background most Christians affirm personal beliefs:

- That in the Scriptures what is happening today was announced before
- That someone powerful is hearing me or that someone knows my sufferings better than I
- That I am supported mysteriously by a caring strength and that I cannot change what is determined by God
- That something better could happen to me
- That relief for my pain is possible and I can have hope
- That I am supported and guided by a mysterious hand and that all that happens to me is the desire of God.

All such beliefs seem to be connected to a religious experience from within, which means from our own experience as human beings. We are always in need of help, consolation, and solidarity. Patriarchal religions seem to have developed a particular way to deal with our anguish, fears, needs, and dreams in a hierarchical way. Always one who is above me can help me; one who is stronger can give me a hand. This logic is very well known in our cultures.

My questions are about feminist theologies beyond all the critique of patriarchal images and interpretations that helped most of us to replace our beliefs. How are we dealing with these human aspirations and needs? Are they provoking us in order to create together new languages to express our deep desires? Are they helping us to propose new places for the experience of transcendence or for new ways of solidarity among poor women?

I am trying to reflect on these questions from a certain distance, so as to capture the consequences in one's personal and collective life. Because of that, I turn to the distinction between *the after suffering* and *the inside of suffering*, especially in its deepest point. In our present culture, during great sufferings patriarchal messages seem to help and support individuals and communities. In an earthquake, a flight disaster, a big storm, or in epidemics of all sorts of diseases, and also in situations of cruel violence against women, it is always Christian patriarchal explanations that come to mind along with collective experiences of worship. Almost always the experience is related to a mysterious God who can hear and help or to the suffering of Jesus, a suffering that is always bigger than the individual's. Or one seeks connection with the Virgin Mary because she knows how to help her child. This connection shows how much believers seem to be linked emotionally to primal experiences regarding vital relations with their mothers.[7]

In these situations, songs and prayers mostly repeat the same traditional patriarchal schema. We feminists still do not have an inclusive musical and poetic schema that could be present in different spaces of our culture and particularly in churches. I am not blaming ourselves but only making a point about the difficulties that we have in patriarchal religious structures.

Some intellectuals can say that this religious behavior of common people is a way to collect energy from the self and has nothing to do with feminist theologies. In my understanding a new challenge arises for the agenda of a pluralistic, twenty-first-century feminist philosophy and theology: to think from the inside about human religious needs.

CRITICIZING FROM THE OUTSIDE

"Let me see your acts and I will know who you are" and "By its fruits we know the tree."[8] Some employ these popular and traditional expressions in order to prioritize actions more than ideas, historical events more than desires and idealistic dreams. They mean that we have to evaluate also from the outside, or from the visible fruits, our beliefs and the efficacy of words like love, sharing, and justice in our daily relationships. The question not only concerns the use of modern theological language without any real transformation in visible relationship but also the challenge of faith from the inside, which is able to show something different on the outside. For example, by praying a rosary, some women and men from the northeast of Brazil took possession of a piece of land and made their community there. The interior piety of these peasants was very traditional in form but produced actions of justice. Relationships between the inside and outside, between individual and collective history, are woven by uncertainty and complexity.

Most religious scientists study religion from the outside, making it an object of research. This exterior perspective means that we are not analyzing the individual suffering of the believer and her/his needs for help, justice, or guidance. Religious phenomena became "what they are" almost only from the outside or from the observation and the research of the scientist. The researcher observes and analyzes a phenomenon with some mediation and a hypothesis, but not necessarily from a personal commitment or involvement in this faith or in the daily life of this people. A scientist of religion does not take this faith as an ethical code or a commandment coming from God but rather is directed by an analytical process, by an ideology, or by some other religious thought and rationality.

As common people, we also act from the outside when we criticize what we consider religious nonsense. Nonsense is not only what is against a good and respectful sense of life but also whatever nonsense is for me or for my milieu. Personally I sometimes lived this extremely difficult situation, feeling divided between my personal research and poor people's lives. Once I was visiting a sanctuary of the Virgin Mary in the city of Juazeiro in the northeast of Brazil. I was in a crowd of people trying to approach the altar of the Virgin Mary, and I was observing the multiple reactions of believers. Suddenly, I was touched by the presence of a curved old man trying to reach the altar. I offered him my help. He took my arm and we walked together. Arriving in front of the image he was astonished. He raised his head and saw the blue eyes and dress of the Virgin Mary and said slowly: "She is so pretty"; "She is so nice"; and we went back out of the crowd.

What happened inside him? What forces were moved on? What desires were satisfied or awakened? I do not know. What I suspect is that he experienced something that has value and gave him something good. Similar experiences can be observed in Muslim pilgrimages, in Buddhist temples, and in other religious settings. Human beings are able to build their own moments of healing and beauty. An esthetic and gratifying moment of beauty cannot be captured by scientific approaches. Such a moment lies beyond descriptive and rational theories.

In this same manner regarding the outside aspect, human rights and women's rights have become more and more widespread in different countries. The consciousness of the cultural oppression of religion and its alliance with politically conservative movements is also growing. Human and women's rights have become criteria to judge religions, personal and collective behaviors, and beliefs. Human and women's rights may have a negative power over our collective beliefs if they are not respecting our lives. Human rights are not necessarily religious rights, and they have, in some sense, the intention to be above religious rights, despite the fact that religious liberty is considered a human right. Regarding religious sciences, we can observe the complexity and the transverse reality of different approaches. Accordingly, we can say that when religious beliefs became a matter of human rights, we opened a new kind of reflection that has to be taken seriously. Feminist theologians bring into question some aspects of patriarchal theologies, claiming they violate women's rights and human rights. A new split is building up inside religious faith and church traditions. All of this invites us to give new reasons for our religious faith and create different organizations able to share pluralistic meanings, traditions, and powers.

FEMINIST CONSOLATION AND CELEBRATION

From the perspective of feminist theologies and biblical feminist hermeneutics, there is a big distance and void between the power of naming our sufferings collectively and being one with another in consolation or in joy in public worship spaces. The production of a theological discourse that church women can accept as part of their tradition is still incipient in Latin America. For instance, we do not have a relevant worship service that can incorporate our religious tradition and cultural elements to celebrate our life, sorrows, and joys beyond the ways offered by patriarchal religions. Efforts made by some feminist women among us were experienced frequently as distant from what most poor women were used to experiencing as worship. Contents, new songs, and new prayers were not as integrated as the old ones. Further, small initiatives that were proposed were considered a threat to the established religious order that still keeps women and laypeople in an inferior place. So we are all challenged to create new artistic expressions, new poetry that touches our hearts and relates to what we are living today.

What we call traditionally "pastoral theology" is not widespread from a feminist perspective because of the impossibility for feminist women to occupy some spaces in institutional churches and have their proposals accepted. We are not encouraged to build a new tradition and new theological languages inside our churches, so we do not use our creativity and strength in this direction.

We feminists need to ask ourselves certain questions. What are our beliefs and what is the incidence of Christian patriarchal tradition in our own personal lives? All of us know that changing religious beliefs only from the outside, or from an analytical and political perspective, is a limited form of change. We must be aware of looking for help from above or from outside ourselves. The challenge now is to recover the strength present in our own selves and in our common solidarity. We have to be educated to develop this solidarity from a global and local perspective. In other words, a new way to do feminist pastoral theology is required within Christian tradition. This new way has to begin by each one of us asking about the meaning of what we call Christian life. With patience and love, we have to ask ourselves what we want to keep, what we want to transform, and what we want to leave out. These are questions from within, questions that could also have negative answers. A negative response means that we can say that Christian tradition has no more meaning inside us in spite of its existence outside or its presence in our historical context.

Of course, our questions about the new challenges of life have no definitive answers. Human needs for consolation, intimacy, and solidarity are still present in all situations of joy and sufferings, and we are always trying to find an answer from places where we have not received them before. Because of that, if Christian tradition has meaning for some of us, we need spaces to exercise our creativity and together build new expressions of our faith, new spaces in which to console ourselves and to celebrate together. Christian tradition has to be revisited with new eyes, new approaches, new hermeneutics more adjusted to our context and necessities. This change is not only a theoretical challenge but a practical one. It invites us to be in proximity to other bodies, to listen more accurately to their questions, and to try to find some new answers together.

FEMINIST RELIGION AS A POLITICAL CAMP OF ACTION

Some feminist scholars in the field of religion deal with the representatives of Christian churches and conservative social groups as if in a battle camp. On one side, we have women's rights, and on the other, persistent patriarchal religious traditions—with their established concepts of right and wrong, of nature and sin, of salvation and the will of God—interfering too much in social and political decisions.

One of the most conflicted issues concerns women's sexuality, particularly reproductive rights. In Latin American churches and countries, sexual issues open a big split inside Christian beliefs and traditions of authority. Our well-known military and clerical authoritarian tradition, founded in a patriarchal interpretation of Christian faith, organized the moral and cultural spaces for women and for men. In these spaces, control of sexuality, particularly of women's sexuality, was important to maintain social order/disorder. Social order/disorder, as we know it, is also maintained by an idealistic patriarchal religion that in fact forgets real bodies' diversity and their circumstances. A kind of masculine theology, similar to a normative sexual ideology and linked to a hegemonic model of living sexuality, is finally called the will of God or natural law. We women denounce this reductionism and control of our bodies by male religious authorities. We continue to criticize this invention of our bodies to serve economic, social, cultural, and religious models of power in the past and the present. We are trying to build among us plural identities and ways to affirm them that respect the right to be different from the established model.

The denunciation of this indecent theology and policy, as the theologian Marcella Althaus-Reid stressed in her book *Indecent Theology*,[9] is the aim of new organizations, which include "Latin American Catholics for a Free Choice." The big battle against churches and some conservative political movements occurs because they present themselves as the representatives of the true moral-sexual-behavioral standards, according to their vision of the will of God. From this perspective, they control the sexual expressions of women as well as different sexual orientation choices based on an established model. Traditional theological concepts have a limiting geography regarding our bodies. They approve only some bodies as perfect, or they reduce our integral body to certain parts that are affirmed as nobler than others. From this limited perspective, they propose a universal behavior, calling it "respect for life." What life is respected?

This battle is intense. It includes women who are not Christians but are upset with the public hypocritical behavior or the inconsistency of the officials of Christian churches. The situation weaves an alliance between Christian feminists and lay feminists against political and religious fundamentalism.

From this tense situation a new gap is born, a gap between an alternative Christian tradition and the patriarchal tradition present in the churches and traditional religious movements. Alternative Christian tradition tries to respond to new situations lived by different groups in different times and spaces. It is not the affirmation of only one tradition for all but the recognition of problems lived by different cultures, in rural areas as well as in the big urban centers of our continent. These groups work hard to recover the humanistic dimension of our Christian Tradition and try to propose different meanings and answers. The alternative seeks a way to unveil women's bodies, women's history, and women's questions in women's voices and actions, thereby offering new Christian insights for our time.

In the present day, a polarization has developed against institutional churches and their influence in political and cultural milieus. The lack of reconstruction of feminist Christian meanings and new feminist pastoral theologies inside different communities grows more severe. For the generation of us between fifty and seventy years, we have to add a sort of fatigue melded with indignation regarding the impossibility of real changes in traditional religious institutions, in interpretation of biblical narratives, and in beliefs. Patriarchal tradition is very much alive and its politics polarize positions and provoke negative turbulences in different cultural milieu. To face this situation we feminist theologians, organized in different countries in Latin American meetings, try to develop new strategies regarding church policies about women's issues. But sometimes we are not far from repeating the same argument given by the other side. We perceive that we are still in the trap of patriarchal discourses and historical interpretations to justify our side. Nonetheless, we seek a liberation path, and we know that to be faithful to the creative call of freedom, new generations have to create other paths. Maybe it is too early to bring collective revolutionary change in the interpretations of religious traditions, but some signs announcing something new are on our horizon. With active confidence, we have to be patient to see what will happen.

CONCLUSION: THE NEW GEOGRAPHY OF TRANSCENDENCE WITHIN THE HUMAN COMPASSIONATE HEART

We are living in a truly special time. Along with Hans Küng,[10] I dare to say that without a worldwide ethic that includes a new dialogue among religions, we cannot survive. This dialogue is not only among national and international leaders but includes necessarily the plurality of religious groups present in our complex societies. The religion of peripheries, of marginalized people in their diversity, is an important aspect of this searching for common survival. It opens up a large conversation among us, which could have many proponents, including feminist movements. This conversation includes recovering some common truths about human life capable of helping us have some essential values for our living together respectfully.

With the present split provoked by religious fundamentalism, the increasing destruction of our planet, and the production of weapons, we are sometimes tempted to discard religion, believing that it is not important to the present context. The danger today is to lose what I consider an important ethical religious tradition that can help us to build new relations among us in a worldwide perspective. For instance, if I take Matthew's Gospel or another one, as a feminist philosopher and theologian, I can find in it an ethic, a new way to live and perceive transcendence, a new logic of life that can emerge from a synthesis of the present reality and the old wisdom. The old wisdom, present in different religions and cultural ethical approaches, recognizes transcendence in multiple compassionate relationships, in the Other different from me who is able to move me to change behaviors, to change my vision because, together, we discover that we need each other to be alive. Continuity and discontinuity occur at the same time. An evolving worldview helps us to get to other theological streets and avenues on which we are still afraid to walk. The challenge is, perhaps, a new moment to improve Christian heritage in an understandable and plural language for our time. It is a time to find together a common passion for the other, a common presence with the other different from me but fundamental to me. It is time to try again to recognize those who live next door—the poor, the prisoner, the orphan, the immigrant, the river, the forest, the animals—as my neighbors, my friends, my image. Without each one, I and we cannot live.

Most churches do not open spaces to transmit new perspectives, nor do radios or televisions (important vehicles for public education). We are in a challenging moment in which it is not possible to see what Christian faith and other faiths will be tomorrow. New situations and paradigms are erupting and challenging our traditional beliefs and ways of life. Because of that situation we are living our hopes in everyday life as ever new starting points in our own individual and collective experiences.

Toward a *new understanding of transcendence* we are led, no longer a metaphysical one that lives in abstract ideas, but transcendence discovered inside the human heart, within our planet with all its forms of life. Each form of life transcends me and provokes me to welcome the beauty and challenge of otherness as the unique condition to living together. This new proposal is not an idealistic one, not a beautiful word that can be pronounced without any action. This word is a word of life inside and outside of us. It is a word that comes from us and invites us to help each other to choose ways to a respectful life. It invites us to consent to the fact that in spite of our individual constitutive dimension, we cannot live alone. We have to repeat this word in different ways, in different places, for different people, and constantly to one another. We are aware—women and men—of our vulnerability, our temptation to betray ourselves and others, our individualistic system to protect us from the other, our fear to change for more equality and freedom. But if we do not choose the direction of solidarity with all its consequences in economy, in policies, in culture and religion, then perhaps it will be too late to overcome the present global crisis of our humanity. I dare to hope that the growth of human solidarity is part of our human hope.[11]

Our daily life challenge and criterion is to learn how to live together with compassion and solidarity. Daily life experience teaches us that we have to begin with small things, learn from them and from our own behaviors. Because of this simple and complex situation, I propose reflection on daily life challenges as a criterion for biblical and feminist theological hermeneutics. Biblical studies and feminist hermeneutics as an expression of a shared wisdom of life must be connected to the values that we are searching for: namely, better human relationships in daily life. Daily life is our life, our ordinary life, our neighborhood, our family, our country, our history, our body, our breath, our dreams of love, joys and sorrows, and the place where meanings are received and constructed individually and collectively. Daily life is the place of our imagination and deep desire to have a land where honey and milk flow, where a child can play with a snake, where five loaves can feed a multitude, where an old woman can be pregnant, where a poem of love can feed us. It is from daily life, from the small events, meetings, sufferings, and joys that old religious traditions touched our hearts and so became a humanistic tradition able to add to our common fountain a new wisdom coming from the present and future human history.

Notes

1. Liberation theology in Latin America began in the 1970s and feminist theology in the 1980s. For an example of recent work, see Ute Seibert, *Espacios abiertos: caminos de la teología feminista* (Santiago: Conspirando, 2010).
2. Ivone Gebara, *Out of the Depths: Women's Experience of Evil and Salvation* (Minneapolis: Fortress Press, 2002).
3. See Zygmunt Bauman, *Postmodern Ethics* (Oxford, U.K., and Cambridge, U.S.A.: Blackwell, 1994).
4. Ivone Gebara, "The Option for the Poor as the Option for the Poor Woman," in *Concilium*, 194 (1987): 110–17.
5. Phyllis Trible, *Texts of Terror: Literary-Feminist Readings of Biblical Narratives* (Minneapolis: Fortress Press, 1984).
6. See, for example, *Religiões em Diálogo: Violência contra as Mulheres*, Yury Puello Orozco (organizadora) (São Paulo: Católicas pelo Direito a decidir, 2009).
7. Ivone Gebara, *Uma leitura feminista da Virgem Maria.In Maria entre as Mulheres* (São Paulo: Paulus e São Leopoldo: CEBI, 2009).
8. Such traditional proverbs echo New Testament sayings, e.g., Jas. 2:18 and Matt. 7:20.
9. Marcella Althaus-Reid, *La teología indecente. Perversiones teológicas en sexo, género y política* (Barcelona: Bellaterra, 2005).
10. Hans Küng, *Projeto de ética mundial* (São Paulo: Paulinas, 2003).
11. See Ivone Gebara, *Vulnerabilidade, Justiça e Feminismos—Antologia de textos* (São Bernardo do Campo: Nhanduti, 2010).

Chapter 14

Do You Understand What You Are Reading?

African Women's Reading
of the Bible and the Ethos of
Contemporary Christianity in Africa

MERCY AMBA ODUYOYE

Christianity is asserting itself as an African religion. In Africa we have been through epochs when Christianity was seen as a foreign religion impinging on Africa's indigenous beliefs, denigrating them as paganism and superstition. This perception resulted from the Western European Christianizing movement in eighteenth-century Africa. The movement was suspect, coming as it did in the wake of the abolition of the trade in human beings from Africa to Europe, the Caribbean islands, and the Americas. After the so-called World War II and the movements to free African countries from European colonialism, Christianity was labeled Western religion, foreign to Africa, and part of the European conspiracy to keep Africa and Africans under European hegemony so that the continent's resources might flow into Europe unimpeded. Yet many were the efforts African Christians made to isolate Christianity from European colonialism and to free it to be a message destined for all nations. African Christians struggled to show that if Christianity has a home on earth, that home is Africa. Leaders highlighted the early church history of Mediterranean North Africa, and African theologians worked intently to relate African culture to Christianity.

Translations of the Bible into African languages enabled Africans to hear and to read the biblical message directly. The result was an explosion of African

Instituted Churches (AICs). Conversely, churches that used to be mission stations of churches in Europe and America—that is, Western Churches in Africa—are now being designated Western Instituted Churches (WICs). (The broad division of African churches into AICs and WICs will be useful in this analysis.) Today the Christianity that is booming in Africa is the Charismatic/ Pentecostal type (C/P). Not only are C/P churches flourishing, but their practices are being adopted by the WICs. One key phrase, "*The Bible says . . .* ," is heard in all three broad types of churches and on the lips of all Christians.

With the Bible in hand, pastors read, preach, heal, deliver, and teach. Round the clock, churches are packed. Under every tree and tent there is a church. Workplaces sport biblical passages and faith statements. Gospel songs fill the airways and sermons are sold on discs. Christianity has prominence in Africa with men in the leadership and women in the audience. More and more the C/P churches exhibit young men, both on TV assemblies and in regular church meetings. Women predominate at prayer sessions. Yet a more complex pattern of women's leadership may be discerned. There were women founders of AICs; now there are women pastors of the C/Ps and many women-led gospel singing groups. Women in clergy clothes are beginning to appear in some WICs. The latest in Ghana are two clergy women in the Anglican dioceses of Accra. Church decision-making bodies now have several women, at least at the lower levels. With the exception of a few C/P churches, uniformed women's groups are clearly visible in almost all churches.

After 1989, African theology ceased to be an all-male enterprise. The Circle of Concerned African Women Theologians (the Circle) was inaugurated that year. Concentrating on research, writing, and publishing, the Circle has produced theological works to join what the men have been doing.[1] "A bird with one wing does not fly"—this African wisdom saying has stimulated the women's initiative. Throughout the Circle's work, biblical scholarship has been a critical component.

READING THE BIBLE WITH WOMEN IN AFRICA— POPULAR PRACTICE, SCHOLARSHIP, AND THE CIRCLE

Africa does not yet boast of many prominent biblical scholars. Much scholarship has been acquired through translations. The dearth of knowledge of biblical languages is evident as "popular" preachers throw in Hebrew and Greek words to try to impress hearers with their knowledge of the Bible. That aside, from preaching and "deliverance," one observes the Bible being read in ways that oppose traditional African beliefs and practices. Most of the time, indigenous ways are cast in negative terms as beliefs to be left behind or negative powers to be neutralized by the power of the name of Jesus. There is little attempt to engage constructively the religio-cultural traditions. The ethos therefore is not much different from that of the Western missionary era.

The core concerns of Africans seem to be marriage and its related challenges. The church's preaching and prayers make this focus clear as do discussions on radio and TV. Sexuality and gender are therefore key to much preaching and counseling. The Bible is the source of counseling that subordinates women to men, silences women, and alienates them from dynamic agency in home, church, and society. In some churches the non-ordination of women to the sacramental ministry continues because "the Bible says so." Women, too, read the Bible and find the same disempowering injunctions. Read by itself, in translation, and by episodes, the Bible is taken at face value as if dictated by God directly to guide Africans of the twenty-first century. The authority of the Bible is not open for discussion; being a holy book its value as a talisman protects it from any notion of critique. Without the Bible you will not be heard on any issue you discuss with Christians on this continent.

A different vignette of contemporary African Christianity and biblical interpretation is provided by the Ghanaian manifestation of "Women Aglow for Jesus International." "Aglow" in Ghana has a dynamism that I have experienced by direct participation and through television. The organization has cell groups throughout the country all studying the Bible. It has a monthly assembly in all the ten regions of the country every third Saturday of the month. The Accra monthly assembly is held at Black Star Square and on special occasions enjoys the presence of regional representatives. This gathering numbers in the thousands. It is ecumenical, and on occasion one can spot Muslim women in the *hijab*. The Bible and prayer take center stage, and biblical symbolic and prophetic acts are enacted. Afenyi Dadzie, a prominent journalist, is the liturgist and the preacher. Her creativity and dynamism know no bounds. Real walls are constructed and broken down if that is what the biblical texts demand. Streams of water are created and crossed if that is what is called for to have people physically cross into a new era. Oil is made to flow on the ground for self-anointing, and bread is broken and shared if that will concretize God's continued sustenance. The Bible is read in several Ghanaian languages and all hear the word of God spoken to them directly. "Aglow" for me epitomizes women's rereading of the Bible to empower themselves. Aglow does not call in men to teach the women.

With the example of "Women Aglow" in mind, I turn to examine the appropriation of the Bible in the writings of African women. The survey concentrates on the literature coming from the Circle of Concerned African Women Theologians and a few others. Nevertheless, the Bible as preached and sung by women is also evidence for women's reading practices.

Beginning in 1989, the Circle planned and executed one pan-African meeting and three biennial institutes to address the "dearth of literature on African women by African women."[2] The goals were not only to enrich study but to enhance women's development and participation in religion and society. In all of the meetings, Bible studies held pride of place, and women preached the Word at the morning prayers. The inaugural conference took as its theme "Daughters of Africa, Arise," from Luke 8:40–56, focusing on the healing of two women—the daughter of Jarius and the woman with severe bleeding. This study also gave the Circle its watchword "*Talitha, qumi,*" ("Little girl, get up"; cf. Mark 5:41), which became the title for the published proceedings. [3] The same Gospel healing story provided the title for the Circle's subsequent 1992 publication, *The Will to Arise: Women, Tradition, and the Church in Africa.*[4] In an epilogue to the volume, Teresa Okure offered an exegesis of the passage calling on African women to arise, to join the disciples in being healers and heralds of the reign of God so that they might "help one another and the whole continent to arise."[5] Okure was (as far as I know) our first and at that time only African woman with a PhD in biblical studies and is now a well-known New Testament scholar.

In 1996 the second pan-African conference of the Circle, held in Nairobi, decided it was time to recognize the specializations within the Circle. One of the four commissions set up was on Biblical Hermeneutics. Another commission on Theological Education and Ministerial Formation was to involve ordained women and to encourage them to publish their sermons. To date I know of only one such publication, from Grace Imathiu, a member of the Circle.[6] Nevertheless, electronic publication of sermons has become the order of the day in Africa, especially among the C/P churches. This practice indicates how hungry Africa is for the Word of God. Now we are beginning to see women as TV evangelists; so there is more evidence of the use of the Bible by women in Africa than I intend to present here.

The writings of African women theologians have caught the attention of others. For example, two leaders from the World Council of Churches included essays from African women in an early volume featuring non-Western women that aimed to foster global dialogue. Barbel von Wartenberg-Potter, a German woman theologian (and then WCC program staff for the sub-unit on cooperation of women and men in church and society) partnered with John S. Pobee, an African New Testament scholar and firm supporter of the Circle (then with the WCC program for theological education). The result was *New Eyes for Reading: Biblical and Theological Reflections by Women from the Third World.*[7] African women's scholarship can now be accessed from biblical commentaries, journals, and other anthologies.

Assessing how widely the Bible is used in Africa, in both popular and scholarly approaches to religion, prepares one further to explore women's use of the Bible as a resource for life (including health and empowerment), for theology, and for understanding African culture. The following discussion continues to focus on the Circle and even there does not claim to be comprehensive. My aim is to give a taste of how the Bible functions and to raise interest in further research and study of our contributions, pointing to further areas of research and collaborators one may find among the Circle women.

The Circle now includes younger scholars whose theses have analyzed biblical themes and who often have acquired facility in the biblical languages. Yet all of us, with or without Hebrew, Aramaic, and Greek, with or without formal biblical studies, are often invited to lead Bible studies or preach at a variety of Christian gatherings. All of us resort to the cultural context of Africa with which the Circle is concerned, and all of us endeavor to be scholarly, but most essentially to communicate effectively and to respect the Bible as the Holy Book of a faith community.

Let me offer myself as an example. My scholarship is in dogmatics/systematic theology. My interest is in how what Christians believe is and was constructed. But this interest comes from my undergraduate studies in biblical and historical theology and early church history at the University of Ghana-Legon. My studies at this level included Hebrew and Greek; I later learned Latin while studying dogmatics at Cambridge-UK. All three languages have atrophied out of disuse, I regret to confess. I therefore do not count myself among biblical scholars and so may stand for the majority of African women holding, reading, and studying the Bible alone or in a group. The Bible is available to the majority of African women not in the biblical languages but in their mother tongue, in one or two European languages, and most universally through preaching. We all study and we all use the Bible and regard it as a resource for understanding our world and guiding our life.

THE BIBLE AS RESOURCE FOR HEALTH, PARTICIPATION, AND RELEVANCE

Called to do a reflection on the book of Ruth for a study on "Women and Healthy Living," this is how I began:

> Bible study is a very delicate undertaking, not to be embarked upon lightly and never without praying, for the affirmation that the Bible is the word of God demands that we listen for the voice of God by way of words that human beings have written over a period of time and during eras that only history can clue us into. History itself is also a human creation. When we pick up our Bible we must know it is Holy because through it God stretches out to draw us into a lifestyle that is wholesome, that is healthy. It is not a book to be worshipped or to be used as a talisman to prevent bad luck. It is not a book to be used as proof-text to back up what we want to say and do. In view of this I would like us to begin with this prayer.
>
> *God, our creator, you have given us the experience of past generations to inform our lives today.*
> *Christ, our saviour, you have promised that when the Spirit of truth comes we shall be led into all truth.*
> *Holy Spirit, companion and guide, sharpen our reasoning, awaken our feeling.*
> *Creator, Christ, and Holy Spirit, we invoke your light of truth on our reading of the word for today.*
> *Grant this for your name's sake. Amen*

With this introduction, I established my approach to the Bible, a book to be read, heard, and mined prayerfully.

At the first Circle conference in 1989, Musimbi Kanyoro coordinated the group of five who provided Bible study. Kanyoro had just come to the Lutheran World Federation (LWF) office at the Ecumenical Centre in Geneva from serving as a consultant for the United Bible Society following her doctorate in linguistics. She summed up the methodology of Bible study as follows: "We begin this Bible study . . . as people seeking for ourselves the joy of experiencing God directly in our lives."[8] She urged participants not to read expecting someone to tell us who we are, what they expect of us, and what we ought to be doing. Rather, participants should expect to hear God's individual address, "Arise, Daughter." In this approach to the Bible as a resource, women come not with a blank sheet but clothed with life experiences of celebration or in search of meaning and inspiration.

In the proceedings of the 1989 convocation, Kanyoro observed:

> During the Bible Study sessions it became clear to us that for women to find justice and peace through the texts of the Bible, they have to try and recover the women participants as well as their possible participation in the life of the text. Secondly, women will need to read the Scriptures side by side with the study of cultures and learn to recognize the boundary between the two. Such recognition will help women to interpret Biblical passages within the proper hermeneutical understanding of ourselves and our contexts as Christian African women. Women will need to sincerely claim Biblical liberation without being apologetic to the cultural set-up in which the message of the Biblical passage has to find its audience today.[9]

Five years later, Christina Landman, contributing to the Eastern and Southern sector process, the third of the Circle biennials, had the following to say on the Circle's appropriation of the Bible. "We tell stories from the Bible with emphasis on relevancy." Her contribution to *Groaning in Faith: African Women in the Household of God* bears the title "A Land Flowing with Milk and Honey: Reading the Bible with Women Who Are Breastfeeding."[10] Her own concern to accompany women in reading the Bible comes from creating an enabling environment "so that women (including ourselves) can be educated theologically, conscientized as to their human dignity; obtain insight into their own situations by learning from everyday problems of women in the Bible." She describes her approach as providing "gender-specific and theologically oriented Bible study which will be both liberating and comforting to women in a particular context, and which will not treat its readers as ignorant lay people, but as people capable of a theology of their own."[11]

In her "Introducing Feminist Cultural Hermeneutics: An African Perspective" Kanyoro makes available the result of her DMin in Feminist Theology studies, pursuing this approach in her reading of the book of Ruth with her own people of the village of Bware in Kenya.[12] One can illustrate this approach from several Circle publications. But I need to cite a few since it appears our output is not well distributed.

Rhoda Ada James encourages reading the Bible to see the empowering roles women played in the Old Testament, the Gospels, and in the early church. She points to Galatians 5:11 where Paul says, "For freedom Christ has set us free. Stand fast therefore, and do not submit again to the yoke of slavery."[13] She urges, "We should not allow culture and social arrangements to block our Christian responsibility."[14] Chipo Mtombeni in a poem urges the "Daughter of Africa" to dig deep into the Scriptures: "Your place is there in the Bible."[15]

Urging adherence to the Bible inevitably leads to probing the authority of the Bible. Why the Bible? We have other texts. On this question, African Christian women theologians fall in line with all Christians on the continent. Meg Umeagudosu states this categorically in *Where God Reigns:*[16] "the Holy Bible serves as the authority and the core of Christian theology. It has unveiled much about human beings . . . ."[17] Women will hold on to the Bible if only for its affirmation of one humanity made up of female and male beings.

The authority of the Bible is upheld by Florence Wuaku in her "Seeking Resources from Theology and Ethics" saying, "The absolute truth of God's word must be preached and young people must be taught to love the values embedded and enshrined in God's word."[18] Writing on HIV/AIDS she refers to 1 Corinthians 3:18–20 to say "the best precaution is abstinence." Such categorical and dogmatic adherence to traditional understanding of the authority of the Bible abounds in the Circle writings as it does in all popular usages of the Bible. On the other hand, one also finds more nuanced and critical use in Christina Landman and others. Landman finds in the Bible a source of healing and wellness for women affected by HIV/AIDS.[19] She finds biblical passages such as Leviticus 15 sources to provide spiritual care with sensitivity and inclusiveness in the face of contagious diseases. She points to how Job and Habbakuk challenge the notion that illness is always and directly linked to personal sin. She lifts up the good news offered by the Bible in the affirmation of the kind and gracious God.

Women go to the Bible to find answers to life's puzzles, the meaning of suffering and the source of healing. Landman provides examples of questions women ask of the Bible from research she conducted in a township in South Africa. In light of HIV, women ask strong questions about the church's theology of punishment as well as about the presupposition that God is helper in times of difficulty. Oduyoye sums this up: "The Bible as a resource and anchor of our theological reflection brings us life in all its variety. As rooted in particular contexts and ages, it is given to us to discern what is necessary for our salvation. And so we must see the debates that go on in the Bible itself and even in the lives and circumstances of individual authors."[20]

BIBLE AS RESOURCE FOR THEOLOGY

The importance of rereading the Bible is highlighted by Kanyoro and Njoroge in their introduction to *Groaning in Faith.* By rereading the Bible, they say women look at the Scriptures and see new things: empowerment, liberation, and a God who is definitely on the side of the oppressed. They continue, "We also search scriptures to discern how they have been interpreted to shape our lives and to see what difference it makes when those scriptures are re-read and reinterpreted through the eyes of women who yearn and long for liberation."[21] They uphold the importance of rereading Scriptures through women's eyes and taking scriptural contexts seriously. From them we are reminded of how all ancient religion and cultural texts have been used and misused to sanction certain attitudes and practices towards women.

"By searching scriptures for themselves, women begin to understand that they were written in and for societies steeped in a patriarchal mindset, where sexism was structurally ingrained into the social fabric."[22] Since African societies are highly androcentric, the women readers of the Bible begin to see themselves in the Bible, not so that they continue in this mindset, but so that they critique and transform what does not make for the enhancement of the image of God in human beings. The authority of the Bible is contextualized through critical studies of the nature of the writings and the different genres of writings. It is not unusual for a woman to ask, "Who was present when God created human beings?" What is the value of the myth and how do we appropriate it? The category of myth is critical in our use of the Bible seeing that myths also exist in our African religio-cultural texts. Mary Getui posits that the Bible gives us a "God-centred approach to life . . . [but that] where men's needs predominate a perversion of relationships occurs."[23] Such messages cease to be a word from God as God does not stand for the downgrading of the humanity that has been created in the divine image. The revelation of God in Jesus supports this approach to the myths and androcentrism. Such passages should not be used to subordinate or "place" women or any other human being. All women and all men come from the same source and should be guided by partnership, participation, and wholeness, as argued by Grace Ndyabahika.[24]

Another view of the authority of the Bible described by Jessica Nakawombe is that "most of the Bible's teaching about women is culturally conditioned and therefore irrelevant or at least safely to be ignored."[25] Nakawombe calls this an extreme position, the other extreme being to simply ensure that biblical teachings are applied. The possibility of irrelevance is not, however, a line that Africans are ready to explore as most will also go along with cultural conditioning. Though separated by millennia and geography, African cultures have remarkable similarities to Semitic biblical cultures as far as the marginalization of women is concerned. This resemblance has fostered many legends of African origins and links with the Fertile Crescent. Cultural hermeneutics is therefore, in my view, a critical area of research and reflection by African Christians and a *sine qua non* for African women theologians and Christians generally.

THE BIBLE AND AFRICAN CULTURE

Here we offer an exercise in hermeneutics as it appears in the theological works of African Women. Araba Ata Sam writes, "Reading the book of the Prophet

Isaiah Chapter 61 today, it seems as if the chapter was written for this age."[26] Verses 1 and 2, which are quoted in Luke 4:18–19, depict the issues that fit lives of African women and the abundant life they search for. The same can be said of Isaiah 58, which describes vividly how in a country like Ghana, where community is vaunted, people regularly "hide themselves from their kin. But does this not happen elsewhere?"[27] In her *Introducing Feminist Cultural Hermeneutics— An African Perspective,* Kanyoro's position is that "to use the text of the Bible to validate any culture is a highly suspicious action."[28] She asks, "What if both the biblical cultures and the culture in question have inherent injustices in them? Injustice is never right, not even if it is in the Bible"[29] Rereading in the African cultural context becomes a real challenge if Christian women's attitude is that because a reading from the Bible "enhanced our culture, then it was good for us." Kanyoro notes, "The women of Bware in 1994 were not ready to debate the authority of the Bible, let alone the authority of culture."[30] The reality they live and the biblical text they read or hear read "become one." The Bible is read "for assurance and for answers to their questions and dilemmas."[31] Kanyoro, along with others in the Circle, have identified "culture as an important key to reading the Bible in Africa and its analysis." She advocates "cultural hermeneutics as a paradigm of a gender-sensitive African theology."[32]

Kanyoro argues that Africans and peoples whose cultures are close to the Bible "hold the Bible in awe." As it is taboo to be counter-culture, so it is with going counter to the Bible. On the other hand, she observes that, for some in the contexts where the culture is more removed from the Bible and is secularized, the Bible becomes fiction. Her position, therefore, is that "Cultural hermeneutics puts *every culture* to scrutiny with the intention of testing its liberative potential for people at different times in history."[33] This test has been the anchor of rereading the Bible among women theologians of Africa. Kanyoro examines this "cultural hermeneutics as a key to reading the Bible in Africa."[34]

The biblical text is used for identifying cultural issues that call for discussion. This is important because in Africa the immediate culture has more influence on the way the biblical text is understood and used in commentaries than the historical facts about the text.[35] It is our experience that popular (non-scholarly) Bible readers do not really care what the scholars think. Kanyoro presents us with six factors concerning cultural hermeneutics as they relate to the reading of the Bible.

- "Sometimes the Bible helps read the culture, while at other times the culture gives meaning to the texts of the Bible."[36]
- Feminist methodologies challenge the assumption that the roles of men and women have been fixed, either by the Creator or by culture.[37] An Akan proverb says, "*wowoo tafoni ba nna onkura ta.*" Persons are not born holding the instruments of their trade.[38]
- Cultural hermeneutics apply to all African theology but more to anthropology; hence the focus on "engendering cultural hermeneutics."

- Communal theology is promoted through communal reading of the Bible.
- Cultural hermeneutics provide a means of sifting out and using usable culture.
- Cultural hermeneutics undermine the myth of certainty.

In the *Global Bible Commentary*, Madipoane Masenya, commenting on the book of Ruth (that Kanyoro also used), says that she presupposes an audience of those African Christians who regard the Bible as "an important spiritual resource." In this context Ruth serves as a model of a person who emerges as a winner despite the many strikes against her: the challenges of identity crisis, the idolization of marriage, and doubts about God's intervention in life.[39] Masenya sees Ruth as a story of courage and hope in the midst of desolation. From the book she identifies women's wisdom for survival in patriarchal contexts that require a son and a husband for survival. Not surprisingly, Masenya asserts that "although marriage is positive when it is not abusive, single people can still experience life in its fullness."[40] Much of what calls up the statement, "It is our culture," happens in the context of marriage, and, in most cases, injustice is being meted out to women.

As Kanyoro points out, in reading Ruth, African women see the story as affirming their culture and so giving them hope.[41] But she issues the caveat that this should not mean that marriage is the only life for women in today's context. She would have readers acknowledge the gap between the time of the biblical cultural event and our time. In doing so we might liberate the word of God from the cultural bonds with which we have chained it, relativize the impact of culture, and read the story as a reminder that we can trust this same God even as we are overwhelmed by different challenges in our own contexts.[42] Masenya points out that in Ruth, two widows allow themselves to be used by God and refuse to be victims of circumstances. She concludes that we, "like Ruth and Naomi, can trust God to make us rise above those circumstances."[43] Thereby she takes us back to Okure's Bible study and the title of the Circle book "*The Will to Arise*."[44]

Hermeneutics appear in Teresa Okure's commentary on Colossians in the *Global Bible Commentary* on the uniqueness of Jesus in religiously pluralistic Africa. Okure explores the message of Colossians that Jesus broke barriers, "especially the anthropological ones—racism, sexism, classism, ethnicism—and all the prejudices that lead us to judge, condemn, and demonize others who differ from us or are not privileged to receive Christ as we have."[45] To present Christ, she says, we should begin where people are. This I see as a call to cultural hermeneutics, for Africans are going to see culture through the biblical text as well as what the colonial period has added to the traditional culture, becoming part of the location from which Africans read the Bible. For this reason, in the context of post-colonial Christianity in Africa, attention has been turned to the post-colonial reading of the Bible.

POSTCOLONIAL INTERPRETATION

Musa Dube identifies post-colonial criticism as an element in African women's reading of the Bible. In her *Post-Colonial Feminist Interpretation of the Bible*,[46] she parallels the colonization of Africa with the colonization of women. The Western missionaries' view was that African culture must not be allowed to influence Christians. Any hint of African culture in church practice or theology was immediately labeled syncretism, abhorred and excised. African theologians who are men tended to defend the African culture and to use its motifs in their efforts to construct African Christian theologies. When the women theologians came along, they said "yes" to this stance but with the proviso that the cultural motifs are not those that demean women's humanity and foster or protect any form of injustice. Dube points to the imperialist stance of the missionaries and also to the fact that at the heart of biblical belief is an imperialist ideology, the ideology of chosenness, which calls for liberating ways of reading for interdependence. She further points out that even among marginalized women there are oppressors and the oppressed, as in the Hagar and Sarah saga at the roots of biblical history.

In the postcolonial reading, African voices and African culture are highlighted as is the participation of women. Transmitting the Bible in the oral culture of Africa, women who idolize the book make liberating readings of the Bible a real challenge. This has presented us with a dual assignment of fashioning a strategy for reading the Bible to decolonize both patriarchal and imperial systems and to seek to articulate the liberation of both women and men and of all races and nations.[47]

In the anthology *Other Ways of Reading: African Women and the Bible*,[48] which Dube edited, the use of storytelling as a method of interpretation and the goal of countering patriarchal and colonizing interpretation are to be found in most essays. Women's reading with and from the perspectives of nonacademic women yields biblical gems not available to historical critical readers of the Bible. We shall review the storytelling method further on. The women bring out how the men theologians are often silent about enculturation when it is in collusion with patriarchy.[49] This anthology raises the need to decolonize and depatriarchalize the biblical translations and to promote theologies that are not devoid of gender perspectives. The authors have a stance of relativizing the authority of the Bible by the recognition that there are several canons at work in our lives. We do not have the Bible alone; we have also the canon of African oral cultures that serves as theories for analyzing or reading. We have non-gendered names and pronouns in a lot of African languages, and the survival of women is at the center of our reading of the Bible.

In hermeneutics and in postcolonial reading, African women theologians' reading of the Bible aims at better understanding the world of today and that of the text; building a world that accommodates diversity and justice; dealing with realities; and asking questions that engage with the struggles of our people.

This hermeneutical task prevents buying into patriarchal prescriptions of the ideal woman.

METHODOLOGY

Looking at the methods used in Bible studies at Circle meetings and in formal presentations to outside gatherings, one finds several approaches depending on the audiences/participants. Presentations and studies that have church women's groups in mind often include dramatization of biblical texts using contemporary African motifs and issues or straight attempts to re-create the biblical episodes. This approach is used in churches especially with young people and usually on festive occasions. The modification is that, with the Circle, there is always a group reflection on what the episode as dramatized tells us. A variant of the dramatic method is one in which groups or individuals act out the story from their perspective or from the perspectives of an onlooker or persons who are silent in the biblical episode itself. The method helps participants think through what the story portrays.

Both in formal presentations and in Circle studies, the method of retelling the story predominates. As Kanyoro puts it, this method enables participants to savor the story itself and draw meanings for themselves. These are then shared and discussed with real life examples in mind. The biblical passage is always read first, either dramatically or in a way that retains the attention of the participants. Often much that goes unnoticed surfaces in the way the reading is done. The way the pericope is marked is also of enormous importance in the storytelling. One does not do the "Widow's Mite" without telling how Jesus in the previous chapter has pointed out the exploitation of widows (Luke 20:47; 21:1–4).[50]

In Okure's "Reflections on Luke 8:40–56," the title *The Will to Arise* springs from the ailing woman's insistence on not settling for the status quo. It underlines her insistence on becoming whole, arising from ill health, marginalization, and impoverishment. The healing of the bleeding woman happens in the context of Jesus' words to the young girl, who was willing to listen to Jesus rather than to those who said she was dead. She acted on the encouragement to arise. Okure sees the episode "enabling the one to arise and confirming the other's determination to be cured."[51] Readers and participants, by this retelling, come to associate women's agency towards wholeness with the will of God.

A favorite method is that of digging for women in the Bible whose stories are not told at all or are slanted to buttress androcentric views—Jael, Rahab, the two Tamars, Rizpah, and others. This method enables the Circle to tap creatively and imaginatively those many images and narratives in the Scripture that speak to women's physical context that could help conscientize women and restore our human dignity. It enables the Circle to live its affirmation that the task of searching and studying must not be the sole preserve of highly educated women and men. The Bible is found in the hands of all Christians wherever they are, in buses, sitting at office desks, on embassy and hospital waiting benches, in shops and in banks. One often asks, "How are they reading?" One gets the urge to walk up to them and ask, as Philip did, "Do you understand what you are reading?" (Acts 8:30). Bible study is construed to generate this process of groups' encounter with the Bible.

Lyrics, poems, sayings, and songs are created out of biblical events or from real situations for discussion. Once in a Hausa congregation in northern Nigeria an often dramatized song—which says, "When you are laboring under a heavy burden who comes to help you? It is Jesus"—became the starting point of studies on Jesus and women in the Gospels. Studies do not only follow pericopes; often they follow themes and current issues in the lives of women. Many Circle Bible studies have been generated by the challenges of the HIV/AIDS pandemic.

In all of this activity the format includes group work and any device that will foster maximum participation of all present. All the studies are backed by technical, scholarly views and expertise that do not become intrusive. Scholarly views are rarely stated for discussion, but they influence how the Bible study is structured and the questions that facilitators ask. The biblical languages hardly feature, except where translations into African languages are biased by cultural givens, like the questions of when a women is a wife (Judg. 19, which Kanyoro discusses). We do stress, however, that we are receiving the word of God through human language and that by the time it gets into an African language, it has passed through many languages and cultures both ancient and modern.

FREQUENT SOURCES

It would be an interesting and revealing exercise to compile an African Women's lectionary of the Bible. It would also repay study to compare women's readings with the malestream readings. Obvious examples of gender biases can be illustrated from the Hagar story (Gen. 16, 21) and from the encounter of the woman who was threatened with stoning (John 8:1–11). We will, however, limit ourselves to highlighting a few of the biblical texts that appear more frequently in African women's Bible studies and other theological offerings. The key passages cover the themes of women's full humanity, participation, partnership, and empowerment. Women as life models and a few attempts at Mariology do appear. The links among patriarchy, sexuality, and marriage are key concerns. The following are a couple of specific examples.

The inaugural passage that has given us *"talitha, qumi"* (Luke 8:40–56) remains with us. On the humanity of women and all attempts at countering the marginalization of women, rereadings of the creation accounts Genesis 1–3 are offered with 1:26–27 as favorites together with the separation of the sexes found in 2:21–25. These often go together with the submission passages in Ephesians 5, with the women reading from the verse that enjoins mutual submission (Eph. 5:21), which the malestream often avoids. Readings from

1 Timothy 2 and the "not counting the women" parenthesis in the feeding the crowds stories (Matt. 14:21; 15:38) are also frequent favorites. These are accompanied by liberative passages: Luke 4:18–19; 13:10–17; Galatians 3:28; 5:11; 1 Corinthians 7:1–5; 14:34–35; John 8:36. Cultural practices that often plague African women are studied with passages from Judges and from Numbers 27:8 on inheritance.

Women frequently resort to biblical passages to highlight women who resisted the status quo, like the Syrophoenician/Canaanite woman of Matthew 15 and Mark 7. Vashti, rarely honored because Esther is the "good woman," is often cited for the need to resist the dehumanization of women even if it means losing material benefits (Esth. 1:12). A woman is worth more than her beauty and the wealth showered on her.

CONCLUSION

In Africa women are hearers of the Bible as read and exegeted by men. Often when they get the chance to speak in public, they echo the malestream, but more and more we are experiencing women's own thoughts and appropriation of the Bible. Even more important is that women are writing. Whether they are being read and listened to is another issue. Nevertheless, women's reading of the rapes and other acts of violence against women of the Bible have taken center stage as the world becomes concerned. Women's identification of empowering stories and their love of the Magnificat (Luke 1:46–55) to demonstrate God's acts against domestication, colonization, and impoverishment are helping them to mine critically this holy book for the word from God to keep humanity whole and holy.

Notes

1. African women theologians did publish before 1989, but after the Circle's formation their work often had a different focus. For example, my volume, *Hearing and Knowing: Theological Reflections on Christianity in Africa*, was published in 1986 (Maryknoll, NY: Orbis Books). It belongs to an earlier genre of African Christian Theology. Only one chapter was specifically gender sensitive.
2. Mercy Amba Oduyoye and Musimbi Kanyoro, eds., *Talitha, qumi! Proceedings of the Convocation of African Women Theologians, Trinity College, Legon—Acra, September 24–2 October, 1989* (repr. Accra-North, Ghana: Sam-Woode Ltd., 2001; first edition, Ibadan, Nigeria: Daystar Press, 1990), 2.
3. Oduyoye and Kanyoro, *Talitha, qumi!* This transliteration of the original Aramaic (cf. Mark 5:41) pays attention to the fact that the verb has to be in the feminine form, that is, end with *i*. Q was preferred to K because Kumi is a Ghanaian name.
4. Mercy Amba Oduyoye and Musimbi Kanyoro, eds., *The Will to Arise: Women, Tradition, and the Church in Africa* (Maryknoll, NY: Orbis Books, 1992).
5. Teresa Okure, "Epilogue: The Will to Arise: Reflections on Luke 8:40–56," in Oduyoye and Kanyoro, *The Will to Arise*, 221–30.

6. R. Grace Imathiu, *Words of Fire, Spirit of Grace: Twelve Sermons from One of the World's Best Preachers*, ed. David Hay Jones, (Porjus, Sweden, and Milwaukee, U.S.A.: True North, 2003).
7. John S. Pobee and Barbel von Wartenberg-Potter, eds., *New Eyes for Reading: Biblical and Theological Reflections by Women from the Third World* (Geneva: World Council of Churches, 1986).
8. Musimbi Kanyoro, "Daughter, Arise. Luke 8:40–46 (*sic*)," in *Talitha, qumi!*, 60–69.
9. Musimbi Kanyoro, "Bible Studies at the Convocation," in *Talitha, qumi!*, 58–59.
10. Christina Landman, "A Land Flowing with Milk and Honey: Reading the Bible with Women who are Breastfeeding," in *Groaning in Faith: African Women in the Household of God*, ed. Musimbi R. A. Kanyoro and Nyambura J. Njoroge (Nairobi: Acton Publishers, 1996), 99–111.
11. Ibid., 99.
12. Musimbi R. A. Kanyoro, *Introducing Feminist Cultural Hermeneutics: An African Perspective* (Cleveland: The Pilgrim Press, 2002).
13. Rhoda Ada James, "The Scope of Women's Participation in the Church," in *Talitha, qumi!*, 192–98.
14. Ibid., 197.
15. Chipo Mtombeni, "Daughters of Africa,"in *Talitha, qumi!*, 249.
16. The outcome of the Circle's second biennial, which was held in Abokobi, Accra. Elizabeth Amoah, ed., *Where God Reigns (Reflections on Women in God's World)* (Accra-North, Ghana: Sam-Woode Ltd. for the Circle of Concerned African Women Theologians, 1997).
17. Margaret A. Umeagudosu, "The Earth Belongs to God: Biblical Expositions through the Eyes of a Nigerian Woman," in *Where God Reigns*, 10. Umeagudosu reflects on Gen. 1:26–27.
18. Florence Wuaku, "Seeking Resources from Theology and Ethics," in *People of Faith and the Challenge of HIV/AIDS*, ed. Mercy Amba Oduyoye and Elizabeth Amoah (Ibadan, Nigeria: Sefer, 2004), 201.
19. Christina Landman, "The Bible as a Source of Healing for Women Affected by HIV/AIDS," in *People of Faith and the Challenge of HIV/AIDS*, 301–12.
20. Mercy Amba Oduyoye, in *African Culture and the Quest for Women's Rights*, ed. Doris Olu Akintunde (Ibadan, Nigeria: SeferBooks, 2001), 6.
21. Kanyoro and Njoroge, introduction, in *Groaning in Faith*, xii.
22. Ibid., xiii.
23. Mary Getui, "Women's Priesthood in Relation to Nature," in *Groaning in Faith*, 31–39.
24. Grace N. Ndyabahika, "Women's Place in Creation," in ibid., 23–30.
25. Jessica Keturah Nakawombe, "Women in the Kingdom of God," in ibid., 40–52.
26. Araba Ata Sam, in Oduyoye and Amoah, *When Silence Is No Longer an Option* (Accra, Ghana: Sam-Woode Ltd., 2002), 96.
27. Ibid.
28. Kanyoro, *Introducing Feminist Cultural Hermeneutics*, 7.
29. Ibid.
30. Ibid.
31. Ibid., 8.
32. Ibid., 9.
33. Ibid., 10
34. Ibid., 18.
35. Ibid., 20.
36. Ibid.
37. Ibid., 26.

38. Elizabeth Amoah, ed., *Poems of Mercy Amba Oduyoye* (Accra, Ghana: Sam-Woode Ltd., 2004), 27.
39. Madipoane Masenya, "Ruth," in *Global Bible Commentary,* ed. Daniel Patte (Nashville: Abingdon Press, 2004), 86–91.
40. Masenya, "Ruth," 87.
41. Kanyoro, *Introducing Feminist Cultural Hermeneutics,* 90.
42. Ibid., 91.
43. Masenya, "Ruth," 91.
44. Oduyoye and Kanyoro, *The Will to Arise.*
45. Teresa Okure, "Colossians," in *Global Bible Commentary,* 490–99.
46. Musa W. Dube, *Postcolonial Feminist Interpretation of the Bible* (St. Louis, MO: Chalice Press, 2000).
47. Ibid., 43.
48. Musa W. Dube, ed., *Other Ways of Reading: African Women and the Bible,* (Atlanta: Society of Biblical Literature; Geneva: WCC Publications, 2001).
49. Ibid., 12.
50. Amoah, ed., *Poems of Mercy Amba Oduyoye,* 40–1.
51. Okure, epilogue, in Oduyoye and Kanyoro, *The Will to Arise,* 221–29.

Chapter 15

With Running Mouth and Hands on Hips

Sapphire and the Moral Imagination

EMILIE M. TOWNES

For the last several years, I have explored evil through an interdisciplinary method that involves literary analysis, social history, and cultural studies, together with ethical and theological analysis, in order to understand the interior life of evil—what I call the cultural production of evil.[1] As I clarified my understanding of evil as a cultural production within the network of relationships we call life and living, I found I had to examine truncated narratives designed to support and perpetuate structural inequalities and forms of social oppression. This exploration led me to investigate the interior material life of evil.

The roots of this quest are found in my childhood, when I was transported to Troy by Homer and devoured all I could about Greek and Roman mythology. The idea of gods seemed quite novel to one who was growing up to "Jesus loves me this I know . . . ." Apollo and Athena took me out of my daily musing on Jesse Helms and fire hoses and colored water fountains, bathrooms, waiting rooms, and cemeteries. I could enter, through Homer's prompting, a different time and place to learn that maybe the holy could be capricious and not always stern.

I learn a great deal from writers and poets like Tina McElroy Ansa, Alice Walker, William Faulkner, Ernest Hemingway, Ayn Rand, Carson McCullers,

Gabriel Garcia Márquez, Jorge Amado, Chinua Achebe . . . ; the list goes on and on. Fine writers help me "see" things in tangible ways and "feel" things through intangible means. Their ability to turn the world at a tilt, to explore our humanity and inhumanity, challenges me in ways that theories and concepts do not quite evoke. Given my Niebuhrian roots (more H. Richard than Reinhold here), I realized that I would be bound in untenable and unproductive ways if I approached a study of evil solely through the realm of concepts and theories. From classic studies by John Hick, Arthur McGill, and Douglas John Hall to more recent work by Wendy Farley, David Ray Griffin, Marjorie Suchocki, and Terrence Tilley, I found helpful ways to think about the *nature* of evil. But the deep interior material life of evil and its manifestations remained untapped for me.

What has the writing life taught me? What have writers like James Baldwin, Patrick Chamoiseau, June Jordan, Toni Morrison, Sonia Sanchez, and Harriet Beecher Stowe said about the struggles and joys of humanity that I can use to understand evil? I begin with Toni Morrison's distinction between truth and fact in her essay "Site of Memory."[2] For Morrison, truth is the key ideal to seek, because fact can exist without human intelligence but truth cannot. From truth and fact, I move to the interplay of history and memory rather than replicate the traditional paradigm of history as scientific and memory as subjective. I work from the perspective that history *and* memory are subjective. This perspective dismisses neither and encourages us to think more circumspectly about the images and stereotypes we have created and disseminated historically and currently.

Coupled with Morrison, I have other articulate resources and strategies to tackle evil, such that we no longer make inordinate appeals to individual will and achievement but lean into a richer and more diverse web of creation. One thing that becomes clear is that the American story *can* be told another way. The voices and lives of those who, traditionally and historically, have been left out are now heard with clarity and precision. These voices can be included in the discourse—not as additives—but as resources and co-determiners of actions and strategies—*as the moral agents they are*—not in crass goals-driven moves, but ones that acknowledge the intimate humanity of our plurality and work with as much precision as possible to name its textures.

Using the interplay of history and memory, I turn to consider how the imagination works within this interaction to create images that buttress evil as a cultural production. Combining Michel Foucault's understanding of the imagination and Antonio Gramsci's use of hegemony, I develop how the imagination—the fantastic hegemonic imagination—"plays" with history and memory to spawn caricatures and stereotypes.[3] The long and short of it is that the fantastic hegemonic imagination traffics in peoples' lives, sometimes caricaturing, sometimes pillaging, so that the imagination that creates the fantastic can control the world in its own image. The rich diversities in our midst are seen as cloying distractions rather than as flesh and blood and spirit. This imagination conjures worlds and their social structures based not on supernatural events, but on the ordinariness of evil. It is this imagination, I argue, that helps to hold systematic, structural evil in place and spawns generation after generation.

INVISIBLE THINGS . . .

To gain a sense of how the fantastic hegemonic imagination works, I turn to the notion of uninterrogated coloredness and that scandalous woman called Sapphire. As a helpful guide to begin the discussion, I turn again to Toni Morrison and her 1989 landmark essay, "Invisible Things Unspoken":

> . . . invisible things are not necessarily "not there"; . . . a void may be empty, but it is not a vacuum. In addition, certain absences are so stressed, so ornate, so planned, they call attention to themselves; arrest us with intentionality and purpose, like neighborhoods that are defined by the population held away from them. Looking at the scope of American literature, I can't help thinking that the question should have never been "Why am I, an Afro-American, absent from it?" It is not a particularly interesting query anyway. The spectacularly interesting question is "What intellectual feats had to be performed by the author or his critic to erase me from a society seething with my presence, and what effect has that performance had on the work?" What are the strategies of escape from knowledge? Of willful oblivion? . . . Not why. How?[4]

Both the academy and religious communities are well practiced at certain silences. This situation is ironic given how much talking goes on in classrooms and at other gatherings. Yet silences haunt us, like so many methodological loose ends and/or mangled analyses. These silences include more than race—ethnicity, sexuality, age, nationality, class—the list goes on and on. There are items on this list that many treat as a threadbare list of gripes. Latter day versions of "What do they want?" or "Well, we elected a Black man president, didn't we?" abound in our musings in print, in professional gatherings, at dinner parties, at social hours, in the offices of colleagues, in the halls of our institutions, and in our hearts, minds, and souls. Somehow, and quite remarkably, a relatively small number of Black women in the church and the academy have become akin to Joel's horde of locusts—cutting, swarming, hopping, destroying. For others, we are Joel's relentless army—not swerving, not jostling, not halted, and entering theo-ethical discussions like thieves (see Joel 1–2, especially 1:4 and 2:3–10).

In dazzling displays of intellectual hubris, orthodox moral discourses ignore the diversities within their (and our) midst in an ill-timed and increasingly irrelevant march toward an objective viewpoint that can lead us toward the [T]ruth. Such inquiries have served (and continue) to preserve a moral and social universe that has mean-spiritedness at one end of its pole and sycophancy at the other when pursued in a world of abstractions that mute the hard stuff of living. A large portion of noblesse oblige often acts as filler and buffer for those who seek to maintain or recapture a dumb and dumber status quo.

In her ever-relevant essay, Morrison notes that the notion of race is still a virtually unspeakable thing. She aptly points out a strong movement within the social sciences (left largely unaddressed by the majority of scholars in the theological disciplines) to question the efficacy of race as a helpful category to explore our social order.

> For three hundred years black Americans insisted that "race" was no use-fully distinguishing factor in human relationships. During those same three centuries every academic discipline, including theology, history, and natu-ral science, insisted "race" was *the* determining factor in human develop-ment. When blacks discovered that they had shaped or become a culturally formed race, and that it had specific and revered difference, suddenly they were told there is no such thing as "race," biological or cultural, that mat-ters and that genuinely intellectual exchange cannot accommodate it . . . It always seemed to me that the people who invented the hierarchy of "race" when it was convenient for them ought not to be the ones to explain it away, now that it does not suit their purposes for it to exist.[5]

These two extended quotations from Morrison underscore the difficulty reli-gious traditions have in addressing race and racism. As people of faith, we simply have not done it adequately or thoroughly. Some see such analysis as veering into public policy; others cannot find an adequate philosophical construct from which to peer into the mysteries of race. Some think in an America with a Black president, our work is done. Nope, none of these stances is true, and I propose that Morrison's question "Not why. How?" provides a faithful framework for the way that coloredness remains inadequately interrogated in the household of God.

Indeed, many discussions on race divorce it from the profound impact that color (un)consciousness plays in our deliberations. Further, we focus on darker-skinned peoples almost exclusively. This focus invites folks of European descent and others to ignore the social construction of whiteness. It allows darker-skinned racial-ethnic groups to ignore their internal color caste system. Often it opens the door for weird bifurcations of class, race, gender, sexuality, age, and so on. Race is a social construction as well as a cultural production. There are both implicit and explicit costs and benefits to collapsing race into uninterrogated coloredness. This move is usually, if not always, wrapped around a spinning top of personal choices and communal power dynamics.

FIND A TOUGH CONDUCTOR

To navigate the rocky terrain of race and coloredness, it is necessary to find a tough conductor. The attitude of Sapphire will be our guide. The Sapphire cari-cature began as a joke of plays and minstrel music shows in the nineteenth and twentieth century and continued as a stock character in more recent situation comedies. Sapphire was smaller than the caricatures of the Black Mammy and

Aunt Jemima, but stout. She had medium to dark brown complexion, and she was headstrong and opinionated. She was loud-mouthed, strong-willed, sassy, and practical.

Some see Sapphire as a negative stereotype and therefore not a likely candidate for an incisive and progressive examination of race and racism. However, I argue that in this stereotype of the masculinized Black female—one who must be subordinated so that the Black male can take his "rightful" place in society and protect whiteness from her furious gaze and analysis—we find the strategic edginess to cut through much of the prattle and utter nonsense that often accompanies critiques of race and racism.

Sapphire is bitchy, loud, bawdy, and domineering. These very characteristics are necessary to disrupt our comfortable racisms. This stereotype of the bitter, hostile, cold, domineering, in-charge Black woman was spawned when, historically, Whites had no "safe" place to put a Black woman who cared for her family, who had ideas and could articulate them, who did not relate to White culture— by choice—and who was fiercely protective of her family, keeping everyone (men included) in line, fed, and cared for as the situation demanded. She is everything the comfortable stereotypes of the Black Mammy and Aunt Jemima are not. And because she is fully human, she had to be demonized to fit the worlds of blackness the White imagination sought to create and the prisons of sex and sexuality that some Black masculinities constructed and now maintain.

Sapphire is threatening to authority—she is *always* in control of herself when her hands are on her hips and she is practicing the fine art of being loud-mouthed. Her rage is precise and her speech is like chicory. Channeling her powerful sass can help us untangle and demystify the intractability of racism. Being polite or dispassionate about it has not worked.

PAUSING TO STOP AND THINK

We tend to use "race" and talk about race, but rarely do we stop to think about what it is that we are talking about when we use the word. What images are being conjured up consciously and unconsciously, with this word? How do those images write themselves large across the academic, theo-ethical, economic, political, and social landscapes? How do these images situate themselves, if not simply plop themselves down, in the life of religious communities? So much of what we have come to understand as race was set before we had a clear understanding of genetics. Now that our knowledge has increased in this area, we are caught with our old categories of skin color (the primary one), the texture and color of hair, the color of eyes, the shape of our noses, the size of our lips as the markers for race. We practice a highly selective process of ranking our biological differences in an enormously nuanced and decidedly unscientific system that ignores the fact that color is the least rigorous way to determine race.

In the United States, such ranking confers social significance to coloredness to an inordinate degree. In our fascination/fixation on coloredness, we have developed a thoroughgoing yet often unconscious color caste system based on degrees of darkness and lightness.[6] Far too often our initial response to one another is built from these color cues we have inherited through history, ideology, and memory. This inheritance is part of the harrowing impact of the fantastic hegemonic imagination. It manifests essentialist racism in its most pristine form: emphasizing hierarchical biological inequalities.

In addressing race and racism, I find the conceptual work of Michael Omi and Howard Winant more helpful and ultimately more rigorous.[7] They argue that race is not an essence, something fixed, or concrete and objective. Rather, race is unstable and decentered. Race is a complicated and interstructured set of social meanings that are always being transformed by political struggle. They call this process racial formation. This understanding of race recognizes the world and our social structures as processes of historical and social transformation. It enables us to explore the dynamic of memory and history with the element of imagination added to this dynamic—often as the spark that fuels racialized fires.

Despite the inadequacies of how we talk about and theorize race, it does exist. It is cabalistic to argue with any level of sophistication or accuracy that a category used to organize entire states such as the Third Reich or Apartheid South Africa *and*, further, a category that is a part of our past and current legal structures does not exist. As a fixed unchanging category—no, race does not exist. As a relational process of shifting boundaries and social meanings constantly engaged in political struggles—race does exist.

With coloredness as a fulcrum, memory, history, and imagination expose race as a phenomenon that is always in formation, as Omni and Winant and others suggest.[8] This perspective provides an excellent window through which to see coloredness as a racial construction. More importantly, it does not allow coloredness to be a phenomenon restricted to darker skinned peoples but extends it to lighter skinned ones as well. In short, whiteness, blackness, brownness, redness, goldenness are *all* historically located, adaptive, and conditional.

Understanding race as a historical process of ongoing transformation, or as relational, reveals that race gets most of its power from appearing to be a natural or biological phenomenon or a coherent social category.[9]

I want to push this understanding beyond the traditional simple (or not so simple) black-white binary we tend to resort to. Antagonistic dualism does not help us address the intractability of racism because it tempts us to continue hackneyed moral and theoretical traps that allow culture to be the convenient escape hatch for avoiding the way in which *coloredness* cultivates the social construction of race. Turning on a black-white primary axis obscures the ways in which whiteness, as a racial construction, functions as privilege and power on national and global stages. Simply put, *whiteness is a concept and a reality that reveals and explains the racial interests of Whites and links them collectively to a position of racial dominance.*

UNINTERROGATED COLOREDNESS

Whiteness is not an eternal or unchanging category. It is susceptible to the same kinds of transformation within political struggle over time as is race. Acknowledging that we have treated whiteness as static, ahistorical, and objective helps to break open its uninterrogatedness. We can recognize the ways in which whiteness tends to be excluded from the list of acceptable and debatable racial nouns.[10]

Whiteness has become an unchanging condition that carries with it clear and distinct moral attributes such as being racist or not experiencing racism, being an oppressor or not experiencing oppression, silencing or not being silenced.[11] In relation to these myths, darker skinned peoples are defined as "nonwhites" who are acted upon by Whites and find their own identity through their resistance to White supremacy. Aside from its being problematic for any group to find its identity through "non-ness," uninterrogated whiteness ignores the pluralities of whiteness itself.

To ring us around a deadly May pole of uninterrogated coloredness is to dance, literally, with the devil. Whiteness has been and continues to be strategically maintained through assuming its colorlessness. The values, belief systems, privileges, histories, experiences of White folks are marked as normal or neutral or natural. All else is the exception. This gigantic superego is absolutely lethal. In an eerily warped way, uninterrogated whiteness uses its own comfort as the measuring stick for how other people should exist.

Maintaining whiteness as colorless, natural, and normal is misshapen hierophany. Whiteness is the invisible thing that *is* there. Perhaps bell hooks is on to something when she notes that most Whites do not have to "see" Blacks, therefore making them invisible, Whites can imagine that they are invisible to Blacks as well.[12] Hooks helps explain, in part, why whiteness functions as an abstraction on a conscious and unconscious level. Such abstraction also is and can be a strategy of subterfuge and suppression that continues feasting on a diet of domination, diminishment, and disavowal.

SAPPHIRE IS A PRECIOUS STONE

Reminder: Sapphire is also a precious stone.

Sapphire does not seek to assign blame; rather she calls us into a radical accountability with one another within community and to other communities in the cultural landscape of the United States as well as globally. To listen to histories and traditions that have not been a part of the standard texts of our lives is hard work. Some (within and without the Black community) respond to such revelations with guilt, shame, and anger. Rather than explore the emotion of the response, too often the rational impulse takes over, creating mincing yet deadly abstractions that result in refusing the invitation to justice and liberatory resistance.

Avoiding the messiness and complexity of race can often involve feeling blamed or held responsible for the sins of the forbearers and/or denying contemporary complicity with practices of injustice. Another response turns to colorblindness to make palatable a bland selective engagement with our genuine differences—differences that are assumed divisive rather than enriching. Much discourse on colorblindness actually brackets and ignores our coloredness. When taken to the extreme, it assumes a noncolored self who, when disrobed, is actually whiteness redux.

In response to all of these often earnest attempts to address the legacy of race and racism, Sapphire appeals to history and tradition and asks the question, How can an authentic ethic of justice be separated from where we have been and who we have been to one another? The contemporary scene did not emerge from a vacuum; it evolved from and in history and is immanently contextual. That context has moments of brilliance and seasons of mourning. We cannot divorce ourselves from the totality of our history and expect even a glimmer of efficacious justice or a vital community that crafts wholeness for its members.

Accordingly, Sapphire urges us to be relentless in our analysis and inclusive in our recovery of history and sociopolitical analysis when prying open and interrogating the previously uninterrogated. Sapphire cannot be content with a justice that addresses only a particular person or group's wholeness. A womanist social ethic that springs from Sapphire's steel-edged tongue must embrace all segments of society if it is to be thorough and rigorous and continue to push us into a critical dialogue that presses the boundaries of our humanness. Class, gender, and race analyses are crucial. But we also need to challenge a host of other matters: ageism (of both the young and the seasoned), homophobia and heterosexism, the myriad issues around accessibility, the color caste system of the United States, issues of the documented and undocumented, the Pandora's box around issues of beauty, and more. The work of womanist ethics guided by Sapphire is not only to eradicate a White cultural, political, and theological hegemony that names darkness as less than, but also to expose, examine, and eradicate the ways that Black folks and other darker skinned folks help that system find *new* ways to deem us children of a lesser God.

Many challenges persist in addressing uninterrogated coloredness. Sapphire, however, never left a situation hanging on the problems or resting with the challenges. As a template for a more faith-filled analysis of race and racism, consider the following moral benchmarks.

First, we must take up the challenges that racism and uninterrogated whiteness present despite the fact that it will hurt and might cause some guilt. Yet we need to understand that guilt, in this case, is a strategy that sanctions oppression. Guilt does not help us if we live our lives in its meandering miasma. To counter this situation, a key goal is building a community in which we are willing to risk. The task takes time, energy, and honesty. It also means learning to stop employing defensive strategies and rationales before we have come to know and appreciate our collective stories. Often we tend to think that this exposure will always be gruesome work—perhaps we focus too much on the Fall. Rather, in facing the pain and the guilt, we will learn that our collective story is far richer than the pathetic master narratives we tend to cling to. Our richness is found in our commonalities *and* in our diversities—creation stories may be a more apt and profound theological resource.

Second, we must work together in the time that we have to put into place new patterns of understanding and analysis. These patterns will require a lifetime of practice beyond who we are now. One way to begin this new work is to find at least one thing each of us can commit to that will be a lifelong commitment to antiracist behavior, thought, and ideology and then to do it every day—perfectly and imperfectly. The point is not success, but commitment and striving for consistency.

Third, we must stop collapsing race into coloredness. Such a conflation can beget an essentialist swamp that blinds us from seeing the ways in which race and racism are parts of the larger web of oppression. This point is obvious from what I have argued thus far. However, like those passages and ideas that appear in Christian Scripture more than once, if a point is important it bears repeating.

Fourth, we must take an uncompromising look at our social locations and the ways in which we are socially constructed beings. We must respond to the rampant individualism that marks contemporary life in the United States, where we often hear sentences that include "I am not personally . . . ." You or I may not personally be doing anything, but socially we are doing a great deal. None of us is in the world alone.

Fifth, we must realize and accept that no one of us can do this work alone, and no one is the unsurpassable expert on race and racism. We are both victim and perpetrator. The difference is largely a matter of where we are standing and to whom we are standing in relation as we move into the varieties of social landscapes in the United States and in global cultures. This variety of stances and relations makes us all, ultimately, experts on race. The question is, Will we acknowledge how much we know and do not know about race—consciously and unconsciously—and then work from that place? To do so means recognizing that the unconscious levels of racial discourses in which we all participate are most deadly. They signal the ways in which the ineptitude of collapsing race into coloredness is one of the most incredibly destructive and seductive uses of power as domination and subordination that persists in ethical reflection.

Sixth, as individuals, we must be willing to be changed, to grow, to admit *our* participation in and *our* resistance to race and racing in the communities of the classroom, the church, the academy, the society. It is far too easy to project onto others that which we do not work on within ourselves. The realities that shape an uninterrogated coloredness depend on such projections to help maintain the status quo. To broaden ourselves as people we must be willing to look within as we recognize that we are also social beings in communities of communities.

Finally, you must give yourself permission to be tired and weary. But also find ways of renewal so that you can be a creative and healthy participant in dismantling oppressions. Burned out, bitter people do not bring in justice.

NOT WHY. HOW?

To return to Morrison—Not why. How? I have only skimmed the tip of this iceberg. As thorny as it can be to shift our attention to coloredness, as we gather all colors around a table of analysis and discernment to understand (methodologically and concretely) the social construction and cultural production of race, we must engage the challenge.

Given all the locust activity womanists are often charged with committing, with Sapphire helping to lead the swarm, it is hard work doing the actual toil we do. Nevertheless, even in the face of the gross intractability of uninterrogated coloredness and high camp drag, I still hold on to a great hope that I will be old when I die. For dying of old age for a Black woman in my generation, who spends a good deal of her life awash in not only uninterrogated coloredness, but gender, sexuality, aging, class, and more . . . For someone like me, and many others, living a long and good life is the ultimate act of defiance and resistance. It is, in fact, living womanism large with Sapphire's bite, Aunt Jemima's good food, Topsy's rope-a-dope, the Tragic Mulatta's passion, Miss Nora's wisdom, and Mama Mary's faith.

Notes

1. This essay is an adaptation of earlier work in my *Womanist Ethics and the Cultural Production of Evil* (New York: Palgrave MacMillan, 2006). It is adapted from and reproduced with permission of Palgrave Macmillan. The full published version of this publication is available from http://www.palgrave.com/page/detail/womanist-ethics-and-the-cultural-production-of-evil-emilie-m-townes/?isb=9781403972736.
2. Toni Morrison, "The Site of Memory," in *Inventing the Truth: The Art and Craft of Memoir*, 2nd ed., ed. William Zinsser (Boston: Houghton Mifflin, 1995), 83–102.
3. See Emilie M. Townes, chap. 2, "Site of Memory: Proceedings Too Terrible to Relate," in *Womanist Ethics and the Cultural Production of Evil*, 11–28.
4. Toni Morrison, "Unspeakable Things Unspoken: The Afro-American Presence in American Literature," *Michigan Quarterly Review* 28 (1) 1989: 11–12.
5. Ibid., 3.
6. For a more thorough discussion of this unconscious color caste system and its particular manifestations within the Black communities of the United States see my chapter, Emilie M. Townes, "Another Kind of Poetry: Identity and Colorism in Black Life," in *In a Blaze of Glory: Womanist Spirituality as Social Witness* (Nashville: Abingdon Press, 1995), 89–119.
7. Michael Omi and Howard Winant, *Racial Formation of the United States: From the 1960s to the 1990s*, 2nd ed. (New York: Routledge, 1994).
8. Other examples include the work of Jayne Choong-Soon Lee, "Navigating the Topology of Race," in *Critical Race Theory: The Key Writings That Formed the Movement*, ed. Kimberlé Crenshaw, Neil Kotanda, Gary Peller, and Kendall Thomas (New York: The New Press, 1995), 441–48, and Martha Mahoney, "The Social Construction of Whiteness," in *Critical White Studies: Looking behind the Mirror*, ed. Richard Delgado and Jean Stefancic (Philadelphia: Temple University Press, 1997), 330–33.

9. Mahoney, "The Social Construction of Whiteness," 330.

10. Alastair Bonnett, "Constructions of Whiteness in European and American Anti-Racism," in *Debating Cultural Hybridity: Multi-Cultural Identities and the Politics of Anti-Racism*, ed. P. Werbner and T. Modood (London: Zed Books, 2000), 173–219; 204.

11. Ibid., 206.

12. bell hooks, "Representing Whiteness in the Black Imagination," in *Displacing Whiteness: Essays in Social and Cultural Criticism*, ed. Ruth Frankenberg (Durham, NC: Duke University Press, 1997), 168–69.

Chapter 16

Why Do Men Need the Goddess?

Male Creation of Female
Religious Symbols

ROSEMARY RADFORD RUETHER

Many contemporary feminists take as a kind of dogma that patriarchal religions, such as Judaism and Christianity, suppress female symbols for the divine. In so far as female personified divinity exists in such religions, it is seen as a "remnant" of a pre-patriarchal women-centered religion. Some feminists also assume that female religious symbols are intrinsically empowering to women.[1] But these are questionable assumptions.

A recent collection of essays by feminist scholars of Hinduism, titled *Is the Goddess a Feminist?*, concludes that most of the Hindu goddesses were created by men to empower men and to keep women in their place.[2] In my 2005 book, *Goddesses and the Divine Feminine*, I come to similar conclusions about the female religious symbols for God and collective humanity in Judaism and Christianity.[3] Gender hierarchy in patriarchal anthropology is a system of stratified relationships. The symbolism of masculine and feminine are two parts of one system. To make the feminine side of this system explicit in religious symbolism does not undermine but rather empowers the masculine side, while restricting women.

In his provocatively titled book *God's Phallus: And Other Problems for Men and Monotheism,* Howard Eilberg-Schwartz suggests that the symbolism of the love relationship between male religious leaders and God is complicated in male monotheism by its anti-homoerotic ethos.[4] This ethos prohibits imagining a male-male love relationship. Thus male monotheism constructs the human side of the God-human love relationship as female. This construction means that men imagine themselves in relation to God in female symbols: as brides and wives wooed and won by a male God as lover and husband.

This symbolic system has some startling consequences. In the Hebrew prophets, such as Hosea and Jeremiah, Israel's unfaithfulness to God is imaged as a sexually promiscuous wife seeking other lovers.[5] God is depicted as acting out the abusive treatment expected of an enraged husband toward an unfaithful wife. "Now I will uncover her lewdness in the sight of her lovers, and no one will rescue her out of my hand," God thunders in Hosea 2:10 (ESV). Modern readers find it hard to realize that such words are not addressed to some errant females in Israel but come from males imagining how God will treat them!

In Christianity, the Song of Songs became the text for an endless elaboration of the love relationship between the church or the soul and God. This highly erotic poem of unmarried love provided florid imagery for the love dalliance of God and the soul (or church). Male mystics imagined themselves as blushing brides led to the marriage bed with their bridegroom, Christ. Bernard of Clairvaux, twelfth-century abbot and mystic, exegetes the opening lines, "Let him kiss me with the kisses of his mouth," by imagining himself not only embraced but impregnated by Christ. His breasts grow full and filled with milk in this pregnant state. "For so great is the potency of this holy kiss that no sooner has the bride received it than she conceives and her breasts grow rounded with the fruitfulness of conception, bearing witness, as it were, with this milky substance."[6] As abbot, Bernard sees himself as nurturing his monks with *his* milk-filled breasts of mothering care.

The heterosexual structure of patriarchal mysticism not only generates female symbols for the human in relation to the divine but also female symbols for the divine in relation to the male human. In the Wisdom tradition in Hebrew Scripture, male sages imagined a rich female personification of the divine as mediatrix between a distant male God and themselves.[7] This female wisdom mediated the relation of God to them in the creation of the world and the communication of God's teachings to them. God also draws them into communion through their love relation with Wisdom. The sage and his students are exhorted to love Wisdom as their dearest possession: "She is more precious than jewels, and nothing you desire can compare with her" (Prov. 3:15).

Some Christian feminists have embraced the symbol of Wisdom as an empowering female image of God for women, while antifeminists in the churches have denounced this cultivation of "Sophia" as a "pagan goddess."[8] Neither group has noticed that women are nowhere to be found in the Wisdom literature as either sages or students. Moreover, this literature is rife with misogyny. Love of

Wisdom as the true bride of the sage's life is constructed to exclude the "bad woman" as evil harlot who draws the sage from God into all worldliness (Prov. 7:10–23). Proverbs does include the praise of the "good wife" who is also "more precious than jewels." Her value lies in hard work as she "seeks wool and flax and works with willing hands" to support her husband (Prov. 31:10, 12). But most women in Proverbs are depicted as the dangerous adversaries of the sage's love of wisdom. A contentious woman is compared to the continual dripping of water on a rainy day, and her beauty is like a gold ring in a swine's snout (Prov. 27:15; 11:22).

In Christianity a celibate spirituality made love of Wisdom or of Mary even more excluding of actual women. Priests were exhorted to love Mary as their true virgin bride in order to exclude the carnal temptations of fleshly women.[9] Catholic Christianity elaborated a rich imagery of Mary as immaculately conceived. She is the fit pure vessel of the sinless Christ. As symbol of the Church, she is the Mother in whom Christians are reborn from their sinful birth from sexual mothers. She is incorrupt in death, ascending into heaven to be crowned Queen of Heaven by Christ and God the Father. But this Marian symbolism is problematic for Christian women. "Our tainted nature's solitary boast"[10] sets Mary as virgin mother against all real women who may be one or the other, but never both at the same time! All women are tempted by their fleshly natures in ways that Mary was not. In modern Catholicism the call to women to become "Marylike" has been a call to a repressive purity and submissiveness that hardly any woman could actually achieve.

Christian love mysticism not only constructed the human self as female in relation to a male God but also imagined God as Lady Love in relation to a male human lover. Both male and female mystics made use of this topos. Thus the thirteenth-century Beguine mystic, Hadewijch, sees herself as a knight errant endlessly seeking the love of a fickle God as Lady Love. The mystic sighs and proclaims her sufferings for the sake of this divine Lady, imagining herself to be riding a proud steed only to be unhorsed. Although Lady Love ever eludes her, Hadewijch endlessly reaffirms her faithfulness to her.[11]

The theme of a divine Lady Love pursued by a male human lover does not disappear with Protestantism. It is reinvented by seventeenth-century Lutheran mystic Jacob Boehme. Boehme imagines a female side of God that arises out of the primal Abyss as God becomes manifest in the creation of the world. This female side of God is the love object of the (male) soul as it seeks to reunite with God. Like Hadewijch, Boehme imagines the soul as a knight errant willing to risk trials for the love of the Heavenly Lady. "For if a man wishes to obtain the noble Sophia, her honor and love, he must make such a vow to her in his resolution and mind." This vow means giving up all worldly honors and comforts rather than the "love of the noble Sophia."[12]

This Sophia spirituality sparked a long tradition in Protestant mystical millennialism that continued into the nineteenth century. One group of followers, the German Lutheran Harmonist Society that immigrated to the United

States in the nineteenth century, cultivated emotional hymns to their "Goddess Sophia." Adopting celibacy, the group saw the love of Sophia as preserving the aspirant male soul from falling into the arms of carnal women. One hymn exclaims, "Sophia, from your glances rapture flows into my heart." Another hymn pleads, "O stay with me, Sophia, let me flee what is distasteful to you. . . . Let no Delilah sneak into my heart and rob me of my strength. Let me be constant and true."[13] Unfortunately no record exists of how female Harmonists connected with this Sophia love mysticism.

Female symbols in Christianity, whether for Mary, the soul, the church, or Holy Wisdom, have been constructed mostly by men in ways that empower themselves, often at the expense of women. Female mystics, such as Hildegard of Bingen and Julian of Norwich, provide a few precious examples of how women interpreted these female and male symbols of God, Christ, humanity, and creation in ways that are more empowering for women. Julian of Norwich freely mixed male and female pronouns and metaphors to declare: "Thus Jesus Christ who does good against evil is our very Mother. We have our being of him where every ground of Motherhood begins, with all the sweet keeping of love that endlessly follows. As truly as God is our Father, so truly is God our Mother."[14]

Modern Christian women, starved for female symbols in what seems like a totally male theological world, have grasped for images such as Wisdom as a welcome draught for a thirsty throat. But they have often done so without sufficient awareness of how these female symbols have been constructed as part of a male dominant ideology. This deepens the task for creating a truly nonsexist symbol system that no longer values one gender against another or sets the masculine and the feminine as "complementary" opposites of active and passive, rationality and emotionality. It is not enough simply to seize upon the feminine symbolism in Christianity to overcome the masculine. Rather the whole system needs to be symbolically (and socially) reconstructed.

Notes

1. For example, see Carol Christ, *The Laughter of Aphrodite: Reflections on a Journey to the Goddess* (San Francisco: Harper and Row, 1987).

2. See Alf Hiltebeitel and Kathleen M. Erndl, eds., *Is the Goddess a Feminist? The Politics of South Asian Goddesses* (New York: New York University Press, 2000).

3. Rosemary Radford Ruether, *Goddesses and the Divine Feminine: A Western Religious History* (Berkeley: The University of California Press, 2005).

4. Howard Eilberg-Schwartz, *God's Phallus: And Other Problems for Men and Monotheism* (Boston: Beacon Press, 1994).

5. See, e.g., Hos. 2:2–13; Jer. 3:1–11, 19–20; Ezek. 16:1–63; 23:1–49.

6. Bernard of Clairvaux, *Commentary on the Song of Songs*, sermon 9:7, in *On the Song of Songs*, trans. Killian Walsh (Spencer, WA: Cistercian Publications, 1972), 58–59.

7. See, e.g., Prov. 3:19–20; 8:1–11, 22–31.

8. This conflict over the figure of Wisdom for God came to a head in the "Reimagining Conference" sponsored by the Presbyterian Church in November 4–7, 1993. While the women at the conference embraced Wisdom

as a feminist image for God, conservatives denounced Sophia as a pagan goddess. For the views on both sides see http://en.wikipedia.org/wiki/ Reimagining_Christian_Feminist_Conference.

9. See John Cihah, STD, "The Blessed Virgin Mary's Role in the Celibate Priest's Spousal and Paternal Love," *Ignatius Insight*, June 2009–June 2010, www .IgnatiusInsight.com.

10. Neil Patterson, "Our Tainted Nature's Solitary Boast: The Marian Dogmas," *Vulgata* 2 (Nov. 2001).

11. See Hadewijch, *Poems*, Stanzas 7 and 8, in *The Complete Works*, ed. Mother Columba Hart (New York: Paulist Press, 1980), 140–65.

12. Jacob Boehme, "On True Repentance," in Peter Erb, ed. *Jacob Boehme: The Way to Christ* (New York: Paulist Press, 1978), 40–58.

13. See Hilda Kring, *The Harmonists: A Folk-Cultural Approach* (Metuchen, NJ: Scarecrow Press, 1973), 113–20.

14. See Julian of Norwich, *Revelations of Divine Love*, chaps. 58–59, ed. John Walsh (New York: Harper and Row, 1961), 159–61. For feminine imagery in Hildegard of Bingen, see Barbara Newman, *St. Hildegard's Theology of the Feminine* (Berkeley: University of California Press, 1987).

Selected Bibliography

Abou El Fadl, Khaled. *Speaking in God's Name: Islamic Law, Authority and Women.* Oxford: Oneworld, 2001.

Abugideiri, Hibba. "Hagar: A Historical Model of 'Gender Jihad.'" In *Daughters of Abraham: Feminist Thought in Judaism, Christianity, and Islam.* Edited by Yvonne Yazbeck Haddad and John L. Esposito. Gainesville: University Press of Florida, 2001.

Abu-Lughod, Lila. *Do Muslim Women Really Need Saving?* Cambridge: Harvard University Press, 2013.

Ahmed, Leila. *A Quiet Revolution: The Veil's Resurgence, from the Middle East to America.* New Haven, CT: Yale University Press, 2012.

Ali, Kecia. *Sexual Ethics and Islam: Feminist Reflection on Qur'an, Hadith and Jurisprudence.* Oxford: One World, 2006.

Althaus-Reid, Marcella. *La teologia indecente. Perversiones teológicas en sexo, género y política.* Barcelona: Bellaterra, 2005.

Amoah, Elizabeth, and Mercy Amba Oduyoye, eds. *People of Faith and the Challenge of HIV/ AIDS.* Ibadan, Nigeria: Sefer, 2004.

Bailey, Wilma Ann. "Baby Becky Menarche and Prepubescent Marriage in Ancient Israel." *Journal of the Interdenominational Theological Center* 37, nos. 1 and 2 (2011): 113–37.

Barlas, Asma. *"Believing Women" in Islam: Unreading Patriarchal Interpretations of the Qur'an.* Austin: University of Texas Press, 2002.

Barnes, Michael, SJ. *Theology and the Dialogue of Religions.* Cambridge Studies in Christian Doctrine. Cambridge: Cambridge University Press, 2002.

Bechmann, Ulrike. *Gestörte Grabesruhe. Idealität und Realität des interreligiösen Dialogs am Beispiel von Hebron / al-Khalil.* AphorismA - Reihe Kleine Texte 24; Berlin, 2007.

Beissinger, Margaret. "Gender and Power in the Balkan Return Song." *Slavic and East European Journal* 45, no. 3 (2001): 403–30.

Bottici, Chiara, and Benoît Challand. *The Myth of the Clash of Civilizations.* London: Routledge, 2010.

Boys, Mary C. *Redeeming our Sacred Story: The Death of Jesus and Relations between Jews and Christians.* Mahwah, NJ: Paulist Press, 2013.

Boys, Mary C., and Sara S. Lee. *Christians and Jews in Dialogue: Learning in the Presence of the Other.* Woodstock, VT: SkyLight Paths Publishing, 2006.

Christ, Carol. *The Laughter of Aphrodite: Reflections on a Journey to the Goddess.* San Francisco: Harper and Row, 1987.

Cohen, Jeremy, ed. *Rethinking European Jewish History.* Littman Library of Jewish Civilization. New York: Oxford University Press, 2009.

Cook, Joan E. *Hannah's Desire, God's Design: Early Interpretations of the Story of Hannah.* Sheffield: Sheffield Academic Press, 1999.

Cooke, Miriam. *Women Claim Islam.* New York: Routledge, 2001.

Dube, Musa W. *Postcolonial Feminist Interpretation of the Bible.* St Louis, MO: Chalice Press, 2000.

Eisenstein, Zilla. *Against Empire Feminisms, Racism, and the West.* London: Zed Books Ltd., 2004.

Exum, J. Cheryl. "'Mother in Israel': A Familiar Figure Reconsidered." In *Feminist Interpretation of the Bible.* Edited by Letty M. Russell, 73–85. Philadelphia: Westminster, 1985.

Fuchs, Esther. "The Literary Characterization of Mothers and Sexual Politics in the Hebrew Bible." In *Feminist Perspectives on Biblical Scholarship.* Edited by Adela Yarbro Collins, 117–36. Chico, CA: Scholars Press, 1985.

Gager, John G. "The Partings of the Ways: A View from the Perspective of Early Christianity." In *Learned Ignorance: Intellectual Humility among Jews, Christians, and Muslims.* Edited by James L. Heft, Reuven Firestone, and Omid Safi. New York: Oxford University Press, 2011.

Gebara, Ivone. *Longing for Running Water: Ecofeminism and Liberation.* Minneapolis: Fortress, 1999.

———. *Out of the Depths: Women's Experience of Evil and Salvation.* Minneapolis: Fortress, 2002.

———. *Vulnerabilidade, Justiça e Feminismos—Antologia de textos.* São Bernardo do Campo: Nhanduti, 2010.

Haddad, Yvonne Yazbeck, Jane I. Smith, and Kathleen Moore, eds. *Muslim Women in America: The Challenge of Islamic Identity Today.* New York: Oxford University Press, 2006.

Heschel, Susannah. *The Aryan Jesus: Christian Theologians and the Bible in Nazi Germany.* Princeton, NJ: Princeton University Press, 2008.

Hiltebeitel, Alf and Kathleen Erndl, eds. *Is the Goddess a Feminist?* New York: New York University Press, 2000.

hooks, bell. "Representing Whiteness in the Black Imagination." In *Displacing Whiteness: Essays in Social and Cultural Criticism.* Edited by Ruth Frankenberg. Durham, NC: Duke University Press, 1997.

Johnson, Elizabeth A. *Ask the Beasts: Darwin and the God of Love.* London: Bloomsbury, 2014.

———. *The Quest for the Living God: Mapping Frontiers in the Theology of God.* New York: Continuum, 2007.

Kanyoro, Musimbi R. A. *Introducing Feminist Cultural Hermeneutics: An African Perspective.* Cleveland: The Pilgrim Press, 2002.

Kinukawa, Hisako. "Mark." In *Global Bible Commentary.* Edited by Daniel Patte, 367–78. Nashville: Abingdon Press, 2004.

Ko, Dorothy. *Cinderella's Sisters: A Revisionist History of Footbinding.* Berkeley: University of California Press, 2005.

Küng, Hans. *Projeto de ética mundial.* São Paulo: Paulinas, 2003.

Levenson, Jon D. *Creation and the Persistence of Evil.* San Francisco: Harper and Row, 1988.

MacKinnon, Mary Heather, and Moni McIntyre. *Readings in Ecology and Feminist Theology.* Kansas City, MO: Sheed and Ward, 1995.

Mark, Elizabeth Wyner. "The Four Wives of Jacob: Matriarchs Seen and Unseen." *The Reconstructionist* 63, no. 1 (1998): 22–35.

McFague, Sallie. *The Body of God: An Ecological Theology.* Minneapolis: Fortress Press, 1993.

Mills, Margaret A. "Gender and Verbal Performance Style in Afghanistan." In *Gender, Genre, and Power in South Asian Expressive Traditions.* Edited by Arjun Appadurai, Frank J. Korom, and Margaret A. Mills, 56–77. Philadelphia: University of Pennsylvania Press, 1991.

Moors, Annelies, and Ruba Salih. "'Muslim Women' in Europe: Secular Normativities, Bodily Performances and Multiple Publics." *Social Anthropology* 17 (2009): 375–78.

Morrison, Toni. "Unspeakable Things Unspoken: The Afro-American Presence in American Literature." *Michigan Quarterly Review* 28, no. 1 (1989): 11–12.

Newman, Barbara. *St. Hildegard's Theology of the Feminine.* Berkeley: University of California Press, 1987.

Niditch, Susan. *Chaos to Cosmos: Studies in Biblical Patterns of Creation.* Chico, CA: Scholars Press, 1985.

———. *"My Brother Esau Is a Hairy Man": Hair and Identity in Ancient Israel.* Oxford and New York: Oxford University Press, 2008.

O'Day, Gail R. "Jesus as Friend in the Gospel of John." *Interpretation* 58 (2004): 144–57.

———. "The Love of God Incarnate: The Life of Jesus in the Gospel of John." In *Life in Abundance: Studies of John's Gospel in Tribute to Raymond E. Brown.* Edited by John R. Donahue, 158–67. Collegeville, MI: Liturgical Press, 2005.

Oduyoye, Mercy Amba. *Introducing African Women's Theology.* Cleveland: The Pilgrim Press, 2001.

Oduyoye, Mercy Amba, and Musimbi Kanyoro, eds. *The Will to Arise: Women, Tradition, and the Church in Africa.* Maryknoll, NY: Orbis Books, 1992.

Omi, Michael, and Howard Winant. *Racial Formation of the United States: From the 1960s to the 1990s.* 2nd ed. New York: Routledge, 1994.

Rebera, Ranjini Wickramaratha. "The Syrophoenician Woman: A South Asian Feminist Perspective." In *A Feminist Companion to Mark.* Edited by Amy-Jill Levine, 101–10. Sheffield: Sheffield Academic Press, 2001.

Reid, Barbara. "The Cross and Cycles of Violence." *Interpretation* 58 (2004): 376–85.

Ress, Mary Judith. *Sin visiones nos perdemos. Reflexiones sobre teología ecofeminista latinoamericana.* Santiago: Colectivo Conspirando, 2012.

Ringe, Sharon. "A Gentile Woman's Story." In *Feminist Interpretation of the Bible.* Edited by Letty M. Russell, 65–72. Philadelphia: Westminster Press, 1985.

———. "A Gentile Woman's Story, Revisited: Reading Mark 7:24–31a." In *A Feminist Companion to Mark.* Edited by Amy-Jill Levine, 79–100. Sheffield: Sheffield Academic Press, 2001.

Rouse, Caroline M. *Engaged Surrender: African American Women and Islam.* Berkeley: University of California Press, 2004.

Ruether, Rosemary Radford. *Gaia and God: An Ecofeminist Theology of Earth Healing.* San Francisco: Harper, 1993.

———. *Goddesses and the Divine Feminine: A Western Religious History.* Berkeley: University of California Press, 2005.

Schaefer, Jame. *Theological Foundations for Environmental Ethics: Reconstructing Patristic and Medieval Concepts.* Washington, DC: Georgetown University Press, 2009.

Schneiders, Sandra. "The Footwashing (John 13:1–20): An Experiment in Hermeneutics." *Catholic Biblical Quarterly* 43 (1981): 76–92.

Schottroff, Luise. "The Creation Narrative: Genesis 1.1–2.4a." In *A Feminist Companion to Genesis*. Edited by Athalya Brenner, 24–38. Sheffield: Sheffield Academic Press, 1993.

———. "The Samaritan Woman and the Notion of Sexuality in the Fourth Gospel." In *What Is John? II: Literary and Social Readings of the Fourth Gospel*. Edited by Fernando Segovia, 157–81. Atlanta: Scholars Press, 1998.

Seibert, Ute. *Espacios abiertos: caminos de la teología feminista*. Santiago: Conspirando, 2010.

Sirin, Selcuk R., and Michelle Fine. *Muslim American Youth: Understanding Hyphenated Identities through Multiple Methods*. New York: New York University Press, 2008.

Townes, Emilie. *Womanist Ethics and the Cultural Production of Evil*. New York: Palgrave MacMillan, 2006.

Trible, Phyllis. *God and the Rhetoric of Sexuality*. Philadelphia: Fortress Press, 1978.

———. *Texts of Terror: Literary-Feminist Readings of Biblical Narratives*. Minneapolis: Fortress Press, 1984.

Trible, Phyllis, and Letty M. Russell, eds. *Hagar, Sarah, and Their Children: Jewish, Christian, and Muslim Perspectives*. Louisville, KY: Westminster John Knox Press, 2006.

Wadud, Amina. *Inside the Gender Jihad: Women's Reform in Islam*. Oxford: Oneworld Publications, 2006.

Index of Bible References

Index of Authors and Editors

257

Index of Subjects

CPSIA information can be obtained at www.ICGtesting.com
Printed in the USA
LVOW11s1056301014

411123LV00002B/16/P